Representation Matters

Thamyris/
Intersecting: Place, Sex and Race

Series Editor:
Ernst van Alphen

Editorial Team:
Murat Aydemir, Yasco Horsman, Isabel Hoving,
Saskia Lourens, Esther Peeren

Representation Matters: (Re)Articulating Collective Identities in a Postcolonial World

Editors
Anette Hoffmann and Esther Peeren

Colophon

Design
Mart. Warmerdam, Haarlem, The Netherlands
www.warmerdamdesign.nl

Printing
The paper on which this book is printed meets the requirements of "ISO 9706:1994,
Information and documentation – Paper for documents – Requirements for permanence".

ISSN: 1570-7253
E-Book ISSN: 1879-5846

ISBN: 978-90-420-2845-6
E-Book ISBN: 978-90-420-2846-3

© Editions Rodopi B.V.,Amsterdam – New York, NY 2010
Printed in The Netherlands

Mission Statement

Intersecting: Place, Sex, and "Race"

Intersecting is a new series of edited volumes with a critical, interdisciplinary focus.

Intersecting's mission is to rigorously bring into encounter the crucial insights of black and ethnic studies, gender studies, and queer studies, and facilitate dialogue and confrontations between them. *Intersecting* shares this focus with *Thamyris*, the socially committed international journal which was established by Jan Best en Nanny de Vries, in 1994, out of which *Intersecting* has evolved. The sharpness and urgency of these issues is our point of departure, and our title reflects our decision to work on the cutting edge.

We envision these confrontations and dialogues through three recurring categories: place, sex, and race. To us they are three of the most decisive categories that order society, locate power, and inflict pain and/or pleasure. Gender and class will necessarily figure prominently in our engagement with the above. *Race*, for we will keep analyzing this ugly, much-debated concept, instead of turning to more civil concepts (ethnicity, culture) that do not address the full disgrace of racism. *Sex*, for sexuality has to be addressed as an always active social strategy of locating, controlling, and mobilizing people, and as an all-important, not necessarily obvious, cultural practice. And *place*, for we agree with other cultural analysts that this is a most productive framework for the analysis of situated identities and acts that allow us to move beyond narrow identitarian theories.

The title of the new book series points at what we, its editors, want to do: *think together*. Our series will not satisfy itself with merely demonstrating the complexity of our times, or with analyzing the shaping factors of that complexity. We know how to theorize the intertwining of, for example, sexuality and race, but pushing these intersections one step further is what we aim for: How can this complexity be understood in practice? That is, in concrete forms of political agency, and the efforts of self-reflexive, contextualized interpretation. How can different socially and theoretically relevant issues be *thought together*? And: how can scholars (of different backgrounds) and activists think together, and realize productive alliances in a radical, transnational community?

We invite proposals for edited volumes that take the issues that *Intersecting* addresses seriously. These contributions should combine an activist-oriented perspective with intellectual rigor and theoretical insights, interdisciplinary and transnational perspectives. The editors seek cultural criticism that is daring, invigorating and self-reflexive; that shares our commitment to thinking together. Contact us at intersecting@let.leidenuniv.nl.

Contents

9	Introduction: Representation Matters	**Anette Hoffmann and Esther Peeren**
31	**I. Concepts of Postcolonial Identity: Contingent Articulations**	
33	Alterity and Identities: The Paradoxes of Authenticity	**Sudeep Dasgupta**
47	Insularity and Identity at Odds in Martinique: 1973 to 2004	**Marc Brudzinski**
67	The West between Culture(s) and Collective Identity: Notes for a Present Problematic	**Nimrod Ben-Cnaan**
83	Ubuntu, the Truth and Reconciliation Commission, and South African National Identity	**Hanneke Stuit**
103	Resistance or Compliance?: The Problem of Orientalism in Osman Hamdi's Paintings	**Gülru Çakmak**
113	**II. Relational Histories**	
115	Romani Identity Formation and the Globalization of Holocaust Discourse	**Huub van Baar**
133	Similarity and Difference: The Appearance of Suffering at the Strokestown Famine Museum	**Niamh Ann Kelly**
155	**III. Rethinking Origins and Indigeneity**	
157	Resignifying Genesis, Identity, and Landscape: Routes versus Roots	**Anette Hoffmann**
175	From Salsipuedes to *Tabaré*: Race, Space, and the Uruguayan Subject	**Vannina Sztainbok**
193	Bolivian Indigenous Identities: Reshaping the Terms of Political Debate, 1994–2004	**Claret Vargas**
205	**IV. Reinventing Tradition**	
207	Performative Constructions of Female Identity at a Hindu Ritual: Some Thoughts on the Agentive Dimension	**Beatrix Hauser**

223	"We Are Like Fish That Were Reeled In": Peasant Understandings of Modernity in Zimbabwe	**Guy Thompson**
237	Silence, Absence, Loss: Chineseness in Post-Authoritarian Indonesia	**Sonja van Wichelen**
253	Moving Identities: Mythology and Metaphor in André Brink's *Praying Mantis*	**Saskia Lourens**
269	The Contributors	
273	Index	

Introduction: Representation Matters

Anette Hoffmann and
Esther Peeren

> I'm not a Derridian in a long-term sense, but I'm a Derridian in a short-term sense in that I think more and more that the most interesting concepts in our field have fallen under erasure in exactly this way. One after the other they tumble from the paradigms where they seem to be settled and come loose in your hands. And then you say: "Shall I stop talking about identity" – but how can you stop talking about identity?
> (Stuart Hall)

Almost fifteen years after the publication of Stuart Hall and Paul du Gay's influential anthology on cultural identities, we are dealing with the hangover that inescapably seems to follow a period of popularity for particular concepts within the academy, in this case the "veritable discursive explosion around the concept of 'identity'" (Hall 1). In the 1980s and 1990s debate about identity politics dominated not only academic discussions in the humanities, but also political discourse (which exhibited a mounting backlash against so-called "political correctness" and "special interests") and popular culture. However, as Hall indicates in the epigraph, instead of leading to more precise definitions, this use across cultural spheres has caused identity to grow ever fuzzier as a concept. Much like the similarly elusive term "culture," identity seems to be everywhere, but in a less and less consequential way – our cover illustration provides an apt example of this emptying out of meaning. As with any fashion, it wears off; hence the various calls to move beyond identity and identity politics.[1] However, unlike legwarmers, which simply disappeared from the late 1980s to their brief resurgence around 2004, identity has a cultural and political function that exceeds fashionability and was therefore never truly superseded. In fact, its meanings proliferated. In his entry on "culture" in *Keywords*,

Raymond Williams points out that the reaction to such a proliferation of meanings around a concept should not be to select "one 'true' or 'proper' or 'scientific' sense and dismissing other senses as loose or confused," but rather to examine the "complexity of actual usage" and to take this complexity seriously (91). Thus, even if we as scholars, along with other consumers of movies, music, clothes, and perfume, are tiring of identity as a catchphrase, it is our responsibility to negotiate its various uses and to make clear why the need to grapple with its meaning, politics, and modes of representation remains. In 1997, Paul Gilroy wrote: "We live in a world where identity matters. It matters both as a concept, theoretically, and as a contested fact of contemporary political life. The word itself has acquired a huge contemporary resonance, inside and outside the academic world" (3). This resonance has not died down and requires further analysis rather than facile dismissal.

Without reliable statistics on the use of the term "identity" in consumer products and advertising, let alone the whole range of cultural production to verify our point, we can suggest its explosion both as trope and title in the movie industry since the 1980s.[2] Of sixty-three apparently popular movies listed in the international movie database (www.imdb.com) that have "identity" in their titles or even as a title, thirty-eight came out between the late 1980s and 2006. These films mainly deal with lost, found, stolen, false, split, multiple, secret, forgotten, recovered, or borrowed identities (the recurring notion of property is significant). In one way or another, their narratives seem to be contending with what Ien Ang has coined "identity blues": the concurrent increase in both the necessity and difficulty of dealing with, representing, and making sense of identities in contemporary societies in terms of their uncertainties, ruptures, fissures, (un)representabilities, and credibilities. Often focusing on the notion of a given or recently discovered uncertainty of identity and the subsequent search for a "true" self, many of the films seem to deal with a putatively current – postmodern and postcolonial – predicament of identity construction, that is, a social context in which identities can no longer be taken for granted but still need to be represented as if they were. Both the array of themes and the sheer quantity of movies dealing with identity testifies to societal concerns in terms of what Zygmund Baumann identifies as an intrinsic part of the concept of identity:

One thinks of identity whenever one is not sure of where one belongs; that is, one is not sure how to place oneself among the evident variety of behavioural styles and patterns, and how to make sure that people around would accept this placement as right and proper, so that both sides would know how to go on in each other's presence. (19)

Looking at film titles in a database certainly does not provide more than a summary glimpse of what may be seen as the conjunctures of a fashionable and marketable concept in popular culture. But if we take popular culture as reflecting on – that is, engaging with and processing – currently relevant societal concerns, the quantity of the films does not simply refer to what could be termed a mere "trend" in popular culture itself.

A film like Doug Liman's *The Bourne Identity* (2002), for example, provides a sophisticated meditation on identity construction in its action-packed story of an amnesiac (played by Matt Damon) who discovers he was a secret CIA assassin named Jason Bourne; this surname cleverly references both a "born" identity (i.e. an identity that one is born with or into, and which is therefore "true" or "authentic") and a "borne" identity (i.e. an identity that is imposed on one, but that can also be discarded), thus evoking the tension between essentialist and constructivist views of identity. As Thomas Byers pointed out in a recent conference presentation, the tension is never resolved, as Jason Bourne discovers, in *The Bourne Ultimatum* (2007), that his "born" identity was not forcibly taken from him, but voluntarily relinquished by himself.[3] In this way, the Bourne franchise rearticulates academic and political debates surrounding identity, thus adding to the complexity of the concept; it also places these debates squarely in the contemporary context of globalization, technologization, and neoliberal and neoconservative politics. Thus, while the vogue for titles that make use of the term "identity" may well reflect a marketing strategy, at the same time it denotes that problems or preoccupations with identity are historically and spatially specific. This volume picks up on this element by featuring localized and historicized readings of identity constructions, ranging from the present-day concerns of Lebanese immigrants in contemporary Sweden, indigenous communities in Bolivia and Uruguay, and Zimbabwean peasants, to the nineteenth-century predicament of an Ottoman painter in Paris.

We want to depart, however, from the way *The Bourne Identity* and most of the other identity-centered films in the movie database present identity as a predominantly individual matter. Taking up Joan W. Scott's criticism of the way the ideology of individualism has led identity politics and the struggle over multiculturalism away from collective action (17–18), we return the focus to collective identity constructions, but in a way that avoids seeing these constructions as unified, stable, or completely determinate of their members' individual identities. The term identity is used with increasing frequency in the media as well as in political debates to label political struggles or violent conflicts between different communities, be it in Africa, the Middle East, or within European metropoles. Such simplifying use of the term identity runs the risk of reducing complex political processes to putatively simple, monocausal "clashes of culture." As Denis-Constant Martin states, by reducing the polysemy of identities, together with their complicated histories and interactions, to homogeneity and permanence, as well as lumping together heterogeneous groups as solid entities of (mainly) "others," the term has lost its analytic power (5). This flattened use of "identity" (in the uncomplicated singular) perpetuates an image of minority communities, immigrants, and gay and lesbian communities, to name some possible actors, as perennially caught up in what is patronizingly and derogatorily called "identity struggle." Whereas collective struggles for the recognition of identities were charged with emancipatory promise in the 1980s (Fraser 107), subsequent genocidal conflicts (e.g. in Rwanda and the former Yugoslavia), the aftermath of 9/11, and xenophobic attacks on immigrants in many societies (often accompanied by a resurgence of virulent nationalism) have caused concern about the essentialist side of identity politics, if not altogether discredited too strong and monolithic ethnic or religious identifications.

Thus, in the post-apartheid states of South Africa and Namibia, where the quest for identification with the new nation-state constituted a political move away from the violent, authoritarian racial oligarchy which had governed the countries for decades, the recent reappearance of publicly staged ethnic identification has been observed with dismay. The 2009 South African elections, in which the presidential candidate of the ANC, Jacob Zuma,[4] actively positioned and represented himself as a Zulu man (to the extent that his supporters wore t-shirts bearing the slogan "100% Zulu Boy"), were criticized as symptomatic of political primitivism (Friedman 116) by analysts who were, in turn, scolded as white middle-class intellectuals. The analysts' discourse intensified when the ANC received a substantial majority of votes in KwaZulu Natal at the expense of Mangosuthu Buthelezi's Inkatha Freedom Party. Many attributed this crucial victory to Zuma's shared ethnicity with the voters in KZN. The complexity of the voters' choices, which certainly spoke as much to questions of redistribution (especially in rural areas the land question is of great importance), unemployment, and housing, to name but a few of the probable motivations, as to any seamless identification with ethnicity, language, and culture, was glossed over (at least in some debates) in favor of a simplifying "identity talk." This is but one example of a situation in which identity is taken to define who the actors "are," precluding the question of what exactly is said, asked, demanded, or promised by whom, where, when, and why. These reductive discourses often trigger arguments for moving beyond identity claims, and, as James Clifford writes, "the effect may be disabling," missing or erasing the historical necessities and the critical potential of conflicts revolving around identity (96).

In place of assuming "born" identities, the detailed analysis of objects and events of representation or the lack thereof renders it possible to elucidate the historical necessities, critical potential, and conflicts Clifford speaks of. Liz Gunner's critical engagement with Zuma's performances on the political stage during the South African (pre-)election campaign is insightful in this regard. She analyzes the complex implications of representation in the mode of a close reading of Zuma's performance of repeatedly singing a political song. This not only re-established singing and song as a political language in its own right, but had alienating as well as mobilizing powers for the South African public. The song, *"Awuleth' Umshini wami"* (isiZulu for "bring me my machine gun"), dates back and refers to the armed struggle against apartheid, speaking of agency and victory in times of crisis; it is "a song from the belly of the struggle" (Gunner 38).[5] Zuma's singing caused controversy not only because of the song's content, which has been said to resuscitate a militant combat tradition (Fikeni 11), but also with regard to the question whether it is proper for a presidential candidate to engage in such public singing performances. Moreover, Zuma commenced his series of performative stagings of the song during the time of the 2005 court case against Shabir Shaik in Durban, in which Zuma, then Deputy President of South Africa, was called to give evidence. Zuma's association with the fraud case severely damaged his reputation, which led former President Mbeki to release him from his office.[6] It was in the aftermath of the trial and during the ANC conference in Polokwane in December 2007, where Zuma was elected the new ANC President by the delegates, that the song became a rallying cry for his supporters.

Instead of dismissing Zuma's performances as a populist recourse to public memory (the anti-apartheid struggle) and traditionalism (sonic genres of performance), Gunner's analysis provides an informed insight into the effect and efficacy of performance and representation in the quest for recognition on the political stage in times of (in)tense campaigning during and before the elections. In the controversy surrounding *Umshini wami*, the recognizable connection of politics with an articulation of cultural genre spoke to the representability of postmodern, African identities, which are much more complex than any outright dismissal of ethnic identifications would have it.

The representation of African identities was also at stake, though in a different manner, in *The Short Century*, an exhibition of African art created between 1945 and 1994, curated by Nigerian-born American Okwui Enwezor in 2001. According to Ashley Dawson, the exhibition foregrounded "the politics of representing non-Western peoples and their traditions of cultural production," but did so in an ambiguous manner (227). On the one hand, Dawson argues, the show emphasized the way cultures are engaged in continuous translations and re-presentations of their histories and identities; yet on the other hand, it put forward a false impression of continental unity, in which art from particular regions is taken to be representative of "Africanness," and it only selected art that would be recognizable in the West as "art" and as somehow related to the project of modernity. Clearly, even in contexts where intentions are noble, representation remains a concept that needs to be carefully parsed: questions like "who is doing the representing?" and "what is the relation between representation and the representative?" have to be asked, especially when dealing with collective identities. For, as Hall has said, representation and identity are intimately interwoven: "identities are . . . constituted within, not outside representation" (10). Moreover, representation itself is understood as constitutive of meaningful realities in the mode of not merely re-staging or accounting for social processes, but creating them in a performative manner. Thus, representation inevitably influences the way identities are constituted and asserted, and while self-representation has its own problems (as is clear in Zuma's case), an inability to control one's own representation can have particularly dire consequences: "Those who are relatively powerless to represent themselves as complex human beings against the backdrop of degrading stereotypes become invisible and nameless. Identity is shaped, in part, by recognition, absence of recognition, or misrecognition by others" (Weaver 243).

While some critics have argued against the centrality of representation and recognition in postcolonial discourse, in favor of a more directly redistributive or materially revolutionary politics,[7] we hold that representation remains crucial in relation to emancipatory projects, but we also argue that not all forms of representation are equally conducive. In order to further the cause of marginalized communities, we need, in R. Radhakrishnan's words, "multi-directional, heterogeneous modes of representation and not the premature claim that 'representation no longer exists.' I do not see how representation 'can no longer exist,' until the political 'no longer exists'" ("Postcoloniality" 765). Whereas in this case Radhakrishnan is referring to the culturalist sense of representation, in "Culture as Common Ground: Ethnicity and Beyond" he draws attention to the double meaning of the term as both *Vertreten* (the right to speak for oneself politically and to be represented on the political stage) and *Darstellen* (the right to culturally "image" oneself and to have a particular worldview) and argues that the two work most effectively through each other (10). It is precisely this interaction that the current volume seeks to explore. The various contributions show that, if representation creates realities, discourses, images, fields of knowledge, and political contestation, then it never occurs accidentally or is inconsequential, but embedded in history, power relations, and current politics. Looking at acts of representation, then, provides analytical tools to analyze the meaning of specific spatially and historically distinct processes of signifying (or signifyin'),[8] defining, shaping, contrasting, but also criticizing, deconstructing, and opening up, or even attacking notions of identity.

The consideration of the intersection of identity and representation in this volume explicitly situates itself in a postcolonial context. In our broad understanding of the term, postcoloniality is not spatially limited to formerly colonized parts of the world (clearly, ex-colonizers are marked by their colonial histories, also because streams of guest workers, migrants, and refugees are now flowing in their direction) and does not denote a temporal closure (the world cannot be said to be comfortably *after* or *over* colonialism). We do not feel it is necessary to insert, as Chris Bongie does in *Friends and Enemies*, a slash in the post/colonial to indicate its ambiguity as a condition in which "the colonial and the postcolonial appear uneasily as one, joined together and yet also divided in a relation of (dis)continuity" and in which "the one continues to haunt the other" (xi). After all, the chronotope of the *post* – not just in postcolonial but also in postmodern and poststructuralist – has revealed itself as less one of departure and transcendence than one of continuous tension and dialogic negotiation. We therefore consider postcolonial critique as operative in revealing the ongoing inheritance of the still acute, distressing effects of colonial modernity; an inheritance that manifests as a haunting legacy that invariably keeps secrets, but that, even though it can only ever be selectively and partially deciphered, compels us to deal with it actively and responsibly in a move towards justice.[9] Postcolonial critique also functions as a counterpoint to narratives of globalization that dismiss or marginalize representations of alterity, as well as to the western bias of many humanist discourses (for example those surrounding human rights). The contributions to this volume present a considerably diverse array of topics bracketed by a shared postcolonial critical and practical commitment. Critically, the volume aims to specify and historicize several concepts prominent in postcolonial studies, while also investigating how such concepts can be translated into practical strategies of grappling with the legacies of colonialism (and its attendant, nationalism), whether such strategies entail the production of counter-memories to re-read and contest colonial histories, the challenging of neo-colonial and resurgent nationalist impulses in the present, or the forging of transnational alliances with other sidelined collectivities to ensure a better future.

Most of the papers selected for this volume were presented in two panels at the 2004 international workshop on Identities/Alterities hosted by the Amsterdam School for Cultural Analysis (ASCA). These panels, centered on "The Politics of Identity" and "Postcolonialism: Formation as Representation/Representation as Formation," dealt with questions of identity politics, with the struggles for and over forms of representation waged in the course of various communities' striving for social and political recognition, as well as with related concepts such as culture, memory, history, tradition, indigeneity, authenticity and hybridity.[10] One of the main aims was to explore the concepts of identity and alterity in the socio-historically specific contexts of postcoloniality and globalization, providing concrete examples of how particular communities (re)articulate and (re)assert themselves as meaningful collectivities to be reckoned with. In terms of Hall's ideas on the politics of identity articulation and representation, the tactical value of the contributions lies in the way they establish identity in terms of shifting alliances and a continuous redefinition of boundaries, without taking this provisional nature to mean that identity no longer matters or that all identity constructions deserve equal protection and consideration. Faced with numerous identity formations and representations in the contemporary postcolonial context, the contributors question whether and how these can be systematically and responsibly accounted for in terms of their specificity as well as their relations to other identities. The essays set out to explore how we deal with identity formations that are open-ended, productive and often ambivalent, yet constitute and represent communities with regard to cultural politics and global economies.

The first section of this volume includes contributions that take well-known and often taken-for-granted concepts from postcolonial theory and proceed to challenge and fine-tune them by exploring their workings in specific case studies and tracing their theoretical roots and meanderings through various disciplines, historical contexts, and social practices. In this way, the concepts in question – alterity, hybridity, insularity, ubuntu, the West, and orientalism – are revealed as what Mieke Bal has called "traveling concepts," with the markings of their wanderings rendered visible and meaningful.[11] The opening essay in this section was the inaugural keynote lecture to the Identities/Alterities conference. In it, Sudeep Dasgupta aims to move beyond the entrenched, polarized debate about identity (essentialism versus constructivism) and to provide an alternative to *différance*-based deconstruction by developing an Adorno-inspired, authenticity-based critique of the concepts of alterity and hybridity that focuses on the otherness of experience (living-in-the-world) to Being as such and on the object as Other to theoretical discourse. Dasgupta insists that a consideration of the object's historical specificity reveals that it cannot be approached through a fixed, abstract perspective, but only through concepts that are "contingently articulated." His reading of the Swedish film *Jalla! Jalla!* (Fares, 2000) stages such a contingent or constellational articulation and proposes a reformulation of the concept of hybridity, against Bhabha, in terms of the acute questions of when and where one is hybrid – in relation to which places, cultures, histories, social relations, and/or economic situations – and which hybridities are institutionally validated in particular socio-political contexts. Although at first sight the film appears to offer little more than a comical clash-of-cultures plot about a Lebanese immigrant in Sweden, its depiction of the complex negotiations, tensions, partial affirmations, and rejections the protagonist, his family, and friends engage in is revealed to disrupt clear distinctions of "bad" authentic cultures versus "good" hybrid lifestyles. Far from enacting abstract concepts, the film stages multiple forms of hybridity, while alterity, in terms of language and culture, turns out to be specifically situated and thus a question of experienced configurations in a time-space of multi-relational and historicized contexts, rather than allowing for a simplifying and convenient practice of nominalism.

In his paper on the concept of insularity and its relation to Martinican identity formation, Marc Brudzinski also insists on terminological specification and historicization. Various Caribbean intellectuals have employed the geography of the island – and the related ones of the sea, the archipelago, and the continent – to symbolically define identity and the process of identification as functions of the Caribbean subject's relation to space and place, but not all of them conceptualize these *topoi* in the same way or attach the same meanings to them. Since the colonial histories of the different Caribbean islands are not consistent and their current statuses diverse (with some independent and others, like Martinique, overseas departments of former colonial powers), insularity needs to be explored both as locally inflected and as potentially generating pan-Caribbean solidarity. As Brudzinski shows, even among Martinican intellectuals there is no agreement on how being part of an island-nation constitutes one's identity. In the work of George Desportes, Édouard Glissant, and Thierry Nicolas, insular metaphors are used in divergent ways depending on the cultural critical affiliations of the writer and the period of writing: in the 1970s, Desportes uses insularity to pessimistically figure Martinique's static isolation and the fragmentation and dependency of the Caribbean archipelago, while Glissant employs it to envision a new, anti-colonial way of thinking Caribbean identity and history; in the 2000s, Nicolas configures insularity as an obstacle to the necessary connection or assimilation between France and its overseas departments (Martinique and Guadeloupe) in a globalized world. In his analyses, Brudzinski shows that geography does not symbolize or determine identity configurations in any straightforward way, but is subject to an ideologically and historically variable conceptualization that may activate any of the (often contradictory) connotations a particular geographical constellation evokes.

The next essay, by Nimrod Ben-Cnaan, interrogates and complicates another geographical marker bearing symbolic meaning in relation to collective identity formation: the West, which may be one of the notions most taken for granted in postcolonial theory. Like whiteness, masculinity, and heterosexuality, the West is that pole of an important, culturally constructed binary that was long thought natural, normative, and invisible. Consequently, it was not considered to require explanation, investigation, or even definition. Of course, the West never did speak for itself as a theoretical concept or even a geographical category, and it does so even less now that its boundaries have become blurred after the fall of the Berlin Wall and globalization has brought westernization to the remotest outposts of the world. If, like the hybrid, the West is everywhere in our postcolonial, globalized world, how useful is this category as a point of reference and mobilizing factor? Probing historical notions of Westernness as well as its intersections with concepts of culture (Williams, Hannerz), collective memory (Nora), and collective identity (Snow, Castells), Ben-Cnaan asks what it means to be Western today. Identifying the assumption that the phenomena of the Western and the "modern" seamlessly converge as one of the major fallacies of critical thought, his essay presents postcolonial critique as a key contribution towards the re-modeling of notions of Westernness as decentered and heterogeneous. While the West must continue to be seen and critiqued as an important power block and privileged collective identity, in both postcolonial studies and globalization theory attention should also be given to its internal bifurcations (expressed, for example, in European resistance to Americanization, the U.S. backlash against everything French in the wake of the Iraq invasion, and Western European disdain for immigrants from the former Eastern Block), as well as to the instability betrayed by its increasingly virulent policing of its boundaries (especially in relation to African and South-American immigrants, and Turkey's possible accession to the European Union).

Ubuntu – as evoked in the Xhosa proverb "*ubuntu ungamntu ngabanye abantu*," which is most often translated as "I am a person because of other persons" – is an ethical concept articulating a specific non-Western way of thinking oneself as part of one's community. While it is perhaps not yet as well-known (and overused) as hybridity and even insularity, the fact that ubuntu was chosen as the name for an increasingly popular open-source computer operating system both shows that its notion of community has broad appeal and that it is not immune to forces of commercialization (Ubuntu may be free to download, but its website includes an UbuntuShop and is run by a commercial company called Canonical).[12] Hanneke Stuit examines ubuntu in the South African context, exploring the term's history and various interpretations, as well as its prominent use within the Truth and Reconciliation Commission. Ubuntu is revealed to be a far from straightforward concept that has undergone its own travels and that positions itself ambivalently on the continuum from an inclusionary humanism to conditional, exclusionary forms of community. Stuit's analyses of various TRC hearings and her reading of ubuntu with (and against) Judith Butler's notion of precarity expose how ubuntu, when it is not seen as an abstract concept but explored contingently, at the level of living-in-the-world, raises important questions about the relationship between identity and alterity (as an inclusive concept, how does ubuntu deal with otherness?), as well as about that between the individual and the community (which should take precedence when it comes to questions of justice and responsibility?).

The final essay in the first section, Gülru Çakmak's "Resistance or Compliance? The Problem of Orientalism in Osman Hamdi's Paintings," takes the concept of orientalism and supplements Edward Said's seminal account by concentrating on its highly specific incarnation as a school in nineteenth-century French painting. At the same time, she repeats Said's perspectival shift (the way he emphasizes the effect of Western orientalism on the orientalized subject) by focusing on the work of the Ottoman painter Osman Hamdi, who was faced with the conundrum of having to represent his own culture through the othering perspective offered by the Orientalist school. In particular, Çakmak examines the way Hamdi's impossible position as an "Eastern Orientalist" has been read in art history. While his paintings depict the irreducible difference, i.e. non-Europeanness, of his subjects by making use of the painterly language of French Orientalism, they have often been interpreted as doing so precisely to produce a counter-hegemonic narrative of Turkish identity. Other critics have read this ascription of a political agenda to Hamdi's works as overly facile and optimistic. Çakmak examines both standpoints and concludes that neither has the last word on Hamdi's agency as a painter or on the effect of Western painterly conventions on the identity of the artist or his work. Her own close reading of the painting *Zeïbek at Watch* locates it as a negotiation not just of Orientalism, but also of particular modernizing initiatives in Academic painting of the time.

The second section of the book is entitled "Relational Histories" and focuses on the way collective identities are constructed, consolidated, and asserted in museum contexts through a particular framing of their history as public memory. In the two cases discussed here – that of the Roma and their persecution in the Second World War, and that of the Irish and their suffering during the Famine – this framing is explicitly *relational*: Romani and Irish identity are not presented as unique configurations or relational only in the sense that they are defined against or in competition with other identities, but as sharing certain characteristics and historical trajectories with other collectivities. This reminds us that alterity, both in terms of history and ethnicity, "is not a mere synonym of difference; what it signifies is otherness, a distinction or separation that can entail similarity as well as difference" (Peeren and Horstkotte 10). Conversely, relationality, defined as an active connectivity, does not imply sameness (there would be no need to actively relate to something completely identical) but rather similarity. Thus, the Romani and Irish communities present themselves as related to but not *the same as* other communities in a similar position: for the Roma, their reference point is the Jewish community and the Holocaust, while the Irish Famine is remembered in the context of present-day African famines. Although elements of opportunism may be discerned in relational strategies of representation (in the case of negative histories of suffering especially, constructive relationality may degrade to a distasteful competitiveness in a hierarchy of victimhood), as well as a danger that significant differences between communities and their histories will be elided, they can also open the way for marginalized communities to engage in collective articulations and assertions of identity across space and time – potentially creating what Appadurai calls "grassroots globalization" or "cellular democratization" (*Fear* 131, 135). Such collective articulations may be more readily intelligible, carry more weight, and thus be more effective in furthering the aim of representation, namely to gain recognition for one's community and its history. In addition, constructing identities relationally could engender enduring solidarity between communities; for this to transpire, however, the identification needs to exceed the level of representation-as-depiction (*Darstellen*) and include effective, coalitional interventions on the social and political level – as occurred, for example, in the case of the indigenous movement, which will be discussed below. The two essays in this section provide a critical perspective on relational histories, highlighting not just the potentially positive aspects, but also the risks inherent to any predication of one collective identity upon another.

Huub van Baar theorizes the political implications of the Roma's inclusion within a globalized holocaust discourse. His essay analyzes the permanent exhibition on the extermination of the European Roma located at the Auschwitz-Birkenau State

Museum, which is considered one of the first opportunities for Romani self-representation with an international scope. Although by providing a documentary account of the Romani genocide, the museum may succeed in bringing about their exit from the peripheral category of "other victims" and establish a more equal standing with the Jewish victims of Nazism, van Baar argues that this advance is predicated on the exclusion of references to discrimination suffered in the pre- and postwar periods and thus on the non-articulation of the differences between Romani and Jewish history. By eliding these differences in favor of a sustained claim to similarity, the exhibition does not – and cannot – provide a space to inform visitors about the current crisis of the Romani communities in Eastern and Southern Europe or incite them to political intervention. In this case, therefore, historical relationality threatens to erase a collective identity's specificity and proves unable to produce a coalitional politics in the present.

Analyzing the displays of the Strokestown Famine Museum, which aims to elucidate the reasons for and effects of the Irish famine, Niamh Ann Kelly provides an account of the museum's strategies of representation with regard to this salient yet underexposed event in Irish history. She reveals how the museum exhibits negotiate between local specificities and national/universal aspects, and how, by emphasizing relations of similarity (comparing the causes and effects of this historical famine in a western colonized country to present-day situations of poverty in postcolonial Africa) as well as difference (accentuating the deprivation of the Irish peasant population in comparison to the wealth of the landed gentry), they encourage the visitor to experience identity in a relational and contingent manner as involving the active negotiation and affiliation of identities and alterities across time and space.

In addition to emphasizing the relational dimension of identity formation and assertion, both van Baar and Kelly point to the mobilization factor of identity and memory politics – uniting the Irish as a now thriving postcolonial nation and the Roma as a still threatened post-nation-state nation – denoting that we are far from getting beyond identity-based claims for recognition, self-determination, and equality. Such claims are central to the third section of this book, which deals with origin narratives and struggles around indigeneity. The three essays in this section show that to further a marginalized collectivity's cultural and political goals in the present, it is essential for this collectivity to construct a (link to the) past that stakes a certain claim to territory, whether in terms of actual land or a more metaphorical belonging, which, in turn, can found a demand for rights and, in some cases, restitution. Rejecting the essentialist notion that such a claim can only be based on an authentic and therefore fixed connection or rootedness, the essays emphasize that it is precisely the constructedness of the relation to the past that renders communities capable, through creative and tactical adaptations, of challenging the colonial or postcolonial state's attempts to either reify or obliterate their histories and identities.

Anette Hoffmann addresses questions of narrated collective identity as related to the history of the community in question, in this case that of the self-representation of the Herero community in praise poetry under and after colonial rule in Namibia. She presents an interpretation of what she identifies as a significant shift from one narration of genesis to another. Whereas in the older story the collective ancestors descended from a tree, in the narration that was recently agreed upon, a journey to and arrival in Namibia is seen as the historical event that constructs ethnic identity together with a notion of belonging. Describing the Ovaherero's articulation of identity as intrinsically connected to their textual construction of landscape, Hoffmann presents these constructions of landscape and identity as fundamentally based upon and mediated by orally transmitted texts. This specific articulation of landscape and identity as communicating and mutually productive forms the analytic premise for her reading of the reasons for and impact of this change on Herero self-representation under a coercive regime. The Ovaherero communities' historically grounded, but also contemporarily operative attempt to appropriate the discourse defining their identity vis-à-vis the state points to the enduring cruciality of Hall's notion of identity as both historically situated and open-ended; origins remain important, but can be molded to the purposes of the present.

This is vital not only when an established origin narrative comes too close to confirming the externally imposed, colonial state's view of a community, as was the case with the Ovaherero's tree story, but also when a hegemonic national origin narrative works to erase indigenous presence altogether. Interrogating the founding narration of Uruguay as a neo-European, white, and modern nation, Vannina Sztainbok asks how its citizens could come to think of Uruguay as so *tan sin indios* 'so indianless.' Her essay identifies the persistent repetition of the narration of the killing of the "last" Charrúas at Salsipuedes as the discursive fetishization of the elimination of the native population and thus as a mode of constructing a national founding myth based on whiteness. The all-encompassing sameness of the population is constructed (in the face of a manifest racial plurality) by narrating the nullification of the Charrúas, which leads to "Indianness" being conceived as the ultimate embodiment of pre-modern alterity. While the present nationalist discourse includes certain Charrúa elements (such as the *garra charrúa* or "Charrúa claw"), it actively forecloses the marking of the native as still present in (and owed by) Uruguayan society. Sztainbok does, however, point to the recent emergence of Charrúa descendents' movements as offering the potential for a reinscription of native identity into Uruguay's present and past. While remaining wary of certain elements of essentialism, unproductive nostalgia, and even racism in this movement, she argues that its growing affiliations with other indigenous movements in the Americas and with Afro-Uruguayans may well open the way for collective counter-narratives able to offer an alternative to Salsipuedes' continuing inscription of whiteness at the heart of Uruguayan identity.

The indigenous movement Sztainbok invokes provides a particularly strong example of the way relationality can strengthen identity-based claims for cultural and political representation. From its quite recent inception – the term "indigenous" was not commonly used to designate human collectivities until the mid twentieth century (Niezen 539) – the indigenous movement has presented itself as a global community that sought to legitimate and support the specific identities of separate groups through a collective appeal voiced on an international level (through the International Labour Organization, various NGOs, and the UN). As Ronald Niezen writes in an article on the way the Internet in particular has facilitated the forging of connections between various indigenous communities:

the collective sense of self, above all the sense of injustice and suffering based upon past wrongs, is not arrived at in isolation from behind closed cultural boundaries, but rather is inspired by and negotiated with others in personal, often professional, relationships and adjusted to the taste of a universal public. The essential features of a community's history and culture are now more than ever an outcome of global collaboration. (538)

While his celebration of the Internet as enabling an "unbridled cultural democracy" (549) appears overly optimistic,[13] Niezen's elaboration of the way the collaborative construction of indigeneity as a platform for demanding cultural and political rights engenders both "a source of global identification" (by linking communities together in a shared struggle) and "a local source of cultural reawakening" (since the framework of indigeneity is broad enough to accommodate various localisms) provides an attractive vision of the way relationality can further a community's aims without effacing its specificity.[14] It needs to be pointed out, though, that, while on the one hand there is "little agreement on precisely what constitutes an indigenous identity," which means that it can be used relatively freely as a strategic term to mobilize communities, on the other hand the fact that the indigenous, on the level of state and international law, has become a legal status with associated rights means that "[i]dentity is expressed as a measurable or quantifiable entity far more for indigenous people than for any other group" (Weaver 240, 248). In addition, as Alfred and Corntassel show as part of a much more pessimistic and separatist perspective on indigeneity, individual communities do not always strengthen each other's claims but are also frequently played out against each other "in battles over authentic histories" (601).[15] Like the concepts discussed in section one, therefore, indigeneity, too, needs to be carefully specified and historicized, since it cannot be assumed to work the same way in all contexts.

One such specification takes place in Claret Vargas's essay, which addresses the rhetoric of indigenous rights in Bolivia in the 1990s. Vargas reveals, by way of Hall's theory of identity, the operational effectiveness of an incomplete, almost utopian, flexible-yet-contested concept of indigenous identity. The practice of "legislating and naming identities," as critiqued by Dasgupta, here appears in a literal sense, as Vargas analyzes the 1994 Law of Popular Participation (LPP). While this law could have transfixed indigenous identity, producing exclusions and a potential struggle for legitimacy between various indigeneities, its lack of definition instead led to the formation of a tactical, fluid, or "thin" understanding of indigenous identity, which allowed various groups to assert themselves and put demands to the state, either separately or in concert. In Vargas's reading, indigenous groups do not necessarily have to anchor their claims in a fixed historical origin, but can use the legal framework (as long as it is not overly constrictive) to develop various tactics to improve their living conditions in the present and their opportunities in the future. The fact that Evo Morales, who is of Aymara descent, was able to unite the indigenous vote with the *campesino* vote in order to be elected as the first fully indigenous Bolivian head of state in 2005 is cited as evidence of the power a "thin" notion of indigeneity can unleash.

While Alfred and Corntassel envision an indigenous resurgence based on "a return to the natural sources of food and the active, hard-working, physical lives lived by our ancestors" (613) – in other words, a return to a tradition that is authentic, stable, recognizable, and retrievable – Morales deliberately instrumentalizes tradition. He does not just invent it in Hobsbawm's sense, where the invention is naturalized to make the tradition appear invariable (1–2), but engages in a continuous pragmatic and overt *re*-invention. This accords with Appadurai's argument, in "Disjuncture and Difference in the Global Cultural Economy," that globalization has complicated the invention of tradition:

in this [globalized] atmosphere ... the invention of tradition (and of ethnicity, kinship and other identity markers) can become slippery, as the search for certainties is regularly frustrated by the fluidities of transnational communication. As group pasts become increasingly parts of museums, exhibits and collections, both in national and transnational spectacles, culture becomes less what Bourdieu would have called a habitus (a tacit realm of reproducible practices and dispositions) and more an area for conscious choice, justification and representation. (18)

Culture and tradition as realms for "conscious choice, justification and representation" are central to the fourth and final section of this volume, which deals with reinventions of specific traditions and their effects on collective identity constructions in the present.

In an interrogation of the concept of agency in relation to the formation, representation, and possible critique or subversion of gendered identities, Beatrix Hauser explores the meaning and function of Mangala *puja*, a votive rite performed by women in Orissa, India, to confirm their religious commitment to the wellbeing of their husbands, brothers, and sons. A case study conducted in Berhampur reveals that the ritual is relatively new to the area and, under the guidance of a senior local woman, has been inflected in creative ways. Although the notion of individual creative input is played down by the woman herself, Hauser argues that she does derive a ritual agency from her role. For the other participants, the rite at once stresses the notion of female suffering while simultaneously transforming this suffering through religious practice and the festive social context. Looking at the efficacy of the rite in terms of the performative construction of at times conflicting features of identity – religion, gender, and individuality – Hauser suggests the need for reconceptualizing the notion of agency, since its common definition as actively willed expression may neglect the (unintended) effects of embodied experience. She argues that the participation in a collective performance – even one designed to reinforce women's subservience – allows for reflexivity and an increasing awareness of gender roles that are usually not questioned. Although the rite is not performed with the aim of altering the self-definition of the worshipping women, the iterative aspect of performativity as that which requires the affirmation of the collective may have the capacity to effect gradual change as the rite is subjected to further reinventions.

Guy Thompson's contribution explores the discourses of residents within peasant communities in Madziwa, Zimbabwe. In these communities, especially older people attempt to capture the ambiguities of their contradictory experiences with modernity through two key Shona terms: *chivanhu*, the way of the people, and *chirungu*, meaning English, European, but also modern and foreign. The juxtaposition of these concepts allows Madziwans to theorize the experience of colonial rule, capitalist expansion, and cultural change in their lifetime. Tracing the history of the two terms from the colonial period via the political debates of the early post-colonial 1960s to their recent essentialist appropriation as anti-western state propaganda by Mugabe's government, Thompson argues that the continued use of the terms by Madziwan peasants should be conceptualized as a politics of popular memory that contains oppositional elements (both in relation to colonialism and the current regime). Interviews reveal that while *chivanhu* is related to oversimplified, nostalgic ideas about the early colonial period, this construction also functions as a counter-discourse to protest a continuing decline in community autonomy. Thus, the retroactive consolidation of tradition is put in the service of negotiating and interpreting the present. Comparable to the revised origin story of the Herero community described by Hoffmann, Madziwans reinvent tradition in order to establish their own reading of a specific, locally defined modernity within which they struggle to define their contemporary identities and protect their material interests.

The problematic imbrication of tradition and authenticity, which suffuses the *chivanhu-chirungu* binary, is also central to Sonja van Wichelen's essay, which analyzes the process of re-sinicization of Chinese-Indonesians in post-Suharto Indonesia. After decades of discrimination and forced assimilation, culminating in the violence of the May 1998 riots, the fall of Suharto's regime that same year opened up a space for this community to begin participating in Indonesia's cultural and political life. By analyzing entries from an Internet discussion forum called *Chinese Culture*, van Wichelen reveals the conflicted nature of the ensuing resurgence of "Chineseness," which involved a diasporic community that did not always speak the languages or have any knowledge of Chinese traditions and ways of life. Using Dominick LaCapra, she argues that in this case, absence (a structural lack of something one never had) is conflated with loss (associated with a historical trauma), causing many Chinese-Indonesians to engage in a nostalgic desire for a "homeland" they never knew, and a quest for authenticity that not only erases the way Chinese traditions have been adapted in their migration to Indonesia, but also prevents the working through of the trauma of the silencing of Chineseness under Suharto and the racist violence preceding his ousting. In this case, therefore, the *re*-invention of tradition is foreclosed in favor of a return to an invented tradition that the community will always be inadequate to.

The final essay in this volume by Saskia Lourens presents a more constructive relation to tradition in its reading of mythology and metaphor in André Brink's 2005 novel *Praying Mantis*. Brink's multi-faceted re-telling of the nineteenth-century life of Cupido Cockroach, South Africa's first Khoi missionary (a historical figure), undermines the traditional opposition between African mythology and western religion and rationalism. In the fact that Cupido is told various incompatible stories about his own origins, myth is transformed from unassailable tradition into a discourse open to appropriation and reinvention, while the inclusion in Brink's novel of lists that resemble and parody the pseudo-scientific tabulations of colonial record, and of a Christianity that cannot deliver the literalness that Cupido seeks in it, reveals the mythological and metaphorical nature of western history and religion (as narrative structures rather than essences). Cupido's life story, as told by Brink's multiple narrators, problematizes the stubborn adherence to a unitary identity that fits into a singular tradition and ultimately privileges a more syncretistic or even "magical" attitude that considers identities and traditions as multiple and changeable. This reflects not only on South African history but also on the current political situation in a country where a variety of identities are supposed to unite under the banner of the post-apartheid nation. As we saw in our earlier discussion of Jacob Zuma, invocations of fixed and unitary identities ("100% Zulu Boy") are not necessarily as helpful in this as the reinvention of traditions in a more inclusionary and relational manner would be.

Significantly, in almost all of the cases discussed in this volume we are dealing with an identity politics that has either abandoned essentialism or adopts it only strategically and self-reflexivity. This causes identity formation and representation to emerge as creative, open-ended processes that are, moreover, no longer designed to exclude or separate, but display a clear relational tendency. The latter tendency could potentially herald a renewed strengthening of the "claims for egalitarian redistribution" that Nancy Fraser saw displaced by claims based on the recognition of difference, without having to subscribe to her individualist "status model" (119). A shift from asserting absolute difference to considering *both* communality and specificity – as displayed, for example, in the indigenous movement – can bring marginalized communities together in a shared quest for political, economic and social justice, rather than allowing the dominant culture to play them out against each other, thus providing (with the appropriate caution about not losing sight of the specificity of each community's position and accountability in the local and global context) a positive answer to Radhakrishnan's question "Is freedom conceivable as a proactive project undertaken in multiple solidarities rather than as a game of mutual negations and objectifications?" ("Globalization" 328). In addition, taking up a view of identities (and their origins and traditions) as constructions that are open to strategic reformulation no longer needs to be seen as robbing decolonized and other marginalized communities of their political grounding or right to self-determination, but, as bell hooks already argued in "Postmodern Blackness," provides a way to challenge the reification of marginalized identities by dominant groups, which often works through essentialism. James Clifford has said that "shelving" identity altogether would "risk being left with a narrowly foreshortened view of contemporary social movements around culture and identity, missing their complex volatility, ambivalent potential, and historical necessity" (1). It is precisely the continued – and renewed – vitality of identity discourses into the twenty-first century that this volume demonstrates by using contingent concepts, relational histories, and reinvented origins and traditions to analyze postcolonial collective identities in concrete case studies from various parts of the world.

Notes

1. This trend was particularly strong in feminist criticism. See, for example, Susan Hekman's "Beyond Identity: Feminism, Identity and Identity Politics," and Mona Lloyd's *Beyond Identity Politics: Feminism, Power and Politics*.

2. Anette Hoffmann thanks her son Simon for the suggestion to check the movie database, but even more for airing the view that identity became an awkward concept, exhausted by its excessive use as a catchphrase to sell consumer products, and therefore almost useless for politics.

3. Byers's presentation was entitled "The Bourne Allegory: Secret Agent, the Grid, and Global Positioning of the Subject of Modernity" and delivered at the 2009 International Conference on Narrative in Birmingham, 6 June 2009.

4. Zuma's candidacy was overshadowed by a corruption trial that was dropped in 2009 and a rape case in which he was found not guilty. Both cases prompted debate on the moral credibility of Zuma as a potential president of both the ANC and South Africa. See, for instance, http://pumlagqola.wordpress.com/2007/05/07/a-year-since-the-zuma-rape-case-judgement/.

5. Gunner is a researcher at the Wits Institute for Social and Economic Research (WISER) at the University of Witwatersrand in Johannesburg who has published on oral genres, as well as on orality and constructions of masculinity in South Africa. At the time when "*Umshini wami*" was causing much controversial debate, her article provided an in-depth analysis of the genre, history, performativity, and polysemic qualities of the song, which was so popular that it became a much-used ring tone for cell phones in South Africa. See also the feature on "*Umshini wami*" in the December 2008 issue of *Art South Africa* (Bloom et al.) and several videos on YouTube.

6. See, for instance, http://news.bbc.co.uk/2/hi/africa/4328360.stm.

7. See Fraser's "Rethinking Recognition" and Bongie's discussion of postcolonial studies' turn to the "properly political" in the Preface and Introduction to *Friends and Enemies*.

8. See *The Signifying Monkey: A Theory of African-American Literary Criticism* by Henry Louis Gates Jr.

9. See Jacques Derrida's *Specters of Marx*, where he argues that "[n]o justice . . . seems possible or thinkable without the principle of some *responsibility*, beyond all living present, within that which disjoins the living present, before the ghosts of those who are not yet born or who are already dead, be they victims of wars, political or other kinds of violence, nationalist, racist, colonialist, sexist, or other kinds of exterminations, victims of the oppressions of capitalist imperialism or any of the forms of totalitarianism" (xix).

10. Selected papers from the other two panels at the conference (on intersubjectivity and postmodern identities) were published under the title *The Shock of the Other: Situating Alterities* as number 15 in the Thamyris/Intersecting series. That volume, edited by Esther Peeren and Silke Horstkotte, includes submissions dealing with the way alterity and its situated negotiations with identity are configured through the body, the psyche, and translational politics.

11. See chapter 1 ("Concept") in Bal's *Travelling Concepts in the Humanities*.

12. See www.ubuntu.com. The "What is Ubuntu?" page explains that "Ubuntu is an African word meaning 'Humanity to others', or 'I am what I am because of who we all are'. The Ubuntu distribution brings the spirit of Ubuntu to the software world."

13. Niezen is not blind to the drawbacks of using the Internet as a platform, noting that its demand for technical prowess may displace the traditional structures of authority in indigenous communities and that its "[u]ncensored cultural representation makes possible the presentation of community ideals that originate in no recognizable community. More than ever before,

it has become possible to express nostalgia for times that one has never experienced and pride towards peoples among whom one has never belonged" (546).

14. A similar positive assessment of the relational or "shared" identities within the indigenous movement can be found in Joy Hendry's *Reclaiming Culture: Indigenous People and Self-Representation* (see, especially, chapter 7).

15. Alfred and Corntassel prefer the term "peoplehood" as a "flexible and dynamic alternative to static political and legal definitional approaches to Indigenous identities" (610).

Bibliography

Alfred, Taiaiake, and Jeff Corntassel. "Being Indigenous: Resurgences against Contemporary Colonialism." *Government and Opposition* 40.4 (2005): 597–614.

Ang, Ien. "Identity Blues." *Without Guarantees: In Honour of Stuart Hall*. Ed. Paul Gilroy, Lawrence Grossberg and Angela McRobbie. London and New York: Verso, 2000. 1–13.

Appadurai, Arjun. "Disjuncture and Difference in the Global Cultural Economy." *Public Culture* 2.2 (1990): 1–24.

———. *Fear of Small Numbers: An Essay on the Geography of Anger*. Durham and London: Duke UP, 2006.

Bal, Mieke. *Travelling Concepts in the Humanities: A Rough Guide*. Toronto: U of Toronto P, 2002.

Baumann, Zygmund. "From Pilgrim to Tourist: A Short History of Identity." *Questions of Cultural Identity*. Ed. Stuart Hall and Paul du Gay. London, Thousand Oaks and New Delhi: Sage Publications, 1996. 18–36.

Bloom, Kevin, et al. "Umshini Wami." *Art South Africa* 7.2 (December 2000): n. pag. Web. 12 November 2009.

Bongie, Chris. *Friends and Enemies: The Scribal Politics of Post/Colonial Literature*. Liverpool: Liverpool UP, 2008.

Clifford, James. "Taking Identity Politics Seriously: the Contradictory Stony Ground…" *Without Guarantees: In Honour of Stuart Hall*. Ed. Paul Gilroy, Lawrence Grossberg and Angela McRobbie. London and New York: Verso, 2000. 94–112.

Dawson, Ashley. "*The Short Century*: Postcolonial Africa and the Politics of Representation." *Radical History Review* 87 (Fall 2003): 226–36.

Derrida, Jacques. *Specters of Marx: The State of the Debt, the Work of Mourning, & the New International*. Trans. Peggy Kamuf. New York and London: Routledge, 1994.

Fikeni, Somadoda. "The Polokwane Moment and South's Africa's Democracy at Crossroads." *State of the Nation*. Ed. Peter Kagwanja and Kwandiwe Kondlo. Cape Town: HSRC Press, 2009. 3–33.

Fraser, Nancy. "Rethinking Recognition." *New Left Review* 3 (May/June 2000): 107–20.

Friedman, Steven. "An Accidental Advance? South Africa's 2009 Elections." *Journal of Democracy* 20.4 (2009): 108–22.

Gates Jr., Henry Louis. *The Signifying Monkey: A Theory of African-American Literary Criticism*. Oxford: Oxford UP, 1989.

Gilroy, Paul. "Diaspora and the Detours of Identity." *Identity and Difference*. Ed. Kathryn Woodward. London: Sage/Open University, 1997. 299–343.

Gunner, Liz. "Jacob Zuma, the Social Body and the Unruly Power of Song." *African Affairs* 108.4 (2008): 27–48.

Hall, Stuart. "Who Needs Identity?" *Questions of Cultural Identity*. Ed. Stuart Hall and Paul du Gay. London, Thousand Oaks and New Delhi: Sage Publications, 1996. 1–17.

Hekman, Susan. "Beyond Identity: Feminism, Identity and Identity Politics." *Feminist Theory* 1.3 (2000): 289–308.

Hendry, Joy. *Reclaiming Culture: Indigenous People and Self-Representation*. New York and Basingstoke: Palgrave Macmillan, 2005.

Hobsbawm, Eric. "Introduction: Inventing Traditions." *The Invention of Tradition*. Ed. Eric Hobsbawm and Terence Ranger. Cambridge: Cambridge UP, 2003. 1–14.

hooks, bell. "Postmodern Blackness." *The Norton Anthology of Theory and Criticism*. Ed. Vincent B. Leitch et al. New York: W.W. Norton & Company, 2001. 2478–84.

Lloyd, Mona. *Beyond Identity Politics: Feminism, Power and Politics*. London: Sage, 2005.

Martin, Denis-Constant. "The Choices of Identity." *Social Identities* 1.1 (1995): 5–20.

Niezen, Ronald. "Digital Identity: The Construction of Virtual Selfhood in the Indigenous Peoples' Movement." *Comparative Studies in Society and History* 47 (2005): 532–51.

Peeren, Esther, and Silke Horstkotte. "Introduction: The Shock of the Other." *The Shock of the Other: Situating Alterities*. Ed. Silke Horstkotte and Esther Peeren. Amsterdam, New York: Rodopi, 2007. 9–21.

Radhakrishnan, R. "Culture as Common Ground: Ethnicity and Beyond." *MELUS* 14.2 (1987): 5–19.

———. "Globalization, Desire, and the Politics of Representation." *Comparative Literature* 53.4 (2001): 315–32

———. "Postcoloniality and the Boundaries of Identity." *Callaloo* 16.4 (1993): 750–71.

Scott, Joan W. "Multiculturalism and the Politics of Identity." *October* 61 (1992): 12–19.

Weaver, Hilary N. "Indigenous Identity: What Is It, and Who *Really* Has It?" *American Indian Quarterly* 25.2 (Spring 2001): 240–55.

Williams, Raymond. *Keywords: A Vocabulary of Culture and Society*. London: Fontana Press, 1988.

I. Concepts of Postcolonial Identity: Contingent Articulations

Alterity and Identities: The Paradoxes of Authenticity

Sudeep Dasgupta

> To exist is to be called into being in relation to an Otherness.
> (Bhabha, "Remembering Fanon" 117)

The car swerves and screeches to a halt as the young driver, Paul, catches sight of his sister on the park bench. She cradles the head of a tall white man who looks up into her eyes. Paul scrambles out of the car and furiously attacks the man gazing at his sister. Classic culture-clash? The siblings are of Lebanese origin, the man Swedish. But what would the word "origin" mean in this context? Or "Swedish" for that matter? The designer-clad Lebanese man drives an expensive car and flashes his bulging wallet at every turn, while the Swede rides a bicycle, wears cheap sportswear, and clears dog shit from the city park. If their visible presence does not bear out cultural stereotypes, neither does the situation. The brother is hell-bent on having his sister married off to a fellow "Lebanese." If this scenario of male authority asserting the right to determine kinship and cultural continuity looks familiar, the irony resides in the fact that the son is taking over the role of the patriarch, whose own ineffectuality and final acquiescence to his Swedish daughter-in-law closes the film.

It is tempting at this point to conclude that here one sees cultural essentialism unraveling as the movement of difference complicates questions of alterity and identity. Is this not *différance* in "action," captured before the camera-eye? By what theoretical assumptions must one proceed in order to read difference into a text? Must one assume a special affinity between a text that broaches the question of cultural difference and the concept of *difference*? I take as my starting point in this essay the question of difference as it crosses (out) the discourse of "self-presence" so that the Self/Other relationship moves beyond the confines of purity-talk.[1] This recognition of difference opens my argument but will develop its theoretical and historical dimensions as the relationship between alterity and identity is analyzed. My chosen epigraph immediately links the question of Otherness to that of Being. What is gained in framing otherness, or alterity, by being as such? For, however relational the understanding of alterity might be, might not a focus on being tend to neglect that this relationality between being and otherness is also related to the Other of being as experience? If a subject's being comes into existence through another subject, which is its Other, Being as such also has its Other in experience as the shifting, lived habitus through which the subject negotiates within and between different fields.[2] And might not the lived experience of being-in-relation to otherness muddy the waters of identity-talk somewhat, so that notions of the hybrid and the pure become untenable? By using authenticity as an orienting-point for analyzing this relationship between alterity and identity, I will interrogate the contemporary discourse on cultural difference. "Authenticity" here will be understood in terms of its referential status vis-à-vis the concept-object relation, as well as a more specifically quotidian mode of living-in-the-world.[3] I will situate this analysis through a reading of the film *Jalla! Jalla!* (Fares 2000; *JJ* from now on) from which the above episode is described.

Left critiques of the contemporary cultural politics around the "Other" are rightly marked by a criticism of the Us/Them discourse couched in terms of civilization, culture, and religion. Thus, questions of alterity and identity, in particular critiques of the essentialist character of such concepts in political discourse, continue to have a bite to them, despite the limits of the essentialism/constructivism debates. However, their valency as intellectual "weapons of the weak" is ambiguous at best,[4] while as discursive tools within the embattled public sphere, they have been blunted by the rise of "extremist networks" across the globe, which seem to contradict all the complexity, contradictory character, and fluidity of "culture" that we cultural analysts are so fond of arguing for. Part of the contention of this paper will be that both circumstances within the geo-politics of current cultural politics and the growing rigidity of "cultural hybridity" talk within the academy have ceded questions of alterity and identity to a familiar discourse where opposing sides endlessly repeat the same discourse. Further, this polarized debate can explain the rise of contemporary "fundamentalisms" only within the bounds of the limiting discursive formation of hybridity versus tradition. It is in this context, tending to hypostasize both cultural identity and cultural hybridity, that I will argue for fine-tuning, developing and critiquing the effectivity of alterity and identity as mobilizing discourses. What is at stake here is not legislating between different forms of identity but inserting the multiple temporalities of contemporary history as they fragment and frame the Other. Recognition of this everyday living through different pasts and presents reorients the question of alterity from a focus on identity towards a critical reflection within postcolonial theory on what Adorno and Horkheimer, in *The Dialectic of Enlightenment*, called "thought thinking itself." I will explore this at first conceptually closed notion by underlining the place of the object as Other to theoretical discourse. Alterity thus figured is not just about cultural difference but about our own theoretical protocols around working with concepts.

Contemporary media productions have been highlighting the complexity through which "culture" is lived in its quotidian dimension. Hanif Kureishi's *My Beautiful Launderette* (1985) was a definitive critique in the period of high-Thatcherism of the emptiness of thinking the "pure subject" of resistance in cultural terms. That critique, however, has become common enough now within certain media fora and the academy. The decision to focus on *JJ* to argue for rethinking cultural difference in all its complexity is based on a number of factors. Firstly, within the contemporary political situation (one which in cultural terms seems to be becoming increasingly global rather than just U.S.-centered after the European capitulation to U.S. demands post-9/11), the enduring manifestation of the desire to belong culturally to a "minority" group seems at odds with the cultural impurity we saw in Kureishi's and other cultural producers' works. Unlike Omar in *My Beautiful Launderette*, who refuses to satisfy his father's desire to see him go to college and prefers to follow his uncle's advice to "squeeze the tits of the system" of upward mobility and free enterprise that Thatcher set in motion, Roro, the protagonist in *JJ*, chooses to negotiate between his family's desire for cultural-familial continuity and a life of his own that already exists outside the family circle. As such, the film highlights the continuing pull that many second-generation immigrants encounter as they negotiate their ambivalent position within European society. Secondly, while Channel 4, whose media profile has tended to be provocative, "thoughtful," and experimental, funded the filming of *My Beautiful Launderette*, *JJ* was made on a tight budget (approximately £630,000), with Josef Fares, who wrote the script as well as directing the film, using his friends and family (his brother Fares Fares plays the protagonist) as cast and crew. *JJ* was shot in thirty days, mostly in Fares's hometown Örebro. While unwilling to make claims about the way institutionalized cultural politics and content might relate, it is worth noting that much contemporary film and television production reproduces old stereotypes of *métissage* without highlighting the enduring pressures that "tradition" might bring to bear on negotiating cultural difference.[5] My point here is that, in certain ways, the most successful hybrids are precisely those who reinforce cultural stereotypes through certain forms of liberal multiculturalism. I use the word "successful" here because the issue is not one of hybrids versus pure identities, but of tracking which forms of hybridity become institutionally validated within different political arenas.

Falling within the genre of "light comedy," *JJ* provides a social commentary and a location through which to interrogate how the mixing of cultural identities within Europe is a social and historical process. In this sense, it provides not so much an example of a concept of hybridity[6] as an object in the sense that Adorno understands the term, as an Other, an alterity that will always disturb attempts at conceptual capture.[7] How one knows, an epistemological question, underwrites how we name, the nominalist moment. Here Adorno's metacritique of Husserl is particularly pertinent in framing my argument that identity-talk is underwritten by claims to authenticity: "Epistemology is true as long as it accounts for the impossibility of its own beginning and lets itself be driven at every stage by its *inadequacy* to the things themselves. It is, however, untrue in the pretension that success is at hand and that states-of-affairs would ever simply correspond to its constructions and aporetic concepts" ("Metacritique" 131, emphasis added).[8]

What sort of disturbance does a film like *JJ* trigger in our conceptual certainties around thinking postcolonial identity? Firstly, the notion of hybridity and complexity that has become common sense within much postcolonial theory is subtended by a claim to authenticity. This authenticity is understood in terms of an adequation between a *notion* of "cultural difference" (Bhabha) and the *empirical object* it designates. For example, the colonizer/colonized relationship is undone in its Manichean formulations as one of contamination, ambivalence and instability. Thus, the instability of the object is captured by a name that attempts to legislate its paradoxical purity as a hybrid phenomenon. However, as names go, the term "the hybrid" cannot ignore the "irreducible hybridity of all language," as Gayatri Spivak has argued (*Critique of Postcolonial Reason* 164; see also 361). Thus, to maintain that one identity is rightly hybrid and empirically true, while claims to purity of origin are ideological or discourse-effects, in effect seeks to assign a closure to what will inevitably be a processual instability in naming. Having argued that a discourse of nominalist stability underscores the authentic claims of alterity as "difference," I want to read *JJ* as evading this sort of conceptual capture. Further, I would contend that this evasion is more historical, empirical, or "other" to the claims of metaphysical thinking than some kind of exemplification (however fraught) of the floating signifier (whose reduction to a theoretical mantra is a telling example of the kind of conceptual imperialism I have discussed above).[9]

History 1: most of the discussions of hybridity, difference, and deference have been formulated through a reading of the colonial archive, with an understandable though generally limiting focus on the Indian colonial experience. Bhabha's influential and compelling argument in "Of Mimicry and Man," for example, underscores the reformulation of colonial epistemic violence (Spivak) through the counter-discourse of the native. This hybrid rearticulation, which precedes what elsewhere he describes as a similar tension between the performative and the pedagogic in the newly independent nation-state's discourse, is compelling but problematic for two reasons: one conceptual and the other historical. For now, I shall focus on the historical element. Take the colonial moment, albeit circumscribed to a particular "Indian" moment. The dynamics and re-articulation of colonial discourse by its unequal interlocutors are conditioned by the modalities of what Albert Memmi, in *The Colonizer and the*

Colonized, calls the "colonial situation." That is, how and why hybridity might emerge must be understood as the consequence of a strategic borrowing of tools, a *bricolage*, of what is at hand *at that time*.[10] The historically specific situation of colonialism determines (in the sense of setting the limits of maneuver, to evoke Raymond Williams's formulation) this exchange between colonizer and colonized. There is, for instance, no simple rejection of native idioms of colonized discourses of alterity; rather, they are reformulated towards combating, under the guise of "sly civility," the privilege of colonial discourse. The ambivalence Bhabha identifies is underscored by the "application" of a particular reading of the split subject of enunciation in Lacan, and of "difference" in Derrida. But in a different historical period (between the wars, in Indonesia as a colonial possession of the Dutch), what Benedict Anderson calls the seriality of discourse manifests itself, where there is a complete overturning of native discourse and a more universal series of concepts is employed by the "natives." This seems to have to do not so much with ambivalence as to be a case of the victory of a universalist paradigm or worldview that was taken up by the colonized subject. A notion of hybridity might not be so apposite in this context, for what emerges is less a *métissage* than a wholesale borrowing. Given that it is a product of a certain encounter, it does not bear any claims to native purity, of course (here the link with hybridity is made halfway), yet it is hardly similar to the sort of mimicry Bhabha identifies in India. The "use" of the concepts of king and bureaucrat are turned to anti-colonial "politics" (another new term) but the terms remain the same.[11] The conclusion must be, then, that ambivalence is not the necessary result of a colonial encounter. And if it does occur, a comparative reading of *differential* appropriations reveals more about the specificities of the "colonial situation" than the concretization of an abstract theory of the slippage of the signifier.

Concept 1: If alterity cannot be marked as absolutely other but grasped as hybridity, how might this understanding be productively deployed at the present time? Can it be simply adequate to use "alterity" when it is so undergirded by a logic of *adequatio*, given the paradoxical easy referentiality that this "differential" term holds? Here the historical conjoins the conceptual as an interruptive encounter between the concept and its possibilities. The historical reading thus suggests that the conceptual designations are not faulty because of a purely internal logical fallacy, but because of the discontinuous relay between the two. Adorno argues that to unlock the history in an object, a single concept remains inadequate (inadequacy will always remain a hallmark of much of the abortive metaphysics that Adorno yearns for). Rather, he suggests a constellative critique where the historical specificity of the object can be unlocked through a contingently articulated illumination of concepts. In small measure, my argument constellates the alterity-identity relation with Adorno's notion of authenticity. His critique of authenticity is specifically leveled against Heidegger's own use of a particular vacant terminology that attempts profoundness.[12] While

Heidegger's notions of authenticity and the *Augenblick* (profoundly cultural terms that themselves legislate between cultural insiders and those who do not belong to a culture) assume an aura of profoundness that is not reducible to the performative possibilities of contaminative hybridity, the structure of the argument remains very similar, since the transportability of the terms is linked to their being cut off from historical specificity, which Adorno sees as one of the prime deficiencies of philosophical work.[13] It is by deploying a series of concepts that struggle to (inevitably inadequately) unlock the history in the object that Adorno argues the philosophical can acknowledge both its vulnerability as well as its recognition of the object as the Other, as the alterity which philosophy cannot subsume.

Given the institutional and historical specificity of *JJ* as a cultural product, what reworkings of notions of immigritude are made available by this object? Firstly, the film offers a disturbance to our received notions of counter-discourses to discourses of hybridity. Rather than setting off a clear distinction between authentic culture (which we know *analytically* to be fabricated) and hybrid postcolonial immigrant subjectivity, the film figures this relationship as one of constant negotiation, of a pull, an embrace, and a tension between familial demands for an impure cultural continuity and assertions of authentic individuality.[14] Roro, as the son of a Lebanese family now living in Sweden, straddles a divided existence between home (marked by his grandmother, Lebanese food, and parental demands to marry another immigrant Lebanese Christian, Yasmin, to whom he is engaged) and his life outside as a park attendant with his best friend Måns, a native Swede, and his (Roro's) Swedish girlfriend, Lisa. Although these two worlds keep crossing (Måns is, for example, not a stranger to Roro's family), such crossings are, however, limited to a line of sexual/kinship relations which cannot be made public. The parents' demands for Roro to get married are not met with outright rejection but a silent acquiescence behind which is marked a secret agreement between the engaged pair to play along for a while. Why?

A notion of hybridity that underscores the mutual contamination of both spheres is readily evident, but unable to explain the enduring pressures that are especially resurfacing in the present historical moment, where arguments of the "rise in fundamentalism," especially around immigrants, are seen as a threat to hybrid realities. The film's intervention I see as lying in its attempt to underscore the enduring pressures to conform to a fabricated tradition of one's roots (as seen from both points of view: the culture in question and the host culture), when as good integrated or critical insider/outsiders we would have given up *that* desire for a fuller integration into the hybrid pleasures and possibilities of a multicultural West. Through comedy, this double pressure is underscored as profoundly hybrid, yet here the term can only be the starting point for analyzing the historical specificity of a particular form of subjectivity. The situation here is not a straightforward choice between the pedagogic function of installing a pure subjectivity or performatively bringing it into being. The family itself is hardly stereotypical and in the very mundane details of its being lived, we encounter a humorous unhinging of the temptation to stereotype the Other. When Måns visits Roro's family home, our first encounter with Arabic is in a series of "conversations" between Roro and the family parrot. The words which issue from the parrot's mouth are "I'm going to fuck your brains out" and "Eat shit." Obviously, swearing is hardly the sole preserve of the English-speaking world, but given the clichés through which we understand Arabic as either the call to prayers that issues from a nearby mosque in the everyday lives of those who live close to one, or the mass-mediated sound and image performances of Islamic clergy from Ramallah to Tehran on our TV screens, for once we hear Arabic and read the translation in all its vulgarity. Later we shall be reminded that Arabic is a language rather than a culture, and that it is the "lingua franca" of Jews, Christians, and many others besides Muslims (Roro's family are Christian). "You and your Arab bird, you are all family," jokes Måns, to which Roro laughingly remarks, "Lebanese bird!" All of this is very subtly spun out through the film, and is striking for those not in the know. Not because of its immense social significance as political tract, however, but because the film's portrayal of very mundane everyday life, the mode of living-in-the-world of a certain kind of immigrant in Sweden, forces us to re-examine our received assumptions of alterity.[15] JJ cautions against making claims about the projected unicity, coherence, and tradition of the stranger inside the host. The grandmother's affectionate repartees with Måns – "What about your bald friend?" she asks Roro, "Is he married?" Måns replies "No I'm not," to which the grandmother responds in Arabic, "First you need to grow some hair" – exemplify the sort of convivial banter that announces cultural incomprehension (his baldness) while seemingly expressing concern for his future (marriage prospects). Such banter is anyway intelligible beneath its face-value, since Måns hardly needs to subscribe to her norms, given the circles he might move in, while she would not expect him to subscribe to hers. This staging of cultural "mis"-communication acknowledges a form of social intimacy fed through each other's cultural scripts rather than evoking a clash between two cultures. These are historical moments of everyday postcoloniality, where inter-subjective relationships mediated through filial and affiliative ties broaden the sphere of what home means, not just for Roro, the young protagonist, but also for his aging grandmother. They play out on *one* side of the supposed pedagogic/performative divide a specific form of hybridity that is not transportable to other forms of postcolonial specificity.

Roro's own hybridity is evidenced in his intimate relationship with Måns, whose problems with sexually satisfying his girlfriend initiate attempts by Roro to help him by buying sex toys and taking him to a native healer from his own community. Even the latter encounter is marked by a hilarity that does not pontificate on cultural difference – Måns undergoes many "treatments," from swallowing a worm to an uncomfortably vigorous massage. "He can't get it up," explains Roro to his healer acquaintance, who snaps back with "he must be a fag then!" Roro translates this for Måns as "he thinks it is strange." The linguistic barrier between Roro and Måns thus facilitates a protectiveness on Roro's part towards his Swedish friend – difference enabling a non-conflictual relationality. Rather than conflicting demands between two alternating discourses of authenticity and purity, then, the alterity of these discourses has more to do with the quotidian living out of friendship.[16] Hybridity does not emerge as the "product" of pure, absolutely Other encounters, but, in Derridean terms, as the mark of a trace where the line between the ontic and the ontological cannot be stabilized. This instability is, however, historically specific and mediated in the film, in a sense which is salient for our historical moment, in which Europe and its culture are up for grabs.

By emphasizing the enduring pressure, the continued salience of conflicting discourses of hybridity that play out on Roro and the other characters, *including* his father and grandmother, the film illustrates through comedy why to legislate hybrid postcolonial identity as politically and empirically existent or desirable falls far short of the current moment. Firstly, the hybrid is everywhere to be seen in this film – even the violent, masculinist privilege of the brother seeking to ensure his sister's marriage to Roro exemplifies a thoroughly western lifestyle. Secondly, conceptually hybridity could not explain the historically specific pull that familial discourses of cultural continuity might have for second-generation immigrants, who, as the triumphalist discourse of Western liberalism would like to have it, have or must have attained "integration" into Western "culture" with all its attendant discourses of free enterprise, bourgeois subjectivity, individual freedom, and the like. As the different forms of hybridity rather than the hybrid/pure identity dyad emerge in the film, the salience of the term "hybrid," or indeed "identity," in thinking cultural difference seems to lose its critical purchase. Further, one sees that Roro's desire to satisfy his family's wish that he get married is not a demand from one side of his supposedly bifurcated life (which I provisionally signaled earlier), but a sense of responsibility towards a *range* of different relationships that form him as friend, lover, fiancé, grandson, etc. The pull to tradition is an inaccurate description not because there is no pressure but because the tradition/modernity divide is an objectively unreal frame through which to understand Roro's actions.

The film's denouement, where Roro ends up leaving his marriage party with the wrong bride (his Swedish girlfriend, Lisa) while his friend Måns runs off with Yasmin, the Lebanese fiancée, could be read as the victory of hybrid immigrant subjectivity over the old guard. Roro's father's own affectionate goodbye and blessing, however, illustrates the pull of love on the other side; the obverse of Roro's affection for his family is represented in the father's concern and love for his son, and his understanding of his decision. Hybridity again is a product not of a normative and disruptive encounter, but evidenced as the doubling or reciprocal intertwining of everyday, familial, and affiliative links across cultures at a particular historical moment.

In "Cultural Criticism and Society," Adorno notes that ". . . no authentic work of art and no true philosophy, according to their very meaning, has ever exhausted itself in itself alone, in its being-in-itself. They have always stood in relation to the actual life-process of society from which they distinguished themselves" (200). *JJ* stages a movement beyond the inbuilt manicheaism which must underwrite the film's claims to difference. For the uninterrogated binarism that underwrites hybridity arguments must eschew the possibility of what Spivak, in her reading of Maryse Condé's *Heremakhonon*, calls "that originary hybrid" ("Staging of Time" 92). This figures hybridity as a more or less universal phenomenon rather than the privileged characteristic of a chosen few, contesting the model in which the immigrant or the diasporic becomes the conclusion of such a glance at alterity.[17] The universality of hybridity, of course, is not the result of an identical logic of difference but, among other things, of the disaggregated planetary coexistence of multiple space-time trajectories within which different subjecitivities are formed and circulate. However, the analytical poverty of stopping at such a conclusion (a quite different one nevertheless from the problematic notions of hybridity in Bhabha) has been evidenced through a historical/conceptual reading of alterity in *JJ*. Distinguishing between different forms of hybridity becomes crucial if one is interested in making interventionary claims around cultural politics. The demand for specificity arises from a methodological investment not so much in transposing a linguistic critique of the sign onto empirical realities, but in disturbing the line between the empirical and the conceptual through a recognition of the fallibility of conceptual reasoning (the historical as lived through everyday experience undermines the empirical-conceptual division).

My argument has moved between a philosophical focus on the problem of authenticity, particularly in Adorno, and the everydayness manifested in *JJ*, which functions as a disturbing counterpart to both the ponderous pronouncements of hybridity and the spurious cosmopolitanism of conservative politics. This everydayness functions as something like the Other of Being in all its profundity and bears some relation to the phenomenology of dialectics that Fredric Jameson brilliantly outlined in *Marxism and Form*. There, he argues that "precisely because dialectical thinking depends so closely on the habitual everyday mode of thought which it is called on to transcend, it can take on a number of different and apparently contradictory forms" (308). I have contended that an uninterrogated espousal of hybricity appears in our intellectual moment as one such "habitual mode of thought." Dialectics, however, does not ascend into the stratosphere of philosophical intricacy to redeem a lost critical moment to stay lodged up there. Rather, "when common sense predominates and characterizes our normal everyday mental atmosphere, dialectical thinking presents itself as perversely hair-splitting, as the over elaborate and the over subtle, reminding us that the simple [the hybrid] is in reality only a simplification, and that the self-evident draws its force from hosts of buried presuppositions" (308). The argument above has attempted to expose some of these presuppositions. If hybridity talk runs the risk of becoming a commonsensical intellectual habit, by reading the cross-relationships in the film I have attempted to show not just a proliferation of multiple hybridities but also a denial of what Adorno thought as resistant objectivity outside the fetish of nominalism.

As argued earlier, the strength or otherwise of alterity talk, of the Other as subject, is reread in this essay as the problem of the Other as the Object of metaphysics. Thus, when "pure philosophy," as Adorno puts it, exhausts itself *in*-itself, it undermines its own authenticity, which comes to being in relation to the "actual life-processes" of society. How banal it might sound, after the conceptual histrionics of Adorno's *Negative Dialectics*, to make appeals to "the actual life-processes of society." But part of the burden of my argument is precisely to descend to, and then ascend above these levels. Jameson makes a particularly apt presentation of this to-and-fro:

When ... after the fashion of intellectuals, we begin to work our way up through a series of abstractions, each one progressively further and further away from the real itself, pervaded as we do so by an uneasy suspicion that the whole teetering construction stands as a monument not to new laws of nature, but rather to the rules of some private mental hobby, then dialectical thought comes as a brutal rupture, as a cutting of the knots that restore us suddenly to the grossest truths, to facts as unpleasantly common as common sense itself. (308–09)

Bhabha's argument of being-in-relation, which opened this essay, has been reworked: firstly, relationality is no longer set up as being in relation to an Other that is historically unspecified; secondly, my argument progresses towards Adorno's insistence that both the work of culture (*Kunstwerk as Arbeit*) and philosophy are authentic insofar as their relation to social life-processes is acknowledged, thus highlighting a reflexive play between conceptual work and everyday practice in its status as objectlike. Bhabha's formulation is thus not just minimal, in setting Self in relation to Other, but a-historical, since his glance is fixed on this dyadic relationship and ignores the broader social/historical processes which Adorno underscores in thinking authenticity. The authentic in conceptual thinking and cultural production is its historically-specific relation with the world within which the Self and its Other are "called into being." Bhabha explicitly underlines his lack of faith in such historical thinking when he writes: "It is one of the original and disturbing qualities of *Black Skin, White Masks* that it rarely historicizes the colonial experience" ("Remembering Fanon" 115). Impressed by this "originality," it is clear that the alleged a-historical character of Fanon's argument does not disturb *him* (Bhabha), but rather the bogeyman of the Enlightenment, here suitably reduced, as in much postmodernist thought, to the "master-narrative or realist perspective that provide a background of social and historical facts against which emerge the problems of the individual or collective psyche" (115). Bhabha must only see history as teleology and therefore of no use in his formulation of alterity. Fanon's original rewriting of the master-slave dialectic becomes deconstruction in Bhabha's hands. Dare one dialectize deconstruction? Adorno, whose critique of teleological thinking hardly needs underlining, does place questions of alterity within the historical resistance of the epistemological object towards the concept. This or that representation of the immigrant and the diasporic is not reducible to the adequation of hybrid nominalism. Authenticity is linked to history, relationality, and the Other, and provides the means to critique both cultural products and conceptual thinking. It is precisely this double agenda, of tracking Otherness in relation with history in the film and situating the concept of alterity in relation to the Object, that the present text furthers by deploying the notion of authenticity.

The philosophical humility of acknowledging the inadequacy of concept to thing is no self-abasing plea for hand-wringing but precisely the sort of productive recognition that enables an improper grasping, however contingent and incomplete, of the specificity of the object (Adorno, "Cultural Criticism"). My reading of Roro, as son, friend, lover, fiancé, and grandson, cannot be definitive but only multi-relational, inseparable from Måns, his father, Lisa, Yasmin, and Paul, or indeed the signifiers of Sweden and Lebanon. Alterity and authenticity as concepts which name, and as metaphors which transform objects, when read within such a constellation of double pressures (Europe and its others) and the instabilities of othering as a universal phenomenon, enable a nuanced and more pointed understanding of alterity as multiple identities. One might still want to hold on to thinking Europe and its Others, not as the recto/verso of a page in the contemporary history of *possessive* individualism (to belong *properly* to a culture implies reading property into the proper), but as a set of shifting relationships which engender multiple forms of alterities. The status of these alterities would need to be rethought as the fraught relationship between the concept and the epistemological object, rather than as the play of difference under the more general sign of "writing."

I have argued that once we make Spivak's seemingly paradoxical "originary hybrid" the starting point for investigating the relationship between alterity and identity, the "resurgence" of certain forms of "barbarism" that the civilized West must contend with cannot be grasped without shifting below the level of ontological arguments of Being. For how postcoloniality is lived in the everyday, within the multiple space-time configurations through which the Other navigates, might be the occasion for moving beyond legislating and naming identities. The Other as Object in and of theory might force us to recognize what true authenticity might mean in our attempts to discipline postcoloniality.

Notes

1. Derrida's loving critique in *Margins of Philosophy* of Heidegger's *Sein und Zeit* (*Being and Time*) is the occasion for reflecting on "self-presence" as the impossibility of fixing an origin. It is one philosophical starting-point for plotting the trajectory of cultural-identity talk, which is never substantially dealt with by those in postcolonial studies who seem so indebted to hybridity talk, such as Homi Bhabha and Stuart Hall. To signal this absent presence is not to privilege it.

2. See Bourdieu's *Logic of Practice*. The "sense" of the book's French title, *Le sens pratique*, more readily than "logic" evokes the everyday dimensions of life rather than the more profound-sounding question of Being-as-existence or metaphysical protocols of conceptual reasoning. "Sense" indicates a more quotidian "feel for the game."

3. "Living-in-the world" rather than "Being-in-the-world" is one way in which I wish to move beyond the seeming profundity of Heidegger's privileging of metaphysics without falling back on the quasi-transcendental "difference" of a Derrida. Hence my thinking of the concept-object relation (Adorno) and "living-in-the-world" as an inflection of Bourdieu's dialectical understanding of the habitus-field relationship. Needless to say, a deconstructive reading tends to focus on undermining the power of the concept from the inside, rather than its relationship with the noumenal world. Spivak's engagement with deconstruction is an interesting attempt at moving beyond this limitation, particularly in her readings of the "axiomatics of imperialism" ("Three Women's Texts" 254).

4. Bernard-Henri Lévi and André Glucksmann are but two of a range of intellectuals in the European media circuit who do not qualify as "weak." Rightist intellectuals have been embraced by the media in the present context, giving respectability to the academy seen as "too Leftist." For a recent critique of the role of intellectuals in the media, see Stabile and Morooka. Bourdieu's *Sur la télévision: suivi de l'emprise du journalisme* provides an unfashionably trenchant attack on media and political discourse.

5. An example is film-artist Isaac Julien's recent historical re-reading of slavery in *Vagabondia* (2000).

6. Derrida, in *Of Grammatology*, has questioned whether an example is simply a concretization of a theory with particular reference to questions of cultural difference in his interrogation of Claude Lévi-Strauss's struggle to place the incest taboo within both a universal and a specific category. The general problem of the place of the particular for my present argument is indebted less to the deconstruction of "western logocentrism" than it is to Adorno's re-reading of the Hegelian dialectic in *Negative Dialectics*. However, at this point, to choose *JJ* is to underline that it is not a concrete example of an abstract principle but one point of entry into interrogating the claims of certain alterist modes of thinking.

7. See Part Two of *Negative Dialectics* (170–189). It might seem counterintuitive to suggest a film is an object, but it is worth noting that, minimally, a film as a cultural product, bought, sold, and inserted into chains of meaning-production is not just a "representation" of an underlying reality.

8. Here the distance between deconstruction and dialectics (negative dialectics' book-length introduction to the intellectual scene took place in 1966; this essay was Adorno's introduction to *Against Epistemology* a decade earlier. Hence, "dialectics" had not yet been transformed into "negative dialectics") can be glimpsed. It is the inadequacy between concept and object that undermines philosophical thinking, not the missed encounter between signifier and signified.

9. Derrida (on Heidegger), in carefully attempting to say what *différance* is, must start through a series of negatives: "*Différance* is not a 'species' of the genus *ontological difference*. . . . It is neither position (appropriation) nor negation (expropriation), but rather *other*" (*Margins* 26n26). The *economy* of the proper traversed by difference is thus the consequence of alterity (the other). To reinscribe this difference would

happen on the scene of the text in general, here understood in the loose sense as the knotted, woven, and endlessly connected web that goes in and out of the text it weaves.

Methodologically, such an argument of course calls up traversing the field of Western metaphysics through an interrogation of different "disciplines" (such as Derrida's own forays in anthropology, linguistics and psychoanalysis), yet the deconstructive reading of postcolonial theory will often use "deconstruction," and particularly "difference," as concepts to "apply" to the results of other disciplines such as Subaltern historiography. This distinction (between Derrida's deconstructive exercises and much postcolonial theory's application of "difference" to identity) is as tenuous as Derrida's own argument about the thin line between example and theory in Lévi-Strauss. For all Derrida's variegated forays into other disciplines, the conclusions and the concepts deployed are surprisingly limited.

10. The richness of Memmi's argument in contrast to the linguistic eloquence but analytical poverty of Bhabha's formulation of hybridity can only be signaled here.

11. The distinction between its use and "the name of the tool or concept" does, of course, make *bricolage* a fuzzy concept, but distinctions must be contingently articulated between the reworking of terms and their straightforward borrowing if one is not to flatten out the difference.

12. The definitive critique of Heidegger's language of authenticity is to be found in Adorno's *The Jargon of Authenticity*. It was intended as a section of *Negative Dialectics*, but its focus on "linguistic physiognomy and sociology" (xvii) did not fit in with the more philosophical critique of that work.

13. Here the difference between Adorno and Derrida's critique of Heidegger becomes apparent. While, for Derrida, it is the temporality of Being underscored by *différance* which makes (im)possible ontological certainty, for Adorno it is the historical blindedness of conceptual development in Heidegger's ontological talk, one intertwined with a conceptual critique of the concept, that establishes his dialectical distance from Derrida's argument about "the trace." Already in "Metacritique of Epistemology," Being, as an ontological first, or the first of *prima philosophica* in Husserl, is read by Adorno as installing either the first or the given as originary. This has less to do with the temporal slippage of the signifier than with a historical question: in a reified world, where the identity principle has become internalized, the adequatio between thought and reality ("the entity" in this essay, the object in *Negative Dialectics*) cannot be undone by purely philosophical speculation, but only by the interruption of the common sense of this identity principle in reified society.

14. This is a knotty problem for media studies. What does one do when the film on the surface itself interrogates authenticity in culturally pure terms? The analyst's work is already done, as it were. Rather than simply concluding with what the film declares on its surface (why analyze it then?), the interest of media analysis would be to take this surface critique (rather than deconstruction) of ideologies of cultural purity further through the interruption of our sedimented critiques of cultural politics.

15. The use of pro-nomials throughout this essay is always inadequate since I cannot assume the reading position of its implied reader beforehand. In a sense, the substance of my argument is linked to this question of who is doing the reading.

16. *Jalla! Jalla!*, the title of the film, eschews profundity by its mundane colloquialism. Signaling in its lack of specificity a range of meanings from "hurry up" to "come on," it is a loquation that animates everyday conversation.

17. Hence Spivak's critique of Derrida's privileging of "diaspora" as the perspective from which to think hybridity ("Staging of Time" 96n4). Roro is not strictly speaking diasporic in this sense, and need not be. This is also why I brought up in an earlier section the difference between different forms of hybrid discourse – that of the Indian colonized subject's mimicry under British rule, and the Javanese adoption of Dutch governmental categories.

Bibliography

Adorno, Theodor W. "Cultural Criticism and Society." *The Adorno Reader*. London: Basil Blackwell, 2000. 195–210.

———. *The Jargon of Authenticity*. Trans. Knut Tarnowski and Frederic Will. London: Routledge, 2003.

———. "Metacritique of Epistemology." *The Adorno Reader*. Ed. Brian O'Connor. London: Basil Blackwell, 2000. 112–36.

———. *Negative Dialectics*. Trans. E.B. Ashton. New York: Continuum, 2000.

Adorno, Theodor W., and Max Horkheimer. *The Dialectic of Enlightenment*. Trans. John Cumming. New York: Continuum, 2001.

Anderson, Benedict. "Nationalism, Identity, and the World-in-Motion: On the Logics of Seriality." *Cosmopolitics: Thinking and Feeling Beyond the Nation*. Ed. Pheng Cheah and Bruce Robbins. Minneapolis: U of Minnesota P, 1998. 117–33.

Bhabha, Homi. "Of Mimicry and Man: The Ambivalence of Colonial Discourse." *The Location of Culture*. London and New York: Routledge, 1994. 85–92.

———. "Remembering Fanon: Self, Pysche and the Colonial Condition." *Colonial Discourse and Postcolonial Theory: A Reader*. Ed. Laura Chrisman and Patrick Williams. New York: Columbia UP, 1994. 112–31.

Bourdieu, Pierre. *The Logic of Practice*. Trans. Richard Nice. Cambridge: Polity Press, 1990.

———. *Sur la télévision: suivi de l'emprise du journalisme*. Paris: Liber, 1996.

Derrida, Jacques. *Margins of Philosophy*. Trans. Alan Bass. Chicago: U of Chicago P, 1982.

———. *Of Grammatology*. Trans. Gayatri Chakravorty Spivak. Baltimore: The John Hopkins UP, 1976.

Jameson, Fredric. *Marxism and Form: Twentieth-Century Dialectical Theories of Literature*. Princeton: Princeton UP, 1971.

Memmi, Albert. *The Colonizer and the Colonized*. Boston: Beacon Press, 1967.

Spivak, Gayatri Chakravorty. *A Critique of Postcolonial Reason: Toward a History of the Vanishing Present*. Cambridge, MA and London: Harvard UP, 1999.

———. "The Staging of Time in *Heremakhonon*." *Cultural Studies* 17.1 (2003): 85–97.

———. "Three Women's Texts and a Critique of Imperialism." *Critical Inquiry* 12.1 (1985): 243–61.

Stabile, Carol A., and Junya Morooka. "Between Two Evils, I Refuse to Choose the Lesser." *Cultural Studies* 17.3/4 (2003): 326–48.

Insularity and Identity at Odds in Martinique: 1973 to 2004

Marc Brudzinski

Identity can take different forms; subjects identify through different modes. This is no less true of the Caribbean than anywhere else. In the twentieth century alone, Caribbean intellectuals have elaborated various ways to identify themselves racially, religiously, linguistically, historiographically, and geographically. In this paper I approach the concept of identity and the process of identification as functions of the Caribbean subject's relationship to space and place. Most specifically, the aspect of geography that concerns me is precisely the "island-ness" or insularity of the lands in question.

In privileging the island as a space for analysis, I am not only identifying a tendency in Caribbean (and pan-Caribbeanist) cultural expression, but also pursuing a line of investigation opened by Caribbean cultural theorists such as Édouard Glissant from Martinique, Antonio Benítez-Rojo from Cuba, and J. Michael Dash from Jamaica. Insularity here becomes particularly important because of its impact on the identity not only of its inhabitants but of the whole region as well: the Caribbean is often constituted as an archipelago, and thus defined by the insularity of its composite lands. Perhaps as a result of this, local and international discourse on this region is seemingly hard-pressed to escape the semantic field of the island: insularity, *insularismo, bannzil kreyol*, etc. The pervasive references to insularity, however, often do no more than serve as the backdrop for analyses of Caribbean society. In fact, interrogations of the notion of "island" or "insularity" are rare. I want to take insularity seriously here, following the proposal of critic Mireille Rosello to see insularity as one of several "systems of explanation that metaphorize the connection between geography and identity" (565). I do so by looking at geographic metaphors for identity in literary works from 1970s Martinique by Georges Desportes and Édouard Glissant. Desportes and Glissant offer contrasting views of the island. Although both authors are critical of metropolitan France's control over Martinique, Desportes uses the negative connotations of insularity to criticize Martinique's dependency, while Glissant subverts the image of the island in order to propose a new way of thinking Caribbean identity. After reading Desportes's *Cette île qui est la nôtre* and Glissant's *Le discours antillais* in the context of the 1970s, I turn to an example of insularist discourse in 2004 from Thierry Nicolas, a geographer at the University of the Antilles-Guyana, to show the tenacity of insularity's hold on Caribbean discourse and to demonstrate how the symbolic field of the island can also be mobilized to express a vision of the Caribbean that is much more oriented towards France than we see in the examples from the 1970s. As I study these texts, I will navigate between the *topoi* of island, sea, and archipelago in order to reach a provisional conclusion about geographic identity and the use of geography to link individual and collective identities.

There are several developments in the 1970s in the Caribbean that give context to writing composed in that time period about the relationship between Martinique and the rest of the world. A large number of workers from Martinique were migrating to metropolitan France, a phenomenon encouraged and facilitated by the French state since 1963 through the BUMIDOM office.[1] As of 1975, official statistics put at 62,265 the number of people born in Martinique living in metropolitan France (Condon and Ogden 506). In 1970, the runway at the Lamentin airport had been equipped for Boeing 747s. In 1972, a telecommunications station was built on the island, and the same year saw the first live television re-broadcast of French programming. These technological developments in the infrastructure connecting Martinique to France (and other places) were instituted in the political environment obtaining after Martinique became a *département d'outre-mer* ("overseas department") of France in 1946, but before the national decentralization measures of the 1980s.[2]

The first text I would like to analyze from this period is Georges Desportes's *Cette île qui est la nôtre* ("This island which is ours"), published in 1973. Criticism on this text is difficult to find, perhaps because Desportes has been classified as a follower of Negritude. In fact, this text does bear many similarities to one of the most famous texts of Negritude, Aimé Césaire's poem *Cahier d'un retour au pays natal* (*Notebook of a Return to the Native Land*). At the same time, the crisis voiced in Desportes's 1973 text is distinct in many ways from that expressed in Césaire's poem. Desportes is writing after the implementation of Césaire's proposal for Martinique (along with Guadeloupe, French Guyana, and Réunion) to leave their colonial status and become French *départements*. Also, since the early 1960s, the French government had sought to bolster a sense of French identity among its West Indian citizens by facilitating temporary or permanent migration from the Caribbean to the metropole through the BUMIDOM office. Desportes continues to write and remains a figure of authority in Martinican letters, despite the comparative lack of international attention his work has garnered. The fact that he was called on to participate in events organized around

Patrick Chamoiseau's 1992 Prix Goncourt-winning novel *Texaco* is an index of the importance he holds for the local literary field.

"Notre dessein? Donner à percevoir la Martinique telle qu'elle est" 'Our purpose? To show Martinique as it is' (9). The simplicity with which the poet states the purpose of the text at the outset belies the confusion to follow. *Cette île qui est la nôtre* is a series of short, disjointed vignettes, by turns poem, prose, and theater. One constant runs through the entire text, which is an extended meditation on Martinican identity, particularly in relation to Martinicans' French nationality. In the theatrical sections, the type-characters represent conflicts between tourists or police officers, taken from the new political economy, and storytellers, magicians, or drum-players (occupations with strong links to idiosyncratic local traditions). In other sections, the anonymous narrator speaks as if he were addressing a metropolitan French audience. The disjointedness of the chapters and the hyperbolic vehemence of the declarations give the text a tone of crisis. The dialogues between the characters allow the crisis to play out as a conflict between allegorical types. At one point a character named "The Prisoner" even shouts questions at his own image in the mirror – "qui suis-je donc? . . . Où me situer dans ce monde . . . ? Toi, mon image, mon reflet, mon autre moi-même! Réponds-moi donc Etranger!" 'Who am I then? What is my place in this world? You, my image, my reflection, my other myself! Answer me, Stranger!' (127) – and then breaks the mirror on the floor in frustration, unable to integrate the different facets of his identity. In scenes like this, the text turns the crisis inward, as Desportes struggles with the implications that his land's *political* status has for his own *personal* sense of identity, which here is also a *communal* identity.

The first discourse that Desportes appropriates in his identity struggle is geography. The first sections of the book, accordingly, portray Martinique using a series of images related to islands. At times using traditional connotations of insularity and at times contesting them, Desportes manages to transpose cultural differences or political imbalances between Martinique and other parts of the world onto a geographical opposition between island and continent. However, in a seeming paradox, he also denies, in passing, that we have anything to learn about Martinique from traditional cartography. What we see on the map when we look at the island is nothing more than a bunch of private property, set one next to another: "Martinique, qu'est-ce que c'est? Terre ou poussière ou chiure de mouche? Pourtant, cela existe bien sur la carte; mais, en réalité, ce n'est tout juste que des propriétés foncières juxtaposées. Mises bout à bout, ça donne une île. La nôtre . . ." 'What is Martinique? Land, dust, or housefly droppings? And yet, it does exist on the map; but, really, that is just a juxtaposition of real estate properties. Put end to end, they make an island. Ours . . .' (16). The only thing to learn from this map is Martinicans' mutual estrangement and exclusion from property. What interests Desportes is not so much the printed map, it seems, as the mental mapping of Caribbean space expressed through poetry.

In his poeticization of these mental maps, readers recognize several commonplaces associated with islands: the island as vacation paradise; the island as far-flung, small, and insignificant; the island isolated from history or the island that floats through space. For example, images abound in Desportes's text linking the island to a sense of stasis and ineffectuality. While for Europe, the inactivity of the island allows it to be a "jardin tropical" 'tropical garden,' the poet experiences this inactivity as frustration, as forward movement that is attempted but diverted into a circle. Sometimes it is the island inhabitants who turn round and round: "Étrangers et indigènes tournent en rond avec cette île, esclaves des vagues et du soleil" 'Foreigners and natives go in circles with this island, slaves to the waves and the sun' (50). Sometimes it is the entire island that moves in circles: "nous sommes aussi cette île qui tourne en rond – toupie dormante sous le soleil" 'We are also this island that turns in circles – a spinning top sleeping in the sun' (17). Desportes states that the limitations felt by Martinicans can be directly traced to the island's "enclosure" by the sea and its other geographical features. "En vérité, comme la géographie et le relief de ce pays, nous sommes aussi tourmentés en notre esprit et découpés dans notre chair. Notre vie, bloquée par la mer, cernée par le paysage, coincée entre la pluie et le beau temps, chute chaque jour dans le marasme" 'Truly, like the geography and topography of this country, we too are tormented in our minds and cut apart in our flesh. Our lives, blocked by the sea, limited by the landscape, stuck between rain and fair weather, fall daily into a deep stagnation' (18). The island becomes a site on which to map his political pessimism.

The anxious, pessimistic tone predominates in Desportes's depictions of the island-space. At the same time, he does invest the island with the possibility of redemption – but even that move is tinged with a strong ambivalence. On the one hand, Martinique's topography represents in the text the source of a potentially dangerous native force that belies its reputation as a vacation paradise. "Vous avez appris que la Martinique était une île? N'y croyez pas, c'est un petit volcan qui a voulu voir le soleil" 'You were taught that Martinique was an island? Don't you believe it; it's a little volcano that wanted to see the sun' (14). Here Desportes is working in the symbolic geography inaugurated by Césaire, for whom the Mt. Pelée volcano and the neighboring *mornes* (hills) represented resistance. Besides the readily understandable symbolism of the volcanic eruption, the hills are where the fugitive slaves lived after their escape from the more low-lying plantations. By denying Martinique's insularity in favor of its geological identity as a volcano, Desportes is denying presumptions of inactivity associated with the developing tourist economy in order to insist on Martinique's defiant or even revolutionary past.

On the other hand, Desportes explains the reasons for the territory's current *assimilated* status (and the inhabitants' collective acceptance of it) in symbolic terms as he continues his myth of Martinique's past. "[Le volcan] a fait un pacte avec la lumière; puis, satisfait de la douceur du climat, il s'entend tout simplement à paresser, à rêver; à la traîne des flots et des nuages, en faisant la planche sur l'océan . . ." 'This volcano made a pact with the light; since then, satisfied with the mildness of the climate, it excells in lazing about, in dreaming; pulled along by the waves and the clouds, floating on its back in the ocean' (14). The influence of the mild climate is held responsible for current local inactivity. In terms of geographic imagery, this pact entails a dramatic change in the island: instead of rising up from the waves in a volcanic eruption, Martinique sets adrift. Without roots or a firm situation on the map, the island floats. Being on the surface of the water rather than connected to the volcanic sea floor implies a loss of historical identity. The floating, which is an image that could have been invested with a recognition of historical evolution or contingency, here signifies a loss of control over the future. The loss of control, coupled with the "laziness" of the island, makes insularity an extremely unappealing symbolic field for Desportes.

As the myth goes, this is a betrayal not only of the potential of Martinique, but of the entire archipelago as well. The islands used to be, in this story, a chain of lands that formed a "bridge" between North and South America. It is only after a mythical earthquake that the "bridge" fell into the water and the Caribbean Sea covered over the past. According to the myth, the Caribbean could have been a model of cross-cultural relations between the islands (expressed through the image of the archipelago), a model of cross-cultural relations between North and South America (expressed through the image of the bridge). But nature, the sea, has turned the islands into a model of fragmentation and precarity.

The poet emphasizes the frailty of the position occupied by the Antilles on the world stage, evoking a new imperialist threat that had arisen since Césaire wrote the *Cahier*, the U.S.: "Mesdames, Mesdemoiselles, Messieurs, nous sommes ici dans l'orbite du Dollar – (avec le vent ou sous le vent) – poussières d'îles qui tournoient dans l'écume pour étaler un monde" 'Ladies and gentlemen, here we are in the orbit of the Dollar – (whether leeward or windward) – island-specks turning in the foam to lay out a world' (12). The French West Indies are imagined as satellites, turning around the gravitational pull of the U.S.'s economic power. The phrase used to name the Antilles – "poussières d'îles" 'island-specks' – uses the imagery of the island to highlight the precariousness of Martinique's position on the world stage. It also evokes a sentence attributed to Charles de Gaulle: "Entre L'Europe et l'Amérique, je ne vois que des poussières" 'Between Europe and America I see only specks of dust.' The latter phrase speaks to the Caribbean's insignificance in the eyes of de Gaulle – almost an abandonment of the islands by France.[3]

This all explains the even more ambivalent geographic imagery with which Desportes begins. The poet turns first to the world map for a couple of symbols of the dangerous potential of the islands. Following the narrator's command to look at the archipelago, one voice compares the islands to "un long serpent désarticulé" 'a long disjointed serpent' and another compares them to "un gros crocodile aux vertèbres brisées" 'a fat crocodile with a broken backbone' (11). The poet continues the comparison, imagining the *serpent-crocodile* confronting the Statue of Liberty, which presides over the misery of black Americans in Harlem. Thus, the archipelago, however broken, represents a possibility of resistance to the new threat to local identity: U.S. imperialism.

We can now notice some recurrent trends in Desportes's use of the island trope as it mixes political metaphors of disunity with psychological metaphors of interiority and alienation. At the same time, we see a strong ambivalence towards the explicative power of insularity, a resistance to the island and insularism as a trap. Elaborating that resistance entails the need to work through some of the negative models for understanding island-space that we noticed above, such as the prison island as a place of social confinement; the floating island as lacking ancestral "roots"; the fractured island, internally as socially fragmented as the Caribbean region; and the peripheral island, isolated but dependent upon a distant colonial center.[4]

These negative images of colonialism and dependency are largely superseded in the second text I analyze here, Édouard Glissant's *Le discours antillais* (*Caribbean Discourse*). This text of Glissant's is not a prose-poem dialogue like Deportes's text; it is normally classified as a collection of essays, which were mostly written for different occasions in the mid-1970s before their joint publication in 1981. The author is now recognized as a pre-eminent Caribbean cultural theorist, largely on the basis of books such as *Le discours antillais*.[5] But he is also a poet like Desportes, and the poetic nature of his essays concerns me here as much as anything else.

Although *Le discours antillais* is rarely read for its geographical imagination, as is done here, in fact Glissant addresses in these essays many of the same preoccupations with insularity that are manifested by Desportes. The essayistic mode allows him to delve into the theoretical depths of identity and global geo-politics, while at the same time he grounds his reflections more conspicuously in Caribbean history. The main difference between the treatment insularity receives in the texts by Desportes and Glissant is that although Glissant shares Desportes's criticism of Martinique's situation since departmentalization, he uses the essay form to address the negative associations with insularity more explicitly as associations. He also turns the clichés of insularity around, giving them a new political purpose – highlighting cross-cultural relations and pan-Caribbean unity.

So, in some ways, Glissant's essays first allow us to get a clearer picture of what may be the economic causes for the lamentable situation that Desportes poeticizes. For example, Glissant analyzes the social and cultural effects of the Martinican economy of the 1970s as a way of understanding the isolation and fragmentation evoked by Desportes. Among that economy's main features are the absence of direct investment; the fear of surplus, explained by a lack of control over an external (French) market, combined with the inexistence of a local market; and the absence of "accumulated capital, technical capacity, creative projects" – all of which Glissant links to a historic dispossession from the land (44). But the primary feature of that Martinican economy that concerns him is the lack of production. Two of the dimensions of this "habit of not producing" are of interest to us here. First, the French state reinvests its surplus into the creation of service-sector jobs in Martinique, most notably civil servant positions, and supplies affordable imported goods to compensate for the concomitant lack of local production, thus creating a "passive consumerism." This, in turn, leads to the isolation of whatever sectors of productivity remain from each other. Second, as the economic isolation and lack of material production intensify, their effects extend into the social and cultural fields, leading Glissant to observe "l'apparition de processus répétitifs révoltes-stagnations, sans dépassements concevables" 'the repeated pattern of revolt, then stagnation, without any idea of how to break free' (103; 44). The economic system of Martinique under the policy of economic assimilation, according to Glissant's analysis, produces the sense of dissatisfied cultural stagnation and social fragmentation we noticed in Desportes's text.

Another of Desportes's images, the floating island, appears in Glissant's essays as well. For Desportes, the floating island signified its surrender to foreign direction. For Glissant, the image has the same significance, and moreover he gestures toward a larger cultural resonance for the image by reporting the following compelling anecdote for what it can show his readers about the slippery border between "floating island" as a symbolic fiction and "floating island" as an element of popular cartography:

... 31 mars 1973, où le journal télévisé annonce (poisson d'avril) que les Antilles ont tendance (dérive des continents) à se rapprocher de l'Europe, alors que le reste du bloc américain s'en éloigne (ce que commente, sous le titre « Le temps d'un rêve », un quotidien du lendemain: « Il faut se rendre à l'évidence : c'était un canular ... En plein carême, quand nous nous sentons loin de tout, avec du vague à l'âme, quand la montagne Pelée se rappelle fâcheusement à notre souvenir, un coup de baguette magique nous arrache à nos cauchemars ... Le jour béni où notre île, ayant largué ses amarres américaines, s'arrimerait à la Métropole, sans pont aérien, ni pont d'aucune sorte, tout octroi de mer aboli, les choses se présenteraient autrement pour nous »). (213–14)

... 31 March 1973 – when the news broadcast announces (an April Fools' Day hoax) that the French Caribbean tends (because of continental drift) to get closer to Europe, while the rest of the Americas drift away (which provokes the comment, under the headline "In a Dream Time," in a newspaper the following day: "We must acknowledge: it was a joke ... In the middle of the dry season, when we feel remote from everything, when the mind wanders, when Mt. Pelée fiercely comes to mind, the wave of a wand can tear us away from our nightmares ... The blessed day when our island, having cast off its ties with the Americas, would be fastened to the Metropolis, without an aerial bridge, without any kind of bridge, all dock duties abolished, things would look different for us"). (56)

The author of the original joke is obviously playing with the same symbology of the "floating island" as Desportes. "Floating," here too, means an uprooting from local culture, and a manifest cultural and political orientation that separates Martinique from its non-French Caribbean neighbors. The joke, in fact, consists of the literalization of the symbolic image as reported geographic fact. The extended comment the next day implies that the joke had some social resonance that warranted the newspaper's attention. Whether the tone of the newspaper commentary was sincere or ironic, it still points to the existence of a common mental geography that places Martinique as contiguous with France. The recognition that this is not a physical fact introduces the vector of time. Complete union with metropolitan France is the desired future, and the most tangible way to realize it is to enable the island to float across the Atlantic. The way that the symbol itself floats from literary to journalistic discourse – as a joke, as a joke that was taken seriously, or as a joke that was expanded in the retelling the next day – also tells us something about the bidirectional relationship between symbolic space and physical space. Viewers of the television news may have been prepared, at some level, to accept a blurry distinction between the *geographical symbolism* of the "floating island" trope and the *symbolic geography* of Martinique's presumed continental drift.

The joke also mentions that the rest of the Caribbean archipelago drifts away from France, negating Caribbean commonalities. For Glissant, the archipelago-form provides a twist in the symbolic space of Caribbean insularity. This is different from Desportes, for whom the archipelago was the picture of a broken unity – a threat to imperialism defused by the sea that divides the islands from each other. Glissant, in his definition of "Caribbeanness," offers an interpretation of the same geography that plays on the potential symbolic freedom suggested by the image of the floating island:

Notre lieu, c'est les Antilles.

L'antillanité, rêvée par les intellectuels, en même temps que nos peuples la vivaient de manière souterraine, nous arrache de l'intolérable propre aux nationalismes nécessaires et nous introduit à la Relation qui aujourd'hui les tempère sans les aliéner.

Qu'est-ce que les Antilles en effet? Une multi-relation. Nous le ressentons tous, nous l'exprimons sous toutes sortes de formes occultées ou caricaturales, ou nous le nions farouchement. Mais nous éprouvons bien que cette mer est là en nous avec sa charge d'îles enfin découvertes. . . .

Dans un tel contexte, l'insularité prend un autre sens. On prononce ordinairement l'insularité comme un mode d'isolement, comme une névrose d'espace. Dans la Caraïbe pourtant, chaque île est une ouverture. La dialectique Dehors-Dedans rejoint l'assaut Terre-Mer. C'est seulement pour ceux qui sont amarrés au continent Europe que l'insularité constitue prison. L'imaginaire des Antilles nous libère de l'étouffement. (426–27)

Our place is the Caribbean.

Caribbeanness, an intellectual dream, lived at the same time in an unconscious way by our peoples, tears us free from the intolerable alternative of the need for nationalism and introduces us to the cross-cultural process that modifies but does not undermine the latter.

What is the Caribbean in fact? A multiple series of relationships. We all feel it, express it in all kinds of hidden or twisted ways, or we fiercely deny it. But we sense that this sea exists within us with the weight of now revealed islands. . . .

In this context, insularity takes on another meaning. Ordinarily, insularity is treated as a form of isolation, a neurotic reaction to place. However, in the Caribbean each island embodies openness. The dialectic between inside and outside is reflected in the relationship of land and sea. It is only those who are tied to the European continent who see insularity as confining. A Caribbean imagination liberates us from being smothered. (139)

In fact, what counts in this vision of the islands is not so much insularity *per se*, but attachment to an archipelago. And the archipelago is not just a chain of land that has been cut apart by the sea, as in Desportes; rather, it is the very "broken-ness" or openness of the connections between the islands that amounts to a physical reflection of the contingency of relations between localities. Instead of being interrupted volcanic roots, the Caribbean is a rhizome – "a multiple series of relationships."[6] Moreover, Glissant sees that the contingent networks of relations that obtain on an archipelagic level also manifest themselves in the microcosm of each island, which "embodies openness."

When Desportes worked with the image of the archipelago, he had imagined the water as an obstacle to Caribbean unity. Glissant, however, in his gloss on the Jamaican writer Edward Kamau Brathwaite's expression "the unity is submarine," uses the water of the Caribbean Sea to make the sea a part of this new geographic identity, in a way that incorporates a "grounding" in history.

Je ne traduis, quant à moi, cette proposition ["The unity is submarine"] qu'en évoquant tant d'Africains lestés de boulets et jetés par-dessus bord chaque fois qu'un navire négrier se trouvait poursuivi par des ennemis et s'estimait trop faible pour soutenir le combat. Ils semèrent dans les fonds les boulets de l'invisible. C'est ainsi que nous avons appris, non la transcendance ni l'universel sublimé, mais la tranversalité. (230–31)

To my mind, this expression ["The unity is submarine"] can only evoke all those Africans weighed down with ball and chain and thrown overboard whenever a slave ship was pursued by enemy vessels and felt too weak to put up a fight. They sowed in the depths the seeds of an invisible presence. And so transversality, and not the universal transcendence of the sublime, has come to light. (66–7, original emphasis)

The islands are linked by geography, by the water that flows between them; but water here is not an abstract cartographic concept. Glissant's saying that the islands are linked by geography is actually tantamount to his saying that the islands are linked by a lived geography, linked by a geography lived over historical time, in fact linked by history. Thus, the Caribbean Sea comes to serve as a reminder of slavery and gruesome forgotten murders.[7]

The common Caribbean history of dispossession – slaves and their descendants being barred from juridical or affective "ownership" of the land – means that, along with the sea, Martinicans need to re-valorize the land of the island. Glissant contends that the affective map of the whole archipelago, and Martinique in particular, needs to be collectively re-drawn to remedy the historic sense of dispossession. "La terre soufferte est délaissée. Ce n'est pas encore la terre aimée. . . . La terre est à l'autre" 'The land of suffering is abandoned. The land is not yet loved. . . . The land is the other's possession' (471; 160). Dispossession, which has characterized the relationship between slaves or their descendants and the land, gives rise in Glissant to a feeling quite different from that expressed in Desportes's text. The lack of control over the land, while bemoaned for historical reasons, creates a kind of poetic awe: "Notre terre est démesurée. Je le sais, moi qui en quelques pas saurai en faire le tour, mais qui jamais ne peux l'épuiser" 'Our land is excessive. I know, since I can in a few steps take it all in but can never exhaust it' (472; 160). The physical scope of the landscape can fit into the field of vision, but the cultural and historic significance of the land has not yet been assimilated, as it were. What is happening here is the recognition that *seeing* the landscape on a daily basis, and *identifying* with it to the point of poeticizing it, are two very different things.

Glissant's perspective on the history and future of the Caribbean allows him to give an interpretation of 1970s Martinique that is different from the anxious cynicism voiced by Desportes. Yet, Glissant still articulates his sense of Martinican identity as an insular or archipelagic cartography. Now, however, the elements of the map have been altered. The closed island becomes open. The floating island signifies adaptability or the recognition of contingency, rather than the surrender of sovereignty. The small, confining prison-island becomes inexhaustible in its import, and the apparently fractured archipelago hints at a submarine regional unity. Instead of the island-space depicted as being removed from history, readers visualize a mental cartography that is grounded in Caribbean history. In this way, Glissant re-invigorates commonplaces of insularist discourse, giving them new political and identitary vigency amid the changing cultural field of the 1970s.

The complex symbology of insularity in that decade gave form to a contestation of political and cultural identity. This identity-struggle was given new urgency by the technological changes introduced in that decade, which tightened links between metropolitan France and its Caribbean *départements*. But insularity as a symbolic field has not ceased to signify in Caribbean discourse. Before reaching my conclusions about the implications of mental cartography for collective identity, I would like to offer a sort of counter-example to Desportes's and Glissant's early use of insularity, taken from 2004. In geographer Thierry Nicolas's interventions, we see that the symbol of the island still has currency, even as it is used to express a political perspective much more sympathetic to Martinique's over-arching Frenchness. In fact, the dream of Caribbean unity proposed by Glissant is in many ways farther from reality than it was in the 1970s. Not least among the reasons for this in Martinique is the increasing economic relevance of Martinique's membership in the European Union (as French territory), and its continued high standard of living, which separates it conspicuously from other places in the Caribbean. But as different as Nicolas's articles are politically from Desportes and Glissant, they are however very useful in suggesting a new idea of spatiality prompted by Martinique's and Guadeloupe's island status.

In his 2004 article in the French magazine *Géo*, University of the Antilles geographer Nicolas makes use of the island *topos*. Although the point of the article is ostensibly to explain the recent renewal of local interest in preserving the natural and cultural landscape of Guadeloupe and Martinique, Nicolas's extensive rhetorical use of the insularity topos to explain that interest actually overpowers his main point about nature conservancy. Consequently, the article ends up telling us more about the persistence of the idea of insularity and its hold on French Caribbean sense of geographical identity than it does about actual Caribbean preservation efforts.

Nicolas identifies technological developments that have brought about a change in the Antilles' relationship with France, and by extension (only by extension) with the rest of the world: for example, air travel and Internet communication. These developments may be seen as steps taken by France to shore up its cultural dominion over the parts of its national territory located in the Caribbean or as unintended consequences of a larger phenomenon of globalization. Whichever is the case, they have no doubt changed the Antilles' place in global information circuits. What is interesting, at the same time, is the picture that Nicolas sketches of the situation *before* these changes. He speaks at some length of

[ces] profonds bouleversements qu'ont pu connaître les Antilles françaises au cours des deux dernières décennies. En effet, ces territoires insulaires vivent une véritable révolution dans leur rapport à « l'ailleurs ». Si, pendant longtemps, la Guadeloupe et la Martinique sont apparues comme des bouts du monde, des refuges préservés des influences extérieures, depuis les années 1980, ce n'est plus le cas. Sous l'impulsion des transports et des moyens de communication, le littoral qui enserre ces îles ne s'apparente plus à une limite qui tracerait une coupure nette entre un dedans et un dehors. . . . [Le] cloisonnement des îles, qui limitait les possibilités d'information, est rompu. Les insulaires ne communiquent plus seulement entre eux et connaissent les mutations du monde en temps réel. (70)

these ground-shaking changes that the French Antilles have seen over the last two decades. Indeed, these insular territories are experiencing a real revolution in their relationship with the "outside world." Though Guadeloupe and Martinique had long been perceived as the ends of the earth, as refuges preserved from outside influence, this has not been the case since the 1980s. As a result of greater transportation and communication, the coastline enclosing these islands no longer resembles a border drawing a clear distinction between an inside and an outside. . . . The compartmentalization of the islands, which had limited the possibilities for getting information, has been broken through. Islanders no longer communicate solely among themselves, and they experience global change in real time.

Now, it would be hard to make a convincing case that until 1980 Martinique and Guadeloupe had been cut off from the "outside world," or that before that decade Martinicans and Guadeloupeans only talked amongst themselves. Our reading of Desportes's and Glissant's writing suggests that these issues were being problematized at least as early as the 1970s. In fact, Nicolas is careful to begin his litany of clichés with a verb of perception ("sont apparues comme des bouts du monde" 'are perceived as the ends of the earth') before sliding into free indirect discourse. Given the nature of the publication, the whole invocation of insularity is made as a concession to non-Caribbean French readers of *Géo* magazine, who are presumed to carry around such *idées reçues* in their heads.

It is therefore not gratuitous that the geographer chooses to explain Caribbean interest in environmental preservation efforts through recourse to these myths of insularity: the islands as distant from some center located elsewhere, the sea as a wall, the enclosed islands cut off from history, and island society as a closed society. In fact, the indulgence in insularist clichés may seem surprising until one realizes the logic underwriting the apparent tangent. The ostensible topic of the article is the resurgence in interest in preserving the Antilles' natural heritage. The idea subtending the description of the recent past as an "insular" time when Antilleans did not value their land is that islands, *qua* islands, cannot be valued. The limits of insularity have to be transcended by technology before islanders can value their own land. The same applies to the cultural effects of those globalizing technological developments: "Cette ouverture sur l'extérieur a paradoxalement réveillé l'aspiration des Antillais à un enracinement et les pousse à manifester leur attachement à leur territoire" 'This opening-up to the outside has paradoxically awakened the Antilleans' aspiration to "re-root" themselves and pushes them to show their attachment to their territory' (70). The implicit resolution of the paradox lies in the idea that the land can be appreciated once it no longer poses limitations on development. The land can be loved when it is no longer an island.

In an article on a similar subject written for a less general audience, Nicolas maintains the conceit. He also describes more clearly what he means by the Caribbean's "opening up to the outside." In this article, published in *Géographie et cultures*, Nicolas discusses the gradual absorption of Martinique and Guadeloupe into the French national economy, culture, and political system – a phenomenon attributed to the success of the French policy of "assimilation," a policy which has evolved but continued since the 1970s, when Desportes and Glissant composed their texts. According to Nicolas, assimilation produced fundamental changes in the economies of Guadeloupe and Martinique over the course of the twentieth century. In the first half of the century, he sees the colonies as hybrid spaces, whose economies remained modeled on the form of the plantation, while their political structure was more and more based on the metropolitan French model. Now, the local economy has also been integrated into the national economy. The proof that Nicolas offers is the ratio of imports and exports. In 1940, Guadeloupe's exports exceeded its imports by a ratio of 2.5, but in the beginning of the twenty-first century exports represent only one tenth of imports. The twin phenomena of an increase in economic dependence and a decrease in capacity of local production Nicolas summarizes as "continentalization." Further indices of the strengthening of human relations between the metropole and former colonies include air travel, re-settlement, and mass communication media.[8]

Nicolas also offers a corollary to the French West Indies' continentalization: their persistent mutual estrangement from other Caribbean lands. The indices he cites are the low level of intra-regional airline service, the lack of regular intra-regional sealine service, and the overall low incidence of travel between the islands. In addition to this, he considers the fact that the French West Indies' membership in the European Union has precluded their inclusion in common market initiatives such as the Association of Caribbean States.

In his discussion of these changes, Nicolas uses "continentalization" to name the effects of the assimilationist policy on France's old colonies, as the effects of maritime distances have been negated. If assimilation is defined as continental, "insularity" logically becomes a term for any "obstacle" to the complete cultural, political, and economic integration of Guadeloupe and Martinique within France and the European Union. His choice of the word "obstacle" to describe cultural autonomy efforts' relationship with the central state (instead of saying that cultural autonomy is a "defense against" assimilation, as Glissant might have done, for example) is significant. Clearly, in this article Nicolas takes a stand for assimilation. He defends this support, in part, because the assimilation of the French West Indies to the central French state still represents a *non-assimilation* to the U.S. neo-colonialism that prevails in the region. As such, the continentalization of Martinique and Guadeloupe may even be a step towards stronger ties with other parts of the Caribbean, inasmuch as it represents possibilities for association with Cuba and Haiti, which also do not share the same degree of economic or cultural dependence on the U.S. that other Caribbean countries do.

The author is careful to use the terms "continentalization" and "insularity" only as metaphors, denying them any geographical referentiality: "Pour celui qui jetterait un coup d'oeil sur une carte et qui saurait de surcroît que les îles ne se déplacent pas sur l'eau, une telle approche pourrait paraître surréaliste" 'To anyone who can look at a map and knows that islands don't move over the water, such an approach could seem surrealist' (39). That is to say, he does not take his "continentalization" argument to the literalist extreme of the 1973 "floating island" joke reported by Glissant. However, although he makes a point of the term's metaphoricity, he does not engage with that metaphoricity. For example, when he defines "continentalization" as the process of transforming the French West Indies to resemble metropolitan France socially and politically, there is no explanation of whether there is anything about the topography of a continent, or the history of continents in general, that could sustain their use as a metaphor for political homogeneity. Instead, we are left to assume that "continentalization" is used only in contradistinction to "insularity" and its longstanding associations with isolation and difference. "Continent" is in effect an "unmarked term" – to use Laclau's notion (33) – defined by nothing more than the exclusion of insularity.

Although Nicolas does not engage explicitly with the metaphoricity of islands and continents, his use of them does provoke him to gesture towards the possibility of non-physical spatialities: "Afin de comprendre cette assertion [que les Antilles sont devenues des appendices continentaux], il faut se démarquer des espaces métriques ou euclidiens dans lesquels on se place traditionnellement. L'espace que nous analysons aujourd'hui, plus abstrait, intègre d'autres variables que la distance topographique, à l'image des 'espaces sociaux' et 'espaces économiques' développés par des sciences sociales voisines" 'In order to understand the claim that the French West Indies have become continental appendices, we must leave aside metric or Euclidean space, in which we have traditionally operated. The space we analyze today is more abstract and involves variables other than topographic distance – similar to the "social space" and "economic space" developed in other social sciences' (39). The spatiality being described is the result of technological changes such as increased air travel, whose consequences are described not just as a reduction in the time necessary to travel across a given distance, but as "la négation de l'espace physique" 'the negation of physical space' (47) altogether.

Instead of referring to physical space, Nicolas works with a mental process that he names alternately "espace symbolique" and "espace abstrait" or "conception du territoire" ("symbolic space," "abstract space," or "conception of territory"). The governing principle of this symbolic space is not the "*cadre*" or surroundings, but rather "polarization" and "gravitation": the continents' magnetic polarization and the gravitation of the islands towards the continents. In other words, more than static location, what is important here is orientation, which is defined as implicit movement. It is a conception of space in which movement is fundamental.

At this point I would like to recall the uses of insularity in Desportes, Glissant, and Nicolas in order to extract some of the subjacent conceptions of place and identity for the case of Martinique. The opposition between *island* and *continent*, in which the island is traditionally distant from the continent but gravitates towards it, attempting by fusion with the continent to achieve the unity it is perceived as lacking, metaphorizes the colonial or neo-colonial dimensions of the relationship between Martinique and metropolitan France. In this way, insularity does not describe places in the Caribbean; insularity suggests a Caribbean spatiality.

The complication introduced by the further symbolic back-and-forth between *island* and *archipelago* in the discussed texts bespeaks other tensions in identity-formation, particularly the struggle between fixed identities and contingent processes of identification. This tension inherent in these depictions of geographic identity anticipates some more contemporary debates about identity and identification. The discursive approach to identity, as described by Stuart Hall, "sees identification as a construction, a process never completed – always 'in process.' . . . identification is in the end conditional, lodged in contingency" (2–3). The possibilities of the archipelago, suggested by Glissant's later use of the Deleuzian rhizome as an alternative to a fixed identity or by Rosello's concept of "insularization" as a way of seeing unpredicted relations between global localities, foreground the contingency of identifications. Identification, as Hall sees it, is necessarily conscious; that is, conscious of its own contingency. Subjects take up identities "always 'knowing' . . . that they are representations, that representation is always constructed across a 'lack,' . . . and thus can never be adequate – identical – to the subject processes which are invested in them. . . . and that in turn places *identification*, if not identities, firmly on the theoretical agenda" (6). Personal or political identifications respond to differing needs; as Hall defines it, identification is the halfway point, the "suture" between social discourses interpellating people into a certain discursive position, and the psychological processes constructing subjectivities; thus, identities are "points of temporary attachment to the subject positions which discursive practices construct for us" (6). We can recognize in this the tightrope that Desportes and Glissant walk between their interpellation as "islanders" and their subjective dissatisfaction with that identity.

The alternance between *island* and *archipelago* also analogizes the struggle between unitary, local identities and transversal, global ones. Patricia Yaeger, in her introduction to *The Geography of Identity*, recognizes that in studies such as the ones contained in her volume, a focus on place may be considered retrograde – a throwback to the stable identities that contemporary cultural studies have discarded. However, for her, a focus on the local means recognizing that each local place is always already hybrid (16). In my analysis of French Caribbean insularist discourse, that kind of "hybrid," in which Martinique evinces links with other places like Paris, is expressed spatially: either as the island's "orientation," or figuratively as the island's physical movement. The island's "gravitation," "orbit," or figurative "drift" towards the European or North American continents metaphorizes the global links already in evidence on the (stationary) island.

When it is not the islands but the island's inhabitants who do the migrating, I think that the relationship between identity and geography becomes more complex. This phenomenon, common to both Martinique and Guadeloupe, brings out similarities between their process of identity formation and those of other formerly colonized places, which together pose a challenge to some unreconstructed disciplinary assumptions about identity:

We need to situate the debates about identity within all those historically specific developments and practices which have disturbed the relatively "settled" character of many populations and cultures, above all in relation to the processes . . . of forced and "free" migration which have become a global phenomenon of the so-called "postcolonial" world. (Hall 4)

This amounts to a recognition that location is only one variable of geographic identity – along with orientation and migration (implied movement and physical movement).

The concept of a geographic identity means, ultimately, that a spatial symbol – such as the "floating island" – is somehow more than just *symbolic*. If Martinicans choose to migrate to France (rather than to the U.S. or to Africa), this is partly because of a spatial symbolism that puts Martinique effectively "closer" to France. This kind of real-historic action taken in symbolic space suggests that the symbolic space is no longer only symbolic. Decisions made on the basis of assumptions grounded in the symbolic realm activate, as it were, the symbolic dimension of real places. Human advances in technology can affect the mental map of the world; but, in turn, symbolic geographies can also change human experience of physical place, and can motivate human transformation of landscape and influence migration decisions. Extending the cycle, these patterns of migration influenced by mental maps can consolidate certain identities. In the case of the French West Indies, mental maps foster alternating identifications as inhabitants of the Caribbean or as members of the European Union.

Given all this, we could say that an "island" identity could be an option for social identification, or, conversely, it could be a pre-emption of it. On a regional level, it is also easier in many contexts for Martinicans to identify as "Martinicans" than as "Caribbeans." In some cases, such as membership in associations of independent Caribbean states, it is impossible for them to identify and be fully recognized as "Caribbeans." On a national level, Martinicans seem to be always already identified as "islanders" in France, before they can fully identify with other Martinicans. In this way, it functions as an imposed identity that precludes a transversal identification with other Martinicans, based on other terms. This difficulty posed by identification with the island – excluding other island inhabitants or excluding oneself from the archipelago – ultimately remains unresolved by Desportes, Glissant, and Nicolas, unless you count Nicolas's idea that the gradual completion of the project of French

Caribbean assimilation to France will cause the category of "island" to lose all significance. It is telling, however, to note the persistence of the "island" concept even among those writing as children of Caribbean emigration or in sociological studies of this migration, such as Alain Anselin's 1990 *L'émigration antillaise en France: la troisième île (Caribbean Migration in France: The Third Island)*. It belongs to a further study to examine how the tropes of insularity change from the perspective of the migrant subject – an experience textualized by Guadeloupean writers Gisèle Pineau in *L'exil selon Julia* (1996), Maryse Condé in *Désirada* (1997), or Simone Schwarz-Bart in *Ti-Jean l'horizon* (1979).

When migration and orientation are factored into the relationship between place and identity, identity is no longer tied to place. It is important, therefore, to separate two different identitary relationships with space. One would be the identification with an actual place, based for example on memories of certain people, flora, fauna, topographical features, or events lived in that place. This would be, for example, the perspective reflected in Nicolas's analysis of French Caribbeans' conservancy initiatives: acting on an attachment to place. Another kind of relationship with space would be the assumption of an identity that is itself spatialized – as a node on the conceptual rhizomatic map. As much as these writers are talking about Martinique or Guadeloupe (places on a map), they are also talking about *islands* (a space, or abstract form) and *insularity* (a spatiality – one kind of human relation to space). Ultimately, the island takes us adrift: from places and identities, to a wider realm of geographic identification.

Notes

1. BUMIDOM is an acronym for the Bureau pour le développement des Migrations intéressant les Départements d'Outre-Mer (Office for the Development of Migrations Concerning the Overseas Departments), which managed the migration of thousands of people from Martinique, Guadeloupe, Guyane, and Réunion to mainland France from 1963 to 1982, when its functions were assumed by the Agence Nationale pour l'insertion et la promotion des travailleurs de l'Outremer (National Agency for the Insertion and Promotion of Overseas Workers).

2. A *département* is a sub-national unit of administration, similar in some respects to a U.S. "state." *Départementalisation* refers to the process of becoming a *département*. Martinique underwent this process in 1946, thereby putting an end to its period of formal colonialism, which had started with the first French settlers of 1635.

3. This is one way of interpreting its inclusion as such as epigraph to Glissant's *Le discours antillais*.

4. Camille Darsières, in a 1974 history of Martinique, also ascribes importance to distance in this assertion of Martinican national identity contained in the conclusion of the historical study: "Martiniquais, nous sommes par la géographie qui nous situe à 7.000 km de la France, et nous ancre en plein Bassin Caraïbe, au milieu d'un archipel identiquement peuplé, colonisé de semblable façon . . . ." 'We are Martinican also by our geography, which places us 7,000 km from France, and anchors us in the middle of the Caribbean Basin, in the middle of an archipelago identically populated, colonized in a similar way' (308).

5. Glissant, after his return to Martinique from studies in Paris in the early 1960s, grew disillusioned with Martinique's new status as a French *département d'outre-mer* (overseas departments) and became a militant for Martinican independence from France. For his anti-French writings and for his political organizing activities (such as founding along with other militants the independentist Front Antillo-Guyanais) Glissant was expelled from France from 1961 until 1965, during which time France furthered its cultural hegemony in Martinique and Guadeloupe through education and programs intended to vernacularize the French language to the detriment of Creole. For a period following his return to Martinique, from 1971 to 1973, Glissant directed the journal *Acoma*, whose purpose was to affirm a regional identity for Martinique, not only among the other French Antilles but also in the wider Caribbean context. In the mission of this journal one sees the beginnings of his theory of Caribbeanness, which would be continually developed until its full expression in *Le discours antillais*.

6. Glissant himself develops this idea from Deleuze and Guattari elsewhere in *Le discours antillais* and in the subsequent book *Poétique de la Relation* (*Poetics of Relation*).

7. It is interesting to note that in 1979 (between Glissant's initial exposition of these ideas and their publication) the St. Lucian Derek Walcott makes a strikingly similar point in his poem "The Sea is History."

8. According to Nicolas's sources, the airports of Pointe-à-Pitre and Fort-de-France processed approximately three million passengers in 1994, with over half coming from Europe. This represents a rise of 200% in passengers originating in Europe in comparison to 1984, while overall travel only increased 33% in the same period. In a related phenomenon, the French West Indian community in metropolitan France reached approximately 350,000 people in 1990 (thirteen times what it was in 1950) and the metropolitan-born community in Martinique and Guadeloupe is estimated to be 56,000 (three times the levels of 1967). In 1992, the two television stations of RFO (Radiotélévision Française d'Outre-Mer) commanded 75% of the viewing public, and 86% of their television programming came from France. On the other channels, the percentage of non-local programming is even higher.

Bibliography

Anselin, Alain. *L'émigration antillaise en France: la troisième île*. Paris: Karthala, 1990.

Condé, Maryse. *Désirada*. Paris: Pocket, 1997.

Condon, Stephanie, and Philip E. Ogden. "Emigration from the French Caribbean: the Origins of an Organized Migration." *International Journal of Urban and Regional Research* 15.4 (1991): 505–23.

Darsières, Camille. *Des origines de la nation martiniquaise*. Pointe-à-Pitre: Désormeaux, 1974.

Desportes, Georges. *Cette île qui est la nôtre*. Ottawa: Leméac, 1973.

Glissant, Édouard. *Le discours antillais*. 1981. Paris: Gallimard, 1997.

———. *Caribbean Discourse: Selected Essays*. 1989. Trans. J. Michael Dash. Charlottesville: UP of Virginia, 1992.

Hall, Stuart. "Introduction: Who Needs 'Identity'?" *Questions of Cultural Identity*. Ed. Stuart Hall and Paul Du Gay. London: Sage Publications, 1996. 1–17.

Laclau, Ernesto. *New Reflections on the Revolution of Our Time*. London: Verso, 1990.

Nicolas, Thierry. "Les Antilles françaises entre insularité et continentalité." *Géographie et cultures* 36 (Winter 2000): 39–56.

———. "La fin de l'isolement antillais." *Géo* 309 (November 2004): 70.

Pineau, Gisèle. *L'Exil selon Julia*. Paris: Stock, 1996.

Rosello, Mireille. "Caribbean Insularization of Identities in Maryse Condé's Work: From *En attendant le bonheur* to *Les derniers rois mages*." *Callaloo* 18.3 (1995): 565–578.

Schwarz-Bart, Simone. *Ti-Jean l'horizon*. Paris: Seuil, 1979.

Walcott, Derek. "The Sea is History." *Collected Poems, 1948–1984*. New York: Farrar, Strauss and Giroux, 1986. 364–67.

Yaeger, Patricia. "Introduction: Narrating Space." *The Geography of Identity*. Ed. Patricia Yaeger. Ann Arbor: U of Michigan P, 1996. 1–39.

The West between Culture(s) and Collective Identity: Notes for a Present Problematic

Nimrod Ben-Cnaan

What does it mean to be Western today? Where is the West, and who are the Westerners? It seems that from our contemporary vantage point these questions and other related queries do not have a clear answer. Academic scholarship does not have a privileged take on this topic, as it is – probably more than any other formal discourse – a Westernizing endeavor. The conventions of the sciences as a particular form and corpus of knowledge have their roots in the European project of modernity, that is, in the core of the traditional West. All scientists worldwide today must adhere to the rules of conduct and engagement of the academic discourse, which are of Western inception. Furthermore, present-day popular culture (particularly urban, industrialized popular culture) is thoroughly infused with public meaningful forms that originate in Western Europe or North America, and it is widely accepted that, with or without the oft-invoked process of globalization, most global popular culture today is to a certain extent Westernized. This state goes well beyond the spread of McDonald's, Coca Cola, or MTV and includes (I argue, more importantly) the economic structure of the late capitalist market, the governance structure of parliamentary democracy, and the moral conventions of universal individual human rights, to name but a few basic examples. If we accept that the world has generally become Westernized, then we must also agree that the West has, at the same time, become a global phenomenon and thus lost its local or regional specificity.[1] As the West is still commonly regarded as a culture (if not a civilization), this dissipation of clear geographical-cultural difference raises questions not just about its present state but also its historical unfolding.

This gradual loss of *difference* is particularly conspicuous when we consider the previously clearer definition of the West, which never relied on the clear definition of boundaries but rather on transgressive and aggressive expansionism, be it Roman, Christian, or modern colonialist and imperialist. In antiquity, the "Western" face of Western Europe, as premised on Classical culture and Christianity, was shaped by several pivotal occurrences: the division of the Roman Empire by Diocletian at the end of the third century; the acceptance of Christianity as the religion of the reunified empire by Constantine at the end of the fourth century; and the church schism six centuries later, which reinforced an ecclesiastical division that corresponded to the old political division of East and West. By the time of the collapse of the Byzantine Empire its Western counterparts were beginning to emerge from what were soon dubbed their Dark Ages and into the conflictive project of modernity. The West as it was defined by its European referents, and later by its North American expansion, was decidedly white and Christian, not to mention male and heterosexist.[2] In the last century, following the bang of the two World Wars and the whimper of the end of the Cold War, an ostensibly "Western" way of life, modeled chiefly on the United States of America, has come to be advocated, if not actually experienced, in most parts of the world. Ironically, most of those who can nowadays regard themselves or their ways of life as Western would have been excluded from inside the former, more rigidly defined Christian West. Still, the West carries for these people a normative and aspirational importance, denoting not just how some of them live their lives, but how nearly all of them would like to live them.

These two facets of contemporary Western-ness illustrate the poverty if not the obsolescence of the noun "West" and the adjective "Western." And yet, they are both in constant reference and will not die out. One might hypothesize along the lines suggested in Derrida's early work that perhaps the ongoing reference to the West serves to conceal an originary lack of substance or foundation, so that there might be a certain common interest in keeping the arcane term in use. However, such a suggestion almost explains away the question, as nothing short of an *a priori* essence or a Neoplatonic emanation can prevent cultures from being foundationally lacking and thus largely constructed. A more useful path of reasoning can be found in Foucault, who saw systems of thought as taxonomies and associations that should be questioned, or, in his words, problematized. Problematization was at the heart of Foucault's concept of a history of thought asking "how and why were very different things in the world gathered together, characterized, analyzed, and treated" as one (albeit composite) phenomenon; his assumption was that "problematization is an 'answer' to a concrete situation which is real," and that it is more than just an epistemic solution but an ethical one as well (171–72). Problematizing the West and its centrality throughout history should not be done at one fell swoop; even so, we can take a closer look at how a certain persistent blind spot was maintained with reference to this archaic term, particularly through the attempts to redefine it as a term that is still valid nowadays. My suggestion is that these attempts of stretching the blanket of scientific definition to cover what the West has come to be might in effect be "saving the phenomena" by saving their collective definition as "the West."

This issue seems particularly pertinent for cultural studies as an academic field and a political project because it goes to the very heart of its definition: the concept of culture, its many meanings, the several discourses around it, and its descriptive and explanatory value. In my discussion, I shall remain within the field (cultural studies) and on topic (the West today) to consider several approaches since the Second World War, not necessarily from mainstream cultural studies. Starting in the 1950s and 1960s, I will discuss the first major cultural critique of Raymond Williams and his definitions of culture. I argue that Williams's early writing is best understood in its local and temporal setting, as well as in the context of postwar sociological modernization theories. Following Williams and his contemporaries in the acknowledgment of "multiple modernities," I shall introduce a definition of collective identity and consider its import for a characterization of the contemporary West, coinciding with the advent of postcolonial critique. The academic discourse of collective identity can be seen as the product of earlier cultural criticism and of the New Left, and as making a central contribution to the identity politics projects from the 1970s to the 1990s. It was accompanied by a widening of the trend of reclaiming collective memory, chiefly by reference to heritage or patrimony and resulting sometimes in a heritage industry. Lastly, I will consider a recent attempt to redefine culture so as to retain its usefulness in the face of a globalizing and dissipating West as well as in the face of newly emergent lifestyles. Throughout this exposition I will examine the usefulness of the various definitions of collectivities for the definition of what "the West" is and means today.

In the history of cultural studies as an academic undertaking a distinguished place is occupied by Raymond Williams, the British cultural and literary critic whose published work spans three decades. There is, however, a tendency to take Williams's thought as a timeless piece of critique or as a source for (new-)leftist war chants for all times. In fact, Williams's real importance lies in the context of his early work, that on English letters and politics in the mid-1950s, against which we can better appreciate his innovation.

Williams's notorious definition of culture as "a whole way of life," in *Culture and Society*, was from the outset meant as polemic. For one, the idea of culture as a whole way of life is but one stage in the unfolding of the history of European ideas of culture. Culture, to Williams, is a whole way of life and not simply the material, intellectual, or spiritual aspect of life. Hence, the study of culture should not be restricted to one discipline. The very idea of culture as a whole way of life was not simply a response to industrialization (or, in Marxist terms, to a change in the means of production), but also to new kinds of relationships emerging in the industrializing, urbanizing, more anonymous society of the nineteenth century.[3] Furthermore, the socially-constructed understanding of culture as a whole way of life characterizes society and the significations it produces as an ongoing process rather than a final conclusion, a dynamic flux rather than a static object. For this reason, culture by definition allows for a plurality of interpretations. This was very important to Williams, who was struggling with the influence of works like Matthew Arnold's 1869 *Culture and Anarchy* on English tradition, which defined culture as *high* or *elite* culture and pitted it against non-culture. To validate popular culture, the culture of the working classes, it had to be wrested from its delegitimized place in this traditional hierarchy and included in "a whole way of life." As Williams states in the title of a famous essay, "culture is ordinary."

Nevertheless, Williams envisions a space of convergence for the plurality of attitudes within culture as a whole way of life in social cohesion or solidarity; some sort of shared premise of what society is and of how it should function. As he asserts, "the development of the idea of culture has, throughout, been a criticism of what has been called the bourgeois idea of society," that is, the criticism of those who "have been unable to think of society as a merely neutral area, or as an abstract regulating mechanism" (*Culture and Society* 328). This is not merely a criticism of the individuated view the bourgeoisie (or just economic liberalists) have of society – encapsulated in Mrs. Thatcher's famous claim that there is no such thing as society – in favor of a more cohesive, more communitarian notion. There is here also an implicit critique, which was later to be made explicit, of the numerous social-scientific definitions common in the practice of (mainly North American) anthropology, which attempt to fix the conceptual usage of "culture" within the discipline, mainly with material reference (cf. "Culture," in *Keywords* 87–93). The very fact of a professor of English appropriating such a staple sociological and anthropological term for his own overtly politicized leftist critique, based on a study of arts and letters rather than on empirical social research, challenged this practice.

Ironically, despite its clear Western and Marxist premises, Williams's definition of culture as a whole way of life is analytically inadequate when applied to the West. The intricacies of a revision of the base-superstructure model do not have significant import when applied to the entire West as culture. The definition is then in clear danger of becoming all-inclusive, especially in a reality where the greatest similarity between the various forms of Western-ness occurs in popular culture, which Williams's definition had set out to validate. Williams does offer his own problematization of the idea of culture, but his whole account of historical changes is placed completely within a Western (mostly European) setting. The effects of modernization on the understanding of the idea of culture have not led to a convergence of ways of life between cultures. In fact, and here Williams followed Marx, they have only come to highlight the divergent "ways of life" and conflicting interests of the two main Western classes: the working class and the bourgeoisie. Moreover, the potential adequacy of culture as a whole way of life to the contemporary West is limited, if only for the fact that it is by definition a sign of the times (as a reaction to changes in forms of production and socialization), and so can only apply to the West since the mid nineteenth century and only until a further change of social relations, which may have already occurred since Williams's death in 1986. Williams's Marxist premises are problematic in that they see society as an insistent struggle between working class and bourgeoisie, and in that they provide the class struggle as the default scheme for social analysis. His is a highly specific viewpoint, as was pointed out as early as Fanon's *The Wretched of the Earth* (1961). However, because of the positioning of the West as a default setting, which self-effaces the Western-ness of the class structure and the Marxist perspective at large, this is easily overlooked.

Most of Williams's famous works of cultural critique – *Culture and Society* (1958), *The Long Revolution* (1961), *The Country and the City* (1973), and *Marxism and Literature* (1977) – were written about and for the British cultural scene; that is, they were generally intended for a British readership. Perceived as part of a larger theoretical and political trend of what was later dubbed the New Left, it signified a turn toward sociology and cultural criticism, and a vote of no confidence in party politics in general, rejecting both the Conservative government and the Old Left of the Labour party establishment in what was considered a show of Commitment (at a time when the original impetus of *engagement* was already exhausted in France). The "anti-politics," or shying away from party politics, had resulted in two things: a general disconnection of the New Left theorists from their public because of their inability to influence the socio-political reality; and a deflection of transformative efforts toward "issue politics" like the Campaign for Nuclear Disarmament (Hewison 175–76). This can be seen as a precursor to other issue politics that were conducted in terms of identity twenty and thirty years later, in which period the view of critical academic writing as transformative action has certainly become a wider trend.

The two main vectors that preoccupied Williams's thought were class and nation, with a possible romanticized third being community, offered as a redemptive alternative to the predicaments of the first two. His critique was insensitive to questions of gender, and only late in life did he address (in a rather minor way) the issue of ethnicity. Like many Marxists, Williams was thinking very clearly within the Western box, with his categories being traditional Western universalistic abstractions. As we have seen, this unselfconscious insiderism is part of the reason his broader definition of culture is not useful in looking at the West itself.

However, we must remember that the social sciences of the 1950s and the 1960s still reflected that Occidentalist point of view. The underlying assumption common to theories of modernization at the time – the period of European postwar reconstruction and global decolonization – was that of convergence around modernity, the only one that Europe had recognized and which is still referred to by some as "first modernity" or "original modernity." Indeed, "it was believed that modernization would wipe out cultural, institutional, structural, and mental differences and, if unimpeded, would lead to a uniform modern world" (Eisenstadt and Schluchter 2–4; see also Hannerz, *Transnational Connections* 44–5). While this may seem naïve or even myopic now, in its time it was the ruling scientific assumption regarding modernization. From our perspective, though, it makes Williams's definition of culture, stemming from a survey of the changing meanings of the English word in British history, look rather more flexible, especially considering its modest intent. In fact, the confident formulation of the assumption of convergence is not dissimilar to the kind of hype, journalistic as well as academic, which heralded the advent of globalization in the 1990s.

The fundamental fallacy of the assumption of convergence was in conflating two phenomena: the Western and the modern. Acknowledging the existence of other forms of modernity and modernization, which have developed separately and sometimes independently of European modernity, leads us to a hermeneutical problem. Having overcome the traditional Orientalism of the Eurocentric outlook, how do we then shed our conceptual and methodological bias and study *multiple modernities* on their own terms? And what would those "own terms" be for societies that were for most of European modernity subjugated to European colonial rule and cultural hegemony?

In this sense, postcolonial critique is both a continuation of and a breach in Western academic scholarship on identity and culture. It is a continuation in the discourse itself and in much of its vocabulary and discursive premises, but a clear breach in that it distances itself from a Western frame of mind, broadening its domain of influences as well as its range of explanation and implication. What is new about postcolonial critique and concomitantly about its brand of identity politics? Firstly and most obviously, postcolonialism effects an epistemic decentering of traditional Western cultural thought. Secondly, it prompts a political decentering toward an understanding of an arena of power and politics that is simultaneously global and local, a "glocalization," as it were (cf. Shenhav and Hever 15–19). A staple of postcolonial critique is its pitting itself across from, and against, Western liberal individualism. It recognizes that one's patrimony or heritage, not to mention one's lineage, is a constant, not a variable, in the construction of one's identity, which is a major step away from the elective and world-constituting construction of the subject according to the traditional Western *episteme*.

Postcolonial critique updated and refined Western cultural thought by its unique sensibility, stemming from its vantage points within and without "being Western," from liminal points along the frontier of Western experience, and from its interaction with other experiences and ways of life. The bulk of postcolonial critical works leans toward understanding both collective memory and identity as narrative, and thus temporal. This endows postcolonial conceptions of identity with a performative quality, a material specificity of place and time that is immediate and that defies universalization, which itself is a common fallacy of Western thinking. A major contribution of postcolonial critique to Western cultural thought is that it questions the supposed need to delineate a singular, characteristic Western identity today. One of the central terms in postcolonial critique is "hybridity," particularly as it has been employed by Homi K. Bhabha. Hybridity, and the reality it denotes, can be taken as signs of our times, and was probably superfluous in traditional or pre-modern societies. It represents a merging of identities and a pluralistic acceptance of both the merge and its constituent elements. I believe the epistemic virtue of the concept of hybridity lies in the way it offers a middle ground between an essentialist understanding of identity and a completely relativist vision. As such, hybridity, like the center/periphery structure, diaspora, and multiple modernities, serves as a setting and an epistemic and political motivation for what was dubbed identity politics.

The concept of identity typically functions as a naming and representing of "us" and "them" categories; that is, as an expression of the need for identity and identification, participation and apartness. Politically, identity is always the bone to be picked: once with the Western liberal project, to uncover its ethnic and cultural bias; and again in the study of history, to renegotiate the discourse of memory and to make room for narratives previously absent from "universal" historical accounts. Indeed, as French historian Pierre Nora suggests in "The Era of Commemoration," the new economy of contemporary cultural consciousness bases itself on three interlinked pillars: identity, memory, and patrimony or heritage (635). Nora himself is less than pleased with the cult of heritage, which, as he sees it, hijacks contemporary politics and poetics (621–32; see also Wood 31–3). However, heritage does fulfill a certain function (and perhaps an underlying need) for the reattachment of subjects to larger and organic frames of identification. Patrimony is there to tap into, a constant rather than a variable in the elements of individual and collective identities.

Like patrimony, memory typically functions as an agent of identity and of social differentiation through the taking of a specific stance toward the past. Furthermore, *public* memory is essentially performative and thus time- and place-specific. It reflects a will or desire to remember, to perpetuate, to construct identity and patrimony (Wood 2–3). Perhaps it is the performative, non-essentialist nature of memory and identity in postcolonial critique that enables one of postcolonialism's greatest merits: its reattachment of the question of identity to the determinant of culture. This is an influence that in secularized and individualized Western cultural thought was relegated to a place of secondary importance, after determinants such as nationality, class, and gender. Postcolonialist critique also reappraised these determinants in their intersections (Shenhav and Hever 12), as in, for example, Anne McClintock's cross-section of gender and economy in *Imperial Leather*; Gayatri Spivak talking and writing of her place as a Bengali woman working in Ivy League American universities; and M. Jacqui Alexander challenging feminist solidarity across cultures or recounting the oppression of homosexuality by national pride in Trinidad.

As we can see, postcolonial critique expands and enriches our common understanding of culture and identity in general and Western-ness in particular. Its principal imports are: the reattachment of identity to culture and patrimony; the consideration of several identity determinants together as they intersect and influence one another; as well as the specific, personal, and performative mode of argumentation that keeps the discourse of identity at eye level and gives it a human face. In this way, postcolonial critique keeps in check the tendency of traditional Western cultural thought to generalize and universalize the subject and its identity denominations. No less importantly, it hits at the very core of Western (formerly "universal") collective memory to reshape and diversify it, thus transforming not only the subject matter of Western identity discourse but also its historical and social foundations (cf. Young; Venn; Chakrabarty).

Among other issues, postcolonial critique raises the question of the validity of culture as a primary constitutive element of identity. Referring to culture still suggests that cultural identity is innate, determinate, and primordial in character – thus rendering culture a reductionist and essentialist identity determinant. Remaining with our specific case, this sort of account is lacking in the way postcolonialism explains the Western element in the experience of people living in Westernized societies around the world, which historically (I am wary of any reference to "origins") were not part of the traditional location of "the West." Nevertheless, the "being Western" element is still very present in such experiences, along with other elements of identity, both private and denominational. How can we work through this complex thicket of identity without resorting to reductionism?

Here is where we arrive at the concept of *collective identity*. Like "culture," collective identity is an elusive notion with numerous definitions that arise from the several disciplines which utilize it in their respective discourses. In general, I shall follow sociological definitions, which themselves already take into account the plurality of uses of the term collective identity and so account for its differentiation from similar-functioning terms. Collective identity can be understood as the construction and perception of a shared status or relation, imagined or concretely experienced (Polletta and Jasper 285). It manifests as a shared sense of collectivity ("we-ness") and collective agency that emerges as an interactive process rather than as a property of social actors: in fact, the process of collective identity is also more important than its outcome or product, the actual in-group. In the shared sense of "we-ness" – its function of animating and mobilizing members on an emotive or cognitive basis, not necessarily by reference to interests or to rational choice – lies the explanatory import of collective identity. Since the process of collective identity formation does not emerge out of nowhere, it is shaped, among other factors, by the discovery of pre-existing bonds, interests, and boundaries, as well as by the available symbols in the society in which it emerges, its center-periphery structure, the character of its public sphere, and other structural elements.

Eisenstadt and Schluchter suggest three modes in collective identity construction: primordiality, civility, and sacredness. Primordiality essentially constructs that which is to be taken as "natural" (or *physis*): the relations and distinctions that shape the in-group, such as language and territory, gender, kinship, and generation. Civility accounts for the *nomos*, the social sphere as constructed by human volition through traditions, routines, and rules of engagement. Sacredness is not to be taken literally but as the linking of the collective "we-ness" to some grander metaphysical entity which validates it, be it a deity or an abstract concept such as reason or progress. By way of these three modes of construction, collective identity facilitates solidarity among members, not unassisted by a sense of similarity between them that supervenes the shared sense of "we-ness" (Eisenstadt and Schluchter 14–5).

Collective identity provides its members with hermeneutic categories and taxonomies for experiencing and making sense of reality. Naturally, these are also used reflexively and form part of the self-constitution of collective identity through ongoing interpretive efforts. Collective identity further serves as an orientational identity, an abstract touchstone, for both the in-group ("we") and the out-group ("them"). This touchstone is in fact not exclusively abstract, for collective identity is performative and expressed in cultural materials – in narratives, symbols, names, appearances, and demeanors. Nevertheless, despite and because of the way it remains always emergent, fluid and relational, not all cultural materials express a collective identity (Polletta and Jasper 298).

D.A. Snow contends that the main approach in the study of collective identity is constructionist: it aims to explore how collective identities are created, expressed, sustained, and modified, especially through generation, invocation, and the maintenance of symbolic resources (commonly dubbed "identity work"), thus constituting collective identity as a "semiotic bricolage" (2215–2216; see also Eisenstadt and Giesen). Snow also sketches out some general tendencies in collective identity scholarship. On a personal level, collective identity must be embraced by the individual member as a salient part of their self. On the social level, the appearance of a collective identity is sometimes taken as indicating the subsided salience of other identity categories among its members. Even so, individual salience is but a part of the potency and intensity of a collective identity, which are determined, among other aspects, by the sharpness of the social difference it implies and by a sense of moral virtue that accompanies the feeling or perception of difference. Collective identities appear in sociological and ethnographic scholarship in all forms and sizes, thus illustrating the flexibility of the term as analytical tool. They are, nonetheless, associated particularly with social change, challenges, and exclusion, as well as with social breakdown and renewal. Indeed, much of the more interesting research has been regarding social change movements like the Greens, women's liberation, and gay liberation. Consequently, collective identities are seen to be an ever-growing phenomenon in the late twentieth century, set against the decline of traditional social institutions, the accelerating pace of life and history, and the corresponding identity crises (Snow 2214, 2218). This is the immediate background for the sociologist Manuel Castells and his interpretation of collective identity.

In a three-tome work of vast scope, Castells has reframed the contemporary late-industrial age as the Information Society, being a new stage in history that is defined by a new structure of societal power relations. In this setting, Castells sees three kinds of collective identity: *legitimizing* identity is an extension of dominant social institutions and their rationalization, and is what generates civil society; *resistance* identity is set up as a survival or resistance trench by those devalued, disempowered, or stigmatized by the dominant social institutions, and thus can generate communes or communities; lastly, *project* identity is the new identity constructed to redefine members' position in society and thus to transform society as a whole, producing subjects in the sense not of individuals but of "the collective social actor through which individuals reach holistic meaning in their experience" (Castells 10). The project of identity is therefore extended into a project of social transformation, reflecting the most radical potentialities of collective identity.

Clearly, even within this flexible definition of collective identity, it would be a demanding task to define the contemporary West as a collective identity. In the perception of an (admittedly loose) shared status of "we-ness," and in the fact that it is an orientational touchstone, the West fits the bill easily. A less easy point to make is how the West as a collective identity can today be a locus of collectively constructed primordiality, civility, and sacredness. Asserting this would necessitate a qualifying claim about the recognition of pre-existing bonds (and rifts), interests, and boundaries. To the extent that the universalistic and individualistic premises of the traditional West are accepted, they – along with other such premises – can be said to be the foundation of a contemporary Western notion of humanistic primordiality, a state- and market-oriented civility of rights and duties, and a sacralization of the Enlightenment project. The formerly oppressed members in this contemporary collectivity cannot and should not relinquish their respective traditions and particular claims. They are, however, expected to pursue them within the flexible confines of the contemporary Western collective identity. If they refuse to do so, then they are seen as challenging Western-ness as a whole and taken – as they have been at least since 2001 – to be outside the collectivity, and consequently somewhat morally inferior. Accordingly, the West (however perceived) as collectivity, as a universal, still evidently serves as a point of reference both from within and from without.

Even so, there remains the central function of mobilization, which occupies most of the literature on collective identity, as it usually deals with smaller and emergent collectivities. The ability of a collective identity to mobilize its members is a covariant of the salience of that identity for them and its relative salience among other identity determinants. It can be safely said that most Westerners today do not see their Western-ness (however perceived) as a major element of their identity, and it is certainly not as important to them as their gender, nationality, ethnicity, faith, and other stock attributes. Moreover, because of its many local interpretations and general ubiquity around the world – all part of its "identity work" – the West no longer creates a sharp difference between its in-group and its others, which is taken as an important mobilizing factor of collective identity. Perhaps most poignantly, by its cultural materials the contemporary West is a product of its tradition and history, so inasmuch as it is considered a project identity, that identity is actually the collective identity of a late-stage Enlightenment project, and not of some new state of affairs framed in experience by a new paradigm of new subjects. Thus, even though at first glance defining the West as a collective identity can be useful in addressing the topic of correspondence between culture and social structure, it s nonetheless still lacking as a basis for accounts of collective action.

A discussion of collective identities allows us to re-examine some definitions of that elusive and more traditional concept, culture. Among other things, it brings back to the fore the more holistic or total definitions of what is commonly understood in the social sciences to be the ideational aspect of a society. We can speak here of Williams's inclusive definition of culture as "a way of life," or of his other catchphrase "culture is ordinary," as valid elements – indeed, prominent ones – in contemporary Western collective identity. This is, of course, provided we understand "ordinary" and "way of life" to be constitutive of the convergence of the individual and the social, rather than as a solipsistic private language or a useless generalization. To Williams we can add the Swedish anthropologist Ulf Hannerz, who offers his own inclusive definition of culture, suggesting it be understood as "the meanings which people create, and which create people, as members of societies" (*Cultural Complexity* 3). Being less of a slogan and more a definition, albeit somewhat poetic, Hannerz's suggestion reflects not only human agency but also membership and partaking, much in the spirit of the concept of collective identity. He proposes to examine the West of today, inclusively defined, as a "contemporary complex culture." Much in the vein of orthodox anthropology, Hannerz defines culture as having three dimensions, from which it can also be examined: ideas and modes of thought (mental); forms of externalization (behavioral); and social distribution, being the systemic picture of the occurrence of the first two dimensions. The novelty of Hannerz's 1992 *Cultural Complexity* was in straying away from the mainstream of anthropological research, which deals mainly with the dimensions of mental "content" and externalization, and turning instead to study the much less addressed distributive dimension of the West as complex culture. Most importantly, Hannerz confronts the customary commitment to "the idea of culture as something shared, in the sense of *homogeneously* distributed in society," which he claims makes "cultural analysis *asocial*" (11–12, emphases added). In so doing, he significantly loosens the definition of culture, while also proposing the problematic of uneven cultural distribution as a valid, indeed central, topic of enquiry.

The move Hannerz performs is not simply an epistemic decision: as he admits himself, adopting his position carries ethical consequences too. As he puts it, "the major implication of a distributive understanding of culture, of *culture as an organization of diversity*, is . . . that *people must deal with other people's meanings*; that is there are meanings, and meaningful forms, on which other individuals, categories, or groups in one's environment somehow have a prior claim, but to which one is somehow yet called to *make a response*" (*Cultural Complexity* 14, emphases added). This also cuts through the aforementioned McLuhanist hype around the advent of globalization toward a more grounded, past-conscious outlook: "postmodern culture cannot be coterminous with contemporary complex culture as the latter exists spread out over the world; postmodernist thought is again Occidentalist" (35).

Hannerz's definition of contemporary complex culture was modeled on what we might call the contemporary West, and in that respect it fits the bill, notably in that intra-cultural diversity is defined as a given. It is Hannerz who intentionally narrows down the scope of discussion: first, by insisting on retaining the anthropological term and concept of culture; and then by choosing to address mainly the questions of cultural distribution and internal congruity, or how people and their "meanings" deal with other people and their "meanings."[4] This is in a way a return to Williams's "way of life" – which had been his version of the ethnographic definition – only to amplify and revise how "ways of life" are to be understood and explored, and with less ideological baggage. As such, it can serve to introduce a discussion of new identities said to have formed in this age. In this context I would mention Marc Augé and his *non-lieux* (non-places) of supermodernity, spaces realized and asserted by human mobility, a view highly influenced by Deleuze and Guattari's *Nomadology* and de Certeau's phenomenology of the everyday; or Arjun Appadurai's *ethnoscapes* – the deterritorialized, transitory states that characterize the everyday lives of modern people, which they take to be constitutive of their identities and a basis for connecting with other people sharing the same experience as an identity denomination. Understanding non-places and ethnoscapes as varieties within the contemporary complex culture validates these definitions and, more importantly, the claims of people who consider them palpable elements of their identities. Alternatively, since collective identities and the contemporary complex culture are not mutually exclusive, they can serve together to highlight different aspects of the new lifestyles/phenomena: the former to questions of mobilization and structure, and the latter to issues of distribution and mutual congruence.

Why then address the West of today as a collective identity or as a redefined culture? The inner differentiation within the contemporary West, and with it the loss of modernity as a distinguishing feature exclusive to the West, necessitate a redefinition of Western identity in a more inclusive manner. This is not only to "save the phenomena" and retain the West as an analytical concept, but mainly to understand Western collective identity today as a social and cultural entity that over the last century has undergone a distinct transformation, along with its persistence in this change. It is not that Western civilization became void of meaning or content; rather, the ubiquity of Westernization preserves the West, while also making Western-ness a more complex and multi-faceted attribute. However, it is clear that traditional Western thought is unable to grasp the change that has occurred in the characteristics of Western-ness, a change that is chiefly characterized by a decentering and a growing heterogeneity, not just of interpretation but also of salience and degrees of participation.

Approaching the West is thus a matter of leveling the playing field and examining it in a way which does not inherently set it apart from all other collectivities and identity factors. More importantly, this has to be done from within its own tradition of thought, in a way that complements the postcolonial gaze from the periphery or the borderline. Clearly, this constitutes a move away from the textuality and high theory that are typical of both Western cultural thought and postcolonial critique. Instead, these new definitions of collectivity relate to the performativity of identity and its materiality, and write off cultural essentialism in favor of a constructionism based on human interaction. In so doing, they are themselves a part of the Western *episteme* of our time.

Notes

1. That specificity or uniqueness can itself be taken as usurpation. Slavoj Žižek suggests that Europe as an ideological concept (derived from Europa, the Classical Greek mythical figure) was born out of two hijackings of an Eastern gem by Western barbarians: firstly, the Roman vulgarization of Greek thought; and secondly, the vulgarization of Christianity by the Western church (143).

2. Despite structural and thematic similarities I shall not use the term "Judeo-Christian Tradition." Granted some cross-pollination, Western European cultures have been predominantly Christian (of some denomination) to the exclusion of all other religious denominations.

3. Williams is critical of the term "mass," which he sees as simply a new appellation of the old pejorative "mob": "The masses are always the other, whom we don't know, and can't know. . . . To other people, we also are masses. Masses are other people. There are in fact no masses; there are only ways of seeing people as masses" (*Culture and Society* 299–300).

4. In this respect Hannerz reads sometimes like he is himself trying to "save the phenomena." As he asserts, "I do not personally think that the culture concept 'will have to go.' We will only have to keep on criticizing it, and reforming it. I believe it is still the most useful key word we have to summarize that peculiar capacity of human beings for creating and maintaining their own lives together" (*Transnational Connections* 42).

Bibliography

Alexander, M. Jacqui. "Redrafting Morality: The Postcolonial State and the Sexual Offences Bill of Trinidad and Tobago." *Third World Women and the Politics of Feminism*. Ed. Chandra Talpade Mohanty, Ann Russo, and Lourdes Torres. Bloomington: Indiana UP, 1991. 133–52.

Appadurai, Arjun. *Modernity at Large: Cultural Dimensions of Globalization*. Minneapolis: U of Minnesota P, 1996.

Augé, Marc. *Non-Places: Introduction to an Anthropology of Supermodernity*. 1992. London: Verso, 1995.

Castells, Manuel. *The Information Age: Economy, Society and Culture. Vol. II: The Power of Identity*. Oxford: Blackwell, 1997.

Certeau, Michel de. *The Practice of Everyday Life*. Trans. Steven Rendall. Berkeley, Los Angeles, London: U of California P, 1988.

Chakrabarty, Dipesh. *Provincializing Europe*. Princeton: Princeton UP, 2000.

Deleuze, Gilles, and Félix Guattari. *Nomadology: The War Machine*. Los Angeles: Semiotext(e), 1986.

Eisenstadt, Shmuel N., and Wolfgang Schluchter. "Introduction: Paths to Early Modernities – A Comparative View." *Public Spheres & Collective Identities*. Ed. Shmuel N. Eisenstadt, Wolfgang Schluchter, and Björn Wittrock. New Brunswick and London: Transaction Publishers, 2001. 1–18.

Eisenstadt, Shmuel N., and B. Giesen. "The Construction of Collective Identity." *Archives Européenes de Sociologie* 36 (1995): 72–102.

Fanon, Frantz, *The Wretched of the Earth*. New York: Grove Press, 1963.

Foucault, Michel. *Fearless Speech*. Ed. Joseph Pearson. Los Angeles: Semiotext(e) – Foreign Agents, 2001.

Hannerz, Ulf. *Cultural Complexity: Studies in the Social Organization of Meaning*. New York: Columbia UP, 1992.

———. *Transnational Connections: Culture, People, Places*. London and New York: Routledge, 1996.

Hewison, Robert. *In Anger: Culture in the Cold War 1945–60*. London: Weidenfeld and Nicolson, 1981.

McClintock, Anne. *Imperial Leather: Race, Gender and Sexuality in the Colonial Contest*. London and New York: Routledge, 1995.

Nora, Pierre. "The Era of Commemoration." Trans. Arthur Goldhammer. *Realms of Memory: The Construction of the French Past, vol. III: Symbols*. Ed. Lawrence D. Kritzman. New York: Columbia UP, 1998. 609–37.

Polletta, Francesca, and James M. Jasper. "Collective Identity and Social Movements." *Annual Review of Sociology* 27 (2001): 283–305.

Shenhav, Yehouda, and Hannan Hever. "The Postcolonial Gaze." *Teoria u'Vikoret [Theory and Criticism]* 20 (Spring 2002): 9–22.

Snow, D.A. "Collective identity." *International Encyclopedia of the Social and Behavioral Sciences*. Ed. Neil J. Smelser and Paul B. Baltes. Vol. 4. Oxford: Elsevier, 2001. 2212–19.

Spivak, Gayatri Chakravorty. *Outside in the Teaching Machine*. London and New York: Routledge, 2008.

Venn, Couze. *Occidentalism: Modernity and Subjectivity*. London: Sage, 2000.

Williams, Raymond. *The Country and the City*. Oxford: Oxford UP, 1975.

———. *Culture and Society: Coleridge to Orwell*. Rev. ed. London: The Hogarth Press, 1987.

———. "Culture is Ordinary." *Resources of Hope: Culture, Democracy, Socialism*. London: Verso, 1989. 3–18.

———. *Keywords: A Vocabulary of Culture and Society*. Rev. ed. London: Flamingo, 1983.

———. *The Long Revolution*. Peterborough: Broadview Press, 2001.

———. *Marxism and Literature*. Oxford: Oxford UP, 1977.

Wood, Nancy. *Vectors of Memory: Legacies of Trauma in Postwar Europe*. Oxford: Berg, 1999.

Young, Robert. *White Mythologies: Writing History and the West*. London: Routledge, 1990.

Žižek, Slavoj. *Welcome to the Desert of the Real: Five Essays on 11 September and Related Dates*. London and New York: Verso, 2002.

Ubuntu, the Truth and Reconciliation Commission, and South African National Identity

Hanneke Stuit

Introduction

This cartoon by Zapiro (pseudonym of Jonathan Shapiro) was first published on the 25th of May, 2008, in the South African newspaper *The Sunday Times* in response to the eruption of xenophobia-inspired violence in South African townships in the course of that year. During this time, groups of black South Africans felt threatened by immigrants from other African countries, claiming that the latter were moving in on resources and job opportunities supposedly designated for "real" South Africans. "Foreign" property was destroyed and burned, hundreds of people were attacked, and thousands were dislocated.[1]

The effectivity of the cartoon consists, as far as I am concerned, of its multi-layered critique of both the disconcerting surfacing of xenophobia and the circumstances under which this violence erupted. The cartoon condemns the violence by bringing to mind the reconciliatory and inclusive discourse that is often associated with the increasingly popular term "ubuntu," especially since its implementation in the truth and reconciliation process. On the one hand, the cartoon suggests that this discourse is past its prime. After all, people having experienced both division and reconciliation in such a relatively short period (i.e. both the end of apartheid and the campaign for reconciliation that followed in its wake), would surely not allow the ostracizing of one group by another? On the other hand, one could say that an ubuntu-inspired discourse is alive and well, but has been transformed in the course of time. In the cartoon, ubuntu's reconciliatory and peaceful tone, as well as its association with a universal humanity, has turned into a way of determining who belongs to the "new South Africa" and who does not. In other words, this term, which is frequently associated with hospitality, empathy, forgiveness, and respect for human dignity (to name but a few of its connotations), is utilized by those who claim to understand its repercussions in order to condemn, violate, and exclude people who supposedly do not know what it means. In addition, Shapiro refers to the fact that, during the xenophobic attacks of May 2008, people were asked to name certain isiZulu words that were slightly archaic as a way to distinguish between foreign and South African isiZulu speakers (Ndlovu). The irony lies in the fact that ubuntu, too, is an isiZulu word. As such, the very term used to emphasize the importance of community in post-apartheid South Africa has become a shibboleth which supposedly protects this community from "outsiders." It has become a boundary marker, a yardstick against which to measure others, a tool for exclusion.

In this way, the cartoon meticulously brings to light some of the issues involved in the analysis of ubuntu as a concept as I will undertake it in this essay. Next to ubuntu's humanitarian interpretations, I will mostly discuss some if its ambivalences in terms of tensions between inclusion and exclusion, individuality and communality, and autonomy and relationality. Considering ubuntu's increasing popularity, this is a necessary approach: it is the name of a popular computer operating system, it is being used in South Africa's PR campaign for the 2010 soccer world cup, and the promotion of ubuntu values was even part of the Congress of the People's (Cope) agenda as formulated for the 2009 elections.[2] However, even though to know what ubuntu means and to claim one practices its values is apparently considered desirable in the South African context, as the term is being used more and more broadly, its meaning becomes less and less specific. Although this lack of specificity is not necessarily problematic and also opens up the possibilities of its use, Mnyaka and Mothlabi point out that ubuntu "has not been immune to misuse and overuse" (216). Indeed, its uses in the context of the world cup and the Cope manifesto in particular imply that it has been reduced to a promotional or marketing tool. Ubuntu, however, has a more extensive background.

Although an exhaustive treatise on the ways ubuntu has been interpreted in different settings over the years falls beyond the scope of this essay, a short introduction is indispensable. It is probably true that ubuntu remains a rather intuitive concept until one can "see" the way it works, for instance in the truth and reconciliation process. Nonetheless, scholars have resorted to quite a number of techniques to provide a description of ubuntu, varying from historical to more anthropologically oriented approaches. Alternatively, quite a few have opted for the field of linguistics in order to deduce a definition. The work of many authors, however, reflects the view that ubuntu is a traditionally African concept that is based on a lively community culture, even though, as historian Christoph Marx observes, 'no historical evidence has been produced to substantiate this alleged community culture. Instead, general references to "tradition" are made to suffice" (52). A possible explanation for this lack of specificity may be that "[u]buntu cultural norms have been orally transferred from generation to generation over a long time, and have never been produced as literature or written form" (Broodryk qtd. in Mnyaka and Mothlabi 216). According to Mnyaka and Mothlabi, however, it is safe to say that generally ubuntu reflects a way of life, "a spiritual foundation, an inner state, an orientation, and a good disposition that motivates, challenges and makes one perceive, feel and act in a humane way towards others" (216). Qualities like "brotherliness, togetherness, hospitality, solidarity and mutual support of each other and the community within which one exists" are regarded as manifestations of this disposition (Barben 6). Many linguistically oriented scholars consider the Xhosa proverb *"ubuntu ungamntu ngabanye abantu"* – which is spelled and translated in several broadly correlating ways, but most often as "I am a person because of other persons"[3] – a leading description of this ethical orientation. Desmond Tutu has described ubuntu as a reflection of the idea that we "belong in a bundle of life" (35) and pitches it emphatically against the Descartian "I think therefore I am" as "I am human because I belong." As such, ubuntu offers a specifically African counterpoint to the individualism of much Western theory. Indeed, the truth and reconciliation process has generated many examples of victims showing involvement in their perpetrators' predicaments, even offering them forgiveness at times. The tangible solidarity and harmony during some TRC hearings show the power and value of this worldview in the face of anger, resentment, and conflict.

What most research does not pick up on, at least not as pertinently as Zapiro has done in his cartoon, is the ambivalence of the concept. How ubuntu relates to exclusion or to issues regarding race, gender, or class is hardly ever specified. Only rarely does research mention ubuntu's changeability over time or its specific historicity. Nor is ubuntu related to other, ethically oriented theories or humanitarian terminology.[4] Unfortunately, there is no room to consider all these issues here. However, ambivalent aspects of ubuntu will be discussed through a focus on its implementation in the setting of the Truth and Reconciliation Commission (TRC) in South Africa. Like Zapiro's cartoon, the discussion of the TRC context is intended to point out how ubuntu can come to function as a boundary marker for belonging and national identity in a postcolonial setting where the existence of a so-called unitary identity (either of individuals or of groups) is greatly complicated (Mbembe 16), but an obvious political need to posit one still remains.

No Future without Forgiveness: Ubuntu and the TRC

When, in 1994, the apartheid government was finally ousted after almost fifty years of complete control over South Africa, the new democratically elected government decided on a course of action that would set an example to many nations around the world. It looked for a way to deal with the country's past that related to restorative justice rather than to punitive justice in order to achieve some form of reconciliation and unity. To this end, the Mandela government installed not only a new constitution, but a Truth and Reconciliation Commission (TRC) as well, which operated from 1996 to 1998 (although it took up to 2001 to complete the amnesty hearings). It consisted of three main structures: the Human Rights Violation Committee, the Amnesty Committee, and the Reparation and Rehabilitation Committee. The task at hand for these structures was, respectively, to unearth what had happened during the apartheid years from 1960 up to 1994 by way of staging testimonies of victims and surviving family members of victims, to grant amnesty to perpetrators who made "full disclosure of all the relevant facts relating to acts associated with a political objective" (National Unity and Reconciliation Act 1995), and to offer some form of reparation to victims. The TRC hoped to spread knowledge of the past throughout South Africa (and the world) and open up dialogue in a disconcertingly divided country.

Legally, the Commission was based on the National Unity and Reconciliation Act (NURA) of 1995. This Act quotes from the postscript to the 1993 interim Constitution of the Republic of South Africa. The following is an excerpt of this Constitution, with the passage quoted by the Act in quotation marks:

The adoption of this Constitution lays the secure foundation for the people of South Africa to transcend the divisions and strife of the past, which generated gross violations of human rights, the transgression of humanitarian principles in violent conflicts and a legacy of hatred, fear, guilt and revenge. "These can now be addressed on the basis that there is a need for understanding but not for vengeance, a need for reparation but not for retaliation, a need for ubuntu but not for victimization." (qtd. in Truth and Reconciliation Committee, *TRC Report Vol. 6* 3)

It is significant that ubuntu is referred to in the founding Act of the Commission, because this places it at the heart of the truth and reconciliation process, and demonstrates how firmly entrenched in South African public awareness the authors presume it to be. Mark Libin rightly observes that the word "ubuntu" is, remarkably, rendered in one of the vernaculars without italics or quotation marks (126), as if it is as straightforward to English-language readers as the ones surrounding it. Whether this is actually the case or not, the use of ubuntu here at least implies that it carries the same semantic importance as both "understanding" and "reparation." Indeed, as Libin suggests, it seems "as though the call for communal regeneration may be located only in an emphatic understanding of the concept of ubuntu" (126).

Considering the positive connotations of ubuntu, this featuring of the word in the Constitution is certainly a welcome sight. Unfortunately, the reverie is disturbed by the problematic construction of the discourse of reconciliation in this particular passage. In it, ubuntu features in a list of three apparent binaries – understanding/vengeance; reparation/retaliation; ubuntu/victimization – of which the poles are presented as mutually exclusive. For instance, there is room for understanding, but not for vengeance. This stylistic maneuver determines the way the rest of the phrase is read: the first part of the binary is emphatically preferred over the second one. As a result, then, reparation is rendered as more desirable than retaliation and ubuntu more so than victimization. This preference seems rather unproblematic, especially in the context of the huge historical momentum of South Africa's transition from apartheid to a democratic government and the consequent emergence of a discourse of reconciliation. However, when giving the passage more thought, difficulty does arise, and it does so precisely from within the frame of reference of reconciliation. For how does one, reasoning from the principle of the oppositions, realize reparation without victimization? If reparation is opposed to the identification or categorization of people as victims, how can their needs be met? Similarly, by constructing reparation and ubuntu as the opposite of victimization, it seems to compel these "victims" to give up their claims for reparation, whereas "perpetrators" gain immediate protection from the fact that, in this particular passage, retaliation is located on the negative side of the binary construction. Even though the general impulse to restore human dignity is surely laudable, does not ubuntu, which, as we will see, in the TRC context largely revolves around tending to the psychological needs of victims, put a spoke in the wheel of materially emancipating those who suffered from apartheid most? Does it not become a pretext for not tending to reparation at all, even though it is obviously named as a "need" in both the Act and the Constitution?

These questions, raised by the way ubuntu formally features in the National Unity and Reconciliation Act, poignantly reveal how the use of ubuntu in this context stresses the tension between individual and communal needs. The promotion of national unity is, or so it seems, clearly preferred over tending to the personal needs of victims. What is more, these personal needs are subsumed to a discourse that is specially devised to present this national need as a personal striving.[5] In what follows, I will demonstrate how this discourse, based on the humanitarian, but ambivalent values implied in the use of ubuntu, relates to a participation in the TRC process in general and to the role of forgiveness in this process in particular.

In John Boorman's 2004 film *In My Country*, which is loosely based on Antjie Krog's book *Country of My Skull*, ubuntu is represented in what is perhaps its most frequent guise. It is explicitly placed in the context of the TRC hearings and is connected to the willingness of one of the victims to forgive his perpetrators. The film dramatizes several hearings based, loosely as well, on some of the most "famous" moments in the TRC process.[6] In one of these scenes, we see a man called Anderson testifying before the Commission.[7] After he has given his testimony, he asks the policeman who has caused him harm: "Now I want to ask this policeman: why did you break my trees? Tell me. Tell me why, so that I can forgive you." Unfortunately, the perpetrator's response to Anderson's request, apart from an uncomfortable glance at his colleague, is not depicted. Thus, the interaction proposed by Anderson, which is crucial to an understanding of ubuntu as a dynamic concept, is foreclosed by the film. Rather than demonstrating the potential force of Anderson's ubuntu-inspired stance towards the policemen, the film stages an explicit explanation of ubuntu. Outside, after the hearing, an American journalist (rendered poorly by Samuel L. Jackson) tells Anderson: "You were great in there, sir! You really showed those bastards!," to which Anderson responds: "I showed them what is ubuntu . . . We are all part of each other. When that policeman hurts me, he hurts you. He hurts everybody in this world, but also himself." In this way, the film highlights Anderson's humanizing attitude and performance, but leaves the importance of his open question, and thus of the responsible and reciprocal interaction between victim and perpetrator, unaddressed. As a result ubuntu is represented not as a mutual responsibility for every relationship or a collective responsibility for every community ("we are all part of each other"), but as uncritically related to forgiveness in the context of the TRC hearing. A similar tendency is reflected in Desmond Tutu's autobiographical work *No Future without Forgiveness*:

> *Ubuntu . . . speaks of the very essence of being human . . . It is to say, "My humanity is caught up, is inextricably bound up, in yours." . . . A person with Ubuntu is open and available to others, affirming of others, does not feel threatened that others are able and good, for he or she has a proper self-assurance that comes from knowing that he or she belongs in a greater whole and is diminished when others are humiliated or diminished, when others are tortured or oppressed.* (34–5)

According to Tutu, the former Archbishop of Cape Town who chaired the Commission, ubuntu is the worldview that "constrained so many to choose to forgive," because it entails a general striving for social harmony (34–5). Forgiveness is a very effective way of restoring social equilibrium, as it allows people to "emerge still human despite all efforts to dehumanize them" (35). By offering someone forgiveness, this implies, you not only help the person you forgive, but yourself as well. In other words, forgiveness is presented as a natural consequence of the notion of ubuntu.

Whereas interaction is foreclosed in the film, a sense of involvement and of its importance for the TRC process does come to the fore in the representation of the first public hearings that the Commission organized. These hearings took place in Port Elizabeth in April in 1996. In the fifth volume of the TRC Report, which was published after the TRC process was brought to a provisional end, these hearings were dubbed the "Cradock Four" hearings and functioned as "a model for future hearings" (2):

The four days were extremely emotional and dramatic. The witnesses included the families of the well-known "Cradock Four", community leaders assassinated in 1985; individuals and the families of those who were killed or injured in bombings carried out by revolutionary activists; and people who were detained, tortured, or victimised in other ways. Deponents were sometimes stoical, almost matter of fact, but others succumbed to tears or expressed their anger as they relived their experiences. The panel of commissioners and committee members was visibly overcome. The public sat silent and spellbound during the testimony, but was occasionally moved to angry murmuring. Tea and lunch breaks were marked by singing and chanting of political slogans. (3)

It is apparent that the recounting of the victim's experiences affected the people present. The commissioners were "visibly overcome," the audience was "spellbound" and "occasionally moved to angry murmuring." Footage of the hearings in Deborah Hoffmann and Frances Reid's *Long Night's Journey into Day* clearly reveals the palpability and intensity of these sentiments. Seeing victims express their anguish on a public platform united the people present sufficiently for them to take up the group activities of "singing and chanting political slogans."[8] The sharing of terrible knowledge about the past and of the ensuing grief and loss thus succeeded in involving the audience in the process.

In some cases, the interaction was not limited to victim, audience, and Commission. Some perpetrators, too, endeavored to become part of the process by applying for amnesty and attending the Amnesty hearings: some of them apologized, others asked for forgiveness, yet others remained uncompromising. But by telling their story, by responding to the consensus in the room that they had to explain themselves, these perpetrators acknowledged the structure of the hearing and adhered to the rules belonging to that setting. Furthermore, the fact that some perpetrators showed remorse implies an acknowledgement of the loss suffered by the victim, provided, of course, that sincerity is being observed. In other words, in the most favorable case, the perpetrator takes part in the rituals of the hearing. According to

George Bizos, who legally represented the widows of the Cradock Four, however, perpetrators do not even have to actively participate in the process of the hearings in order to produce the desirable effect of involvement and interaction. Presence alone is enough to provide for a literal staging of the perpetrator that results in a kind of catharsis:

The audience actually plays the role of a chorus in an ancient tragic play. Here we are, the actors on the stage – it's unusual to have a judicial proceeding on a stage, but here we are on a stage and an audience, and when they see them [the perpetrators] squirm, it's part of the . . . it's part of the cathartic process. Here you were, the all powerful that would come and arrest us in the middle of the night and not give account to anyone, you "white masters," and now you are not the super humans you thought that you were. You are subjected to cross-examination by a person who's on our side. I think that that is an important aspect of the TRC's work. (qtd. in *Long Night's Journey Into Day*)

In Bizos's frame of reference, then, a bond is created through a communal condemnation of a certain participant, rather than through the sincere and well-intentioned participation of all parties involved. This view on the "cathartic" function of the hearings as a platform where a sense of community is constructed through the staging of a scapegoat, throws further light on Zapiro's criticism of ubuntu in the cartoon. Its shrill disharmony with the ubuntu-inspired discourse as brought forward by Archbishop Tutu, with its emphasis on forgiveness, makes visible that ubuntu, in this case through scapegoating, can be used as a means to close ranks, rather than to open them.

The Healing of Our Land: Ubuntu and South African National Identity

During the Cradock Four hearings, this tension between inclusion and exclusion comes to the fore once more when Tutu, in his role of Chair, gives prominence to the desirability of forgiveness. The subsumption of individual experience is explicit here, as Tutu pulls the events of these first hearings to a "higher," exemplary and national plane:

We are proud to have people like you and your husbands, and the reason why we won the struggle is not because we had guns; we won the struggle because of people like you: people of incredible strength. And this country is fortunate to have people like you . . . We have a tremendous country, which has tremendous people, and you are one example of why we make it in this country. And that she, your daughter, should say, "I want to forgive, we want to forgive", after what she has experienced and seen what happened to her mother and to her father, and she says, "we want to forgive, but we want to know who to forgive". We give thanks to God for you, and thank you for your contribution to our struggle, and thank you, even if it was reluctant in a sense, rightly, thank you for sacrificing your husbands. (Truth and Reconciliation Commission, *TRC Report Vol. 5* 359)

It is crucial that this passage features in the TRC report, where it is staged as a successful instance of human dignity being restored to victims. In this particular passage, Tutu emphatically addresses the willingness of one of the widows' daughters to forgive as exemplary. However, what the context of Tutu's words in the report does not and what the full transcripts of the hearings do disclose (as does the coverage of these hearings in the documentary *Long Night's Journey into Day*) is that the widows of the Cradock Four were not actually interested in offering forgiveness to the killers of their husbands. In fact, all four widows opposed the amnesty applications of the policemen in question. The only person to show any willingness to forgive, applauded by Tutu in the passage above, was the daughter of one of the widows. Thus, it becomes apparent that the singling out of this young woman by Tutu and the subsequent reference to this situation as a success story in the TRC report effectively silence the actual course of both the hearing and its aftermath.[9] One could say, therefore, that, in this case at least, the microlevel of the hearing (the attempt to discover what happened to the Cradock Four and the revelation of suffering on the part of their widows) is framed in such a way as to fit the needs of the macrolevel, namely the representation of the hearings as exemplary and successful. As such, the women become part of the TRC's attempt to forge national unity out of its proceedings through an ubuntu-inspired discourse.

In one of the most infamous special hearings another such attempted affirmation of the TRC setting and its discourse comes spectacularly close to its refutation by a pivotal figure in apartheid resistance. I am referring to the nine-day Mandela United Football Club hearing (MUFC), also known as the Winnie hearing, during which Winnie Mandela's complicity in human rights violations was closely examined, and not with a terribly favorable outcome.[10] Although many people stepped up to testify, Mrs. Madikizela-Mandela vigorously denied all allegations brought against her, discarding statements as either "ludicrous" or "ridiculous" (*Country of my Skull* 391; MUFC hearing transcript). By refusing to admit to any role in the violence that clearly emanated from her direct entourage and by deeming testimonies from victims hallucinatory, she forcefully negated and disrupted the ultimate goal of the hearing, namely to have a public figure like herself engage, as a perpetrator, with her victims and affirm the reconciliatory narrative of the TRC under full media attention. For in order to achieve reconciliation and unity, it needed to be demonstrated that the TRC "worked," that people like Winnie Mandela, the "Mother of the Nation" and one of the key figures in the struggle against apartheid, acknowledged the process of truth and reconciliation. To obtain Mrs. Madikizela-Mandela's cooperation would signify a supreme confirmation of TRC discourse. Therefore, when the hearings were drawing to a close on the ninth day and Mrs. Madikizela-Mandela remained adamant that she was innocent, Tutu, in his official role as chairperson of the Commission, but also as a close friend of the Mandela family, tried once more to change her mind:

"*If you were able to bring yourself to be able to say: 'Something went wrong . . .' and say, 'I'm sorry, I'm sorry for my part in what went wrong . . .' I beg you, I beg you, I beg*

> *you please . . . You are a great person. And you don't know how your greatness would be enhanced if you were to say, 'I'm sorry . . . things went wrong. Forgive me.'" And for the first time, Tutu looks directly at her. His voice has fallen to a whisper. "I beg you."*
>
> *Time freezes. Tutu has risked . . .*
>
> *everything.* (Krog, *Country of my Skull* 391)[11]

Tutu, by literally begging Mrs. Madikizela-Mandela to show some form of remorseful involvement in the hearings, is indeed risking "everything." His effort lays bare the crux of the problem: without the establishment of a bond between antagonistic parties on an individual or microlevel, the work of the TRC will not be able to resonate on a larger scale, namely that of the national or macrolevel.[12]

This move from the micro- to the macrolevel also surfaces earlier during the same hearing. When some of the family members of the people that testified are preparing to leave the room, Tutu interrupts the proceedings to address them as follows:

> *I just want to say that on behalf of our country, we hope that the pain and anguish of so many will be something that goes towards the healing of our land. We want them to know our very deepest sympathies for them for what they have suffered and we thank them and hope that they will have it in their hearts to reach out to those who may have caused them pain, to reach out in order for our land to be healed. Thank you very much.* (MUFC hearing transcript)

This speech clearly demonstrates how "the pain and anguish of so many" is collapsed into "the healing of our land." Tutu, from his position of authority, instigates the victims to offer forgiveness. He appeals to them to subsume their personal suffering, and that of their families, to the need to forgive, to the need to further the promotion of the road to reconciliation.

This subsumption is mirrored in Jennifer Wilkinson's analysis of ubuntu in relation to her argument that race and racial differences are important to the feminist project in (South) Africa because gender cannot be isolated from other aspects that constitute a person's identity. In her article "South African Women and the Ties that Bind," she elucidates how the experience of oppression in South Africa has been radically different for black and white women. In this context she refers to white and black South African girls being equipped with different coping mechanisms in order to deal with their social environment. White girls are taught "the niceties of good social behavior to enable them to become both supporters of their men folk and more recently . . . to strive for personal fulfillment" (356). Although this view is probably (hopefully!) slightly outdated, it is true in general that black girls in South Africa receive a different education than their white peers. One only has to think of the conditions of public schools in the poorer areas of South Africa in order to realize that this is no overstatement. Wilkinson claims that black girls "learn how to care for the weak and aged, to share equally with an extended family and to respect custom and tradition, although given the history of political upheaval they have also learned to extend this consciousness to the wider context – first to black liberation and more recently to black empowerment" (356). Although this argument raises the question of the primacy of the individual over its community and vice versa, it also signals the necessity for some subjects to negotiate their individuality more than others, in this case women and men respectively.

According to this view, the interests of black women are subsumed to the importance of the community and its liberation from white rule, creating the so-called double repression of women in colonial situations. Although the emancipation of women is not always subsumed to the color of their skin (a point in case being the important role of women's movements in the anti-apartheid struggle, which fought not only for black liberation, but also and specifically for the liberation of black *women*),[13] Deniz Kandiyoti argues in "Identity and its Discontents: Women and the Nation" that in postcolonial societies the emancipation of women was often conflated with the self-professed modernity of nationalist movements (387). This caused their emancipation to serve as a marker for the agenda of a particular movement, instead of actually improving the situation of women. Female nationalists often had to "articulate their gender interests within the parameters of cultural nationalism, sometimes censoring or muting the radical potential of their demands" (388). Social progress, then, does not necessarily mean improvement of the position of women:

Wherever women continue to serve as boundary markers between different national, ethnic and religious collectivities, their emergence as full-fledged citizens will be jeopardised, and whatever rights they may have achieved during one stage of nation-building may be sacrificed on the altar of identity politics during another. (382)

Although Kandiyoti's argument focuses primarily on postcolonial situations in the Middle East and in South East Asia, her point can be extended to the South African context. The interests of the widows of the murdered Cradock Four, for instance, are, in line with Kandiyoti's point, initially subsumed to black liberation and, later on, once the political paradigm has shifted, to black empowerment; not only because they are crucial witnesses in what the TRC has deemed a "model hearing" and are thus turned into an example, but also because of the way they are represented afterwards in the TRC report. There, the case of the Cradock Four widows (I am aware of using these four women as a cluster here; they are, of course, not a homogenous group) is mentioned, among others, under the heading "Silences" in the chapter on special hearings on women (Truth and Reconciliation Commission, *TRC Report Vol. 4* 295). It unambiguously states that, although some of the women were themselves harassed, detained, and tortured, the public hearings in which they gave testimony were not about the violation of their own rights, but about that of their high-profile husbands. What the report does not state, although it clearly signals awareness of this fact, is that after having lived their lives in the shadow or in support of the struggle of their spouses, the role the widows are given in the TRC process seems to once more subject their identity to a larger project, namely that of reconciliation in post-apartheid South Africa.

In a similar vein, Winnie Mandela is literally staged by the Commission in a special and public hearing in order to tie her name to the project of national reconciliation. (Of course, a significant difference exists between the case of the "Cradock Four" widows, who were victims, and that of Mrs. Madikizela-Mandela, who acted, and possibly perpetrated violence, from a position of power and privilege.) Tutu tries to persuade Winnie Mandela to admit to, take responsibility, and apologize for her role in human rights violations in Soweto in the 1980s. He attempts to force her to denounce what she might have felt was acceptable damage in the name of the struggle against apartheid, so that she can be orchestrated as an adherent to a new kind of struggle: the road towards reconciliation and unity. In line with Kandiyoti's argument one could argue that Tutu attempts to relocate the iconicity of her identity – reflected in nicknames like "Mother of the Nation" and forged in a specific moment in South African history – from one particular framework of identity politics to another.[14] Winnie Mandela's attitude during the public hearings of which she was the subject, although mind-boggling on first encounter, can be read as a refusal to acknowledge the Commission's claims of authority. Mrs. Madikizela-Mandela effectively negates a determination in terms of its discourse and does not allow it to read her situation in terms of a victim-perpetrator dichotomy. By refusing to perceive herself as a perpetrator, Winnie Mandela distorts the clarity of this binary. As a result, some of the problematic aspects of the post-apartheid construction of community are made visible: What kind of community is being constructed? With which other communities must this community co-exist? And who determines the way these communities are organized? Beyond the signaling of a need for national unity in the Act, these aspects are not adequately addressed by the ubuntu-inspired discourse of reconciliation. Who is to be judged, punished, grieved, or acknowledged as such and, what is more, by whom, thus remains an open-ended question.

The Old, the New, and the Yardstick

Even though the TRC process certainly reflects a clear condemnation of South Africa's apartheid past, the way it attempts to create national unity through an uncritical adaptation of ubuntu, is also reason for concern. Christoph Marx, for instance, is profoundly troubled by the TRC proceedings and its appropriation of ubuntu, especially by its emphasis on the importance of community, of which the nation is, in cultural nationalistic terms, the ultimate incarnation. As Marx discusses in his article "Ubu and Ubuntu: On the Dialectics of Apartheid and Nation Building," the accentuation of ubuntu in the TRC process – as expressed by Tutu during the Winnie hearing, for instance – plays a definitive role in the separation of cultural nationalism from the racist connotations it had during apartheid. Thus, it has been able to return to the realm of acceptability (54).

Marx's account of the use of ubuntu in the reconciliation process closely resembles Benedict Anderson's description of nationalism. According to Anderson, people act by investing their actions with nationalistic sentiments, not out of self-preservation, but out of a nationalistic zeal devoid of personal interest. In his chapter on patriotism and racism in *Imagined Communities*, Anderson explains how this type of nationalism works. Because the country is always referred to in terms of kinship and home, it comes to be regarded as something to which one is "naturally tied": "In this way, nation-ness is assimilated to skin-color, gender, parentage, and birth-era – all those things one can not help" (131).[15] Ergo, anyone who does not fit the description is excluded and, what is more, not recognized as a person. In other words, the idea that nations provide "natural" ties can serve as a way to exclude those that do not fit the prerequisites. At the same time, the comparison of the nation to family allows the protection of the nation to be regarded as an act without self-interest:

[T]he family has traditionally been conceived as the domain of disinterested love and solidarity. So too, if historians, diplomats, politicians, and social scientists are quite at ease with the idea of "national interest," for most ordinary people of whatever class the whole point of the nation is that it is interestless. Just for that reason, it can ask for sacrifices. (Anderson 131)

Marx underlines this point in relation to the capacity of perpetrators to commit horrible crimes in apartheid South Africa:

Cultural nationalism offers the exculpation as well as the clearance of the conscience, the means as well as the legitimation for [someone's] own dehumanisation and degradation into a beast. (49)

This is not only true, however, of the justification of crimes against humanity committed by perpetrators under apartheid; it also closely resembles, as was pointed out above, the way ubuntu has been appropriated in the Commission's discourse on unity and reconciliation. This leads Marx to claim that ubuntu is the "Africanist version of integral nationalism" (58). Not to participate in this process equals, in the discourse of the TRC, failing to undergo a crucial rite of passage, and thus failing to become part of the "new South Africa." In addition, adherence to the process can be interpreted as another subsumption to the category of the nation:

Within the TRC process, the [perpetrator] was confronted with Ubuntu as an ethnicised value that represented the victims. But, within this process, the victims, because of their moral superiority, became representative of the "Nation," and were consequently "anonymised" once again. (Marx 53)

According to Marx, then, both ubuntu and the victims professing it are gobbled up by the need for national unity.

How, then, can we counter these problematic aspects of ubuntu, namely the dominance of its discourse and the unequal sacrifices required from victims and perpetrators? Here, I want to turn to the work of Judith Butler, who has argued that in order to resist oppressive systems, we have to understand "that lives are supported and maintained differentially, that there are radically different ways in which human physical vulnerability is distributed across the globe" (24). She continues:

Certain lives will be highly protected, and the abrogation of their claims to sanctity will be sufficient to mobilize the forces of war. And other lives will not find such fast and furious support and will not even qualify as "grievable." (24)

Thus, physical inequality and violence is, although not exclusively, the result of an antecedent violence on the level of discourse, where each community determines what it considers vulnerable, grievable, even human. As soon as we are born (and arguably even before that, in the womb) we become part of such discursive practices. We are inevitably vulnerable to other people and profoundly influenced by interhuman relations. This, Butler argues, is the very premise of our existence as subjects. We are, for example, racialized, gendered, and made citizens of a particular nation. As such, we are and simultaneously are not the owners of our bodies and – without conflating them – identities. Because others are the conditions of our existence and because we live in relation to them, we are, literally, "ec-static."

The similarities between Butler's argument and ubuntu's dictum that "I am a person because of other persons" are striking. In both cases, the subject is understood to exist as inevitably constructed through its ties to other people and in both cases the importance of the community is highlighted. There is, however, at least one important difference between Butler's stance and the problematically uncritical uses of ubuntu discussed above. As Butler points out, there is a definite need to recognize people's vulnerability, to realize exactly how precarious life can be, and to understand that subjects are dependent on each other (since this potentially creates room for empathy and solidarity). Being dependent on others, however, is not the same as being subsumed to others or to a community as a whole. Consequently, Butler argues that there is a simultaneous need to defend the body as "one's own," that there should be some sort of limit on the control of others or the discourse to which they introduce us:

In a sense, to be a body is to be given over to others even as a body is, emphatically, "one's own," that over which we must claim rights of autonomy. [These claims] are part of the normative aspiration of any movement that seeks to maximize the protection and the freedoms of sexual and gender minorities, of women, defined within the broadest possible compass, of racial and ethnic minorities, especially as they cut across all other categories. (20–21)

In other words, Butler discerns a clear political need to posit autonomy simultaneous to and exactly because of the subject's inherent relationship (and vulnerability) to the other. Striking a balance in the dynamics of the tension between these two realities could provide an important condition for making ubuntu a workable and negotiable concept, rather than turning it into an oppressive discourse.

Conclusion

However, the realization of such a state of equilibrium, where ubuntu does not become a means of exclusion or a way to subsume certain people's interests to those of the group to an unacceptable degree, is, to use Butler's term, precarious. This was amply demonstrated by the outbreak of xenophobic violence in South Africa in May 2008. The extent to which a realization of people's inevitable dependence on each other will have a long-lasting effect on the occurrence of violence is questionable, especially as long as the category of "human" remains exclusionary; similarly, ubuntu will only be able to fulfill its striving for a more harmonious community when it is not tied too strongly to a particular national identity or turned into a shibboleth to determine who is and who is not a "person." Still, although the ways in which they can be put into practice effectively remain unclear, both ubuntu-based philosophies and Butler's attempt at a more global, ethical approach are valuable, since they envision the possibility of more inclusionary and relational forms of communality. In the end, the truth and reconciliation process, despite the way the TRC's nationalistic tendencies infused the hearings and the TRC report, did succeed in allowing people to share their grief and loss, as well as in foregrounding alternative ways of relating to each other (as sharing a sense of humanity rather than as being of different races).

The way ubuntu was appropriated during the TRC process has caused a close association with the latter's dictum of reconciliation and forgiveness. The focus on these terms obscures the way ubuntu, under the guise of "we belong in a bundle of life" (Tutu 35), can work to exclude or subsume certain people. As the case of Winnie Mandela suggests and as Butler emphasizes, not everyone is automatically considered as (an equal) part of a community, or even as a "person"; certain prerequisites have to be met. Mrs. Madikizela-Mandela's refusal to adhere to the discourse of the Commission and to the role this discourse had designated for her reveals this point of tension. If, as Tutu suggests, one belongs because one shares, people who do not share automatically do not belong. When a community has to deal with people that do not meet the set standard of personhood, the dictum "I am a person because of other persons" can easily change into "I am a person because of other persons like me." This much is suggested by Zapiro's cartoon, which effectively captures how ubuntu-inspired post-TRC South Africa can function in practice, with people who were victims before appropriating the term not to include, but to separate themselves from others. The cartoon shows how ubuntu came to be used as a boundary marker for belonging and national identity, while simultaneously pointing out the irony of this use.

It is, however, important to note that neither the TRC nor ubuntu can be considered as unified wholes. There were, in the case of the TRC, innumerable factors that influenced each separate hearing and hence led to very different outcomes. Similarly, ubuntu cannot be defined merely on the basis of its role in the TRC process. Indeed, it is exactly the ambiguity of ubuntu as a concept that provides it with the necessary dynamics and flexibility to be both criticized and reformulated in constructive ways. The relation between ubuntu discourse and Butler's emphasis on a more ethical, transnational approach to the formation of communal identities points towards a possible direction in which ubuntu can be both enriched en re-articulated. Thus, in line with Butler's argument in *Excitable Speech* about the subject's agency in relation to language (which is always circumscribed by language's history, but can nevertheless effect gradual and partial rearticulations), we have to continue to reshape ubuntu in order to be able to use it in ways that prevent it from becoming an oppressive discourse and that accentuate its most promising aspects.

Notes

1. See *The Mail and Guardian*'s special report on xenophobic violence: http://www.mg.co.za/specialreport/xenophobia; reports by the BBC and *The Guardian* at http://news.bbc.co.uk/2/hi/africa/8070919.stm and http://www.guardian.co.uk/commentisfree/2008/may/20/failingitspeople; and *The Sunday Times* for more recent developments: http://www.timeslive.co.za/news/article198408.ece.

2. See, respectively, www.fifa.com/worldcup/destination/southafricafromatoz/letter=u/ and www.congressofthepeople.org.za.

3. See, among others, Sparks 14; Mnyaka and Mothlabi 218; Barben 6; Marx 52; Battle qtd. in Libin 126; and Krog, *Ik Spreek* 34.

4. Some significant exceptions are, among others, Sanders ("Reading Lessons"; *Complicities*); Marx; Praeg; Coertze; and Libin.

5. This will become clear from the discussion of the Mandela Football Club Hearings, where Desmond Tutu explicitly mentions to Winnie Mandela that to offer apologies would "enhance" her "greatness" (*Country* 391).

6. The film seems to collapse the Human Rights Violation hearings into the Amnesty hearings. Perpetrators were not always present during HRV hearings; usually they were subpoenaed because of the evidence that was unearthed during these hearings or they were heard during their own Amnesty hearings.

7. This scene is based on what Antjie Krog calls "The Shepherd's Tale" (*Country* 320).

8. See, for instance, the 2002 documentary *Amandla! A Revolution in Four Part Harmony*, which highlights the role of music in the struggle against Apartheid.

9. *Long Night's Journey into Day* shows that the policemen's application for amnesty for the killing of the Cradock Four was denied, because one of the victims was not a political figure and could thus not have been killed under the pretence of a political motive.

10. For the full transcript of the Winnie hearing see http://www.doj.gov.za/trc/special/index.htm#mufch.

11. I have referred to Antjie Krog's book here and not to the official transcript. In my opinion, they are not so different. In a way, Krog's so-called fictional account is just as much a transcript of these hearings as the original ones, since she was present as a radio reporter. On the other hand, Krog's work offers only a selection of what happened during the hearings, whereas the official transcript attempts to give a full account. Unfortunately, the flaws and omissions in the actual transcripts make them difficult to follow and raise questions of reliability. Krog provides a narrational framework that renders the events more accessible to the reader. This fictional shell does not automatically imply that her account is less "true," only that it is rendered in a different way, independent of the Commission. Krog discusses the Winnie Hearings in chapter 20 of *Country of My Skull*, entitled "Mother Faces the Nation" (367–94).

12. In response to Tutu's entreaty, Mrs. Madikizela-Mandela is prompted to express what Dirk Klopper calls a reluctant and vague apology "for whatever it was that had 'gone wrong'" (454).

13. See Roger G. Beck's *The History of South Africa* (140–41).

14. Mrs. Madikizela-Mandela, although subpoenaed by the TRC, never applied for amnesty and thus was granted none. However, since the hearings she has not been tried or convicted for the human rights violations the Commission strongly suspected her to have committed or masterminded. In 2003, she was charged with and convicted of theft and fraud, but was not imprisoned because the High Court overturned the theft conviction.

15. Winnie Mancela's acquisition of the nickname "Mother of the Nation" during the anti-apartheid struggle is significant in this respect.

Bibliography

Amandla! A Revolution in Four Part Harmony. Dir. Lee Hirsch. Lionsgate, 2002.

Anderson, Benedict. *Imagined Communities: Reflections on the Origin and Spread of Nationalism*. London: Verso, 1983.

Barben, Tanya. "Umntu Ngmuntu Ngabantu ('A Person Is a Person Because of Other Persons'): The Ethos of the Pre-colonial Xhosa-Speaking People as Presented in Fact and Young Adult Fiction." *Quarterly Bulletin of the National Library of South Africa* 60.1–2 (2006): 4–20.

Beck, Roger B. *The History of South Africa*. Westport, CT: Greenwood Press, 2000.

Butler, Judith. *Excitable Speech: A Politics of the Performative*. New York and London: Routledge, 1997.

———. *Undoing Gender*. New York and London: Routledge, 2004.

Coertze, R.D. "Ubuntu and Nation Building in South Africa." *South African Journal of Ethnology* 24.4 (2001): 113–18.

In My Country. Dir. John Boorman. Chartoff Productions, 2004.

Kandiyoti, Deniz. "Identity and its Discontents" *Colonial Discourse and Post-Colonial Theory. A Reader*. Ed. Patrick Williams and Laura Chrisman. New York: Columbia UP, 1994: 376–91.

Klopper, Dirk. "Narrative Time and the Space of the Image: The Truth of the Lie in Winnie Madikizela-Mandela's Testimony before the Truth and Reconciliation Commission." *South Africa in the Global Imaginary*. Ed. Leon de Kock, Louise Bethlehem, and Sonja Laden. Pretoria: U of South Africa P, 2004: 195–213.

Krog, Antjie. *Country of My Skull*. London: Vintage, 1999.

———. *Ik spreek en verhef uw hart: kosmopolitisme, vergiffenis en het voorbeeld van Afrika*. Amsterdam: Volkskrant boekenfonds, 2006.

Libin, Mark. "Can the Subaltern be Heard? Response and Responsibility in South Africa's Human Spirit." *Textual Practice* 17.1 (2003): 119–40.

Long Night's Journey into Day. Dir. Deborah Hoffmann and Frances Reid. Reid-Hoffmann Productions, 2000.

Marx, Christoph. "Ubu and Ubuntu: On the Dialectics of Apartheid and Nation Building." *Politikon* 29.1 (2002): 49–69.

Mbembe, Achille. *On the Postcolony*. Berkeley: U of California P, 2001.

Mnyaka, Mluleki, and Mokgethi Mothlabi. "The African Concept of Ubuntu/Botho and its Social-Moral Significance." *Black Theology: An International Journal* 3.2 (2005): 215–37.

Ndlovu, Nosimilo. "The 21-st Century Pencil Test." *Mail & Guardian Online*. 24 May 2008. Web. 4 Dec. 2009. <http://www.mg.co.za>.

Praeg, Leonhard. "An Answer to the Question: What is [ubuntu]?" *South African Journal of Philosophy* 27.4 (2008): 367–85.

Sanders, Mark. "Reading Lessons." *Diacritics* 29.3 (1999): 3–20.

———. *Complicities. The Intellectual and Apartheid*. Durham: Duke UP, 2002.

South Africa. Office of the President. No. 34 of 1995: *Promotion of National Unity and Reconciliation Act*. 1995. Web. 20 March 2007. <http://www.doj.gov.za/trc/legal/act9534.htm>.

Sparks, Allister. *The Mind of South Africa: The Story of the Rise and Fall of Apartheid*. London: Mandarin, 1991.

Truth and Reconciliation Commission. *Transcript of Mandela United Football Club Hearing.* 1997. Web. 8 Dec. 2008. <http://www.doj.gov.za/trc/special/index.htm#mufch>.

———. *Truth and Reconciliation Commission of South Africa Report.* Vol 4. 1998. Web. 8 Dec. 2008. <http://www.doj.gov.za/trc/report/>.

———. *Truth and Reconciliation Commission of South Africa Report.* Vol 5. 1998. Web. 8 Dec. 2008. <http://www.doj.gov.za/trc/report/>.

———. *Truth and Reconciliation Commission of South Africa Report.* Vol 6. 2003. Web. 8 Dec. 2008. <http://www.doj.gov.za/trc/report/>.

Tutu, Desmond M. *No Future without Forgiveness.* London: Rider, 2000.

Wilkinson, Jennifer R. "South African Women and the Ties that Bind." *The African Philosophy Reader.* Ed. P.H. Coetzee and A.P.J. Roux. New York and London: Routledge, 2003: 343–60.

Zapiro. "I Could Tell He Was a @#&* Foreigner!" *Sunday Times.* 25 May 2008. Web. 4 Dec. 2009. <http://www.timeslive.co.za/sundaytimes/>.

Resistance or Compliance?: The Problem of Orientalism in Osman Hamdi's Paintings

Gülru Çakmak

Osman Hamdi Bey (1842–1910), director of the Imperial Archaeological Museum in Istanbul and founder of the School of Fine Arts, produced Orientalist paintings at the end of the nineteenth century. Hamdi was among an early wave of students from the Ottoman Empire to study fine arts in Europe, taking part in the emergence of an easel painting tradition in Ottoman art in the nineteenth century. Today, his paintings are considered among prominent examples of Orientalist painting, yet he is carefully classified as an "Eastern Orientalist" (Lemaires 268; MacKenzie 61). His body of work, over a century after its production, continues to provoke opposing interpretations among art historians. Mainly known for his late work, where he painted Eastern-looking people in exotic settings in canvases that have the finished look and polished surface of Academic painting, was he an unoriginal adherent of Jean-Léon Gérôme (1824–1904), at whose studio in Paris he received his art training in the second half of the 1860s, or were his paintings part of a strategy of resistance against European cultural and political hegemony, aimed at subverting stereotypes?

One note about the term "Orientalist painting" before I go any further: by the 1860s, in French art criticism, the term *peinture orientaliste*, or *école orientaliste*, was established as a subgenre in painting. Starting in the 1840s, art critics had noted the emergence of a new artistic tendency, as more and more artists traveled to North Africa and the Middle East, returning with notebooks filled with studies that claimed to capture the everyday life of the various peoples populating these lands. Orientalist painting in the mid nineteenth century was thus closely associated with activities of artist-travelers, whose sketches and paintings were considered to have a documentary value by art critics. Distinct from Orientalist representations of the imaginative eighteenth century, this interest in depicting the quotidian was the outcome of a more general need that emerged in French painting in the mid-century, that of defining the conditions of a new painting that represented contemporary life.

Another clarification which needs to be inserted here relates to defining Hamdi as an Orientalist painter. When art historians talk about Hamdi's Orientalist work, they refer to a specific group of paintings in the artist's overall oeuvre. These were large canvases, at times painted in two versions, and known to have been exhibited in France. These paintings displayed what might be called the Orientalist visual language of the day, whereby architectural elements, costumes, and accessories were chosen and arranged according to the codes that conveyed to the viewers the notion that the context was the Other, the exotic Orient. In addition to his Orientalist paintings, Hamdi produced a wide array of "non-Orientalist" portraits and landscapes, which have not received much attention from art historians to this day.

A question that has preoccupied art historians in Turkey is how to account for Hamdi's Orientalist imagery, in which he depicted *our* irreducible difference rather than demonstrating *our* equal share in the modern world.[1] An alternative question is why the artist did not aspire to develop a specifically Turkish visual language in his oil paintings, and instead subscribed to the language of French Orientalism (Tansuğ 107). Scholars have attempted to address this problem by reading a pedagogical motivation in Hamdi's work: correcting Western stereotypes about the East. In recent years, a growing number of studies on the artist have concurred that Hamdi did appropriate Orientalist imagery in order to produce counter-hegemonic narratives. According to this reading, Hamdi's work is underwritten by a self-assigned mission to correct Western stereotypes about the Ottomans, a political agenda whereby he produced uplifting representations of the Ottoman historical heritage.

Before offering a summary analysis of the art historical literature on Hamdi, I would like to note a prevalent tendency in this body of writing whereby "Ottoman," "Turkish" and "us" are rendered interchangeable, therefore conflating the late-nineteenth-century identity politics in the Ottoman Empire with a more recent incarnation of Turkish nationalism. The following quotation from Mustafa Cezar, author of the only monograph on the artist, is representative of this slippage in language:

In Osman Hamdi, who was an Orientalist painter, there is a different atmosphere, a different rendering of the subject matter, which separates him from European Orientalist painters. The magic ingredient that creates this important difference is no doubt the fact that Osman Hamdi is a member of these lands, of this society. *Of course he would approach the subjects representing* this country *with a different sensitivity than the Westerner, and would reflect his feelings in his works. . . . Even if most of the costumes he represented are not* Turkish, *the real elements that cry their belonging to* us *are architectural elements, architectural ornamentation and accessories.* (Cezar 349–351, emphasis added)

When scholars give Hamdi's peaceful and conservative scenes of daily life pride of place, their reading of Hamdi's "good Orientalism" tends to go hand in hand with an oversimplification and demonization of Orientalist painting by European artists. Consequently, Hamdi's work emerges as a unique phenomenon countering the "bad Orientalism" of European provenance. Semra Germaner, for instance, maintains that Hamdi's politically correct and ethnographically realistic representations essentially differ from Orientalist scenes rendered by European artists, which seek merely to denigrate the Eastern Other (4). Depictions of young men and women reading books or playing instruments of classical Turkish music and people discussing religious issues in Hamdi's oeuvre, contends Germaner, articulate the acquisition of knowledge and enlightenment as a characteristic of the East (4). Zeynep Çelik makes a comparable argument, suggesting that Hamdi appropriated the West's own visual language to teach them the truth about the East. For Çelik, Hamdi's paintings are "critiques of the Orientalist school by a 'resistant' voice whose power derives from the painter's thorough acquaintance with the school's techniques and conventions. These paintings are carefully composed essays on Ottoman society, expressed in a Western vocabulary" (41).

A number of scholars have offered nuanced interpretations of Hamdi's work, not taking the Orientalist imagery's claim to realism at face value. Nonetheless, these readings still perpetuate a simplistic and overgeneralized reading of French Orientalism. According to Wendy Shaw,

Throughout his professional career as museum and Academy director, Osman Hamdi continued to paint in the style of his teachers, Gérôme and Boulanger. . . . With their juxtaposition of colourful costumes against intricate architectural settings, Osman Hamdi's paintings reflect a particularly strong influence from the work of Gérôme. However, while Gérôme presented a romanticized, salacious East with a deceptively transparent realism, Osman Hamdi adopted the style of his master to represent a glorified and dignified vision of Ottoman heritage. (425)

Yet another scholar, Ahmet Ersoy, interprets Hamdi's work in terms of a Romantic quest for roots in the Islamic past and an idealized vision of a historical identity (87). Ersoy notes that it is not easy to decide whether Hamdi was indeed an Orientalist like Gérôme, or whether he should be considered the Eastern counterpart to the romantic-nationalist historicism of the early nineteenth century (86). Representing stylized and romantic reconstructions of a fantasized Islamic Golden Age, Ersoy contends, Hamdi's paintings contributed to the construction of a collective memory, reinforcing the image of an ideal, virtuous Ottoman identity (86).

One theoretical question lurking beneath these discussions is whether an Orientalist mode of representation can be appropriated to produce counter-hegemonic narratives at all, or whether the language of Orientalism is always already biased, not allowing such a liberty with its rules. What is crucial to underscore at this point is that what Hamdi learned during his student years in Paris was not only how to paint well, but a particular way of seeing and articulating according to a certain set of visual codes. Hamdi's paintings were legible because of their very subscription to a visual language; an allegiance that would always already predetermine the perception of the subject matter of these paintings as the exotic Other. My intention is not to argue for a homogenous and fixed Orientalist pictorial language. However, there were certain codes for contemporary viewers to infer that certain motifs denoted the everyday life elsewhere: Arabic script, pointed arches, costumes, turquoise tiles, certain types of abstract, geometrical, arabesque designs, etc. As Inge Boer suggests, a multitude of details would "inform the ideological background from which to read the paintings; the details are all indexes for 'otherness,' for 'non-Westernness' and more specifically the Orient" (212). To refer back to Zeynep Çelik's words, the "Western vocabulary" was the very tool used to organize and construct such a reality at the first place. This visual vocabulary provided "the lenses through which the Orient is experienced," in Edward Said's words, and not only experienced, but, furthermore, constructed (58).

Even when attempts are made to counter the homogenizing gaze of Orientalism by representing specificities of the other culture, such as Hamdi's so-called emphasis on the Ottomanness, or even more specifically, the Turkishness, of his themes and settings, this hardly plays a subversive role in relation to the mainstream order of Orientalist representation, for it can always be relegated to a variation on the theme: the alterity and exoticism of the Orient. As Meyda Yeğenoğlu notes, "to pose the 'truth' of the Orient as distinct from the Orientalist discourse and to construct a nativist position outside Orientalism is indeed to reproduce the division imposed by Orientalism" (122).

"Turkishness" was a variant in the nineteenth-century French Orientalist imaginary. One of the earliest formulations of Hamdi's "Turkishness" – which had a lasting influence on later generations of art historians – came from Adolphe Thalasso. In his *L'Art Ottoman: Les Peintres de Turquie* (1910), Thalasso argued that Osman Hamdi's paintings did not depict generic Muslim types, but specifically Turkish people, ornaments, architecture, and landscape.[2] These paintings could have been realized only by an artist who was Turkish, Thalasso contended.

Distinct from contemporary art historians, who anachronistically read in Hamdi's work a Turkish nationalist agenda, Thalasso's interpretation of Hamdi's Orientalism belongs to the tradition of the nineteenth-century French art critical discourse that understood Orientalist paintings as documentary products of artist-travelers. More than half a century before Thalasso, writer and art critic Maxime Du Camp had made a corresponding claim in relation to the work of Alexandre-Gabriel Decamps (1803–1860), one of the foremost Orientalist painters in France at the time. Having seen a wide array of Decamps's works at the Fine Arts section organized in conjunction with the Universal Exhibition in Paris in 1855, Du Camp suggested,

From the moment he had seen the Orient, M. Decamps felt himself in his element, in his truth, and he rendered and translated it with an exactitude which astounds me. The Orient of his preference, the one he knows and loves, is not the blond Egypt, it is not the bountiful Hindoustan, neither is it the infinite deserts of Libya, it is Asia Minor: Asia Minor with its kiosks, its cities divided by narrow streets, its blue mountains, its high cypresses, its bushes of myrtles, its beautiful children with singular gazes, its pensive camels, its brooks full of tortoises, its fields filled with storks, its veiled women. . . .
(Du Camp 130)

This enumeration of different Orients, and the consequent breakdown of each Orient into its idiosyncratic characteristics, was the foundation on which Orientalist art criticism and artistic production was based in the course of the nineteenth century. From this viewpoint, to the extent that Orientalism is the formulation of a body of organized knowledge, Osman Hamdi's works are not subversive, for they comply with the most basic rule: articulating the Orient as an identifiable and knowable entity. But can this be the last word on Hamdi's agency as a painter? I do not think so. On the contrary, I believe that we still have a lot to research and recover to come even close to understanding Hamdi's paintings. It is time we started analyzing his body of work in the context of artistic and art critical discussions surrounding modern painting and Academic conventions in France in the nineteenth century. In what follows, I would like to take a preliminary step in that direction.

When Hamdi arrived at Gérôme's studio, the illustrious master had departed for a voyage to Egypt, entrusting his students to Gustave-Clarence-Rodolphe Boulanger (1824–1888), whom he had known intimately since their student days at the studio of Paul Delaroche in the 1840s. Hamdi thus received his artistic training from Boulanger in a pedagogical and artistic environment which was strongly influenced by Gérôme's understanding of the stakes of contemporary painting in France. Very little is known about Hamdi's early work, apart from the fact that in 1866 and 1868 he took part in the Salon exhibitions organized by the Academy of Fine Arts. In both Salon catalogues, he featured as "Osman Hamdy [sic], born in Constantinople, student of M. Gustave Boulanger." Exhibiting one canvas at the Salon of 1866 entitled *Femme turque*, Hamdi submitted two paintings to the following exhibition in 1868: *Portrait de Mme de H...* (*Portrait of Mme de H...*) and *L'Escamoteur juif à Constantinople* (*Jewish Conjurer in Constantinople*).[3] In between the two Salons, Paris hosted the Exposition Universelle in 1867, which gave Hamdi a major opportunity to exhibit his work among the displays of the Ottoman Empire.[4]

La Turquie à l'Exposition Universelle de 1867, the official guide published under the auspices of Salaheddin Bey, the commissary of the Ottoman exhibition, commences its account of the Ottoman exhibits at the fine arts section by talking at length about the three paintings submitted by Osman Hamdi: *Halte de Tchinganès* (*Stopover of the Gypsies*), *Zeïbek à l'affût* (*Zeïbek at Watch*), and *Mort du Zeïbek* (*Death of the Zeïbek*).

While two of these paintings have not been identified among the extant work by the artist, the third one, *Zeïbek at Watch*, is most probably the canvas which is in a private collection in Turkey.

The Zeïbek, alternately referred to as *bazhi-bazouk*, was a recurrent motif in Gérôme's Orientalist scenes of everyday life. In many pseudo-ethnographic scenes, Gérôme depicted these mercenary soldiers engaged in activities of leisure. Zeïbeks dancing, smoking, and playing backgammon start appearing in Gérôme's work as early as 1859. Salon viewers would be familiar with such scenes of leisure from seventeenth-century Dutch genre painting, as well as from the work of Gérôme's contemporaries such as Ernest Meissonier, who painted numerous small scenes of male figures in historical costumes engaged in leisure activities, such as playing chess.

Zeïbek at Watch depicts a male figure lying at the edge of a cliff, observing the distant landscape, the main feature of which is the sky and the light reflected by the setting sun. His torso, the central element of the traditional male nude, is buried under an amorphous vest. We cannot tell where his shoulder ends and where his back begins. The contours outlining his body merge with the landscape. The entry in the official guide offers the following interpretation: "Without giving his Zeïbek at watch a theatrical pose, without learnedly grouping the figures of frightened travelers, without covering the sky with black clouds to obscure the situation and bringing back at the same time the light on the principal subject, [Hamdi] succeeds in conveying the drama as it exists, and not as one sees it on the stage. This bandit, in a landscape of pure lines and rosy hues, tranquilly watching his victim, simply gives one the shivers" (*La Turquie* 142). The painting operates on the fiction that we are given a glimpse of a warrior on watch duty, who is carefully observing a distant spot invisible from our vantage point. Hamdi's Zeïbek does not seem to pose. He seems to be oblivious to the fact that he is being watched by the viewer. As if his *profile perdu* does not hide him sufficiently, the face is further screened from our sight by the falling tresses of the elaborate headpiece. This headpiece defies gravity as it stands on top of the emaciated body. The foregrounding of the costume, especially the prominence of this complex headpiece, functions as a fetishistic compensation for the vulnerability of the supple body.

Wendy Shaw interprets Hamdi's 1867 exhibition entries as complicit Orientalist representations denigrating the Eastern Other, for they were suggestive of "hyperbolized bellicosity and languor typical of Orientalist paintings and befitting the work of a student of Gérôme and Boulanger" (424). A close analysis of the *Zeïbek at Watch* reveals this painting to be a far more complex and ambitious project whereby the young artist aspired to render an Orientalist genre motif according to the Academic conventions of history painting, engaging in a dialogue with contemporary art criticism.

The pose of Hamdi's Zeïbek is closely connected to two models of ideal masculinity in the classical tradition: the body in action – with its discourse of the heroic body in motion – and the body at rest – a discourse of the heroic body in a state of unconsciousness. As Thomas Crow demonstrates in *Emulation: Making Artists for Revolutionary France*, the ideal of a heroic masculinity was brought to the center of Academic painting at the end of the eighteenth century in the work of Jacques-Louis David and his students. In 1785, in the *Dying Athlete* (oil on canvas, 1.25 m. × 1.82 m., Louvre Museum), Germain-Jean Drouais, a star pupil of David's, transformed the studio exercise of the male nude – the *académie* – into a representation of virtuous martyrdom (Crow 56). *Dying Athlete* depicts a supine nude, in the company of a sword and shield, in an unconventional blend of extreme pain and intense alertness, his left hand covering and at the same time revealing a bleeding wound on the left thigh. Drouais's life-size figure of a dying athlete/wounded warrior (both were recognized titles for the painting) provided a powerful codification of an androgynous male hero, subverting the conventional distinction between active and resting male bodies (Crow 61). As Crow demonstrates in the rest of his seminal study, this imagery was to be repeatedly deployed in a number of canonical paintings produced by David and his students at the turn of the century.

In Osman Hamdi's Zeïbek figure the categories of the male body in action and the male body in repose are similarly collapsed: the Zeïbek's body below the waist seems to recline in a leisurely manner; the feet and legs do not convey a posture of alertness but one of repose, while the upper half of the body is ready to act, as he raises himself on his left arm to gaze into the distance. The languor interpreted by Shaw in Hamdi's work as a signal of decadent Orientalism was, therefore, an integral part of Academic tradition: this was Hamdi's attempt to inscribe himself into the Davidian line.

Even before Hamdi, the motif of the warrior Zeïbek was deployed in Orientalist imagery in the works of Alexandre Decamps in the 1840s as well as in Gérôme's Orientalist genre scenes starting in the late 1850s. In one aspect, however, Hamdi's figure radically differs from these previous models: while both French painters carefully set their Zeïbeks in Orientalist settings, Hamdi stations him on a mountaintop, his exotic costume being the only indicator of his iconographical and geographical provenance.[5] The aforementioned conventional codes whereby the setting would mark the otherness of the Orient are eschewed in this unconventional presentation. By deeply embedding his figure in the Davidian model of heroic masculinity, Hamdi framed the Zeïbek motif, itself borrowed from Decamps and Gérôme, as a contemporary model of heroism. In this painting, Hamdi does no less than offer his own version of what a modern history painting could look like. The display of the painting in the Ottoman section of the Exposition Universelle bolstered its implicit fiction of contemporaneity.

Emerging in the late 1850s, Gérôme's Orientalist genre scenes, often referred to as *peinture ethnographique* by his contemporaries for lack of a better category, responded to a growing and urgent need to invent a new painting that aspired to transform academic conventions into meaningful representations of life at present, albeit the life of other people in other places. It was this element of otherness that provoked Jules-Antoine Castagnary in the mid-1860s to protest vehemently against Orientalism. A proponent of naturalism and realism, and above all a fervent advocate of French landscape painting, Castagnary accused the Orientalists of an escapist drive to avoid the here and now, to "flee Paris, to run away from the world around them, to escape the obsession with the real and the present. There is nothing they would not prefer to what is" (211). By setting his Zeïbek in a generic landscape devoid of the codes of an Oriental setting, by establishing a fiction of heroic action, and above all by exhibiting this painting in the Ottoman section of the Exposition Universelle in 1867, Hamdi captured a golden opportunity to respond to the urgent issue of engaging with the here and now, albeit the here and now of Ottoman Turkey.

I am weary of reading Hamdi's 1867 painting in terms of a resistance to and subversion of Gérôme's "bad Orientalist" imagery. The *Zeïbek at Watch* is clearly the work of a student, as betrayed by the figure's awkward anatomy and faulty foreshortening. However, its shortcomings do not cancel out the ambition of the young artist's project: a painting of contemporary heroism, in other words, a modern history painting. If we are to look for possibilities of agency in Hamdi's early work, we should take into account the prevalent sense of urgency which shaped French art during this period: an urgency which materialized in the works of ambitious painters as nothing less than a revision of Academic conventions, a necessity to make high art matter to the contemporary audience again. Such a reading allows us to have a glimpse of Hamdi's preoccupations at this junction in his life when he –as a young and aspiring artist from Istanbul—reflected intensely on the discussions surrounding modern painting and Academic tradition.

Notes

1. This problematic emerges as a politically urgent one in the context of late-twentieth-century Turkey, echoing ongoing discussions around the vexed question of the country's pending accession to the European Union.

2. Adolphe-Marie-Antoine Thalasso wrote on a variety of subjects, ranging from Eastern poetry to French theater. He was the editor of the periodical *Revue Orientale Journal Littéraire, Artistique et Scientifique*, published in Istanbul in 1885 and 1886.

3. As none of these paintings are extant, and there is no known written account of them, all one can say about them has to remain in the realm of speculation. However, it is interesting to note that the *Escamoteur juif à Constantinople* echoes the title of a Salon success by Jean-Louis Hamon, the *Escamoteur, le quart d'heure de Rabelais* exhibited in 1861, and acquired by the government for the Fine Arts Museum in Nantes the same year. Hamon was in the close circle of Gérôme and Boulanger, forming a group called the néo-Grecs while still students at the studio of Paul Delaroche. Hamon's *Escamoteur* is a dense allegory set in a pseudo-antique scene. It is tempting to think of Hamdi's *Escamoteur juif* as a genre version of Hamon's neo-Greek allegory, transported to a contemporary setting.

4. The Ottoman sultan Abdulaziz traveled to France to visit the exhibition, being the first in the history of the Ottoman Empire to pay a visit to the monarchs of a European country for peaceful purposes.

5. *Zeïbek at Watch* provides us with an iconographical and technical anomaly in Hamdi's oeuvre. Neither his studio studies, in which he rendered nudes as well as models posed in costume, nor his later genre scenes featuring Zeïbeks, correspond to this single heroic male figure in a landscape.

Bibliography

Boer, Inge. "This is not the Orient: Theory and Postcolonial Practice." *The Point of Theory: Practices of Cultural Analysis*. Ed. Mieke Bal and Inge E. Boer. Amsterdam: Amsterdam UP, 1994. 211–19.

Castagnary, Jules Antoine. "Salon de 1864." *Salons (1857–1870)*. Vol. 1. Paris: Bibliothèque-Charpentier, 1892. 183–220.

Cezar, Mustafa. *Sanatta Batı'ya Açılış ve Osman Hamdi*. Istanbul: Erol Kerim Aksoy Kültür, Eğitim, Spor ve Sağlık Vakfı Yayını, 1995.

Du Camp, Maxime. *Les Beaux-Arts à l'Exposition Universelle de 1855*. Paris: Libraire Nouvelle, 1855.

Ersoy, Ahmet. "Şarklı Kimliğin Peşinde: Osman Hamdi Bey ve Osmanlı Kültüründe Oryantalizm." *Toplumsal Tarih* 119.19 (November 2003): 84–89.

Germaner, Semra. "Sanayi-i Nefise Mektebi Mimar Sinan Üniversitesi Kurucusu Osman Hamdi Bey." *23 Şubat-23 Mart 2001 Arası Düzenlenen 'Osman Hamdi Bey' Sergisi Kataloğu*. Istanbul: Yapı Kredi Yayınları, 2001.

La Turquie à l'Exposition Universelle de 1867. Ouvrage publié par les soins et sous la direction de S. Exc. Salaheddin Bey, Commissaire Impérial Ottoman près Exposition Universelle. Paris: Librairie Hachette & Cie, 1867.

Lemaires, Gérard-Georges. *The Orient in Western Art*. Italy: Könemann, 2001.

MacKenzie, John. *Orientalism: History, Theory and the Arts*. Manchester: Manchester UP, 1995.

Said, Edward W. *Orientalism*. New York: Vintage Books, 1994.

Shaw, Wendy. "The paintings of Osman Hamdi and the Subversion of Orientalist Vision." *Essays in Honour of Aptullah Kuran*. Ed. Çiğdem Kafesçioğlu and Lucienne Thys-Şenocak. Istanbul: Yapı Kredi Yayınları, 1999. 423–34.

Tansuğ, Sezer. *Çağdaş Türk Sanatı*. 6th ed. Istanbul: Remzi Kitabevi, 2003.

Thalasso, Adolphe. *L'Art Ottoman: Les Peintres de Turquie*. Istanbul: Arkeolojive Sanat Yayınları, 1988.

Yeğenoğlu, Meyda. *Colonial Fantasies: Towards a Feminist Reading of Orientalism*. Cambridge: Cambridge UP, 1998.

II. Relational Histories

Romani Identity Formation and the Globalization of Holocaust Discourse

Huub van Baar

A Dialectic of the Local and the Global

Over the last decade, there has been a growing tendency among Romani elites and organizations to participate in a globalized holocaust discourse to deal with processes of Romani identity formation. This article scrutinizes the consequences of this participation by focusing on debates about the role of the Nazi genocide of the Roma in these processes of identity formation, and by analyzing the exhibition on the extermination of the European Roma in the Auschwitz-Birkenau State Museum in particular. As we will see below, from this analysis arises the general question of how the processes of Romani identity formation in general, and their reliance on the Roma's various histories of marginalization and persecution in particular, have to deal with their own specificity.[1]

The visitor to the Auschwitz-Birkenau State Museum in Poland who follows the route suggested in the museum's guidebook will end her or his tour with a visit to the recently established permanent exhibition on the extermination of the European Roma. This exhibition is located in barrack 13 of the former Auschwitz I extermination camp (the so-called *Stammlager*). The barrack is the last one on the recommended route along the fifteen camp barracks that together make up the museum's exhibition. Established in August 2001, the exhibition on the Roma marks a rather unique part of the museum's exhibitions. For the first time in the museum's history, a particular exhibition has been dedicated to the suffering of the Roma. Moreover, since it was realized by various national Romani organizations, it can be considered as one of the first opportunities for Romani self-representation at such an internationally important site of memory.[2] At the moment of its establishment the exhibition was the most modern and remarkable exhibition of the museum, and it still is in many ways. Moreover, besides the exhibition titled "Struggle and Martyrdom of the Jews," it is the only permanent exhibition not dedicated to a particular nation-state. From this point of view, the Jewish and Romani exhibitions break with the museum's tradition to present its exhibitions along the lines of the nation-state. Furthermore, the Romani exhibition is established in the barrack in which the exhibitions on Denmark and the German Democratic Republic were housed in the past. Like Bulgaria, these countries are no longer represented in the museum. Once we realize the implications of these changes, we are in the midst of a discussion on the past, present, and future of holocaust remembrance, and its interrelationship with debates on nationalism, globalization, and identity politics.

The removal of the former exhibitions in barrack 13 belongs to a long history of various removals and renewals. The exhibitions were already re-organized during communism. The first Hungarian exhibition, for instance, was established in 1960, and new or restyled ones replaced it in 1970, 1980, and 2004 successively. Hence, the Romani exhibition belongs to a whole series of new and renewed exhibitions (cf. van Baar, "Memorial Work").[3] The tendency to change the exhibitions regularly indicates that we have to be attentive to "how much forgetting is always entailed in the production of memory" (Sayer 16). Not only does this imply that the production of memory can intentionally or unintentionally coincide with the erasure of other memories that were produced in the past, it also implies that memory can be considered as a very particular regulation of remembering and forgetting. When we analyze the institutions involved in memory production, we need to be aware of the ways in which memory intrinsically implies selection and, therefore, oblivion as well. Hence, we need to scrutinize which kinds of regulation and selection the exhibited materials embody and the extent to which both are related to concrete socio-cultural and political developments.

Undoubtedly among these developments are the nationalization and globalization of memory and of holocaust memory in particular. The museum's guidebook mentions the Romani exhibition at the top of a list of "national exhibitions." This is all the more interesting when we realize that Romani elites and organizations are striving for the recognition of the Roma as a nation at a European level. The declaration of the Romani nation, presented by the International Romani Union (IRU) at its fifth world congress in Prague in 2000, says in its first paragraph:

We, a Nation of which over half a million persons were exterminated in a forgotten Holocaust, a Nation of individuals too often discriminated, marginalized, victim of intolerance and persecutions, we have a dream, and we are engaged in fulfilling it. We are a Nation, we share the same tradition, the same culture, the same origin, the same language; we are a Nation. We have never looked for creating a Roma State. And we do not want a State today, when the new society and the new economy are concretely and progressively crossing-over the importance and the adequacy of the

State as the way how individuals organize themselves. (qtd. verbatim in Acton and Klímová 216)

Notwithstanding the unclear status of the IRU among the Roma and the questions raised by both Roma and non-Roma on whether all Romani communities do indeed share what has been stated here, the declaration is remarkable for its reference to Martin Luther King's "I have a dream" speech and for its use of the concept of "a nation without a state" as a post-nation-state formation. Within the scope of this article, however, it is most important to note that the unity of the Romani nation is first and foremost associated with the holocaust and the Roma's long history of suffering, and, at the same time, with their shared tradition, culture, origin, and language. This is in line with what Romani intellectuals such as Andrzej Mirga and Nicolae Gheorghe consider to be the way in which Romani national consciousness is created. Romani political elites "advanced other elements of the concept of nation; the common roots of the Romani people, their common historical experiences and perspectives, and the commonality of culture, language, and social standing. The experience of the Porrajmos, the Romani holocaust during World War II, played an important role in providing the Romani diaspora with its sense of nationhood" (Mirga and Gheorghe n. pag.). This quote clarifies that the IRU's link between Romani national identity and the Roma's Second World War history is not a singular one. Throughout Europe, and Eastern Europe in particular, there is an increasing tendency among Romani elites and organizations to refer to the genocide of the Roma alongside the Jewish holocaust on the one hand, and to rely on holocaust references in Romani identity building processes on the other (cf. Kapralski, "Auschwitz"; "Identity Building").

These references to the Jewish holocaust are part of a worldwide tendency to speak in terms of "forgotten," "other," "unknown," or "new" holocausts. Whoever browses the website www.holocaustforgotten.com, for example, finds information on the Nazi mass murder of the Roma, homosexuals, the disabled, Black Africans, Jehovah's witnesses, and Poles. Moreover, the term "holocaust" is not exclusively used for the mass murders during the Second World War and on the European continent. Events in different periods and on various continents are increasingly framed as holocausts: e.g. the mass murder of the Herero by the Germans in Namibia in 1905; the one of the Armenians by the Turks in 1915–16; Stalinism in general; the massacre in Nanking, where Japanese soldiers slaughtered Chinese civilians in 1937; the violent displacement of the Palestinians in 1948; and the brutal reductions of the indigenous populations of the Americas and Australia. Furthermore, recent large-scale ethnic cleansings, such as the ones in the former Yugoslavia, Rwanda, and the Sudanese province of Darfur, are referred to as holocausts as well. Without judging the value of these holocaust references, all of them rely on a comparison with the Jewish holocaust in one way or another, while simultaneously trying to certify their own specificity. Because of this increasing tendency to use the holocaust as "a universal trope for historical trauma," Andreas Huyssen has suggested to speak of a "globalization of Holocaust discourse" (23). As he wrote, this discourse concerns a dialectic of the local and the global. A global awareness of similarities between present and past holocaust-related events has emerged from the local events in Bosnia, Kosovo, and Rwanda, while past or present violent local conflicts could be mediated and identified as "holocausts" or "genocides" by the very existence of something like a globalized discourse. In the case of the Roma, however, as in those of the disabled and homosexuals, we have a paradoxical situation. While their sufferings during the war were spatio-temporally conflated with those of the Jews, though neglected for decades, both the spread of knowledge about the Nazi genocide of the Roma and the public identity derived from it are highly dependent on a general discourse in which disjunctive holocausts are presented as "of the same kind." When spatio-temporally different events are formally lumped together under the term "holocaust," each loses some of its specificity. In order to analyze the consequences of such a loss, we first have to scrutinize the ways in which holocaust discourse operates globally.

The Globalization of Holocaust Discourse: Three Stages
Over the last two decades, the scope of holocaust discourse has widened through the various controversies about how it could and should be represented. Events such as the establishment of holocaust and genocide studies centers in different countries, the opening of the U.S. Holocaust Memorial Museum in 1993, the controversies around various artistic representations of the holocaust, the post-1989 rise of international tourism to the former Nazi camps, and the organization of international holocaust conferences, are but a few of the ways in which holocaust discourse achieved its actual form. Paradoxically, the de-nationalization of holocaust discourse started with its Americanization. The debates surrounding the U.S. Holocaust Memorial Museum exemplarily illustrate what Daniel Levy and Natan Sznaider have called the "loss of the monopoly position of the heroic national narrative" in favor of "a skeptic self-reflexive cosmopolitan" holocaust discourse (234).[4] The museum has been criticized for various reasons, which can roughly be summarized under three different types of critique. First, because the museum pays little attention to holocausts other than the Jewish one, it has been criticized for privileging the latter. Second, since the museum emphasizes the liberation of the Nazi death camps by American soldiers, through its prominent representation at the very entrance of the permanent exhibition, some critics have considered it one-sided and have accused the museum of nationalizing the holocaust. Finally, since the route through the museum and the representation of "the stages of suffering" in particular recall Christ's *Via Dolorosa*, the museum has finally been accused of the Christianization of the holocaust (cf. Young, *Texture of Memory*; Linenthal; Finkelstein).

Yet, although the Americanization of the holocaust has certainly resulted in its nationalization, from the very beginning the museum's project has also been presented as something larger than American life. Because, firstly, it universalized America's Bill of Rights and then considered the Nazi crimes as its ultimate violation, the Holocaust Memorial Museum could be defended as an institution beyond the national scope and with universal value (cf. Young, *Texture of Memory* 336). The U.S. Holocaust Memorial Council, which was responsible for the museum's project, expressed its approach as follows: "An event of universal significance, the Holocaust has special importance for Americans: in act and word the Nazis denied the deepest tenets of the American people" (qtd. in Young, *Texture of Memory* 337). From this point of view, the museum's adaptation of the holocaust to American secular Christianity did no more than effectively link American citizens to the universal "holocaust story," resulting in both the deterritorialization and universalization of holocaust discourse, albeit in American-centric forms. I consider this the first of three interrelated stages in which holocaust discourse has started to become globalized.

The second stage, which is not strictly separated from the first one, is dominated by the more popular understanding of Americanization as commercialization. Holocaust memory has become inextricably bound up with its distribution by mass media. Therefore, we cannot discuss issues related to holocaust discourse without taking into consideration the various ways in which it is globally commodified. Over the last few decades, the U.S.-dominated mediascape has effectively been transformed into a global one, in which "the holocaust" has become a large-scale consumable product. However, unlike Theodor W. Adorno suggested in his critique of mass culture, commodification does not amount to forgetting, and holocaust commodification does not necessarily amount to banalizing the original historic events and their traumatic consequences. Phenomena like autobiographical, artistic, and academic holocaust representations, as well as international tourism to the former Nazi camps, war relics, and museums cannot simply be split into serious and "trivial" memory. Instead, these phenomena "compel us to think traumatic memory and entertainment memory together as occupying the same public space, rather than seeing them as mutually exclusive phenomena" (Huyssen 29).

The encoding of holocaust memory implies the production and reproduction of images and narratives that can be transported by global mass media, which does not necessarily entail the homogenization of memory. The globalization of culture, and of holocaust discourse in particular, "is not the same as its homogenization, but globalization involves the use of a variety of instruments of homogenization . . . that are absorbed into local political and cultural economies, only to be repatriated as heterogeneous dialogues . . . in which the state plays an increasingly delicate role" (Appadurai 42). To understand the full-scale political and cultural impact of both the aforementioned aspects of the Americanization of holocaust discourse, we thus need to reflect on the ways in which globally commodified holocaust memory is decoded locally, e.g. nationally or regionally. Indeed, "the *political* site of memory practices is still national, not postnational or global" (Huyssen 26, original emphasis). This means we need to analyze not only local memorial practices such as the Romani exhibition in Auschwitz, but also the extent to which international political decisions are influenced or even controlled by the ways in which globalized holocaust memory is decoded *nationally*, and then re-encoded globally. To do the latter, we first need to explain the way in which the first two stages are transversally linked with a third one in the process of the full globalization of holocaust discourse.

Huyssen, Levy, and Sznaider emphasize the overriding importance of the massacres in Bosnia for a decisive turn in holocaust discourse. The images of the Serbian "death camp" in Omarska that swept the world's television screens in 1992 convinced the global audience that it had to worry about a "new" holocaust on the European continent. When we analyze the different national debates that the Bosnian war unleashed, like Levy and Sznaider did for the American, German, and Israeli ones, we notice that the Bosnian war was increasingly framed in holocaust terms. Simultaneously, many of the national debates started to focus on the issue of intervention and the violation of human rights, while the passive spectator mentality was increasingly interpreted as a failure of the national governments (and the U.N.) to fulfill their moral duty. Hence, the ways in which the Bosnian war and its interrelated holocaust references were decoded nationally, as in the cases of the Rwandan and the Kosovo conflicts later on, were charged with morality and closely related to compliance with the Charter of the United Nations. This is what characterizes the third stage of the globalization of holocaust discourse: its moral encoding. Admittedly, holocaust discourse was always intimately related to morality. What has changed is the way in which it is globally deployed to denounce violations of human rights, and how it becomes intrinsically linked with the International Charter of the United Nations. Hence, in the third stage, a further deterritorialization and universalization take place, and by linking holocaust discourse to the general frame of human rights, entirely other post- or neo-colonial contexts could be incorporated in the discourse as well. However, the more "universal" and deterritorialized holocaust discourse becomes, the more important it becomes for the groups in question to develop a strategy to relate their own case to the globalized discourse effectively. Levy and Sznaider suggest that such strategies bring together victimhood and morality in a particular way:

The oppressed have to be "guiltless", and those who violate human rights, have to be "evil". Nazis and Jews form the constituents of this new global religion. Consequently, those who claim that their human rights are violated, have to relate their suffering to the one of the Jews, and have to bring the perpetrators symbolically at the level of the Nazis. . . . The holocaust has become a universal "container" of memories of indistinguishable victims. It has resulted in "the globalization of evil." (222–23)

This strategy of claiming victimhood could explain why it is meaningful for Romani elites and organizations to inscribe Romani history in a globalized holocaust discourse.

Yet, Dimitrina Petrova, executive director of the Budapest-based European Roma Rights Center (ERRC), claims that, "while we see very little in-fighting and a tendency to strong consensus among Roma over human rights issues, identity issues are increasingly sensitive and controversial. . . . The struggle over identity at this stage does not unite the Roma in Europe. Is identity then the dividing principle, as opposed to Human Rights?" (4). This question could be answered negatively, once we accept that Romani identity building and its reliance on a globalized holocaust discourse are now intrinsically linked with a call for the compliance with human rights. This link returns in the IRU's declaration, which, as we saw above, starts by relating the Romani nation to the holocaust and ends by connecting their nation to the U.N. Charter: "We, the Roma Nation, have something to share, right by asking for a representation, respect, implementation of the existing International Charter on Human Rights, so that each individual can look at them as at existing, concrete warranties for her or his today and future" (qtd. verbatim in Acton and Klímová 217). The question remains how the inscription in a globalized holocaust discourse actually *works* in the Roma's case. Therefore, in the next section, I return to the Romani exhibition to analyze in detail a particular example of such an inscription.

Cultivating Victimhood and Periodizing History in the Auschwitz-Birkenau State Museum

The Romani exhibition is roughly divided into two parts. The room visitors enter first has a floor that is raised thirty centimeters. The displays in this space concern, on the one hand, the rise of National Socialism and its implications for the Roma and, on the other, the history of the persecution and deportation of the Roma state by state. This central room is diagonally placed on the "original" floor of the barrack and does not touch its outer walls. The thirty-centimeter-high floor in its turn has two levels: the upper consists of grey nature stone tiles, the lower of orange-brown bricks, which resemble the barrack walls seen from outside. The soft, orange-colored and orange-lighted panels that display documents and photographs from the pre-war period stand on the highest level, while the steel elements that display documents and photographs concerning the wartime period stand on the lower floor (cf. Figure 1). The visitor who leaves the latter level enters the second part of the exhibition at the same time; it has been put on the original floor, which has been painted white. The panels that stand on this floor predominantly concern the Roma's suffering in

Figure 1 Overview of the central exhibition room (Huub van Baar, 2003).

Auschwitz and their extermination. The catalogue explains the exhibition's structure as follows:

The central room, which stands for the persecuted people, does not blend in well with the existing architecture and also stands in contradiction to the original room in every respect: the axes of both rooms are not identical, here pleasant, safe forms, there hard and severe forms, here warm, earthy colours, there cold blue-white, here faces of people, laughter and family life, there typewritten documents of the captors. The wedge-shaped steel elements as symbols of persecution and violence dissect the central room, gliding more or less on the invisible axes of the original room and finally break it up completely. (Rose 317)

While the exhibition has been well-designed and thoughtfully created, I would like to make some critical remarks with reference to my earlier reflections on the globalization of holocaust discourse.

First of all, it is striking that the pre-war past is almost exclusively represented by photographs and brief explanatory captions. These images are predominantly portraits and group photographs of families, school classes, sports clubs, bands, and little orchestras. Few images show working Roma, and only very few are shots of Romani villages or caravan dwellers. Since the displayed photographs are mainly snapshots of members of Romani elites on holidays, the part of the exhibition that

Figure 2 Images of pre-wartime Roma in the former Czechoslovakia (Huub van Baar, 2003).

concerns the pre-war period mostly shows peacefully and harmoniously living individuals and groups all over the represented European countries. Furthermore, these images are not complemented by texts other than the brief captions (cf. Figure 2). Hence, the visitor passes by images from the pre-war period from which poverty, hard times, the differences between various regional groups, and national forms of marginalization or persecution different from the Nazi ones, are practically excluded. The omission of the latter, in particular, creates a radical, inaccurate contrast between the pre-war and the wartime period. By underrepresenting anti-Roma measures taken in pre-war European countries other than Nazi Germany, the Roma from the countries that are included in the exhibition become indistinguishable victims of one and the same brutal aggressor that occupied their "peaceful" rations.[5]

In fact, a lot of European countries took restrictive measures with regard to their Romani populations, in particular in the interwar period. To mention but a few examples: a Czechoslovakian law from 1927 "condemned the Roma as asocial citizens, limited their personal liberty, introduced Gypsy identity cards, and decreed that Romani children under 18 be placed in special institutions" (Barany 99; cf. Nečas 41); a Hungarian law from 1928 "ordained semiannual Gypsy police raids in order to weed out the criminal and parasitic elements from the Romani communities. As in Czechoslovakia, special regulations required the fingerprinting and registration of all

Roma" (Barany 100; cf. Szabolcs 38). From the 1920s onwards, Ante Pavelić's Croatian *Ustaše*-movement increasingly endangered the position of Roma and Jews in the former Yugoslavia, while during the Second World War the pro-Nazi *Ustaše*-regime was responsible for the extermination of about 25,000 Roma, mainly in the camps surrounding the Croatian town of Jasenovac (cf. Acković; Glenny; Reinhartz). Furthermore, countries such as France, Belgium, and the Netherlands had already taken restrictive measures against Roma and other travelers during the migration waves at the end of the nineteenth and the beginning of the twentieth century (cf. Hubert; Gotovitch; Lucassen). These national differences and local anti-Roma sentiments and measures are underrepresented in the exhibition, creating the impression of a homogeneous European Romani people, which began to suffer as soon as, but not before the moment Nazi terror penetrated the occupied countries. In this particular conception of their victimhood, any possible aggressive element against the Roma is excluded from the non-German national territory and history, and projected abroad. The good and peaceful nations on the one hand, and the evil and foreign aggressor on the other are largely polarized and a moral logic à la Levy and Sznaider's appears.

What is true for the pre-wartime period is also true for the post-wartime period. By displaying the wartime period on steel elements into which the related documents and photographs are entirely integrated (the pictures are not fixed onto, but reproduced on the panels themselves), it seems that the memory of the wartime is guaranteed "forever" (cf. Figure 3). However, when we consider post-war and current situations in many European countries, we can easily list a number of local cases in which it is questionable whether the memory of the Roma's war history is safeguarded at all. One of the most delicate examples is the neglect by the Czech authorities of the former Roma concentration camps in Lety and Hodonín (cf. Nečas; Pape; van Baar, "The Way out of Amnesia?"). At the sites of these former camps stand a pig farm and a cottage park respectively. It is even worse in some of the Balkan countries. The mass graves of both Roma and Jews in Transnistria in today's Moldova, to which about 25,000 Romanian Roma were deported by the Antonescu regime, are still hushed up by local and national authorities (cf. Crowe; Heim; Kelso; Mihok). Last but not least, the Bosnian wars of the 1990s have radically disturbed the museum that was established in 1968 at the site of the former Jasenovac camp at the border of today's Croatia and Bosnia-Herzegovina. From 1991 to 1995 Serbian soldiers occupied this site. Afterwards, the area was mined and part of the museum's collection has been 'removed' to Belgrade.

The topicality of this issue leads me to another point. Objects, documents, and photographs that depict the lives and suffering of the Roma in the pre-war and wartime period are relatively scarce; they mainly concern the elites or are based on what remains from the Nazi administration. Moreover, only very few Romani war testimonies

Figure 3 Panels displaying the wartime suffering of Roma in Auschwitz-Birkenau (Huub van Baar, 2003).

and diaries are known (among the few exceptions are Bernáth; Hübschmannová; Meijer; Lacková; Danielová, Zajoncová and Haragal'ová). Memory related to the war period is consequently largely dependent on oral testimonies from a rapidly decreasing number of survivors and representatives of the following generations. Therefore, Romani holocaust memory relies increasingly on what Marianne Hirsch and James Young have respectively termed "postmemory" and a "vicarious past" (Hirsch; Young, *Memory's Edge*).[6] The Romani exhibition in Auschwitz has excluded such references, instead attempting to provide what Andrew Hoskins calls "a literally 'documentary' past" (10) by carefully displaying as many original documents and pictures as possible. By thus isolating wartime experiences from both pre- and post-war ones, history becomes conceptualized in terms of disjunctive periods. The war experiences seem to have neither predecessors nor successors, and the wartime period itself is represented as a "distant past."

Concluding Remarks

The establishment of the Romani exhibition marks a historical opportunity for Romani self-representation at such an internationally crucial memorial site. Disappointed by the scarce attention paid to the Roma in the U.S. Holocaust Memorial Museum in Washington D.C., the Romani linguist Ian Hancock expressed the hope that "we will eventually be moved out of the category of 'other victims' and fully recognized as the only population, together with the Jews, that was slated for eradication from the face of the earth" (59). To some extent, the opening of the Romani exhibition in Auschwitz illustrates that Hancock's hope was not in vain. Since the Romani and the Jewish exhibitions are the only ones dedicated to a particular group of victims, it could be claimed that the Roma are not in the periphery of holocaust memory anymore. Once we arrive at this point, however, we also need to ask ourselves, as Edward Linenthal did with regard to the U.S. Holocaust Memorial Museum, to what extent groups that argue that they belong within the boundaries of the holocaust define their position always *"in relation to the Jewish center"* (249, original emphasis). When we consider the debates and studies that have been published on the genocide of the Roma, we indeed have to acknowledge the considerable effort that has been expended on the (in some cases rather fanatic) demonstration that the scale and the manner of the atrocities are of the same kind as in the case of the Jews.

Nonetheless, the definition of the Roma's position in relation to the Jews is finally not evidence of competition, but of a striving to occupy a place as unique and important as that of the Jews in post-war Euro-American history. This is one of the main reasons why participating in a globalized holocaust discourse could help improve the visibility of the Roma. Two partly incompatible interests seem to play tricks on the Roma's case, though. On the one hand, the participation in the globalized holocaust discourse, since it is linked with the denunciation of the violation of human rights, meets the wishes of many Roma to see recent or current dramatic events with regard to their group in terms of the wartime past. Hancock strongly makes such a claim: "Today, the Romani population faces its severest crisis since the Holocaust; neo-Nazi race crimes against Gypsies have seen rapes, beatings, and murders in Germany, Hungary, and Slovakia; anti-Gypsy pogroms in Romania and Bulgaria, including lynchings and home burnings, are increasing. For my people, the Holocaust is not yet over" (55). It may be said that the participation in a globalized holocaust discourse enables the Roma to make a local translation to the present-day situation and, furthermore, to represent themselves collectively, as a non-territorial nation.

On the other hand, the inscription in a globalized holocaust discourse results in the loss of the specificity of the Roma's own histories. This not only includes losing sight of the specificity of various Romani groups, but also, most important in the context of my argument, losing the specificity of the history of the Eastern European Roma in particular. By focusing on a conception of victimhood that excludes both the pre- and the post-war (communist) anti-Roma measures that were taken in most of the region's countries, the treatment of the various Romani communities within the different national contexts becomes undertheorized. A better understanding of the ways in which Roma and non-Roma were historically related to each other at a national level, as well as a better contextualization of the ways in which the communist victimization of many of the inhabitants of the former Eastern Bloc is related to the suffering of the Roma, are of paramount importance to formulate a concept of victimhood beyond artificial polarizations. Until at least these conditions are fulfilled, the Roma's case seems to remain dominated by the paradox of gaining an identity through the loss of its specificity.

Notes

1. I use the term "Roma" and its adjective "Romani" to indicate all the different groups that are often called "Gypsies" in English-speaking regions. Hence, when referring to the Roma, I often also implicitly refer to the Sinti and other Gypsy groups who prefer to be distinguished from the Roma.

2. The exhibition on the genocide of the Roma and Sinti in the Auschwitz-Birkenau State Museum was an initiative of the Documentation and Cultural Center of German Sinti and Roma (Dokumentations- und Kulturzentrum Deutscher Sinti und Roma, Heidelberg). This center intensively collaborated with the Auschwitz Memorial and the Association of Roma in Poland. Furthermore, national Romani and Sinti organizations from Austria, the Czech Republic, Hungary, Serbia, Ukraine, and the Netherlands participated in the realization of the exhibition. The exhibition was designed by the Atelier für Gestaltung, under supervision of Wieland Schmid. In fact, the monument established in the former so-called "Gypsy camp" (*Zigeunerlager*) in Birkenau, can be considered as the first opportunity for Romani self-representation in the museum. This monument was an initiative of the Association of Sinti in Germany (Verband der Sinti Deutschlands) and was established at the site of the 28th barrack in the former BIIe section of the Birkenau camp in 1973.

3. Remarkably, the former exhibitions are not archived by the museum, and the museum direction does not know what has happened to the exhibits. Since the national exhibitions are property of the corresponding nation-states, the museum's direction does not hold itself responsible for what happens to a particular exhibition after its removal (cf. Oleksy, Świebocka and Zbrzeska).

4. The translations from German into English of Levy and Sznaider are mine.

5. Silvio Peritore and Frank Reuter suggest that the photographs that were made by Sinti and Roma before the war and that are displayed at the exhibition counterbalance those of the Sinti and Roma that were made by the Nazis during the war. This is true to some extent, but, nevertheless, the selected photographs of the pre-wartime period give a one-sided, romanticized image of this period. Interestingly enough, representatives of three of the Romani organizations that contributed to the development of the exhibition told me that the Documentation and Cultural Center of German Sinti and Roma in Heidelberg made a pre-selection of the photographs to be displayed. They also told me that the center did not select the photographs of poor and not very well dressed Roma and Sinti that these three organizations had collected during their research (see Lhotka; Váradi and Kardos; Weiss).

6. Hirsch characterizes postmemory as "the experience of those who grow up dominated by narratives that preceded their birth, whose own belated stories are evacuated by the stories of the previous generation shaped by traumatic events that can be neither understood nor recreated" (22). She distinguishes postmemory "from memory by generational distance and from history by deep personal connection" (22). Since Hirsch considers the condition of exile from the space of identity as a characteristic aspect of postmemory, it is of high importance to analyze more extensively the ways in which Romani holocaust postmemory relates to contemporary processes of Romani identity building. Young's concept of a "vicarious past" is mainly based on Hirsch's concept of postmemory and characterizes a vicarious past as "the memory of the witness's memory," in its various mediated forms (*Memory's Edge* 1–2).

Bibliography

Acković, Dragoljub. *Roma Suffering in [the] Jasenovac Camp*. Belgrade: Roma Culture Center, 1995.

Acton, Thomas, and Ilona Klímová. "The International Romani Union: An East European Answer to West European Questions?" *Between Past and Future: the Roma of Central and Eastern Europe*. Ed. Will Guy. Hatfield: U of Hertfordshire P, 2001. 157–219.

Appadurai, Arjun. *Modernity at Large: Cultural Dimensions of Globalization*. London and Minneapolis: U of Minnesota P, 1996.

Baar, Huub van. "Memorial Work in Progress: 'Auschwitz' and the Struggle for Romani Holocaust Representation." *Cultural Politics*: forthcoming.

———. "The Way out of Amnesia? Europeanisation and the Recognition of the Roma's Past and Present." *Third Text: Critical Perspectives on Contemporary Art and Culture* 22.3 (2008): 373–85.

Barany, Zoltan. *The East European Gypsies. Regime Change, Marginality, and Ethnopolitics*. Cambridge: Cambridge UP, 2002.

Bernáth, Gábor, ed. *Roma Holocaust (Kodola seron, kon perdal zhuvinde – Túlélők emlékeznek – Recollections of survivors)*. Budapest: Roma Press Center, 2001.

Crowe, David. "The Gypsy Historical Experience in Romania." *The Gypsies of Eastern Europe*. Ed. David Crowe and John Kolsti. London and Armonk: Sharpe, 1991. 61–79.

Danielová, Helena, Dana Zajoncová, and Jana Haragal'ová, eds. *Pamětí Romských Žen (Kořeny 1)*. Brno: Muzeum romské kultury o.p.s., 2001.

Finkelstein, Norman. *The Holocaust Industry: Reflections on the Exploitation of Jewish Suffering*. London and New York: Verso, 2000.

Glenny, Micha. *The Balkans: Nationalism, War and the Great Powers, 1804–1999*. New York: Viking, 1999.

Gotovitch, José. "Verfolgung und Vernichtung Belgischer Sinti und Roma." *Sinti und Roma im KL Auschwitz-Birkenau 1943–44. Vor dem Hintergrund ihrer Verfolgung unter der Naziherrschaft*. Ed. Wacław Długoborski. Oświęcim: Verlag Staatliches Museum Auschwitz-Birkenau, 1998. 209–25.

Hancock, Ian. "Responses to the Porrajmos: The Romani Holocaust." *Is the Holocaust Unique? Perspectives on Comparative Genocide*. Ed. Alan Rosenbaum. Oxford and Colorado: Westview Press, 1996. 39–64.

Heim, Susanne. "Sinti und Roma im Rahmen der Nationalsozialistischen Bevölkerungspolitik in Südosteuropa." *Sinti und Roma im KL Auschwitz-Birkenau 1943–44. Vor dem Hintergrund ihrer Verfolgung unter der Naziherrschaft*. Ed. Wacław Długoborski. Oświęcim: Verlag Staatliches Museum Auschwitz-Birkenau, 1998. 144–61.

Hirsch, Marianne. *Family Frames: Photography, Narrative and Postmemory*. London and Cambridge, MA: Harvard UP, 1997.

Hoskins, Andrew. "Signs of the Holocaust: Exhibiting Memory in a Mediated Age." *Media, Culture & Society* 25.1 (2003): 7–22.

Hubert, Marie-Christine. "The Internment of Gypsies in France." Trans. Sinéad ní Shuinéar. *In the Shadow of the Swastika: The Gypsies During the Second World War Vol. 2*. Ed. Donald Kenrick. Vol. 13. Interface Collection. Hatfield: U of Hertfordshire P, 1999. 59–88.

Hübschmannová, Milena. *"Po Židoch cigáni": Svědectví Romů ze Slovenska 1939–1945*. Vol. 1: 1939 – August 1944. Prague: Triáda, 2005.

Huyssen, Andreas. "Present Pasts: Media, Politics, Amnesia." *Public Culture* 12.1 (2000): 21–38.

Kapralski, Sławomir. "Auschwitz: Site of Memories." *Polin. Studies in Polish Jewry*. Ed. Antony Polonsky. Vol. 15. Focusing on Jewish Religious Life, 1500–1900. Oxford and Portland: The Littman Library of Jewish Civilization, 2002. 383–400.

———. "Identity Building and the Holocaust: Roma Political Nationalism." *Nationalities Papers* 25.2 (1997): 269–83.

Kelso, Michelle. "Gypsy Deportations to Transnistria: Romania, 1942–1944." *In the Shadow of the Swastika: The Gypsies During the Second World War Vol. 2*. Ed. Donald Kenrick. Vol. 13. Interface Collection. Hatfield: U of Hertfordshire P, 1999. 95–129.

Lacková, Ilona. *A False Dawn: My Life as a Gypsy Woman in Slovakia*. Trans. Milena Hübschmannová and Carleton Bulkin. Ed. Alice Bialestowski and Astrid Thorn Hillig. Vol. 16. Interface Collection. Hatfield: U of Hertfordshire P, 1999.

Levy, Daniel, and Natan Sznaider. *Erinnerung im globalen Zeitalter: Der Holocaust*. Frankfurt am Main: Suhrkamp, 2001.

Linenthal, Edward. *Preserving Memory: The Struggle to Create America's Holocaust Museum*. New York: Penguin, 1995.

Lhotka, Petr (Museum of Romani Culture). Personal interview. Brno, Czech Republic. 2003.

Lucassen, Leo. *"En men noemde hen zigeuners…" De geschiedenis van Kaldarasch, Ursari, Lowara en Sinti in Nederland: 1750–1944*. Amsterdam and The Hague: Stichting Beheer IISG/SDU, 1990.

Meijer, Mia, ed. *Het wilde vuur: Sinti en Roma aan het woord. Verhalen vanaf WO II tot heden*. Hoogmade: Uitgeverij De Sirenen, 2004.

Mihok, Brigitte. "Die Verfolgung der Roma. Ein verdrängtes Kapitel der rumänischen Geschichte." *Rumänien und der Holocaust. Zu den Massenverbrechen in Transnistrien 1941–1944*. Ed. Mariana Hausleitner, Brigitte Mihok and Juliane Wetzel. Berlin: Metropol, 2001. 25–31.

Mirga, Andrzej, and Nicolae Gheorghe. *The Roma in the Twenty-First Century: A Policy Paper*. Princeton: PER, 1997.

Nečas, Ctibor. *The Holocaust of the Czech Roma*. Prague: Prostor, 1999.

Oleksy, Krystyna, Teresa Świebocka and Teresa Zbrzeska (Board of the State Museum of Auschwitz-Birkenau). Personal interview. Oświęcim, Poland. 2003.

Pape, Markus. *A nikdo vám nebude věřit. Dokument o koncentračním táboře Lety u Písku*. Prague: G Plus G, 1997.

Peritore, Silvio and Frank Reuter. "Die ständige Ausstellung zum Völkermord an den Sinti und Roma im Staatlichen Museum Auschwitz: Voraussetzungen, Konzeption und Realisierung." *Die Kunst ist der Zerstörer des Schweigens. Formen künstlerischer Erinnerung an die national-sozialistische Rassen- und Vernichtungspolitik in Osteuropa*. Ed. Frank Grüner, Urs Heftrich, and Heinz-Dietrich Löwe. Cologne, Weimar and Vienna: Böhlau Verlag, 2006. 495–513.

Petrova, Dimitrina. "Competing Romani Identities." *Roma Rights* 4.3 (1999): 4.

Reinhartz, Dennis. "Damnation of the Outsider. The Gypsies of Croatia and Serbia in the Balkan Holocaust, 1941–1945." *The Gypsies of Eastern Europe*. Ed. David Crowe and John Kolsti. London and Armonk: Sharpe, 1991. 81–92.

Rose, Romani, ed. *The National Socialist Genocide of the Sinti and Roma: Catalogue of the Permanent Exhibition in the State Museum of Auschwitz*. Heidelberg: Dokumentations- und Kulturzentrum Deutscher Sinti und Roma, 2003.

Sayer, Derek. *The Coasts of Bohemia: A Czech History*. Princeton: Princeton UP, 1998.

Szabolcs, Szita, ed. *Tények, Adatok. A Cigányok Háborús Üldöztetésének (1939–1945). Tanintézeti

Feldolgozásához. Budapest: Holocaust Documentation Center, 2000.

Váradi, Istvánné, and Ferenc Kardos (Roma Minority Self-Government). Personal interview. Nagykanizsa, Hungary. 2004.

Weiss, Lalla (National Sinti and Roma Organization). Personal interview. Best, the Netherlands. 2004.

Young, James. *At Memory's Edge: After-Images of the Holocaust in Contemporary Art and Architecture*. London and New Haven: Yale UP, 2000.

———. *The Texture of Memory: Holocaust Memorials and Meaning*. London and New Haven: Yale UP, 1993.

Similarity and Difference: The Appearance of Suffering at the Strokestown Famine Museum

Niamh Ann Kelly

Introduction

The Great Hunger, or famine, in Ireland began in 1845 and continued to wreak a devastating effect on the land's population through the 1850s. As the single most significant event for the demographic alteration of Ireland in modern history, it is a peculiarly quiet and understated presence in the representational practices of Irish museums and art. There are, however, small cottages devoted to recounting local histories of the famine throughout Ireland, in counties as far apart as Kerry and Donegal. In such examples, one of the recurring methods of representation is to show the famine through the display of various domestic and farming objects with labels providing a famine-centered historical context. As there is no evidence of direct photographic images of the famine era in Ireland, these objects become the primary means by which representations, though scarce, are created in Irish material culture. In a postcolonial reading, these representations of the famine are logically imbued with questions of identity. Namely, the presentation of artifacts and information in museum settings explores the famine as a historical event by encouraging the visitor or reader to recognize and interpret notions of social similarity and difference.

The primary museum devoted to the famine in Ireland is the Strokestown Famine Museum, situated in Co. Roscommon in the midlands of the country. Throughout this museum, representations of famine occur on two distinct levels: firstly, accounts of both the victims of suffering and the contributors to that suffering are presented; and secondly, the displays overtly correlate the past to the present day. The site of the museum provides the first indication of the representations to follow, and the first exhibition room tells a particular local history that is presented as an utterance of both a broader national history and what is perceived as a trans-national, trans-temporal condition of modern famine more generally. Strategies of recognizing similarity and difference, seeing "sameness" and "otherness," are apparent throughout the museum. Displays and artifacts are presented in carefully constructed conversations with each other, and as the reader moves through the museum the sequence of revelation central to the exhibition forces the staging of various identities and (their) alterities, in order to understand the famine as it is re-membered at this location.

Indication – Situating the Museum

The Strokestown Famine Museum tells the story of one estate decimated during the famine of the 1840s. In this case, a landlord-driven policy of emigration resulted in the depletion of an agri-dependent population. The assassination of the landlord in question was followed by the trial and hanging of the supposed assassin. The museum, first opened to the public in 1994, lays a claim to authenticity by locating its primary voice within the fabric of the buildings and grounds: the museum displays are contained in the former stables, the Big House is open for guided tours, and visitors can also stroll through the sprawling parkland and walled gardens. This luscious context provides a marked contrast to the tale of deprivation told in the museum's exhibits and information panels. Strokestown Park was formerly the estate of the Mahons, a family of local wealth and power whose story, as it is now told, casts them as a stereotype of the landed gentry of colonized nineteenth-century Ireland.[1]

The site exudes a sense of the worthy wealth contingent on Anglo sympathies of a former era. Located in the center of the town it spawned, the estate opens with a sweeping driveway. A grey stone wall to its left masks the stables and courtyard and, further on, the walled gardens. The house is an eighteenth-century three-storey mansion of grey stone with a pillared portico and a standard classical system of diminutive scale windows per storey. The façade is symmetrically balanced: both sides are adorned by white servants' blocks connected to the owner's residence by Palladian-style curved wings. The single-storey whitewashed stable building contains the museum and a paved path leads through the loose gravel to its entrance.

Beyond the casual atmosphere of the pay booth, a dark green door announces the beginning of the museum proper through the medium of an A4 laminated printout of heraldic iconography (Figure 1). This bears the simplified form of a green seven-pillared temple plotted on a lighter green marbled background below some text in red, bold, capital Times print that reads: "Famine Museum Entrance." Though the production value of the sign is informal, the choice of iconography is cause for thought. It calls to mind the austerity of a shrine, strongly echoing the historical relationship between the museum and the temple. As Susan Pearce writes, in general terms: "Museums are the modernist heirs to the European tradition in the long term which has created an organically related sequence of holy repositories . . . in which collected material of abiding community significance can be stored and (usually) displayed" (387).[2]

Figure 1   Museum Sign (Niamh Ann Kelly, 2004).

The sign is clearly intended to portion off whatever lies on the other side of the green door from all that constituted the journey up to it. What I am about to enter is a sanctuary of some kind; what I have passed through to get here is of a different order. Duncan and Wallach write of the significance of both the spatial and architectural structures of museum and gallery spaces (448–69). They explore the interrelationship between such visual and material cues and the construction of citizenship through the "scripting" of exhibitions.[3] The signage up to the entrance of the Famine Museum, the context of the site itself, and the situating of the museum in the stables, clearly iterate an awareness of such a scripting, though the nature of the "citizenship" is only finally revealed in the exhibits beyond the Museum Entrance sign.

This marking off of territory is a historical compound of the tradition of museum spaces as "other" than the everyday, while still, in theory, by modern description accessible to all. Historians and cultural analysts alike are aware of this desire for distinction on the one hand and, on the other, the parallels often implied between museums and other public spaces, such as botanical gardens, parks, and zoos. Historically, pleasure gardens and, later, amusement parks replaced the traveling fair, reflecting an emergent element of modern town and city planning that promoted designated spaces to be developed as leisure areas. Similarly, zoos were planned to replace the more transitory form of the circus, in recognition of the fast-growing stationary urban populations of modernity.[4]

Increasingly, such observations tend to equate an urban-centered desire for social distraction with the more aggressive consumer-driven advent of museum marketing. Pearce emphasizes that the emergence of the modern museum coincided with a rise in capitalist concerns with market values and the advent of consumer society in the West (116). Brawne also identifies museums as "not only places of social pilgrimage but also components of the service industry catering for our leisure" (56). Susan Sontag, writing on the difficulty of defining an appropriate space for the display of photographs of suffering, states that the "chief model of public space is the mega-store (which may also be an airport or a museum)." She goes on to describe the museum:

Once a repository for conserving and displaying the fine arts of the past, the museum has become a vast educational institution-cum-emporium, one of whose functions is the exhibition of art. The primary function is entertainment and education in various mixes, and the marketing of experiences, tastes and simulacra. (107–9)

The secluded rural location of the Strokestown Famine Museum, however, indicates that it is unlikely to be merely a space intended for the distraction of the, usually urban, masses. Instead, the location of the museum enters its representations into a postcolonial paradigm in which Ireland's national identity is tied closely to perceptions and perpetuations of ruralism as integral to Irishness, interwoven with a problematic notion of linear time in the shift from Ireland as a colony to a Free State.

The Utterance of History: Re-Telling Tales

Gayatri Chakravorty Spivak's exploration of the mechanisms and implications of appropriating alternative history or histories undermines the easy identification of rupture in the supposed transition of a society or culture from colonized to free. With a cautionary tone, she advises that "we are obliged to deal in narratives of history, even believe them," and further that "neocolonialism is a displaced repetition of many of the old lines laid down by colonialism" (272, 274). Attendant to this is the, for Spivak, necessary counterintuitive tendency to focus on repetitive negotiations within a supposed point of rupture, which therefore negates rupture as finite or even as an appropriate concept in this context. She denies the possibility of decolonization in any essential form and speaks, instead, to a neo-colonial globe in danger of supplementing a postcolonial elite. Those who appropriate alternative histories I suggest we could call "survivors," as they claim to speak for those previously subjugated or submerged by processes of historical power. Such a survivor may also, according to Spivak, unwittingly or otherwise, rehearse internal patterns of colonization within cultures in the process of re-making history, namely in the telling of that colonial history in a postcolonial context. This questioning of the definition of post-colonialism as a discrete break, or even a meaningful transition from colonialism bears significant relation to the means of representation at work in the Strokestown Famine Museum.

In the first exhibition room, "The Ascendancy," the tale seems a simple one: a basic account of the land and the succession of its owners that provides a description of the ascendancy in Ireland in general (Figure 2). The introductory panel informs visitors:

Following the Cromwellian Plantation of the 1650s, Catholics owned approximately one-tenth of the land. Thirty years earlier they had owned nearly two-thirds. One of the planters, the "adventurer" Nicholas Mahon (d.1680) was granted approximately six thousand acres at Strokestown for his services under Cromwell . . .

This text is the opening remark of the first set of freestanding panels bearing the headings "The Landed Gentry" and "The Dublin Parliament." Comprised of a brief text accompanying three illustrative images, these panels give a terse outline of their designated subjects. Clearly devised to make the specific genesis of the Strokestown estate of relevance to the economic context of the history of the famine as a whole, the text panels throughout the museum continue this pattern – leaping from the general to the specific and back again.

The first section of the panels is illustrated, inexplicably, by a reproduction of a watercolor, captioned "The Linen Hall, Dublin, 1783." The collapse of the cottage linen industry in southern Ireland in the 1820s, unable to compete with the modernization taking place in Britain and the north of Ireland, left a significant proportion of the rural communities of several counties, including Roscommon, suddenly without income or occupation (Gray, "Ideology and the Famine" 23–24). As this is not explained on the panel, the watercolor's relevance assumes a historical awareness on the part of the reader.

The following two panels devoted to "The Dublin Parliament" are illustrated with a reproduction of a garishly colored *Punch* magazine cartoon entitled "Lady Rock Settling the Half Year Account with the Tithe Prod," and a black-and-white print "The Irish House of Commons in Session, 1790." The cartoon image depicts the central figure of a caricature of Ireland as a buxom, ruddy-faced woman complete with traditional red shawl, wielding some sort of prod or whip as she grasps at a man running from her. The man must be a middleman – that is, a man who ran the estates of often absentee landlords – as he has a hat and is wearing riding boots, the likely attire of someone of a middle-income bracket. Behind them is a clergyman, hence the pun on "prod." The middleman has dropped his riding whip and a piece of paper, probably a tithe agreement, which would outline that one tenth of a laborer's income was to be paid to the church. The background is a bland rural scene, save for the obvious church spire on the right. The language of this cartoon is standard *Punch* fare – the indigenous Irish typically drawn with stocky build, exaggerated facial grimacing, enacting violent and/or, at times, drunken behavior.

Alongside this cartoon, the interior view of the Irish House of Commons in full session looks distinctly sober, with the sunlight streaming onto the chequered marbled

Figure 2 Views of "The Ascendancy", the first exhibition room (Niamh Ann Kelly, 2004).

Figure 2 (continued)

floor of James Gandon's grand chambers at College Green Dublin. The all-male members sport the requisite chamber wigs, which, along with their breeches and tapering braided jackets, clearly date the image to the eighteenth century. The upper-floor viewing galleries are full with an orderly crowd of seated onlookers. This image shows a splendid scene of politics at play: the classical symmetry of the interior is offset by the dramatic compositional trigger of a darkly dressed lone figure, presumably agitator for Catholic rights Henry Flood, who has taken the floor, standing with his hand raised in an emphatic gesture.

The presentation of these images suggests a coupling of the historical-political context of Ireland during the famine with the localized tale of Strokestown, comprised of its lists, objects, images, texts, and maps of a particular people and place. This is perhaps a necessary co-joining of two potentially disparate traditions of historiography. It is a delicate balance to attempt to weigh up the local, often personal, stories with a wider, in this case predominantly national, history. In an effort to contextualize her work on the tradition of female representations in famine literature, Margaret Kelleher refers to the alternatives set out by Paul Ricoeur, who wrote of two modes of encountering a (hi-)story: "a ruinous dichotomy between a history that would dissolve the event in explanation and a purely emotional retort that would dispense us from thinking the unthinkable" (qtd. in Kelleher 13). The first dissolution of meaning through explanation would no doubt be attendant to the more universally told history, such as that of a national or global situation, while the second denial of meaning by way of emotional retort would more likely emerge from an encounter with a personal or localized story. In a seeming contradiction, Ricoeur is further quoted by Kelleher as saying: "the more we explain in historical terms, the more indignant we become; the more we are struck by the horror of events, the more we seek to understand them." The complexities inherent to both perpetuating meaning and seeking to understand retrospectively, through a historical account, are most readily the subject of Ricoeur's comments. Kelleher is referring specifically to the individuation of famine through the portrayal of victims in literature as a necessary and sometimes effective strategy to depict horror (6). However, the tactic taken at Strokestown is potentially more illuminating, as it attempts to individuate the famine through the portrayal of perceived contributors to suffering, as well as single sufferers, such as various evictees.

In the first set of panels, the focus is primarily on providing historical context by way of introduction to the local story to come. The first of the three images presented is ostensibly a neutral historical illustration, consisting merely of a visual account of a center of business at a particular time (though its relevance is not indicated as such or otherwise). The second is a highly charged cartoon, which, both literally and metaphorically, colors the text. The third is, on close reading, equally provocative through its deceptively innocuous classicism, which masks the intensity of a fraught political situation. As three images broadly contemporary to famine times by different illustrators and artists, they present three types of representation common for the period. They are also three types of two-dimensional representations typically deployed in retrospective views of the famine, though all seem concerned with a historical explanation of a national context for the famine. In this reading, these first images utter a prelude to the localized site of famine to be revealed in this room and throughout the museum.

Discussion of these types of historical images – the illustration, the cartoon, and the watercolor/painting – and their social function occurs from different standpoints according to the visual material analyzed in the writings of scholars as diverse as Catherine Marshall, an art historian and curator; Tom Dunne, Helen Litton and Noel Kissane, historians; Margaret Crawford, social historian and Peter Gray, historian and illustration analyst. Marshall, for example, in her quest to understand the lack of artistic interest in portraying the reality of Irish life during the nineteenth century, surmises: "the problem was not the depiction of poverty . . . but rather the politicisation of that poverty in a colonised country" (49). Similarly, historian Tom Dunne, in "The Dark Side of the Irish Landscape," reflects that this gap between reality and representation was defined largely by the relationship of art to politics and to the marketplace. This dearth of evidence of artists in Ireland portraying the famine or even the general impoverishment endemic for the whole of the nineteenth century is remarkable on two counts. First, as Campbell draws attention to in his essay on the historical context of the famine, the Poor Law Inquiry of 1832 stated that some three million people were at poverty level, and later that the total population in 1841 was 8,175,124 (15). It is reasonable to assume the poverty level of these decades remained, at best, close to 35% of the population. Second, as Marshall points out, elsewhere in Europe a trend of so-called realism was emerging that depicted and even sanctified the peasant lifestyle (cf. Millet and Breton in France; Watts in Britain), while none such was manifest in Ireland. Logic surmises that had artists looked to the peasant life they would have been confronted with, and perhaps felt obliged to visualize, an unspoken poverty. In indirect response to Marshall's wondering, Dunne suggests that the Irish context was witness to a Romanticism in art, one which distracted artists with a vision of political idealism and prevented them from seeing or even looking at the peasant reality around them. Duffy offers a more mercenary explanation when writing on topographical art in Ireland in the early nineteenth century and underlines the significance of the social class of most artists and viewers. He distinguishes between viewer and viewed: "Everyday squalor and poverty would have offended most artistic eyes (and noses), and only the most dedicated illustrators faithfully recorded living conditions that were quite alien to their class" (34).

Crawford pursues a different focus on visual material relating to the Irish famine. Interrogating both the commissioning briefs and the final results of the images in *The Illustrated London News*, she emphasizes the significant discrepancy between verbal accounts, which horrified readers, and images, which broadly beautified scenes of starvation or more usually relief (75–88). Crawford also draws attention to the discrepancy between the severity of written accounts and the comparatively beautiful visual descriptions to be seen in the etchings of illustrators such as James Mahony, as well as the inaccuracy of the "human features of famine" that British readers would have been unfamiliar with. Litton, whose *The Irish Famine* comprises a concise illustrated history of the Irish famine, relies considerably on the images from the *London Illustrated News*, though contains little critical account of them.

A perhaps surprising point of view is outlined by Gray in his exploration of the political implications of the cartoons in *Punch*. He approaches these visuals as historical documents and argues that they are highly pertinent to serious retrospective consideration of the famine as they shaped contemporary perceptions as well as providing satirical commentaries where written account was absent ("Punch and the Great Famine" 26–32). Kissane adopts an all-inclusive approach as he presents a history molded from various documents, ranging from government reports and recipe lists to survey maps and drawings. His bringing together of such a variety of visual evidence suggests an equivalence of authority between illustrations and more official documents. Inadvertently, Gray also requests this parity by his declaration of *Punch* cartoons as historical documents. Such a designation is by no means typical for a historian and indicates the re-assessment of visual and material culture as evidently as useful as more traditional modes of historical record such as documents, data, statistics, and surveys.

The re-consideration of what may tell and re-tell the stories of the famine has the potential to address Spivak's provocative denial of the supposed rupture between colonial and postcolonial situations. It seems that the utterance of the traces of history presents both the possibility to rehearse a colonial pattern and the potential to transcend it. At Strokestown, the research and curatorial engagement is undoubtedly one of deep consideration that struggles between these outcomes, chiefly through two differing conceptual devices: there is the generation of a spectacle of transhistorical representation and simultaneously the promotion of a historical, ultimately local, narrative. Aspects of both broader histories and specific personal accounts are the material of each of these conceptual endeavors. Processes of forged identities and alterities come forcefully into play throughout the museum in the attempt to distinguish between these strategies of representation. The agenda at Strokestown is, it seems, to find a space for representation between Ricoeur's notions of explanation and horror and, further, to move beyond indignation toward a meaningful exploration of the conditions and outcomes of the famine. From a close reading of the first exhibition room, it becomes apparent that this exploration at Strokestown is also assumed to provide an understanding of the Irish famine that is potentially transferable across temporal and geographical conditions.

Seeing Sameness: Identity

Beyond the three images discussed above, set in a small alcove at a height of approximately five feet, is a cluster of figurines labeled "Rural Irish figures, early 20th century" and protected by a sheet of Perspex (Figure 3). Consisting of five adult figures, including a woman with a baby wrapped in her shawl, and a goat, the group stands a mere ten centimeters high. The figurines are a curiosity. Informative in terms of dress of a time some fifty to sixty years after the famine, they are made of crudely cast ceramic that is brightly colored. Atypically, each of the figures is wearing shoes. The two older-looking women wear red headscarves, the younger woman has a red skirt, and both of the men don red shirts. According to Bourke, the recurrence of red, brown, black, and dark blue clothing was common in rural Ireland (68–70). The figures are clothed almost exclusively in red- and brown-colored garments, with the exception of a blue skirt on one of the older women. Each member of the group appears to have a robust physique despite the widespread poverty in Ireland from the eighteenth up to the early twentieth century. It is commonly noted by nutritionists and historians alike that, though a perilous dependency, the potato-centered diet contributed to one of the healthiest, most nutrition-rich diets in northern Europe, giving the Irish a physical strength and longevity unusual for such poverty. The quasi-heroic stance of the figures and the bareness of their presentation – vulnerably alone in a whitewashed alcove – traps them somewhere between Jack Yeats's iconic 1957 painting *Men of Destiny* and tourist mementos incidentally placed in a serious museum setting.

Figure 3   Rural Irish figures, early 20th century (Niamh Ann Kelly, 2004).

Figure 4 A Cottier Tenant and his Family, 1830s (Niamh Ann Kelly, 2004).

Nearby, on the wall, is a framed and mounted copy of a black-and-white drawing entitled "A Cottier Tenant and his Family, 1830s" (Figure 4). The image depicts a family lying huddled beneath a blanket in front of an open hearth with a bullock tethered behind them sharing the heat. As is well accounted in various histories, the livestock would sleep at night on the hearth alongside the family, so as to make best use of the dying embers. This cottier – a farm laborer who rented land from the landlord each year – owns a chair, a table, a stool, and a dresser filled with crockery. While the rendering of each of these furnishings is individually accurate to common contemporary description, it would have been unusual for one cottier to own so many possessions. Even towards the end of the nineteenth century the ownership of a dresser was the exception rather than the norm and this amount of crockery less likely. Furthermore, were a cottier the proud owner of a full dresser, he would likely have another room for the livestock. Add to this Foster's summary of the census of 1841, which demonstrates that 40% of the Irish population lived in one-room huts and 37% lived in two- to four-room huts (334), and the discrepancies between this image and an average cottier's domestic interior are obvious.

The drawing is by Wexford landlord James Connery. His view seems to have been from a low seated position on the floor, looking upwards. The result of this unique focalization is that half of the image depicts the interior roof space, a thatch that rests on the crude brickwork of the wall. Though this image is indicated as representative of one particular reasonably well-off cottier tenant, its placement in the first room of the museum is no doubt intended to describe nineteenth-century Irish

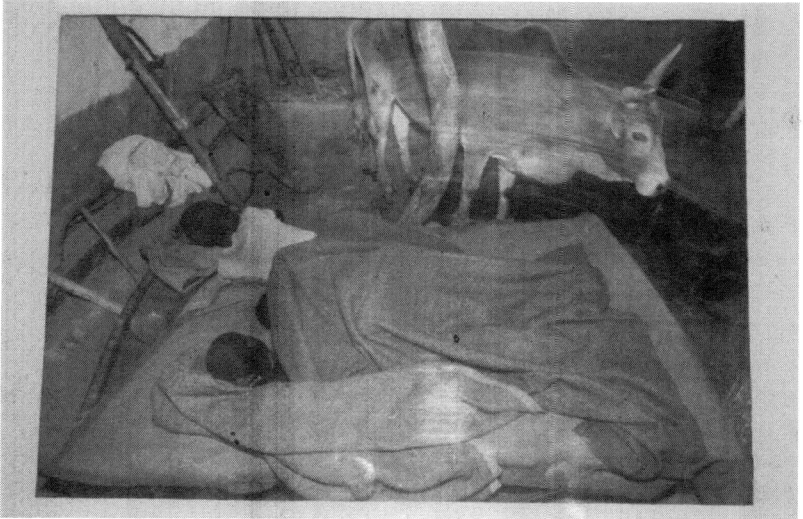

Figure 5   Eritrea, April 1991 (Niamh Ann Kelly, 2004).

poverty in general. In the interests of depicting the signs of rural life in Ireland, the choice to display this drawing here seems to compromise the more likely absence of possessions in favor of positive signifiers of rural poverty.

Hanging alongside Connery's drawing, again framed and mounted, is a color photograph, "Eritrea, April 1991" (Figure 5). On the floor of what appears to be a mud hut, three children lie beneath an old blanket on a makeshift mattress for a bed. In the background is a bullock and, resting against ochre mud walls that have been part whitewashed, are various basic farm implements, such as a hoe and a spade. The photograph has been taken looking downwards, from a standing height, with a slight fish-eye view that emphasizes the closeness of these cramped quarters. While "A Cottier Tenant and his Family, 1830s" is a black-and-white drawing, one of the most primary of visual communicative forms, the color photograph of "Eritrea, April 1991" is of the present day, or at least a more recent past. The shared compositional elements of these two images speak to the reader just as loudly as the temporal differences. The message seems clear and is echoed throughout the museum: what happened then, here, is still happening now, elsewhere. Not articulated in the text panels, it is the juxtaposition of these two images that introduces this core agenda of the museum. As noted by Mary Robinson, President of Ireland, in the Preface to the Museum book:

> Now, if we look at it thoughtfully and clearly, and with the factual assistance of this book and the Famine Museum, that past has the power to do something more: it can construct and strengthen our understanding and our sympathy in the present. (7)

There is a worthwhile comparison to be made here to a dichotomy raised by Joep Leerssen between Lessing's notions of *Nacheinander* and *Nebeneinander*, or consecutiveness and contiguousness[5]: "artistic representations can concentrate either on the spatial arrangement of objects into a spectacle, or the temporary concatenation of events into a narrative." He further relates this to the telling of history: "one way of unifying history proved to be to rearrange its consecutive events from a narrative order into a spectacle, a conspectus of juxtaposed 'freeze-frame' images" (7). At Strokestown, this two- tiered approach to (re)presentation is manifested in the curatorial choices of display that move from presenting historical narratives to creating spectacles of contemporary relativity.

That the documented historical account of the Mahon estate can be usefully brought to bear on and, in some ways, compared to the photographed present-day famines is reiterated in the exhibits. Indeed, throughout the museum, prints, paintings, and drawings of the Irish famine are juxtaposed with photographs of latter-day African famines. A similar comparison is suggested between furniture, as later in the museum a three-legged Irish stool in one room bears visual relation to an African stool or *gambur*, possibly from Somalia, in the final exhibition room. The alliance created between the past and the present assumes that visually identifying similarity can produce political, social, and economic empathy across colonial and post- or neo-colonial experiences through the recognition and formation of shared identities. The effectiveness of this utterance seems to rest primarily on the ability of the photographic image to enrapture, for, as in "Eritrea, April 1991," the supposed realism of the camera rudely takes the viewer out of the lull of distant facts and generalizations on the past.[6] This image is quiet, there is no harbinger for it; it appears alongside the historical drawing so as to change how it is seen.

Seeing Otherness: Alterity

The difficulty in visually representing the context of modern famine (invariably poverty) is created by the lack of material evidence it entails. One strategy to counter this curatorial quandary at Strokestown has been to emphasize the material wealth of the landlord class (colonizer) in contrast to the comparatively lesser possessions of the cottier class (colonized). However, it is difficult to make this distinction without actual visual cues, and so images and objects have been appropriated by the museum for this purpose.

Opposite "Eritrea, April 1991" hangs a portrait of Major Denis Mahon (Figure 6). With finely penciled detail, mounted, and gilt-framed, the drawing conveys a stately sense of poise. It is the portrait of a gentleman of property, shown seated in an armchair by his writing desk, indicated by an ink jar and quill. As per the contemporary neo-classical trend, it is a prescription three-quarter-length portrait with the sitter rendered in clear draughtsman's detail against a sketched suggestion of drapes in

Figure 6   Major Mahon (Niamh Ann Kelly, 2004).

the background. At this first encounter, Major Mahon seems slightly apprehensive, leaning uneasily in his chair, hands clasped on his crossed knee, his facial expression stern, if not a little impatient. The label on the wall beside states simply that: "Major Mahon was the cousin and heir of Maurice, Baron Hartland. He inherited the Strokestown estate in 1845 but was assassinated two years later."

The dark collar of his evening jacket is velvety in texture; his cravat, waistcoat, and jacket are all indicators of his wealth and contrast with the rural figurines on the other side of the room. His cushioned armchair belongs to a world apart from the hut interiors imaged on the wall opposite.

Between "Eritrea, April 1991" and "Major Mahon" is a free- standing panel, "After the Union," with an enlarged reproduction of an early-twentieth-century photograph of the last members of the Mahon Family (Figure 7). They are posed for a family portrait, the panel recounts, at the back of the house, over the underground tunnel built to keep servants out of view. Fashionably attired, the group is resplendent: the four women wear elaborate hats, the older man a bowtie, the younger a cravat, and the girl-child seated at the front has placed her wide-brimmed hat on the ground. The text begins: "In the late 19th century, the dominance of the Irish landed gentry diminished greatly . . ."

Figure 7   After the Union (Niamh Ann Kelly, 2004).

and concludes: "The child in the foreground is Olive Pakenham Mahon . . . Her death in 1982 brought ascendancy life in County Roscommon to an end."

In a glass case mounted higher than any other in the room rest "The 2nd Baron Hartland's Pocket Watch," its elegant winding key, and a brief printed account of the four Barons preceding the notorious Major Denis Mahon of the 1840s. The pocket watch, inscribed in 1835, is definitively a man's timepiece, and as such connotes a masculine tradition of governance where, in a country of mass poverty, such a luxury item symbolic of status and wealth was an uncommon possession. In discussing the illustrations for the *Illustrated London News*, Crawford observed: "A precise representation of famine was less important than the overall atmosphere of misery that the engravings were seeking to portray" (82). This comment identifies a common theme for historians and a conundrum for cultural analysts representing the famine. The very lack that predetermined the famine, the impoverishment that sustained it, and the absence it subsequently created, on bodily, material, and geographical levels, is apparently impossible to describe in its own terms. And so it is hardly surprising that in the first room of the Strokestown Famine Museum, the poverty of the early-nineteenth-century rural Irish population is indicated by a drawing of an interior domestic scene of the 1830s and a set of figurines of the early twentieth century, both of which show more material possessions than historians claim was typical. By prescribing a particular visual description of alterity, the museum promotes the visitor's identification with the colonized.[7]

At Strokestown, the visitor's recognition and formation of alterities – through their reading of the representations presented in the exhibits – engenders a sympathetic tone to their comprehension of the visual accounts, which ultimately encourages the appearance of a unified event or narrative. The advocacy of "seeing" poverty is further emphasized through contrast with the relative luxury of the Mahon family, to be viewed here dressed in finery, owning a big house, a plush armchair, and, not least, an elegant pocket watch.

Imaginary Orders: The Difficulty of Documentary[8]

In the center of the room, a glass case positioned at waist height displays a maquette of the sprawling townland of Gortoose/Strokestown (Figure 8). This gives a bird's eye view of what the visitor just walked through en route to the museum, putting across in miniature language the relationship between the layout of the town as it now stands and the physical extent of the estate that effectively provided its livelihood until famine times. It is near impossible to peer into this case without seeing various exhibits and panels in the room reflected in its protective glass covering. It is therefore impossible to view it without an acute awareness of what Edward Said termed the "invention of geographical space," as these representations around the room interfere with the visitors' reading of the miniature landscape in front of them.

Said first articulated the notion of imaginative geography in *Orientalism* (1978) and *Culture and Imperialism* (1993), as a concept firmly rooted in the postcolonial territorial anxieties of an imperial west. He also wrote of the constructed nature of

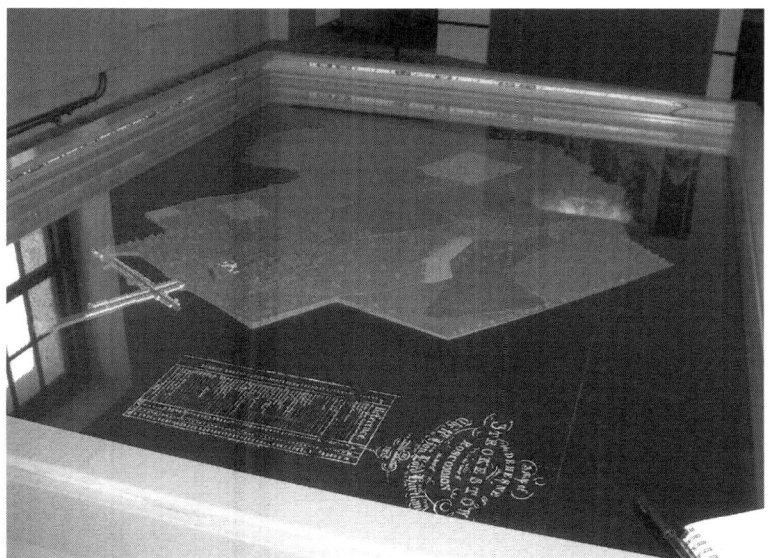

Figure 8   Maquette of Townland of Gortoose/Strokestown (Niamh Ann Kelly, 2004).

the relationship between a place and various connected traditions, such as the emergence in France of Bastille Day in 1880:

The invention of tradition is a method for using collective memory selectively by manipulating certain bits of the national past, suppressing others, elevating still others in an entirely functional way. Thus memory is not necessarily authentic, but rather useful. ("Invention" 244–5)[9]

With specific reference to Palestine, he usefully articulated that:

. . . the interplay between geography, memory, and invention, in the sense that invention must occur if there is recollection – is particularly relevant to a twentieth-century instance . . . which instances an extraordinary rich and intense conflict of at least two memories, two sorts of historical invention, two sorts of geographical imagination. ("Invention" 248)

Whilst Said wrote of still bloodily contested territory, a quieter contestation continues in post- and neo-colonial climes, to which Spivak refers in the passage quoted earlier. This negotiation of strategies of re-making history – re-telling the tales, in short, of re-claiming the past – recalls Sontag's recent proclamation on the problematic concept of memory. Sontag negated the notion of collective memory and proposed that there is only "collective instruction" (76–9). Such a statement marries well to Said's suggestion that there cannot be a neutral notion of shared memory, only constructions of identities bound, for multifarious reasons, superficially to particular spaces.

The initial indications at the Strokestown Famine Museum speak, in the first instance, directly to a post- and neo-colonial context such as Spivak evoked: public access to the gardens, parklands, and Big House are, quite literally, the "old lines" of colonial power, marked out territorially and further re-iterated in the maquette of the estate in the first exhibition room. The title of this room, "The Ascendancy," announces the intention to continue indoors the narrative of historical dominance begun en route to the museum, in the voice of its location, by the presentation of objects, text, and visuals as documentary evidence. Within the galleries, the narrative becomes more cluttered as the devices of colonial difference are overtly reversed – albeit intentionally, in the way Homi Bhabha might describe as "a sense of the new as an insurgent act of cultural translation" (7) – to project "otherness" onto the colonizer re-membered. Meanwhile, seeing "sameness" through reading visual similarity engenders the affiliation of momentarily constructed identities across geographical, temporal, and cultural divides. These visually cued translations of objects, images, and histories are together intended to transcend the problem of documenting an event defined by absence, by emphasizing visible tangible signs and, in doing so, to make suffering appear.

Acknowledgments. All images by the author, by kind permission of the Famine Museum Strokestown Park. Thanks to Catherine Marshall, for access to her research files, and to Tom Dunne.

Notes

1. This stereotype is frequently contested by various historiographers, from as early as Maria Edgeworth writing in 1847 (Kelleher 130). By contrast, the writings of Donnelly, which chronicle various evictions countrywide during the famine, are difficult to ignore as evidence of widespread attitudes and actions that mirror those of Major Mahon at Strokestown ("Mass Eviction" 155–173; *Great Irish Potato Famine* 132–168). The differentiation between guilty and blameless landlords is but one aspect of the greater conflict between what are typically perceived as more nationalistic-driven histories and self-consciously revisionist histories, such as the 1994 anthology *The Great Famine: Studies in Irish Histories, 1845–52*, edited by R.D. Edwards and T.D. Williams. Most post-revisionist accounts tend to acknowledge the inheritance of this controversy and overtly state their various viewpoints at the outset. See, for example, Ó'Gráda; Donnelly.

2. Further to this, Brawne writes of the art museum: "Art and the temple have a long association . . . but the temple . . . was a place of social significance open to the public as part of a ritual which went beyond everyday experience" (17), and Lorente, in *Cathedrals of Urban Modernity*, likens the generic art museum to "an urban cathedral."

3. In this instance, their focus is specifically on the princely art collections, which were, nominally at least, replaced by those of public ownership with the rise of modern nation-hood. Hence, the viewing subject became the reading citizen.

4. Stallabrass provides an insightful account of the Vauxhall Pleasure Gardens in London, which I am taking as a generic type (170–207). Bennett explores the complexities of the museum-fair polemic in relation to the concept of the amusement park (3–4).

5. Leerssen discusses the permutations of the relationship between these two concepts with respect to literature and, in particular, the writings and imagery of James Joyce.

6. Sontag presents a thoughtful account of the relationship between photography and memory when she writes that, by comparison to non-stop stream imagery, "the photograph has the deeper bite. Memory freeze-frames; its basic unit is the single image . . . the photograph is like a quotation, or a maxim or proverb" (19).

7. This is not always the case in retrospective representations of the famine, as exemplified in one parallel literary analysis where the axis of difference has been identified in reverse. Kelleher discusses the relationship between the Big House and famine as portrayed in some such early-twentieth-century literature. She emphasizes an agenda often apparent in this genre, as evident in Edith Somerville's 1925 *The Big House of Inver*, where an effort is made to re-write the roles played by the landlord class during the famine. For example, she notes: "Within the genre of Big House writing and its representations of famine recurs a striking motif: the encounter between upper-class woman and poor peasant in which food is exchanged for disease. The giver of fever, the 'other' from whom contagion is received, is cast in shadow; the heroic ancestor is named and remembered" (134).

8. The notion of imaginary orders is alluded to in Donald Preziosi's essay "Brain of the Earth's Body: Museums and the Framing of Modernity," a critique of curatorial authority in museum and gallery practice. The idea of documentary in film and its difficult affiliation to interpretative practice is discussed by Trinh T. Minh-Ha in "The Totalizing Quest of Meaning."

9. The term "Invention of tradition" refers of course to ideas discussed in Hobsbawn and Ranger's anthology *The Invention of Tradition*.

Bibliography

Bennett, Tony. *The Birth of the Museum*. New York: Routledge, 1995.

Bhabha, Homi K. *The Location of Culture*. London: Routledge, 1994.

Bourke, Marie. "Rural Life in Pre-Famine Connacht: A Visual Document." *Ireland: Art into History*. Ed. Brian P. Kennedy and Raymond Gillespie. Dublin: Town House & Country House, 1994. 61–74.

Brawne, Michael. "Museums – Mirrors of Their Time?" *The Architectural Review* CLXXV (February 1984): 17–9.

Campbell, Stephen J. *The Great Irish Famine: Words and Images from the Famine Museum Strokestown Park, County Roscommon*. Roscommon: The Famine Museum, 1994.

Crawford, Margaret. "The Great Irish Famine 1845–9: Image Versus Reality." *Ireland: Art into History*. Ed. Brian P. Kennedy and Raymond Gillespie. Dublin: Town House & Country House, 1994. 75–88.

Donnelly Jr., James S. *The Great Irish Potato Famine*. Stroud: Sutton Publishing Ltd., 2001.

———. "Mass Eviction and the Great Famine." *The Great Irish Famine: The Thomas Davis Lecture Series*. Ed. Cathal Póirtéir. Cork: Mercier Press, 1995. 155–73.

Duffy, P.J. "The Changing Rural Landscape 1750–1850: Pictorial Evidence." *Ireland: Art into History*. Ed. Brian P. Kennedy and Raymond Gillespie. Dublin: Town House & Country House, 1994. 26–42.

Duncan, Carol, and Alan Wallach. "The Universal Survey Museum." *Art History* 3 (1980): 448–69.

Dunne, Tom. "The Dark Side of the Irish Landscape: Depictions of the Rural Poor, 1760–1850." *Whipping the Herring: Survival and Celebration in Nineteenth-Century Irish Art*. Ed. Peter Murray. Cork: Crawford Art Gallery & Gandon Editions, 2006. 46–59.

Edwards, R.D., and T.D. Williams, eds. *The Great Irish Famine: Studies in Irish Histories, 1845–52*. Dublin: Lilliput Press, 1994.

Foster, Roy. *Modern Ireland, 1600–1972*. London: Penguin, 1988.

Gray, Peter. "Ideology and the Famine." *The Great Irish Famine: The Thomas Davis Lecture Series*. Ed. Cathal Póirtéir. Cork: Mercier Press, 1995. 86–103.

———. "Punch and the Great Famine." *History Ireland* 1.2 (Summer 1993): 26–32.

Hobsbawn, Eric, and Terence Ranger, eds. *The Invention of Tradition*, Cambridge: Cambridge UP, 1983.

Kelleher, Margaret. *The Feminization of Famine: Expressions of the Inexpressible?* Cork: Cork UP, 1997.

Kissane, Noel. *The Irish Famine: A Documentary History*. Dublin: The National Library of Ireland, 1995.

Leerssen, Joep. *Remembrance and Imagination: Patterns in the Historical and Literary Representation of Ireland in the Nineteenth Century*. Cork: Cork UP, 1996.

Litton, Helen. *The Irish Famine: An Illustrated History*. Dublin: Wolfhound Press, 1994.

Lorente, J. Pedro. *Cathedrals of Urban Modernity: The First Museums of Contemporary Art*. Aldershot: Ashgate, 1998.

Marshall, Catherine. "Painting Irish History: The Famine." *History Ireland* 4.3 (Autumn 1996): 46–50.

Minh-Ha, Trinh T. "The Totalizing Quest of Meaning." *The Postmodern Arts*. Ed. Nigel

Wheale. London/New York: Routeledge, 1995. 258–78.

Ó'Gráda, Cormac. "The Great Famine and Today's Famines." *The Great Irish Famine: The Thomas Davis Lecture Series*. Ed. Cathal Póirtéir. Cork: Mercier Press, 1995. 248–58.

Pearce, Susan. *On Collecting*. London: Routledge, 1995.

Preziosi, Donald. "Brain of the Earth's Body: Museums and the Framing of Modernity." *The Rhetoric of the Frame: Essays on the Boundaries of the Artwork*. Ed. Paul Duro. Cambridge: Cambridge UP, 1996. 96–110.

Robinson, Mary. "Preface." *The Great Irish Famine: Words and images from the Famine Museum Strokestown Park, County Roscommon*. Ed. Stephen J. Campbell. Roscommon: The Famine Museum, 1994. 7.

Said, Edward. *Orientalism*. London: Penguin, 1978.

———. *Culture and Imperialism*. London: Vintage, 1993.

———. "Invention, Memory and Place." *Landscape and Power*. Ed. W.J.T. Mitchell. Chicago: U of Chicago P, 2002. 241–59.

Sontag, Susan. *Regarding the Pain of Others*. London: Penguin Books, 2003.

Spivak, Gayatri Chakravorty. "Who Claims Alterity?" *Remaking History: Discussions in Contemporary Culture*. Ed. Barbara Kruger and Phil Mariani. Washington: Bay Press/Dia Art Foundation, 1989. 269–92.

Stallabrass, Julian. "A Place of Pleasure: Woodwork, Vauxhall Spring Gardens and Making Audiences for Art." *Occupational Hazard: Critical Writing on Recent British Art*. Ed. Duncan McCorquodale, Naomi Siderfin, and Julian Stallabrass. London: Black Dog, 1998. 170–207.

III. Rethinking Origins and Indigeneity

Resignifying Genesis, Identity, and Landscape: Routes versus Roots

Anette Hoffmann

Introduction

> *Roots, I sometimes think are a conservative myth,*
> *designed to keep us in our places.*
> (Rushdie 86)

> *Tribal groups have, of course, never been simply "local," they have always been*
> *rooted and routed in particular landscapes, regional and interregional networks.*
> (Clifford, "Diasporas" 310)

Michael Taussig has asked: if "most of what seems important in life is made up and is neither more (nor less) than, as a certain turn of phrase would have it, 'a social construction' . . . why don't we start inventing?" (xv–xv). What if people already do, especially where theory and poesis are so inextricably interwoven that we cannot separate the practice of articulation from its theoretical implications, as John and Jean Comaroff (1987) have suggested? This is not to argue for the continuous and unregulated re-telling of history in societies where the social texture of life is or was constituted by oral texts.[1] The interpretation of history (everywhere) changes with(in) societal discourse, and, where landscape is closely tied to these constructions, so does the landscape. Perhaps the idea of the social constructedness of life – as of landscape, identities, history, and the like – is not altogether new or strange to a society where a conversational poetics of social construction as that which molds and makes a person, and as that which is constantly negotiated, is common cultural practice; a practice that is neither veiled nor naturalized but, instead, is seen as the medium for the ongoing production of the being-as-becoming of social existence.

This essay explores the re-construction of a landscape of origin by means of the replacement of one genesis story with another by Ovaherero in Namibia. This radical shift in the terms of an articulation of landscape and identity took place under the duress of apartheid, where people drew on and retold the origins of their community in order to socially survive the epistemic and physical violence of the regime, but also in order to think of their community in an altered way. Whereas in the older genesis story the notion of continuity and rootedness connected to ancestry stood at the center, the newer story emphasizes the deliberate choice to travel. In the latter story, mobility as well as collective journey marks the beginning of cultural identity and the origin of the Ovaherero community.

The more recent story, which came to circulate during the time of the South African regime in Namibia, deploys the notion of a community as mobile yet routed. This story, I suggest, enabled the community to at once construct another past and create an agreeable present. Moreover, it created a self-representation that allowed the community to think beyond the impasse of racist definitions of "locals." As will be shown later on, this narration of genesis is still constitutive within the discursive field of social identification of Herero communities in Namibia.

The Voiced Landscape

In order to explore how and why a story of migration became the dominant narration of origin within the Herero communities of Namibia, an understanding of the specific textual and performative construction of the landscape and identity that Ovaherero people regard as their own is crucial. The Otjiherero-speaking communities in Namibia refer to themselves as OvaHerero (Herero people); they are seen and regard themselves as a single ethnic group with a shared cultural background and language within the multiethnic society of Namibia. Within the cultural productions of the Otjiherero-speaking communities, orature has a prominent position. Annemarie Heywood gives a lucid definition of orature as comprising much more than praise poetry, oral history, and folktales:

By orature we mean the whole body of art, science, history and philosophy by which a speech community gives meaning to itself and its world, which is not stored in print but in human minds. . . . Orature depends on a succession of human carriers and is "published" in specific social contexts. (qtd. in Kavari, "Form and Meaning" 1)

Initially constructed by orature, the landscape of the OvaHerero is not to be seen but, instead, is performed by signifying speech acts and constructed by recitations of praise poetry. Landscape, in this case, is a cultural activity of poetic construction based on words, voices, and poetic artworks rather than on visible objects like pictures, paintings, photographs, or films.[2] In order to come to an understanding of the landscape the OvaHerero construct, a change of conceptualizing registers is necessary; we need to move from privileging the visual to an emphasis on the auditory, which is transmitted by the human voice in sung and spoken performances of praise poetry.

The OvaHerero community shares a mainly orally transmitted textual culture that produces and reproduces a social and aesthetic landscape. Every named settlement, but also graves, wells, and borders, are characterized, conserved, and mapped within praise poetry. This practice of naming and identifying entails the textual signification of usufruct rights. Within this system of signification, omitandu (singular omutandu, related to the verb okutanga, to praise), or praise poems, were and to some extent still are the poetic transmitters of a system of land allocation. In pre-colonial times the scheme of land rights as mediated by omitandu had legal status for the members of the OvaHerero communities. There was thus clearly an instrumental dimension to praise poetry, since the texts were used to consolidate a socio-economic pattern of land use. Whereas land allocation was seen as rightfully achieved by the settler who initially appropriated an area, for his heirs the right to stay on and use the land was established by means of a praise poem that was composed at the event of the burial of the first settler. By means of the omutandu composed for the deceased, he (or sometimes she) was characterized in relation to the landscape and poetically lodged in it. Within this omitandu, which was created during the death lament, genealogies and territories were tied together. The ties to the land were thus not simply inherited, but enacted by means of the iterated performative speech acts that were memorialized and thereby guaranteed the poetics of relation they established.

Hence, if one could state a beginning to all Otjiherero praise poems, this beginning would be related to a person's death. The praise poems for a settlement or place would then be based on this omutandu for the first deceased of the area. Today, praise poetry continues to articulate a network of relations between genealogies and territories; that is, it constructs people's history as specifically located, but also as related to cattle, which are often mentioned in place of their owners. A vast textual network is created by means of cross-referencing between the texts, but also through the mode of accumulating stanzas. In this way, poetry is interwoven into a body of orature that creates a socially and historically significant space. The area that, even today, is often referred to as ehi rOvaherero, the land of the OvaHerero, is therefore filled with a network of related and specifically located genealogies.[3]

Located Identities

Places and the landscape of the Ovaherero have survived colonization through these acts of re-signifying cultivation. I use the notion of cultivation here in the sense of artfully culturalizing the environment into a landscape that appears to consist of a similar texture or thread, to borrow Clifford Geertz's image of culture as a web, as that which provides elements of the fabric from which cultural identities are constructed.[4]

This may sound like an oversimplifying systematic and, indeed, orature is not an all-encompassing meaning-producing machine.

What I wish to establish by means of the image of the web that people spin for themselves is the notion of an interacting, communicating fabric of social practice that embraces the making of landscape and personal identities alike: not only does orature characterize and identify people and landscapes, but the same *omitandu* elementarily signify people as tied to the landscape and the landscape as essentially connected to people. Thus, the mode of production is similar and the oral texts interact, building a flexible body or network of texts that identifies places and people, enabling the Herero communities to think, narrate, and perform places and people as intrinsically interconnected. It is, therefore, the collective activity of performing, speaking, and remembering that transforms the land from a physical environment into a landscape of meaning and beauty, harboring the experiences of the past and invested with the ability to speak this past in the present. I regard Herero productions of landscape as at once social constructions and artworks. The landscapes created in this way provide the process and vehicle that focus interpretations of the past in the present and that mediate current and historical articulations of identity. It is for this reason that the change from one narration of origin to another is telling: it speaks about a re-definition of collective identity.

This is not to say that orature today, or in the past, equips OvaHerero with a general, all-encompassing means to work out identities. Instead, orature is but one element in the process of building up personal identities within the "relational positioning [that] is the work of culture" (Clifford, "Identity Politics" 95). Elements that provide the fabric of what OvaHerero see as their identity may stem from irreducibly specific local sources and the societal interactions mediated by local cultural practice, but they are also – like everywhere else – informed by enactments of sameness and difference, as performed by the consumption and display of "branded commodities," lifestyles, income, and education – in short, all the elements that are part of social interaction within societies in a globalized world.

The reason I bring up orature as an element of the figuration of identities in relation to landscapes is that I seek to explore the closeness between landscape and personal as well as collective identities as cultural constructions. If we understand orature as bestowed with the suturing efficacy to link articulations of identity to specific locations, the issue is not how orature reflects on identities, but how it produces them together with a landscape of meaning. This suturing efficacy of orature can be described as a form of articulation in Stuart Hall's sense. Hall assigns the term "articulation" a twofold meaning: it signifies uttering or expressing, but also a strategic bringing together of elements that do not necessary belong together at a specific place and time:

> *An articulation is thus the form of connection that can make a unity of two different elements, under certain conditions. It is a linkage which is not necessary, determined, absolute and essential for all time.* ("Who Needs Identity?" 141)

In line with this, the proximity of landscape and people does not speak for an ecological narrative of natural ties to the land. Instead, what I want to stress is a specific articulated closeness, established by cultural practices that counter the construction of landscape as that which is completely outside the self. In her work about landscape and nature conceptions within artworks in the Western world, Petra Halkes writes:

> *Through centuries of Western culture, landscape has provided an attractive screen for the projection of desire to transcend the inadequate self into a larger, seemingly boundless entity. "Landscape" indicates a human conception of nature: it is generally defined as that what the human eye can encompass at a given time and place, of "nature," which always exceeds the landscape. In the Western tradition "nature" embraces a seemingly infinite accumulation of objects that are* outside the self. (8, emphasis added)

The concept of landscape has to travel quite a bit here: from that which can be seen, acts as a screen for projection, and is conceptualized as outside of the self, as Halkes describes it, to a landscape that is spoken, performed, heard, and belongs to the cultural text in which the narrated self as part of a relational social construction is located.

Another important aspect in the construction of Herero landscapes is the notion of time. If the existence of every place of meaning begins with a speech act of orature – one that names, claims, and characterizes – and if this act of signification is connected to deceased community members whose life gave meaning to the places, then both performing *omitandu* and listening to it enacts a landscape that is steeped in history. For the Herero, therefore, landscape is not encompassed at "a given time and place" but always extends into the past of the communities. The same is true for a notion of identity as intrinsically linked to specific locations. A change within the cultural construction of identity must therefore expand into the past and we must analyze orature as merging the present and the past; that is, as producing a meaningfully located present by means of conjuring a collective past, as well as the communities' memories and historiology.

Creating a Different Past

During my visit to Namibia in 2004, the year in which the colonial war of the German *Schutztruppe* against Herero and Nama communities (1904–1907) was commemorated all over the country, I had the chance to interview Usiel Kandji, one of the organizers of an exhibition on Herero history in Namibia. The exhibition was set up by members of one of the commemoration committees and took place in Katutura, a former township of Windhoek.[5] One of the topics of the exhibition was the migration of the Herero community to Namibia. To my questions about this, Usiel Kandji answered:

> Nobody knows exactly when and from where the Ovaherero came to Namibia. But our oral tradition agrees upon an exact point of entrance into what is now Namibia: A place called Okarundu Kambeti. This is transmitted through orature. Herero people came to Namibia some 500 years ago. They came together as a group via Angola from the Great Lakes area of East Africa.

This recent story of origin, invested with the authority of orature, has replaced another one that was also transmitted orally. Both revolve around origins, but with different images, metaphorical contents, and, I suggest, different agendas. In the following, I will compare these stories in order to explore Herero constructions of origin, from which not only claims to the land derive, but to which, albeit less explicitly, different definitions of identity are also tied. The aim of the comparison is to analyze why and under which circumstances one story became inappropriate and another one was regarded as more productive in the theorizing of identity.

The OvaHerero communities living in Namibia do not claim indigeneity in the sense of firstness in the region. The nationally accepted reading of Namibian history clearly puts the San of Namibia in the position of "first people." The Otjiherero name for this group is *Ovakuhura*, which loosely translated means "first people" or "people who have always been here."[6] Present-day Herero discourses narrate their community's origin as a story of traveling, dwelling in different places, war, interdependencies, and tensions with other groups. The versions of the modern myth of origin say that the community came to central Namibia from another area, searching for new regions to graze their cattle. The locations vary in different versions. In all cases, however, the story begins with travel. The origin of the Herero as a community or ethnic entity is thereby extended into an even more distant past, a past that cannot be known.

This was not always the case. The existence of a presumably older narration of origin that was replaced by the currently privileged one speaks for the flexibility of the Herero community in its selective and decisive restructuring of the symbolization of origins and continuity. In older descriptions of Herero culture by anthropologists and missionaries, the poetic myth of coming out of the Omumborongbonga tree appears to be the Herero story of origin as told by themselves. In this story, which also exists in different versions, Mukuru, which means "the old one," and his wife Kamungarunga, are the ancestors of all Ovaherero. In all versions, Mukuru and Kamungarunga descend from the tree. Two central motifs are important for the comparison with the more recent narration of origin that begins with travel: the tree as an evocative symbol of rootedness and the notion of ancestral origin. The tree appears in all versions of the Omumborongbonga story I draw upon, but the notion of genealogy, which explains relatedness and difference, varies in different versions. Whereas in Brincker's written account the people who descend from the tree are referred to as *ovandu*, which means people or men in general, in the versions of Vedder, Katjivena, Irle and Köhler it is not clear whether people in general or specifically Ovaherero are meant.[7]

However, in the two versions written down by Irle (1907) and the one published by Katjivena (1988) the distinctiveness of the Ovaherero is established in different ways. In the story as retold by Katjivena, the grandcaughters of Mukuru and Kamungarunga are the ancestral mothers of different ethnic groups. Kazu, the mother of the Herero, is married to Ndeo and they become pastoralists, whereas the descendants of Nangombe, the other granddaughter, are the Oshivambo-speaking groups. The presence of men who did not descend from the tree and are not related to these two women suggests that the story does not speak about the genesis of people in general, but about that of a group of people with a common origin. The same holds for one of Irle's versions, in which the ancestral couple descends from the tree together with the cattle, whereas other people (the so-called Bergdamara) descend from a rock together with other animals, small stock, and baboons. In the second version written down by Irle, a difference between groups is established, but only after the birth from the tree. Here, black (Herero) and red (Nama) people gain their skin color through eating different parts of a cow that is slaughtered to celebrate the birth of the first daughter. Although the people who turn red are not related to the ones who will be the Herero, the difference emerges belatedly, not through birth. The stories thus deal with origin and the emergence of difference. But the notion of difference itself is established in various ways, which appear to be conflicting in terms of the mode by which this difference is constituted.

Although the stories were written down between 1886 and 1988, it is difficult to date their emergence or define periods in which different variations were popular. As with most orature, authorship is not relevant and thus not referred to. Further, different versions of the stories may have existed synchronously and thus do not allow the privileging of a dominant version. Dealing with versions that variously focus on difference or commonness of ancestry and versions that do not mention other communities at all, I cannot retrieve a discourse that accounts for a common position in terms of distinctive communities. What can be said, though, is that, whether related to other groups or completely distinct from them, a common ancestry of all Herero is constituted. This ancestry is tied to a region in the north either Kaoko or Ovamboland (again depending on the version).

Asked about this story in 1999 and 2000, the reactions of Herero people were often mildly amused, suggesting that my question showed nothing more than my naivety. Recalling the situations in which I asked these questions about the

Omunborongbonga tree now, the situation seems to be comparable to asking people in Amsterdam, say, in the tram, about Adam, Eve, and the snake. James Weiner writes that myths of origin "ask the listener to consider things that cannot possibly have an origin" (387). They provide a symbolical language with a set of images that codify established relations of difference between groups of people or origins that cannot possibly be known *post facto*. Thus, even if both the Omumborongbonga myth and the one that succeeded it do not represent what may count for real, their allegorical language and contents may be seen as more or less appropriate to symbolizing origin and establishing a meaningful relation between the current life-world and its beginnings. What interests me here, therefore, is the conflicting discursive relation between different stories of origin, including scholarly views of the ethnogenesis of the Herero.

Asking about the Omumborongbonga tree in 1999 in Namibia, nobody seemed to know or would tell the story. Instead, I was told that Herero people came to Namibia some five hundred years ago. Only later did I learn from Dag Henrichsen, a Namibian historian, that until the 1980s older men used to visit Omumborongbonga trees on a farm in north-west Namibia. The farmer told Henrichsen that the men would stay near the trees for a couple of days to "discuss things." What exactly was discussed and which function the trees had in this, he did not know. Though the trees may therefore retain some importance, as a story of origin the Omumborongbonga tale has been replaced. Taking both stories into account, the question is not which is more authentic or traditional. If re-placing one teleology of origin with another is part of a politics of articulation in which different "elements of tradition get hooked onto elements of modernity," and then "these hybrid elements get re-connected with elements from the past – notions of kinship, place, revived tradition – to construct current forms of indigeneity" (Clifford, "Identity Politics" 1), the notion of authenticity has to be given up altogether. Rather, what interests me here is the notion of conjunctures: the selective, transformative creation of meaning as representing and producing current conditions of life.

Consequently, I suggest that both stories belong to the mythic idioms of a cultural archive. Johannes Fabian writes that Foucault's notion of the archive

might help to find an alternative to an oversimplified concept of culture as the depository of beliefs and values. According to Foucault the archive is not the sum of all texts of a culture; nor does it designate the institutions, which record and preserve texts. Rather, it "is the first law of what can be said, the system that governs the appearance of statements as unique events." (91)

Defining what can be said and specifying how it can be said, this notion of the archive creates a certain regulation of discourses, but it does not completely obstruct transformative or manipulative conduct. Instead, it "enables statements both to survive and undergo regular modification" (Foucault 130). Looking at a process of societal transformation, the concept of the archive limits the notion of invention, yet at the same time allows for radical re-signification; in this case, it allows for the creative replacement of a founding myth with a more adequate narration. Thus, the archive is both resource and restriction; it allows for re-imagination and a selective use of elements within a cultural practice in the process of symbolic production, but "with inherited resources and not under the circumstances of our own choosing" (Gilroy 127).

With this in mind, I return to the question of conjunctures. If the process of cultural change in the (post)colony is not just a series of "breakdowns of 'traditional culture'; and [is] not made up of ill- or half-understood 'reactions' to the onslaught of Westernisation" (Fabian 19), how are we to understand this radical shift from roots to routes? With respect to the change of tropes from a community whose ancestors descended from a tree to a community that decided to travel thousands of miles, the inevitable question is why and under which circumstances one story replaced the other.

Both stories belong to the realm of orature. They are cultural productions that reflect and articulate social processes and conditions of life. Their preservation or disappearance is selective but never accidental, mirroring what people regard as vital. If "nothing survives without someone's conscious decision that it should" (Miller 12), forgetting as the other side of remembering implies agency as well. Moreover, orature as a genre of re-told or versioned narrations comprises a certain flexibility, a capacity for creative transformation, as performers ingeniously react to the situational context and alter the stories.[8] If the forgetting or vanishing of an entire story of origin, together with the disappearance of an evocative symbol, is not accidental, there are grounds for the assumption that this symbol of natural rootedness must have lost its value as identificatory imagery at a certain point. I suggest that the multifarious forms through which people construct, remember, and lay claim to places or origins must be seen in the light of their history, but also provide clues about the politics inherent in these constructions.

The Omumborongbonga tree, located and rooted in the remote north-west of Namibia, evokes a notion of immobility, a natural tied-ness to a certain territory and soil. As a result of the forced sedentariness of the Herero communities under apartheid – their virtual incarceration in the reserves – as well as their opposition to these restrictions on their mobility, the image of a tree as a point of origin, that is, of spatio-temporal stasis as "natural" and therefore given, may no longer have been "good to think with." While the Omumborongbonga myth likely had other, more complex implications for the Ovaherero communities themselves, it may have come too close to the discourses and practical restrictions of the apartheid regime, which maintained and forcefully manifested a concept of native culture as rooted, stable, and territorially segmented.

Anthropological discourse, which often naturalized the locatedness of the so-called natives, problematically served to translate indigenous claims upon territories into a physical belonging to certain areas. In this way, Arjun Appadurai notes, natives became "not only persons who are from certain places, and belong to those places, but . . . those who are somehow incarcerated, or confined, in those places" (qtd. in Malkki 29). Such a naturalization of belonging implied an ideal adaptation to a specific ecological environment, which again connects ethnic communities to a territory in a language of biology. A typical example of this convergence of biological and anthropological discourses in a conceptual fusion that suggests the comparability of ethnic groups with biological species can be found in J.S. Malan's *Peoples of Namibia*; although characterizing "the Herero" as nomadic pastoralists, the schematic description begins with the heading "natural environment," under which the geography and vegetation of "Hereroland" are depicted.[9]

The justification of the spatial incarceration of the so-called natives operated through connecting notions of territoriality with the distinctive ascription of the native's status based on his or her "race." The politics of territorializing race and culture under apartheid entailed a moral discourse that pathologized so-called up-rootedness: mobile people, willing to leave the place the colonial regime had designated for them, where regarded as detached from the location defined as the natural environment of their culture, and therefore regarded as a danger to the project of civilization. Liisa Malkki has pointed out that sedentarist metaphors like "natural rootedness" operate to re-affirm the partitioning of space into neat segments perceived as distinctive territories of nations, cultures, or, as in this case, races (31). In colonial Namibia, mobility, if only for the so-called natives, was linked to amorality and the loss of "tribal" culture.

Thus, not only did the notion of travel as the origin of a distinct cultural identity (discursively) transgress the discrete spatial partitioning of the territory, but the intentional deracination of the older genesis story also mobilized the collective past in the mode of re-locating the origin of the community in the event of a collective journey. Unmooring the narration of origin from its spatio-temporal metaphor of rootedness, the alternative story produced an insurgent re-signification of origin: it rejected apartheid's definition of natives as locals, along with its essentialist ascriptions of natural origin and innate place-boundedness, by means of privileging the socio-economic, cultural practice of traveling. Hence, the more recent story of origin, which begins with a collective journey, replaces the notion of the givenness of a natural origin with an emphasis on a cultural practice that implies choice and mobility as opposed to stasis, and thus stresses history and agency. Further, the currently privileged narration of origin promotes a version of history that stresses cultural continuity rather than ancestral origin. According to the recent story, the Herero arrived in Namibia as a distinct community, in some versions coming from the area of the

Great Lakes in East Africa. Searching for a region to graze their cattle, the group split up in the area of today's Angola, where a part of the community stayed and became agriculturalists, whereas the others traveled further towards the south.[10]

At first sight, this narration seems to be a delayed adaptation to the privileged scholarly reading of history as enunciated by missionaries and anthropologists since the nineteenth century.[11] However, historians have come to doubt this version in the last decades, deconstructing the view of ethnic groups as neatly distinguishable and static. Jan-Bart Gewald, revising his own findings, writes:

The work presented by Henrichsen suggests the existence of a particular pastoralist stratum in the central Namibian highlands at the beginning of the 19th century. Essentially they shared a set of core ideas regarding, relating to and revolving around the ownership of cattle and a pastoralist economy. It was in drawing upon this, as yet ethnically undefined, stratum that Herero society developed, in the second half of the 19th century. Consequently the "Herero" did not come wandering into Namibia from the Great Lakes region over the course of the 16th century. (188, emphasis added)

From the perspective of both discourses – the early scholarly one of the missionaries, which promoted the idea of wandering tribes, as well as the current, mainly historical line of argumentation, which considers Herero ethnicity as a formation of the late nineteenth century – the contemporary Herero narration of origin could easily be discarded as unquestionably essentialist and backwards. But things are not that simple.

A closer look at the contemporary version of the myth of origin circulating within Herero communities makes clear that although some elements could stem from the theory of the "wandering tribes" as told by the missionary Hahn, the narration also emphasizes other aspects. The Herero's specific version indicates an evaluative re-articulation of the theory pioneered by Hahn and perpetuated in the writings of other missionaries, which emphasized the notion of racial difference and drew on the assumption that the Herero were of Hamitic ancestry and therefore clearly distinguishable from the "Negro-type."[12] In the versions of the narration of origin I came across in Namibia, however, a relation to the Oshivambo-speaking communities, which according to some of the missionaries would have belonged to the Negro-type, is established: the community split up in the north and some of the people became peasants. According to Alexander Kaputu, who is a local historian and probably the community's most prominent interpreter of Herero culture in Namibia, the close relation between the two ethnic groups is evident from the similarity of the languages spoken by them. The link that is established between the communities thus articulates both a proximity of languages and a difference in terms of socio-economic lifestyles: the shared cultural identity claimed for the Herero as a community is thus not an absolute (racial) difference but an alterity of socio-cultural practice. Furthermore, the notion of racial superiority, as deployed by missionary Vedder and his colleagues, is absent in the Herero versions I found. This means that although the story of origin may have been influenced by scholarly discourses of the nineteenth century, it does not draw on the same categories, but has been fundamentally altered through the re-signifying practice of orature. The differences deployed within the stories reflect on the radical incongruity between the politics of the OvaHerero communities and those of the colonial regime.

The representational function of the narration sheds light on the question of why elements of an older scholarly grand narration are privileged over the recent historical deconstruction of the origin of ethnic categories. I assume that, much like the current critique of tribalism, the discussions of ethnogenesis and the deconstruction of primordial ethnicity have not passed by the Herero communities unnoticed. Yet, recent anti-essentialist academic characterizations of Herero culture as a relatively current construction are actively rejected. What is at stake in establishing an authoritative narration of origin is the emergence of what I understand as "strategic theory." With this term I designate the selective appropriation-cum-transformation of discursive elements for identity politics under historically identifiable conditions. It inevitably implies the requisition of the power to define the self.

As in many cases where *omitandu* provide an alternative reading and making of public history vis-à-vis colonial inscription, the power of the narrative functions to promote alternative realities or life worlds. Salman Rushdie writes:

[R]edescribing a world is the necessary first step to changing it. And particularly at times when the state takes reality into its own hands, and sets about distorting it, altering the past to fit the present needs, then the making of the alternative realities of art, including the novel of memory, becomes politicized. (qtd. in Murphy 38)

In the case of the Herero narration of origin, this connotes that even if elements have been taken from a missionary-colonial grand narrative, the form, content, and meaning have been transfigured. The recent narration of origin expands a notion of continuity and communal cohesion into a pre-colonial past, no longer by means of a metaphor of rootedness but by narrating the historical praxis of mobility as well as asserting a deliberate choice for a certain territory.

By strategically emphasizing continuity, the Herero community insists on a self-representation that is *not* the result of the epistemic power of the colonial state. Instead, collective identity is constituted within Otjiherero orature; invested with the authority of oral texts, collective identity is grounded in the community's version of history and oral self-representation. Replacing the older myth of origin with a narration of origin that begins with travel and a community's deliberate choice for a pastoralist lifestyle of mobility, the recent story of origin can be seen as the product of a resignifying practice that extends into the past. Since this mobile way of life was constrained by colonial law and by the restrictions imposed during the colonial war of 1904–1907 and thereafter, the story comments on the forced alienation from a mobile way of life and the disappropriation of the land under colonialism.

Today, mobility forms a central trope in Herero orature; most of the life stories that are constructed by and within the textual web of orature stress the notion of life as travel. In these accounts of the history of prominent members of the community, mobility denotes sovereignty, social status, but also bravery and wisdom; in short, all ingredients that make "lives worth narrating." Traveling freely in the region is referred to a social practice that signifies and perhaps sometimes romanticizes pre-war conditions of life. Speaking to the colonial situation, the restriction of mobility becomes the condensed image for the restriction of cultural practice, the loss of a lifestyle.

Mobility is therefore much more than a spatial practice; it entails what Lakoff and Johnson have described as "metaphors we live by." Seen in this way, life as travel is a conceptual metaphor that structures not only the practice of life, but the very conception of lives in time and space. Mobility in this sense is not determined by its spatial reference, as it may refer to a sense of being-as-becoming that transgresses notions of "the local." The concept of identity as constructed in orature is "therefore not essentialist, but strategic and positional" (Hall, "Who Needs Identity?" 3). By looking at the specific historical situation, discursive environment, and strategic moments of the re-signification of OvaHerero's narrations of origin, I have sought to move beyond the notion of "social constructedness" as an almost exhausted assertion. Drawing on the notion of the archive as both resource and limitation, and looking at a historically definable period and specific community, I contend that this re-articulation of genesis, landscape, and identity makes use of the signifying capacities of orature in a move to re-appropriate the community's self-definition. In my reading, this allows for an assertion of alterity vis-à-vis the colonial and early scholarly definition of "racial" communities. Thus, the newer version of the genesis story not only reflects on discourses within Otjiherero orature, but actively de-colonizes Herero history as well.

Notes

1. "Text" in this essay refers to initially oral compositions that may or may not have been written down. Henry Louis Gates Jr., drawing on the work of Walter Ong, argues that the English word "text" is etymologically more compatible with orature or oral utterances than with the notion of literature as referring to letters, "because of its Latin root *textus*, past participle of *textere*, 'to weave'" (25). Weaving, in this case, is a very appropriate image to describe the element of composing or cutting-and-pasting that is crucial for the activity of orally performing while synchronically re-composing or interweaving elements from various known poems with new ideas and tropes that are related to the topics of the current performance.

2. Namibia's landscapes have been excessively photographed. My argument here is not that these photos are meaningless or do not circulate within Otjiherero-speaking communities. Ovaherero, as anybody else in Namibia, take, own, exchange, and in multifarious ways make use of landscape pictures. My argument is, rather, that visual representations are not the basis of their artful construction of landscape. For a more detailed discussion of this point, see Hoffmann.

3. Unfortunately, a reading of some examples exceeds the scope of this essay. For detailed examples and readings of *omitandu*, see Hoffmann.

4. Geertz writes: "Believing, with Max Weber, that man is an animal suspended in webs of significance that he himself has spun, I take culture to be those webs, and the analysis of it to be therefore not an experimental science in search of law, but an interpretive one in search of meaning" (5). I use the web here as an image for the multilinear spinning of cultural practice, without wishing to attach a notion of culture to this image. For I believe, along with Mieke Bal, that definitions of culture are "inevitably programmatic" and that it is therefore "presumptuous to pronounce on what 'culture' is, except perhaps that it can only be envisioned in a plural, changing, and mobile existence" (9).

5. Two committees, at times competing but also collaborating, organized the commemorative events during 2004, one led by Bishop Kameeta and the other by Arnold Tjihuiko. Usiel Kandji explained that the people around Tjihuiko saw the bishop's committee as too all-embracing and collaborative with the government, which he said "watered issues down."

6. I use the problematic collective names (San, Ovakuhura) for the different Khoisan-speaking groups of Namibia, because these names are used by the Herero. I am aware of the fact that I am referring to these groups with names that are not their own. Suzman refers to the term Ovakuhura (and Ovabusmana) as a name the Mbanderu (an Otjiherero-speaking community in Botswana) use to describe Ju/'hoansi (97). The term Ovakuhura is also used by Ovaherero in Ovitoto. Although the name itself acknowledges the "firstness" of these communities, this does not mean that Herero recognize their land rights. Suzman was told by a Mbanderu informant: "The Bushmen may claim to be the owners of this land, because they were here first, but it is not their land, it is Mbanderu land. If the Bushmen were the owners of the land, they would have stayed and fought, instead of running away, as they did when they saw the Mbanderu coming. The Mbanderu did not notice the Bushmen when they came. The idea that the Bushmen own the land is an idea of the whites to keep the blacks down" (97).

7. Brincker wrote down a version in Otjiherero: "*Kuza ovandu va za m'omunborongbonga, u ri k'okooko, n'ouo omuti omunene tjinene, nu u n'ondovi n'ouo mbua kuala ovandu*" (One says that men come out of the Omunborongbonga tree, it is a big tree in Kaoko and it has a hole out of which men are born) (247, my translation from German). In all other versions the story is retold in English or German (See Irle 75–76; Katjivena 24–25; Köhler 82–83; Vedder, *Manuskripte* 106).

8. David Coplan ("Times of the Cannibals" 25) and Karin Barber ("Obscurity and Exegesis" 40) point out that changing metaphors in orature

reflect changes in life circumstances. Coplan writes: "A good example is provided by Cope's summary of the historical shift in values and images in Zulu royal praises (*izibongo*). During the eighteenth century, when the Zulu were a second-rank Nguni clan, praises resembled lyrical odes in which shrewdness, reciprocity, and diplomacy were emphasised. Animal metaphors portrayed Zulu chiefs as small species admired for cunning, quickness and beauty. With the rise of Shaka and Zulu imperial power in the nineteenth century, these images were replaced by lion, leopard, buffalo and domestic bull, reflecting the strength, aggressiveness, authority, confidence and social order of a monarchical state" (25).

9. J.S. Malan worked as an ethnologist for the government during apartheid. The first edition of *Peoples of Namibia* was published in 1980; the present publication, still available, stems from 1995.

10. These contents were displayed at the 2004 exhibition in Katutura and told to me in interviews with Wisconsin Hekemo and Alexander Kaputu in 1999.

11. Bollig and Gewald describe the idea of the long-distance movement of solid, distinct tribes as promoted by the missionary Carl Hugo Hahn in the nineteenth century. This idea, they suggest, was informed by the concept of the *Völkerwanderung* that was virulent in contemporary German historians' discourses: "Hahn invented the Herero as a racial category and described them as 'beautiful black Negro people.' Hahn's theory was widely accepted among missionaries, whose categorisations preceded those of anthropologists. However, it is to the missionary Vedder that full credit must be given for developing and fleshing out the image of the Herero such as it exists in most of the academic literature of the present day" (9–10).

12. Bollig and Gewald write that "Herero origins in the Great Lakes are based on the racist hypothesis of Hamitic migrations to Africa. In the early decades of this century (see Meinhof, K. 1912. Afrikanische Religionen. Berlin) linguists believed to have found evidence for a major migration of peoples from the Near East to all parts of Africa" (10). Vedder suggests that the Herero "differ too much from the Negro-type to warrant our including them in the negro-race without further investigation" ("The Herero" 156).

Bibliography

Bal, Mieke. *Travelling Concepts in the Humanities: A Rough Guide*. Toronto, Buffalo and London: U of Toronto P, 2002.

Barber, Karin. *I Could Speak until Tomorrow*. Edinburgh: The Edinburgh UP for the International Africa Institute, 1991.

———. "Obscurity and Exegesis in African Oral Poetry." *Oral Literature and Performance in Southern Africa*. Ed. D. Brown. Oxford: James Currey, 1999. 27–49.

Bollig, Michael, and J.-B. Gewald. "People, Cattle and Land: Transformations of a Pastoral Society." *People, Cattle and Land*. Ed. M. Bollig and J.-B. Gewald. Köln: Rüdiger Köppe Verlag, 2000. 3–54.

Brincker, Heinrich. "Die Omunborongbonga-Sage der Herero (Cva-Herero) und ihre ethnologisch-mythologische Bedeutung." *Globus* 50 (1886): 247–66.

Clifford, James. "Taking Identity Politics Seriously: The Contradictory Stony Ground." *Without Guarantees: In Honour of Stuart Hall*. Ed. Paul Gilroy, Lawrence Grossberg, and Angela McRobbie. London and New York: Verso, 2000. 94–112.

———. "Diasporas." *Migration, Diasporas and Transnationalism*. Ed. S. Vertovec and R. Cohen. Cheltenham: Edward Elgar, 1999. 302–38.

Comaroff, John, and Jean Comaroff. "The Madman and the Migrant." *American Ethnologist* 14.2 (1987): 191–209.

Coplan, David. "Popular History, Cultural Memory." *Critical Arts* 14.2 (2000): 147–69.

———. In the Times of the Cannibals. The Word Music of South Africa's Basotho Migrants. London and Chicago: U of Chiago P, 1994.

Fabian, Johannes. "Popular Culture in Africa: Findings and Conjectures." *African Popular Culture*. Ed. K. Barber. Bloomington, Indianapolis and Oxford: Indiana UP and James Currey, 1997. 18–28.

Foucault, Michel. *The Archeology of Knowledge*. New York: Harper Colophone Books, 1976.

Gates, Henry Louis, Jr. *The Signifying Monkey: A Theory of African-American Literary Criticism*. New York and Oxford: Oxford UP, 1988.

Geertz, Clifford. *The Interpretation of Cultures*. New York: Basic Books, 1973.

Gewald, Jan-Bart. "Colonization, Genocide and Resurgence: the Herero of Namibia 1890–1933." *People, Cattle and Land: Transformations of a Pastoral Society in Southwestern Africa*. Ed M. Bollig and J.B. Gewald. Köln: Köppe, 2000. 187–225.

Gilroy, Paul. *Against Race: Imagining Political Culture Beyond the Color Line*. Cambridge, Massachusetts: The Belknap Press of Havard UP, 2000.

Halkes, Petra. *Aspiring to the Landscape: Investigations into the Meaning of Nature in Works by Wanda Koop, Stephen Hutchings, Susan Feindel and Eleanor Bond*. Amsterdam: ASCA Press, 2001.

Hall, Stuart. "Negotiating Caribbean Identities." *Postcolonial Discourses: An Anthology*. Ed. G. Castle. Oxford. Blackwell, 2001. 280–92.

———. "Who Needs Identity?" *Questions of Cultural Identity*. Ed. Stuart Hall and Paul Du Gay. London, Thousand Oaks and New Delhi: Sage Publications, 1996. 1–17.

Henrichsen, Dag. "Herrschaft und Identification im vorkolonialen Zentralnamibia: Das Herero- und Damaraland im 19. Jahrhundert." Diss. University of Hamburg, 1997.

Hoffmann, Anette. "'Since the Germans came, it rains less': Landscape and Identity of Herero Communities in Namibia." Diss. University of Amsterdam, 2005.

Irle, Jacob. *Die Herero. Ein Beitrag zur Landes-, Volks- und Missionskunde*. Gütersloh: Bertelsmann Verlag, 1907.

Katjivena, Uazuvara. "Ndjambi und die Ovakuru. Meine afrikanische Tradition." *Ein Land, eine Zukunft. Namibia auf dem Weg in die Unabhängigkeit*. Ed. N. Mbumba, H. Patemann, and U. Katjivena. Wuppertal: Peter Hammer Verlag, 1988. 144–62.

Kavari, Jekura. "The Form and Meaning of Otjiherero Praise." Diss. School of Oriental and African Studies, 2000.

———. *The Form and Meaning of Otjiherero Praises*. Köln: Rüdiger Köppe Verlag, 2002.

Köhler, Oswin. "Der Ahnenkult der Herero." *Afrikanischer Heimatkalender* (1956): 80–88.

Lakoff, George, and Mark Johnson. *Metaphors We Live By*. London and Chicago: U of Chicago P, 1980.

Malan, J.S. *Peoples of Namibia*. Wingate Park: Rhino Publishers, 1995.

Malkki, Lisa. *Purity and Exile: Violence, Memory and National Cosmology among Hutu in Tanzania*. Chicago: U of Chicago P, 1995.

———. "National Geographic: The Rooting of Peoples and the Territorialization of National Identity Among Scholars and Refugees." *Cultural Anthropology* 7.1 (1992): 24–44.

Miller, J.C. *The African Past Speaks*. Folkestone. England: Dawson, 1980.

Murphy, David. *Sembene: Imagining Alternatives in Film and Fiction*. Oxford and Trenton: James Currey and Africa World Press, 2000.

Rushdie, Salman. *Shame*. London: Knopf, 1983.

Suzman, James. *Things from the Bush: A Contemporary History of the Omaheke Bushmnen*. Basel: Schlettwein, 2000.

Taussig, Michael. *Mimesis and Alterity: A Particular History of the Senses*. New York and London: Routledge, 1993.

Vedder, Heinrich. "The Herero." *The Native Tribes of South West Africa*. Ed. C. H. Hahn, L. Fourie and H. Vedder. Cape Town: Cape Times, 1928. 153–207.

———. *Manuskripte ohne Jahresangabe*. Vol. 4. Windhoek: ELCIN Archive, n.d.

Weiner, James. "Myth and Mythology." *Encyclopedia of Social and Cultural Anthropology*. Ed. A. Barnard and J. Spencer. London and New York: Routledge, 1996. 386–89.

From Salsipuedes to *Tabaré*: Race, Space, and the Uruguayan Subject

Vannina Sztainbok

> When we speak of the "nation" or "identity," we could say,
> actually, that we are being "spoken" by those words.
> (Verdesio, "La República" 97)[1]

Introduction: The Nation as Told through Indigenous Genocide

Starting in school, Uruguayan children learn that they are mostly the descendants of Europeans. They are taught that the Charrúas, the indigenous nation most identified with the region, were almost all killed in an ambush at Salsipuedes in 1831.[2] This historical moment is narrated in history and anthropology texts, in literature, and in the arts. There are also commemorative ceremonies, field trips, and there is a monument of the "last Charrúas" in central Montevideo. In this essay I consider how the narration of this historical episode underpins the construction of the national space and of a hegemonic national subject. I suggest that the story of Salsipuedes constructs Uruguay as a neo-Europe, setting it apart from the rest of Latin America, and simultaneously allows for a metaphoric cultural hybridity that roots the nation in the land.

Uruguay's identification with whiteness and Europe is not unique. During their formation, most of the American nation-states attempted to minimize the presence of racialized peoples and cultures (Radcliffe and Westwood; Wade; Skidmore). This Eurocentrism was driven by the desire to be considered among the modern and rational nations, when modernity and rationality were constructed as white, European virtues (Mignolo). One of the aspects that distinguishes Uruguay, however, is its almost complete erasure of indigenous presence and the rejection of *mestizaje* (racial hybridity) as a national marker.[3] As has been well documented, the discourse of *mestizaje* is one of the ways in which Latin American nations have "managed" racial diversity. By incorporating colorful elements of indigenous and African cultures, a unique national identity is articulated (Wade; Radcliffe and Westwood). At the same time, *mestizaje* tends to retain a hierarchy that privileges whiteness and is inherently about diluting the "darker" elements and "whitening" the population (Wade, *Race and Ethnicity* 32). Yet some Latin American elites, exemplified by Argentine statesman Domingo Sarmiento (1811–1888), decried any form of racial miscegenation. Sarmiento saw *mestizaje* as one of the fundamental obstacles impeding Argentina's and Latin America's path towards progress and modernity. His views were deeply influential in the Southern Cone, so that "while Mexicans preached racial hybridity to construct the 'cosmic race' proposed by Vasconcelos, Argentines imagined themselves as a chunk of white Europe tacked on to the southern part of the continent, and Uruguayans 'stated' that they were already purely white because they did not have the 'Indian problem'" (Sapriza 23).

I am not the first to draw attention to Uruguay's neo-European identity and understand my research as building upon the work of scholars who have been pointing to the Eurocentric basis of the Uruguayan imaginary. Verdesio notes that the "expert knowledges" of history and archaeology have been complicit by at best minimizing and at worst inferiorizing the presence of the indigenous societies that preceded the Uruguayan republic (*La Mudable*). Hugo Achugar ("El Parnaso") and Gerardo Caetano show how identification with Europe was encouraged via the educational system, immigration policies, the arts, and literature. Along with others (Cosse and Markarian; Porzecanski; Sapriza; Rodríguez), they have noted the racializing implications of the myth of *La Suiza de América*, "The Switzerland of America." Relying on an identification with Eurocentric ideals, the myth is that Uruguay was (in its golden age, until the 1960s) an exception in Latin America, because of its perceived relative prosperity, the level of education of its citizens, its history of democratic government, and its cosmopolitanism. At the crux of this myth is the absence of an indigenous population. Alicia Migdal puts it bluntly, "Uruguay was like a sum of exceptionalities . . . so literate, so cultured, so European, so Indianless" (184). How did Uruguay become *tan sin indios*, "so Indianless"? I suggest that the fact that Uruguay could think of itself as neo-European or white is not a simple reflection of the origin of the population, but of how the national space was discursively produced.[4]

To begin my argument, I reiterate the claims that the nation is "imagined" (Anderson) and "narrated" (Bhabha). As Étienne Balibar contends, "no modern nation possesses a given 'ethnic' basis, even when it arises out of a national independence struggle" (221). This challenges the idea that nations are based on a primordial attachment between the people and the land, or that there is an "essential" national character. The meaning of the nation is produced in and through narratives in multiple sites, including history, literature, theater, television, newspapers, and the many "texts" that comprise the national discourse (Achugar, "El Parnaso"; Alonso, "The Politics of Space"; Radcliffe and Westwood; Sommer). Nations are also constituted by symbolic and material practices – such as singing anthems, marking borders, and building monuments – that create an emotional and physical attachment to the territory (Radcliffe and Westwood 58). Space is constituted by discourse and in turn constitutes the subject and social relations (Soja; Lefebvre). This process is not unidirectional; rather, discourse and space are mutually constitutive. Attending to this reciprocal constitution of discourse, subjectivity, and space, I pose the following questions: What does it mean to narrate the nation as having eliminated the indigenous inhabitants from the national territory? What kind of space is produced by the story of Salsipuedes? What kind of subject does it constitute?

I start by approaching Salsipuedes as a narrative. I consider how the national space – and consequently the national subject – has been produced by the representation of the Charrúas and Salsipuedes in history, anthropology, and various other sites. The texts examined include early-twentieth-century histories by Eduardo Acevedo 1916; 1919), Pablo Blanco Acevedo (1900), and Alberto Zum Felde (1900). These are foundational works that continue to inform how historians take up indigeneity in Uruguay. I consider the above texts alongside more recent histories written by Eduardo Acosta y Lara (1998), Benjamín Nahum (2000), and Mauricio Schurmann Pacheco and María Luisa Coolighan Sanguinetti (1985). I also look at anthropological texts by Aníbal Barrios Pintos (1991), Renzo Pi Hugarte (1998), and Daniel Vidart (1997). Next, I draw on postcolonial critic Radhika Mohanram to think through the significance of the removal of the Charrúa figure from Uruguayan territory. In *The Black Body: Women, Colonialism, and Space*, Mohanram stresses the centrality of a spatial/racial logic in the imagining of the national space and national subject. She holds that dominant subjectivities are produced in relation to the racialized body, and that this body is constituted by its constructed relation to place. Lastly, I posit that the centrality of Salsipuedes in Uruguay's collective memory is inextricable from two "dilemmas": the desire for national legitimacy and anxiety about being perceived as a racialized nation.

El Problema Indio, "The Indian Problem"
Sal si puedes means "flee if you can" and is the name of the site and incident where the "last of the Charrúas" are said to have been killed. The official story is that there were only 150 to 200 Charrúa families left in Uruguay by 1831, but the Creole elites felt that containment was necessary. Rodolfo Martínez Barbosa recounts that the Charrúas were portrayed as barbaric, nomadic, and in effect "uncontainable" (23). This representation constituted them as a problem and gave permission for their "elimination." Although small, Uruguay had vast unpopulated areas which were difficult to police. The Creole population was said to be concentrated in the urban

centers, while the outlying land was parceled into very large *estancias*, "ranches." The problem, according to the landowners, was that the "Natives" moved around a lot (Martínez Barbosa 39); they could not be pinpointed to specific sites and did not recognize the boundaries of the *estancias*, moving freely between them. By 1831, landowners were clamoring for a solution to the "Indian problem." Historian Eduardo Acosta y Lara documents the many letters going back and forth between landowners, the government, and military officials. General Fructuoso Rivera, the first president of the republic, responded by planning an ambush. He convinced the Charrúas to join his troops to fight against Brazil, which was not an unusual request since they had been allied before against this common enemy. In return, he promised them land. There was some dissent among the Charrúas, but history tells us that the majority did march to the site only to be met by death at the hands of Rivera's troops.

Subsequent accounts in the press established that the Charrúa nation had been decimated (Acosta y Lara; Martínez Barbosa). Rivera followed up by sending his nephew, Bernabé, to "finish" the mission with a series of smaller attacks. Much was made of "the last Charrúas," a group of four people (Tacuabé, Guyunusa, Vaimaca, and Senaqué) who suffered the indignity of being transported to Paris for exhibition. There was some criticism of Rivera's actions (Acosta y Lara; Martínez Barbosa; Reyes Abadie and Vázquez Romero), but whether the story was told approvingly or critically, the effect was the same: the indigenous presence east of the River Uruguay had been erased. Historical accounts place the survivors in marginal spaces such as the Falkland Islands (Barrios Pintos) and other sites outside of the national territory (Zanón). Those historians and anthropologists who recognize the presence of Charrúa descendants in contemporary Uruguay locate them within the poor, rural classes, the *pobrerío* (Barrios Pintos; Pi Hugarte; Zanón).

The Production of History

At first glance, this seems a straightforward account of abhorrent colonial actions. What I am interested in, however, are the productive effects of the narrative. Critical historians insist that there is no such thing as a straightforward representation of the past (Alonso, "Politics of Space"; Scott). Instead, histories must be viewed as constitutive of that past. Ana Maria Alonso argues "for understanding how histories produce effects of power/knowledge" ("Politics of Space" 389) and Walter Persaud suggests that we should read historical texts not so much to find the "facts" but to "examine them for what they do" (290):

It would require of us to conceive of texts not only in this documentary capacity but also as sites in which a complex political machinery of management, administration and production is at work. In other words, and to return to Foucault's idea of discourse, we need to see signification as a process which does more than just use words to tell us about the world; we need to see language as a practice whose goal is to produce knowledge as truth. (292)

Most compelling in this instance is the repetition of the narrative. Whether Salsipuedes is referred to explicitly or not, the "elimination" of indigeneity has a prominent place in most histories of Uruguay. The results of Salsipuedes and the other massacres are described in the literature as "disappearance" (Pi Hugarte 13; Zum Felde 10), "annihilation" (Barrios Pintos 163; Pi Hugarte 183; Zanón 167), "extinction" (Pi Hugarte 139, 161), "elimination" (Pi Hugarte 139; Vidart 94), "extermination" (Acevedo, *Manual* 14; Barrios Pintos 115; Nahum 15; Pi Hugarte 147; Zanón 171) and "genocide" (Pi Hugarte 139, 142, 148) In fact, several historical and anthropological texts *begin* by stating the "disappearance" or "extermination" of the Charrúas from the national territory, suggesting the importance of this narrative for articulating the nation's foundation (this includes Acevedo, *Manual*; Blanco Acevedo; Nahum, Pi Hugarte; Schurmann and Coolighan). The "inevitability" of their disappearance has also become part of the narrative (Acosta y Lara; Vidart). Barrios Pintos indicates that the ongoing fascination with Salsipuedes has led to a play, a novel, and an art exhibit (163). In addition, the "last Charrúas" have been memorialized in a monument in central Montevideo, the *Monumento del Prado*. Achugar complicates the effects of this commemoration:

Paradoxically, these monuments supposedly meant to honor the memory of vanquished or defeated people end up honoring the erasure of the individuals or groups intended to pay homage. This is the case with the monument to the last aborigines in Uruguay, known as "Monumento a los últimos charrúas" or just "The last Charrúas" . . . In this case, through a perverse – maybe not deliberately – ideological operation this monument commemorates the death of "The last Charrúas." ("Monuments" 5–6)

Attending to the productive effects of Salsipuedes, what stands out is how its narration precisely and economically delimits the nation as a non-indigenous space. I argue that Salsipuedes is a site where "power and memory are most intimately embraced in the representations of official histories which are central to the production and reproduction of hegemony" (Alonso, "Effects of Truth" 50). The absence of indigeneity in Uruguay is, at least in part, a result of the unrelenting historical production of the national space as having "eliminated" the Charrúas. Thus imagined, the inhabitants of the space are effectively whitened. This construction is not merely inferred. For instance, the introduction to Alberto Zum Felde's *Proceso Histórico del Uruguay* states that, "as to the Charrúas, we have already said that they disappeared without leaving a minimal trace. All of the elements that have formed the Hispanic-Creole society and that determine the future of the nation come from Spain or from America" (10). While Zum Felde was writing in 1920, contemporary histories provide continuity. In 2000, the first page of Benjamín Nahum's *Manual de Historia del*

Uruguay 1830–1903, Tomo I lists the historical and geographical factors that have informed the "national reality." Foremost among these factors is the absence of an indigenous population:

*The **few Indigenes** who were present upon the arrival of the Spanish, and their subsequent rejection and extermination, prevented the birth of a mestizo culture, as happened in the rest of the South American continent. The Spanish transplantation was almost pure in a region that was practically uninhabited.* (15, bold print in original)

In this short paragraph, Nahum dispenses with the "few Indigenes" of Uruguay and naturalizes their "extermination." He consciously distances Uruguay from the rest of the continent by citing the absence of a *mestizo* culture. And, using arboreal imagery, Nahum explicitly connects the lack of indigeneity to the "purity" of European transplantation, a process that has been identified as key to the construction of settler identities (Malkki).

Spatial Marginality of the Charrúas and the National Subject

How *is* the Uruguayan national subject constituted vis-à-vis the alterity of the Charrúa? Many scholars have theorized how dominant identities are articulated in relation to an inferiorized Other (including Bhabha; Hall; Morrison; Said; and Verdesio, *Forgotten Conquests*). Mohanram draws attention to the spatiality of these relations by suggesting that the hierarchies characterizing modern nations are connected to specific discursive moves that specify the relation between the body and geography. She notes that the mind/body dualism underpinning "Western thought" has negotiated the existence of other binaries such as male/female, human/nature, rational/irrational, and Western/Native.[5] The positive valuation of one side of the binary over the other leads to the hierarchical ordering of bodies as subjects become inscribed as superior and inferior via their constructed relation to the body and space. In this schema, the racialized body (the native, black body) is anchored to its place of origin. Mohanram cites the work of Claude Lévi-Strauss as an example. For Lévi-Strauss, the difference between the Western and the Native scientist is that the former can make deductions and abstractions, while the latter gains knowledge only from the observation of his direct environment. Mohanram believes that "when he links ways of knowing with scientific thought, Lévi-Strauss' work becomes problematic, not for what he says but for the effects of his analysis" (8). Here, Mohanram is elaborating on Arjun Appadurai's argument about the "incarceration" of the native in Western discourse, where "natives are those who are somehow confined to places by their connection to what the place permits" (Mohanram 37). The anchoring of the racialized body – what Mohanram refers to as the "black body" – to place makes that subject a slave to its body (its knowledge, needs, and passions) and its origins. This mooring constitutes its opposite – the white (masculine) body – as rational, mobile, and entitled to full citizenship.

The constitution of a dominant subjectivity in relation to the spatial entrapment of alterity resonates with the role of the Charrúa figure in the imagining of Uruguay and "its" people. To read the history of the Charrúas is to read a story of symbolic and material containment. Most historical accounts emphasize that the indigenous population was very scarce even prior to conquest (see, for instance, Acevedo; Blanco Acevedo; Nahum; Schurmann Pacheco and Coolighan Sanguinetti; Vidart; and Zum Felde). The trope of *terra nullius* was often a strategy of colonization (Goldberg; Smith; Verdesio, *Forgotten Conquests*), since constructing the land as sparsely populated legitimated its taking – it could not be considered theft if nobody was on it. Verdesio documents that the territory of what is now Uruguay was described as empty by the earliest European navigators and explorers. The land was imagined as barren and waiting to be inhabited by the only logical inhabitants – Euro-Christians (Verdesio, *Forgotten Conquests* 81).

A further containment occurs in terms of the actual spaces that indigenous peoples are said to have occupied. Most historical accounts situate them on the river banks and in the woods, thus making them peripheral to the emerging nation. Furthermore, the Charrúas (standing in for all aboriginals) are described as nomadic, a condition that renders them "rootless" to Eurocentric eyes. Liisa Malkki writes that the valuation of a "sedentarism . . . actively territorializes our identities, whether cultural or national" and suggests that it "enables a vision of territorial displacement as pathological" (31). Under this logic, only people who are seen to "settle" on the land – by cultivating it, building, and "putting down roots" – are perceived as truly entitled to it. Nomadism constructs an ephemeral people that do not seem to belong in any place. So, paradoxically, the indigenous Other is both tied to the land (in Mohanram's sense of the native being bound by origins) and rootless due to the negative connotations of a perceived nomadic existence. In the following excerpts, rootlessness, geographic marginality, and numeric scarcity emerge as key descriptors of the region's first inhabitants. Thus, the nomadic label is implicated in constituting and containing the Charrúas' "marginal" presence.

In *Historia De La República Oriental Del Uruguay* (1900), Pablo Blanco Acevedo establishes both the scarce numbers and peripheral location of the indigenous population prior to conquest:

The territory that makes up the Republic of Uruguay today was populated, as were other South American nations, by different Indian tribes that inhabited the coastline. Each tribe was made up of a group of Indians that varied in number, but were generally not numerous. (1)

Eduardo Acevedo situates different indigenous nations as inhabiting the literal margins. He states that they lived in the coastal areas, the islands of the Río Negro, and the "margins of the Paraná" (11). Acevedo also refers to the nomadic nature of the Charrúas: "'Here today, there tomorrow' – wrote the historian Lozano – always migrating and always in their homeland, finding their tools anywhere, and enjoying the fruits of the country, according to the season" (11). Significantly, Zum Felde links marginal location and a nomadic lifestyle to an absence of morality:

They were warring and sullen tribes; they lived on the margins of the rivers and streams, naked and roaming. They were hunter-gatherers; they killed venison for their hide, which they used as tents and blankets. Given their condition, these locals did not interest the Spanish whatsoever, whose objective was to find riches. (10–11)

Although their numbers were allegedly few, most accounts also establish that the Charrúas were the most numerous indigenous group on Uruguayan territory (Schurmann Pacheco and Coolighan Sanguinetti). According to these accounts, this makes them "our indigenes" and "our Charrúas" (Barrios Pintos 100–101). Schurmann Pacheco and Coolighan Sanguinetti suggest that it was due to geographical factors that the territory was sparsely populated. They argue that in warmer climates, the Guaraní could practice a semi-sedentary lifestyle, build villages, and live in larger communities. In contrast, the Eastern Province (*Banda Oriental*) was only suitable for a hunter-gatherer society and a nomadic lifestyle with smaller communities (26). Several anthropological texts corroborate this view. Renzo Pi Hugarte states that, "from the point of view of natural resources, the territory of Uruguay presented difficult conditions for human habitation" (13) and Daniel Vidart estimates that the land could only have supported one to two thousand hunter/gatherers (13–14). It is interesting that, in this way, the land itself is constructed as not being compatible with large numbers of indigenous inhabitants. Some investigators question the small population estimates and the lack of agriculture, but they do not represent the dominant historical record regarding the Charrúas (Abella; Antón; Zanón).

I am not concerned here with determining the actual location, numbers, or livelihood of the original inhabitants. My intent is to foreground how conceptualizing a people in a certain way constitutes them and the space they inhabit. In this instance, the predominant characterization of aboriginal people as hunter-gatherers constructs them as scarce and almost vanishing prior to European occupation. Hence, I appropriate Mohanram's observation that "the discursive construction of blackness is metonymically linked to the schematization of space and the function of the signifier" (22) to remark upon indigeneity. Historically, indigenous peoples in general – and the Charrúas in particular – have been constructed as primitive, barbaric, warring, and at best noble savages. Consequently, for the Latin American nation to be constituted as "Indianless" – through the repetitive narration of indigenous absence – is to enter the realm of civilization and modernity.

The juxtaposition between civilization and barbarism as an intrinsic and dangerous difference between the "races" is epitomized in an epic poem written in 1888 by "The Nation's Poet," Juan Zorrilla de San Martín. *Tabaré* is set during the early stages of the Spanish conquest. It is the tragic story of a *mestizo*, Tabaré, who is born of a white Spanish mother who was raped by a Charrúa cacique, "chief." *Tabaré* differs from the Latin American romantic novels studied by Doris Sommer, where there is some reconciliation of racial conflict through romance. In *Tabaré*, the possibility of *mestizaje* dies with the violent death of the protagonist. At the heart of the story are the "inevitable" disappearance of the Charrúas and the emergence of a new nation. There are many passages referring to the vanishing of a race: "There are still Indians awaiting death,/cautiously wandering in the woods," and "Not even your bloodstains/are left on our soil" (53, 51). Tabaré constitutes and is constituted by the national schema of indigenous "extinction." Although the epic poem features both Charrúa and Spanish characters, I believe it is implicitly about the construction of a Uruguayan or Creole identity. In the course of the narrative, the Spanish become more and more rooted in the land: rooted by birth, by death (of the disappearing Charrúas), and by their moral (Christian) superiority, which entitles them to the land.

From analyzing the historical, anthropological, and literary narration of indigenous presence in Uruguay, it is evident that not only did a brutal genocide take place, but it was accompanied by a discursive campaign that sought to assure the nation that indigeneity had been eliminated.[6] Salsipuedes thus provides a glaring example of how difference was produced and land was secured through "the symbolic and material organization of space" (Alonso, "Politics of Space" 381); materially through the marginalization and murder of indigenous people, and symbolically by eliminating any space where people and communities could be defined as indigenous.

References to Salsipuedes or indigenous absence also make their way into other types of narratives. The following is a passage from Uruguay's Ministry of Sports and Tourism website:

The population of Uruguay is of European origin, primarily Spanish and Italian; there is no prejudice against other nationalities due to an open door immigration policy. There is the small presence of the black race, which arrived in the country from the African coasts, and was greatly reduced during the times of Spanish domination. As to the indigenous population, it has been over a century since the last Indians disappeared from the national territory, which distinguishes the Uruguayan population from the rest of Hispanic America. (Ministerio de Turismo y Deporte Del Uruguay)

This passage was first accessed in the year 2000 and was still present in December 2006, despite the fact that the site had been completely revamped, probably following the change in government in 2004. The only modification made is that there is no longer a reference to the "predominance of the white race" (present until April 2004). Still, whiteness is implicitly and explicitly invoked to signify difference between Uruguay and other Latin American nations. Tourism websites usually present a narrow view of the nation meant for foreign consumption, so it is somewhat perplexing to find a tourism blurb – usually intended to paint a pretty picture – making veiled references to the violent evictions of racialized populations. Although there is certainly an obfuscation of the violence of conquest and slavery, it is still markedly there: the black population is referred to as having "arrived" and then being "reduced." Similarly, the "Indians" are said to have "disappeared," in a country where the word "disappearance" can never be uttered without ominous connotation. Through this reference to disappearance, the passage constructs the white Euro-descendant as the normative citizen. Perhaps whiteness is part of the "pretty picture" being marketed, and must be established whatever the cost. There is an admission of blackness – indeed, Afro-Uruguayan cultural expressions are often promoted as a tourist attraction – but it is discursively contained. I believe that this paragraph evinces the tension between two ongoing dilemmas that have haunted the postcolonial American nations: dilemmas regarding racial purity and national legitimacy.

Dual Dilemmas: Racial anxiety and National Legitimacy

The insistence on narrating Uruguay's non-indigeneity is not so puzzling when we contextualize the emergence of the nation. Societies born of colonialism were beset by anxieties over racial mixing and racial ambiguity (Stoler, "Carnal Knowledge"; *Race*). Indeed, imperial and colonial projects were implicated in constituting the very categories they relied on for social stratification (Said; Stoler). The colonial encounter posed a problem for the European or Creole elites who needed to clarify the boundaries between the entitled (whites) and the un-entitled (indigenous inhabitants) in a setting where the lines were blurred by geographic, and sometimes conjugal, proximity. Anxiety over racial ambiguity was deeply felt and even more complicated in nineteenth-century Latin America. As the nation-states were being formed, Enlightenment thought dictated that northern Europe was the birthplace of civilization, modernity, and rationality (Mignolo 441–42). Southern Europeans were deemed lower on the hierarchy, given their geographic and genetic proximity to what were constructed as the "inferior" races of Africa and the East. In addition, the former Spanish and Portuguese colonies were (like the rest of the world) racially diverse. For those invested in identifying the new Creole nations with civility and modernity this posed the "Latin American Dilemma" (Graham). The challenge for southern elites was to project their nations as civilized and respectable, when they were considered barbaric and backward vis-à-vis the North. Thus, the ruling classes of Latin America were no less committed to racist thought than the North, being actively engaged in modifying the same theories to prove the racial superiority and modernity of their own societies (Graham; Skidmore; Wade, *Race and Ethnicity*).

I read narratives such as Salsipuedes and *Tabaré* as manifestations of, and responses to, anxiety over racial mixing and ambiguity. *Tabaré* in particular foregrounds Ann Laura Stoler's thesis that meanings about race, gender, and sexuality are constructed through each other. Stoler considers the significance of narratives of the rape of white, Dutch women by indigenous men in the nineteenth-century Dutch

East Indies, maintaining that race and gender difference were constituted through the production of a vulnerable white femininity and a degenerate indigenous masculinity. The tale of white women captured and raped by "savage" natives is also present in *Tabaré*. In this poem, two Charrúa men are the instigators of rape and Tabaré, the *mestizo*, has questionable desires for Blanca, a white woman who reminds him of his mother. It is the Spanish men who are seen as in control of their sexuality, and they are the ones who must defend the honor of Spanish women. White women are ambivalently positioned; they are dominant in relation to Charrúa men and women, who are disappearing and have no place but at the same time they are always at risk of being tainted by contact with native men. Their vulnerability marks them as unable (or perhaps unwilling) to fully maintain the racial boundaries, and leaves them subordinate to men. *Tabaré*'s storyline establishes racial and gender difference, while justifying both the domination of the indigenous inhabitants and the policing of women's bodies. Thus, "it becomes obvious that racial lines also construct notions of gender while being constructed by those same notions" (Mohanram 86).

These interlocking hierarchies are at the core of *mestizaje*, which underscores the role of gender and sexuality in the racial reproduction and alteration of the nation (Wade, "Racial Identity" 852–53). As previously stated, *mestizaje* involves the incorporation of certain racialized elements, while ultimately seeking to "whiten" the population. It is important to note that *mestizaje* does not quite describe the way that Uruguay has been officially narrated. After all, Salsipuedes and *Tabaré* attempt to foreclose racial fusion, foregrounding Wade's observation that "there is also a hierarchy of mixed nations, according to the degree of mixture and where this places each nation on a global scale of whiteness" (849). This hierarchy of nations is palpable in the tourism passage cited above, where a distinction is made between Uruguay and the rest of Latin America based on the racial characteristics of the population.

Uruguay's connection to indigeneity, however, is not altogether disavowed by the national discourse. A symbolic hybridity is also invoked. Mythical Charrúa attributes that draw on the classic trope of the brave, noble savage are often mobilized to define the national character. This phenomenon is epitomized by the claiming of the *garra charrúa*, the "Charrúa claw," to describe the strength of the Uruguayan character, particularly the nation's prowess in soccer. In *La Construcción De La Identidad Uruguaya*, Carolina González Laurino studies the roots of this trope. The early origin narratives by historian Francisco Bauzá (1849–1899) and novelist Eduardo Acevedo Díaz (1851–1921) called up a romantic Charrúa ancestry.[7] Bauzá described the Charrúas as "the tribe 'who held the destiny of Uruguayans' in their hands'" (qtd. in González Laurino 109). González Laurino credits these two writers with founding the narrative of *orientalidad*, in which the Creoles assume the noble characteristics of the original inhabitants. In these texts the Uruguayan nation is constructed as the natural heir of the courageous, but disappearing, Charrúas. The take-up of "Charrúaness" was not wholesale. González Laurino notes that while the Charrúas could be taken up as ancestors, they could not be narrated as national subjects. Acevedo addresses this problem through the hybrid figure of the *gaucho*; this figure bestowed the national character with some uniqueness, but its coarseness, rurality, and racial mixedness were not desirable as national markers. Thus, González Laurino and Acevedo identify a tension facing the young nation. On the one hand, the nation needed to naturalize its existence – which was by no means uncontested – by appealing to a rightful, primordial ancestry. On the other, identifying too closely with the native inhabitants was to be "tainted" by their alleged "barbarity" and "primitivism." This national quandary is inextricable from the racial anxieties outlined above.

The texts examined by González Laurino, moreover, draw attention to the theme of national legitimacy. Sherene Razack holds that this is one of the central dilemmas facing a "white settler society" (2). How does it legitimate its existence on the territory, given its brutal eviction of the original inhabitants? Because the initial violence never goes away – it is the basis of the national racial hierarchy – it must be erased through national narratives or mythologies that are a "disavowal of conquest, genocide, slavery" and that naturalize the rightfulness of the nation-state (2). Legitimizing occupation relies on a claim to innocence, "a belief that we are uninvolved in subordinating others" (14), while the idea that power has been exercised legitimately is central to the notion of being a modern, enlightened state (Jacobs 17). Uruguay, like the rest of the American states, was established "in the spirit of liberalism" and Enlightenment (Anderson 51). In this context, the invocation of the Charrúas as the progenitors of the Uruguayan nation can be understood as a stake for innocence and legitimacy. Unlike in North America, however, where the official story is that the land "was peacefully settled and not colonized" (Razack 2), Uruguay's national narration foregrounds indigenous genocide.

Despite the atrocious history, legitimacy is claimed through the narration of General Rivera (the president responsible for Salsipuedes) as a traitor to the ideals of the nation, and, as noted by González Laurino, through the appropriation of a figurative Charrúa heritage for all Uruguayans. María Inés de Torres indicates that this opens up the possibility of national reconciliation, rather than culpability:

The national identification with the values that were attributed to the Charrúa tribe only became possible with the verification of their complete disappearance. Upon the desolate image of extermination was founded the legend of the indigenous community, which constructed a national kinship based on the idea of a mythical, autochthonous group. The ethnic plurality dissolves into a new "race," which germinates from the singular environment of the native land and is configured within the symbolic limits of the nation. (qtd. in González Laurino 116–17)

A national ethnicity is forged from the "blend" of a mythical Charrúa and Creole-European heritage. My contention is that in Uruguay the tension between racial anxiety and historical legitimacy is evinced and negotiated via the story of indigenous absence. The story of Salsipuedes means that everyone and no one can make claims to "Indianness." No one can make land-based claims, which would detract from the nation's sovereignty and whiteness, but the nation as a whole can claim an indigenous heritage in a bid for innocence.

Conclusion: Counter-narratives to Whiteness from Charrúa Descendants and Afro-Uruguayans

Recent years have seen the emergence and growth of a Charrúa descendants' movement, including the organizations Asociación de Descendientes de la Nación Charrúa (ADENCH) and Asociación Indigenista del Uruguay (AIDU), both formed in 1989, and Integrador Nacional de los Descendientes de Indígenas Americanos (INDIA), formed in 1998. In an earlier work, I consider their discursive and material practices, concluding that, despite the intentions of the actors, the movement is problematically implicated in reiterating the story of Uruguay's non-indigeneity (Sztainbok). Very briefly, the actions of the descendants focused on commemorating Salsipuedes, calling for the repatriation of the remains of the four Charrúas who were forcibly sent to France in the nineteenth century (some remains have now been repatriated), and searching for evidence of a genetic Charrúa heritage within the Uruguayan population. What kind of subject is produced by the descendants' discourse and actions? Verdesio is critical of this movement's tendency to essentialize aboriginal predecessors and its reduction of all indigenous nations on the territory to the Charrúas (*La Mudable*). He also recognizes that claiming an indigenous identity in Uruguay today is fraught with many challenges, given the lack of continuity in terms of cultural transmission.

My original reading was that the descendants' identity was not that different from that of the *mestizo*, who appropriates ennobling aspects of indigeneity. Because of *mestizaje*'s implication in whitening throughout Latin America, I problematized the descendants' stance and was skeptical about whether their discourse and practices constituted a disavowal of whiteness. In raising this critique, I was also aware of being complicit in denying Uruguay's indigeneity, which was not my intention. Here, I want to draw attention to the possible productive effects of the descendants' practices and also to complicate my initial interpretation. In Uruguay, after all, the admission of *mestizaje* is not necessarily a move towards whiteness, as it has been in other nations. Moreover, the movement is made up of heterogeneous actors who have different relations to indigeneity and whiteness. Lastly, the movement keeps evolving and there is now greater evidence of its political identification with other indigenous nations throughout the Americas, as well as with Afro-Uruguayans.

This shows a shift from the identification with a noble ancestry that marked the previous efforts. There is, however, a critical point from my previous analysis which I believe is still valid. Salsipuedes, or the narrative of indigenous absence, remains a powerful schema for narrating the nation and makes it almost impossible to raise the possibility of indigenous presence in Uruguay without in some way reinscribing the story of disappearance or fetishizing what it means to be indigenous (as a matter of genetics, or as a certain way of looking, acting, etc.). Here, I concur with Radcliffe and Westwood, who write that "that ideological hegemony is powerful in part because it is unstable and it brings together the dominant and the subordinate" (81).

In critiquing the narration of Salsipuedes, I am not denying that aboriginal people suffered great losses in this land. My aim has been to consider how this narrative may be implicated in articulating an ongoing racial hierarchy. After I presented a version of this paper at a conference in Havana in 2002 someone asked, "What would be a good way to narrate such a history?" While this is not a question I dismiss, my own question has to do with why there is a continuous *need* to retell Salsipuedes. I have suggested several effects of this story here; primarily that it produces a normative national subject who is neo-European and white. I am arguing that it is difficult for this narration not to reify whiteness, and here I include my own writing, since I am aware of the constant tension of reproducing this story in my work.

Absent from my discussion of how the disavowal of indigeneity within Uruguay's national narrative produces whiteness is the urgently needed discussion of how the national racial order is also constituted with respect to other Others, particularly Uruguay's Afro-descendants. Therefore, this essay ends where another one needs to begin. In concluding, I would like to remind myself that the construction of a national subjectivity is a process that cannot be over-determined. As Alonso points out, "ideological hegemony is not monolithic and static, fully achieved and finished but constantly negotiated" ("Effects of Truth" 48). It is not my intention to suggest that the narratives reviewed here are the only way that the nation is being imagined. In Uruguay, the growth of an anti-racism movement led by Afro-Uruguayans – namely through Organizaciones Mundo Afro – and involving the indigenous descendants' groups, attests to the existence of counter-narratives.[8] In the coming years, these interventions will likely play a key role in shifting the discourse of whiteness of "La Suiza de América."

Notes

1. This and all other translations from Spanish to English are my own. Works are cited with their title in the original, published language.

2. Charrúa is the hispanicized version of the name of one of several aboriginal nations that inhabited the general region now named Uruguay.

3. Argentina has a similar national narrative that for the most part occludes the indigenous presence.

4. Throughout this paper, the categories "neo/European" and "whiteness" are used in reference to how these terms have been deployed to constitute superiority in the civility/barbarity binary vis-à-vis blackness or indigeneity. I do not mean to suggest that there are "true" Europeans as opposed to constructed ones. As the scholarship of Shohat and Stam, Said, and others shows, Europeanness is also an imagined category.

5. Other theorists who develop this theoretical point include Butler; Goldberg; and Rose.

6. This type of discursive erasure is not unique to Uruguay. Muriel Nazzari documents how shifting racial categories in seventeenth-, eighteenth- and early-nineteenth-century São Paulo led to the collapsing of indigenous peoples into mixed-race classifications that assumed a European/African heritage. In Argentina, the discursive elimination of the black and indigenous populations has been documented by Lucía Dominga Molina and George Reid Andrews.

7. González Laurino refers to Bauzá's *Historia de la dominación española en el Uruguay (1880–1882)* and Eduardo Acevedo Díaz's *Ismael, Nativa, Grito de gloria* and *Lanza y sable*.

8. Luis Ferreira provides an overview of the Afro-Uruguayan political movement in the last two decades.

Bibliography

Abella, Gonzalo. *Nuestra Raíz Charrúa*. Montevideo: BetumSan Ediciones, 2000.

Acevedo, Eduardo. *Historia Del Uruguay: Tomo II*. Montevideo: Imprenta Nacional, 1919.

———. *Manual De Historia Uruguaya: Tomo 1*. Montevideo: Impresora "El Siglo Ilustrado," 1916.

Achugar, Hugo. "El Parnaso Es La Nación O Reflexiones a Propósito De La Violencia De La Lectura Y El Simulacro." *Las Otras Letras: Literatura Uruguaya Del Siglo Xix*. Ed. Leonardo Rossielo. Montevideo: Editorial Graffiti, 1994. 27–44.

———. "Monuments, Commemoration and Exclusion; Politics of Memory in the Construction of the Uruguayan National Imaginary." University of Laval, History and Memory, 2000. Web. 15 November 2004. <http://www.fl.ulaval.ca/celat/histoire.memoire/histoire/confcapethm.htm>.

Acosta y Lara, Eduardo F. *La Guerra De Los Charrúas En La Banda Oriental: Volumen 2 (Periodo Patrio 2)*. Montevideo and Buenos Aires: Talleres de Loretto Editores, 1998.

Alonso, Ana Maria. "The Effects of Truth: Representations of the Past and the Imagining of Community." *Journal of Historical Sociology* 1.1 (1988): 33–57.

———. "The Politics of Space, Time and Substance: State Formation, Nationalism, and Ethnicity." *Annual Review of Anthropology* 23 (1994): 379–405.

Anderson, Benedict. *Imagined Communities: Reflections on the Origin and Spread of Nationalism*. Revised ed. London and New York: Verso, 1991.

Andrews, George Reid. *The Afro-Argentines of Buenos Aires, 1800–1900*. Madison: U of Wisconsin P, 1980.

Antón, Danilo. *El Pueblo Jaguar: Lucha Y Sobrevivencia De Los Charrúas a Través Del Tiempo*. Montevideo: Piriguazú, 1998.

Appadurai, Arjun. "Putting Hierarchy in Its Place." *Cultural Anthropology* 3.1 (1988): 36–49.

Balibar, Étienne. "The Nation Form: History and Ideology." *Race: Critical Theories*. Ed. Philomena Essed and David Theo Goldberg. London: Blackwell, 2002. 220–30.

Barrios Pintos, Aníbal. *Los Aborígenes Del Uruguay: Del Hombre Primitivo a Los Últimos Charrúas*. Montevideo: Librería Linardi y Risso, 1991.

Bhabha, Homi. *The Location of Culture*. London and New York: Routledge, 1994.

Blanco Acevedo, Pablo. *Historia De La República Oriental Del Uruguay*. Montevideo: Dornaleche y Reyes, 1900.

Butler, Judith. *Gender Trouble: Feminism and the Subversion of Identity*. New York: Routledge, 1990.

Caetano, Gerardo. "Identidad Nacional e Imaginario Colectivo en el Uruguay: La Síntesis Perdurable Del Centenario." *Identidad Uruguaya: Mito, Crisis o Afirmación*. Ed. Hugo Achugar and Gerardo Caetano. Montevideo: Ediciones Trilce, 1992.

Cosse, Isabella, and Vania Markarian. "Entre 'Suizas' y Charrúas." *Uruguay Hacia El Siglo XXI: Identidad, Cultura, Integración, Representación*. Ed. Gerardo Caetano. Montevideo: Ediciones Trilce, 1994. 13–28.

Ferreira, Luis. *El Movimiento Negro en Uruguay (1988-1998): Una Versión Posible*. Montevideo: Ediciones Etnicas-Mundo Afro, 2003.

Goldberg, David Theo. *Racist Culture*. Cambridge and Massachusetts: Blackwell, 1993.

González Laurino, Carolina. *La Construcción de la Identidad Uruguaya*. Montevideo: Universidad Católica, 2001.

Graham, Richard. "Introduction." *The Idea of Race in Latin America, 1870-1940*. Ed. Richard Graham. Austin: U of Texas P, 1990. 1–6.

Hall, Stuart. "The Spectacle of the Other." *Representation: Cultural Representations and Signifying Practices*. Ed. Stuart Hall. London, Thousand Oaks, CA and New Dehli: Sage Publications, in association with The Open University, 1997. 225–90.

Jacobs, Jane Margaret. *Edge of Empire: Postcolonialism and the City*. London: Routledge, 1996.

Lefebvre, Henri. *The Production of Space*. Trans. D. Nicholson-Smith. Oxford: Blackwell, 1991.

Malkki, Liisa. "National Geographic: The Rooting of Peoples and the Territorialization of National Identity among Scholars and Refugees." *Cultural Anthropology* 7.1 (1992): 24–44.

Martínez Barbosa, Rodolfo. *El Ultimo Charrúa: De Salsipuedes a La Actualidad*. Montevideo: Rosebud Ediciones, 1996.

Migdal, Alicia. "Formación de la Opinión Cultural." *Cultura(s) y Nación en el Uruguay de Fin de Siglo*. Ed. Hugo Achugar. Montevideo: FESUR, 1991. 177–89.

Mignolo, Walter D. "Coloniality of Power and Subalternity." *The Latin American Subaltern Studies Reader*. Ed. Ileana Rodríguez. Durham and London: Duke UP, 2001. 424–44.

Ministerio de Turismo y Deporte Del Uruguay. "Uruguay Natural: Información General." 22 December 2006. <http://www.turismo.gub.uy/>.

Mohanram, Radhika. *Black Body: Women, Colonialism, and Space*. Minneapolis: U of Minnesota P, 1999.

Molina, Lucía Dominga. "El Negro En Una Sociedad Pretendidamente Blanca." ALAI, América Latina en Movimiento, 1995. 8 December 2004. <http://alainet.org/active/show_text.php3?key=1006>.

Morrison, Toni. *Playing in the Dark: Whiteness and the Literary Imagination*. Cambridge: Harvard UP, 1992.

Nahum, Benjamín. *Manual De Historia Del Uruguay 1830–1903*. Montevideo: Ediciones de la Banda Oriental, 2000.

Nazzari, Muriel. "Vanishing Indians: The Social Construction of Race in Sao Paulo." *The Americas* 57.4 (2001): 497–524.

Persaud, Walter. "Benevolent Rationality: A Foucauldian Reading of the Historiography of East Indians in 19th Century British Guiana." *Forging Identities and Patterns of Development in Latin America and the Caribbean*. Ed. H.P. Diaz, Joanna W.A. Rummers, and Patrick D.M. Taylor. Toronto: Canadian Scholar's Press, 1991. 289–311.

Pi Hugarte, Renzo. *Los Indios Del Uruguay*. Montevideo: Ediciones de la Banda Oriental, 1998.

Porzecanski, Teresa. "Uruguay a Fines del Siglo XX: Mitologías de Ausencia y de Presencia." *Identidad Uruguaya: Mito, Crisis o Afirmación?* Ed. Hugo Achugar and Gerardo Caetano. Montevideo: Ediciones Trilce, 1992. 49–61.

Radcliffe, Sarah A., and Sallie Westwood. *Remaking the Nation: Place, Identity and Politics in Latin America*. London and New York: Routledge, 1996.

Razack, Sherene H. "Introduction: When Place Becomes Race." *Race, Space, and the Law: Unmapping a White Settler Society*. Ed. Sherene H. Razack. Toronto: Between the Lines, 2002. 1–20.

Reyes Abadie, Washington, and Andrés Vázquez Romero. *Crónica General del Uruguay. El Estado Oriental*. Vol. 1. Montevideo: Ediciones de la Banda Oriental, 2000.

Rodríguez, Romero Jorge. *Racismo y Derechos Humanos en Uruguay*. Montevideo: Ediciones Étnicas, Organizaciones Mundo Afro, 2003.

Rose, Gillian. *Feminism and Geography: The Limits of Geographical Knowledge*. Minneapolis: U of Minnesota P, 1993.

Said, Edward. *Orientalism*. New York: Vintage Books, 1979.

Sapriza, Graciela. "Nuestro racismo corriente: Los sustentos ideológicos e institucionales de la discriminación en el Uruguay del siglo XX." Choike.org: Un Portal sobre la Sociedad Civil del Sur, 2003. Web. 12 November 2004. <www.choike.org/documentos/sapriza.pdf>.

Schurmann Pacheco, Mauricio, and María Luisa Coolighan Sanguinetti. *Historia Del Uruguay*. Vol. 1. Montevideo: Editorial A. Monteverde, 1935.

Scott, Joan W. "Experience." *Feminists Theorize the Political*. Ed. Judith Butler and Joan W. Scott. New York: Routledge, 1992. 22–40.

Shohat, Ella, and Robert Stam. *Unthinking Eurocentrism : Multiculturalism and the Media*. London and New York: Routledge, 1994.

Skidmore, Thomas E. "Racial Ideas and Social Policy in Brazil, 1870–1940." *The Idea of Race in Latin America*. Ed. Richard Graham. Austin: U of Texas P, 1990. 7–36.

Smith, Linda T. *Decolonizing Methodologies: Research and Indigenous Peoples*. London and New York: Zed Books, 1999.

Soja, Edward. *Postmodern Geographies: The Reassertion of Space in Critical Social Theory*. London: Verso, 1989.

Sommer, Doris. "Irresistible Romance: The Foundational Fictions of Latin America." *Nation and Narration*. Ed. Homi Bhabha. London: Routledge, 1990. 71–98.

Stoler, Ann Laura. "Carnal Knowledge and Imperial Power: Gender, Race, and Morality in Colonial Asia." *Gender at the Crossroads: Feminist Anthropology in the Postmodern Era*. Ed. M. di Leonardo. Berkeley, CA: U of California P, 1991. 51–101.

———. *Race and the Education of Desire: Foucault's History of Sexuality and the Colonial Order of Things*. Durham: Duke UP, 1995.

Sztainbok, Vannina. "From Salsipuedes to Tabaré: Race, Space and the Uruguayan Subject." MA thesis University of Toronto, 2002.

Verdesio, Gustavo. *Forgotten Conquests: Rereading New World History from the Margins*. Philadelphia: Temple UP, 2001.

———. *La Mudable Suerte Del Amerindio En El Imaginario Uruguayo: Su Lugar En Las Narrativas De La Nación De Los Siglos Xix Y Xx Y Su Relación Con Los Saberes Expertos*. University of Michigan, 2005. Web. 12 November 2004. <http://us.es/araucaria>.

———. "La República Árabe Unida, el Maestro Soviético y la Identida Nacional." *Identidad Uruguaya: Mito, Crisis O Afirmación?* Ed. Hugo Achugar and Gerardo Caetano. Montevideo: Ediciones Trilce, 1992. 97–108.

Vidart, Daniel. *El Mundo De Los Charrúas*. Montevideo: Ediciones de la Banda Oriental, 1997.

Wade, Peter. *Race and Ethnicity in Latin America*. London: Pluto Press, 1997.

———. "Racial Identity and Nationalism: A Theoretical View from Latin America." *Ethnic and Racial Studies* 24.5 (2001): 845–65.

Zanón, Angel J. *Charrúas, Minuanes, Chanáes, Guaraníes: Pueblos y Culturas Aborígene del Uruguay*. Montevideo: Rosebud Ediciones, 1998.

Zorrilla de San Martín, Juan. *Tabaré*. 1888. Montevideo: Collección de Clásicos Uruguayos, 1956.

Zum Felde, Alberto. *Proceso Histórico Del Uruguay*. 1920. Montevideo: Arca, 1991.

Bolivian Indigenous Identities: Reshaping the Terms of Political Debate, 1994–2004

Claret Vargas

In the 1990s, discourses of indigenous rights became common currency among development and aid organizations, among them the World Bank, USAID, the Canadian International Development Agency (CIDA), and the United Nations.[1] The Bolivian Law of Popular Participation (LPP) was part of this trend, at least at the discursive level. Passed unanimously in 1994, it gave the impulse for several constitutional changes that inserted Bolivia's heterogeneity into the definition of the nation. It was, however, plagued by unevenness in the implementation of the law, an educational reform still in the making, and multiple failures at every level of the administrative ladder, which hindered the dreamed-of efficient communication between OTBs (Organizaciones Territoriales de Base), municipal government, and the central state apparatus. This essay is not a study about the administrative and practical failures of LPP. Rather, it is a study of the changing rhetoric of indigenous rights, the tactical deployments of indigenous identities by indigenous actors themselves, and the perhaps unwitting results of the Law of Popular Participation. In its wake, the LPP left an arsenal of laws that were idealistic or ill-conceived and lacked the logistical support to render them effective.[2] As the government's enthusiasm for the LPP waned and a new government entered into power, the reforms proved to be largely rhetorical, if potentially effective at least on the educational front.

Nevertheless, the LPP provided an unexpected springboard for the deployment of indigenous identities as a politically effective tool. Indigenous and other activist groups that could, in some way, align their claims along the lines of cultural and ethnic rights used the LPP, among other laws, to reconfigure political debate in Bolivia. Although Popular Participation is a reform imposed "from above," a number of indigenous and rural groups[3] seized upon it to articulate their own political projects and to contest the State on issues ranging from environmental policy to economic development. The Council of Mallkus and Amautas, for example, framed a protest against the State as an affront both to Aymara peoples and the Constitution.[4]

The timely engagement of indigenous groups in Bolivia with a discourse that external agencies had already adopted and indigenous groups elsewhere in the hemisphere were also deploying, gave additional legitimacy to Bolivian indigenous demands for political debate and spaces of contestation organized around identity. It was particularly important that the LPP did not attempt to define the term "indigenous," but claimed instead to recognize "indigenous and rural" communities as political actors with the right to participate in governmental decisions. The law effectively left indigenous peoples' self-definition untethered and lent legitimacy to ethnic rights as a politically viable category without trying to define what constituted indigenous identity – whether this was an oversight or a conscientious rejection of the traditional discourses of *indigenismo* remains unclear. It is, however, what indigenous political actors have inscribed on the law that reflects the productive possibilities of an incomplete definition of identity.

The period from 1994 to 2004 provides a glimpse of the ways in which indigenous identity asserts its validity as a shifting, often wavering category in political contestation and in the definition of Nation. The Bolivian State left the definition of "indigenous" open in its formulation of the LPP and provided the means for local communities to acquire "legal personhood" (*personería juridica*), a gesture that abandoned the age-old practice of promoting indigenous identification with externally defined markers of "indianness." This move allowed indigenous identity to remain a functional factor in political mobilization, regardless, or perhaps because, of its malleability.

The theoretical implications that I seek to tease out of this case study concern multiplicity. Taking Stuart Hall's gesture of inflecting the concept of identity with the instability of a discursive, constantly changing process of identification (rather than identity formation), I propose to look at the case of Bolivian indigenous movements of the past decade as an example of fluid identities that continue to be contested and resist any attempts to formally define them. It is precisely at particular points of sharp contestation that indigenous identity seems to be at once redefined and reaffirmed, anchoring its redefinition both in recent laws that have validated, but not defined, indigenous identity, and in a number of assumed markers of group identity, which inject a complicated variable into economic and legal arguments.

It is also at these points of contestation that indigenous identity is at its thinnest and, paradoxically, at its strongest in symbolic terms. What I mean by "thin" is that indigenous identity, because of the sheer number of groups who claim it as a principal source of political solidarity and a powerful vehicle of mobilization, becomes defined and encapsulated in a single symbol at times when unity is the priority: for example, the coca leaf, the special relationship with the earth, or even the resonances of particular grievances with those of Tupac Katari's movement.[5] The possibility of translating an identification with a discreet cause (be it the water wars of Cochabamba, the gas wars that ousted Gonzalo Sanchez de Lozada in October 2003, or the rejection of a complete eradication of coca crops) into a politically effective group identity transforms this thinness into a tactical strength rather than a sign of lost identity. This fashioning of identity as a negotiation between what has traditionally been part of the cultural practices of certain indigenous groups and what comes to define indigenous causes at a particular point in history provides an interesting insight into Hall's definition of identity as a process in contestation and in formation:

> [T]hough they seem to invoke an origin in a historical past with which they continue to correspond, actually identities are about questions of using the resources of history, language and culture in the process of becoming rather than being: not "who we are" or "where we came from," so much as what we might become, how we have been represented and how that bears on how we might represent ourselves. (4)

This fluid conceptualization of identity is grounded in practices of self-representation and negotiations of symbolic capital, which, in the case of Bolivian politics, have provided at least part of the foothold for one of the most powerful grassroots political movements in the past ten years. I am referring, of course, to Evo Morales's Movimiento al Socialismo (MAS) party. By the late 1990s, the coca leaf growers' union had attained significant notoriety and, in Morales, had a single candidate for the House of Representatives. The party grew stronger through alliances with indigenous and *campesino* groups, and with urban groups that were focused on a single cause. In 2000, this cause was the rejection of the privatization of water services in the city of Cochabamba in favor of a foreign company named Aguas del Tunari. After a number of marches and a week of blockades that paralyzed all commerce to and from Cochabamba, Aguas del Tunari was forced out. By 2003, the MAS obtained over 20% of the votes in the presidential elections, and in the December 2005 elections, two years after the Gas Wars, Evo Morales obtained an unprecedented 54% of the votes in the national election. He became the first indigenous president of Bolivia ("Los datos").

Since the enactment of the LPP, a number of changes in the relations of rural communities to municipal and national government agencies redefined not only what was conceived of as indigenous identity by external observers, but also the symbolic arsenal that indigenous activists deployed in order to advance demands that might or might not be directly linked to questions of cultural and ethnic rights. A punctual example of this realignment of indigenous demands and grievances along the lines of Constitutional interpretation, rather than appeals to the historical weight of colonialism, is the formation of the Aymara Parliament. Supported by institutions such as the Instituto Interamericano de Cooperación para la Agricultura (IICA), the Aymara

Parliament anchored its participation in an international forum on water management in age-old grievances against what is still conceived as colonial control, as well as on specific and fairly recent laws:

What is the Aymara People's Parliament? Founded at the border of Perú, Bolivia and Chile on June 16, 1996, and strengthened at Chukiapu Marka on April 27, 1999, it is the only political and ideological instrument of the [Aymara] representatives – Jilakatas, Jilakata Taikas, Mallkus y Mama Thallas, Jacha Mallkus and Jacha mamas, Jilir Mallkus y Jiliri Mamas, Amautas – from the Ayllus, Markas and Suyus, and other forms of regional organizations. The Parliament declares itself an organism of international indigenous rights (Convention No. 169 of the International Labour Organization; the Universal Declaration of the Rights of Indigenous Peoples, and other national and international instruments). The Parliament delegates its responsibilities to a Council of Mallkus and Amautas, as the directive and executive branch. The Apu Mallku and the Jach'a Mallku are the principal authorities.[6]

The representatives of this parliament couched their arguments in constitutional terms, in terms of international law and human rights, and in terms of indigenous tradition. Faced with a project that threatened to drain some of the Altiplano's (the Andean plateau) most important sources of water, the council appealed both to the IICA forum and to the United Nations with very similar claims to legitimacy: the International Labour Organization (ILO) Convention No. 169,[7] as well as the Constitutions of each of the three states involved (Peru, Bolivia and Chile). Significantly, the Aymara People's Parliament "declares itself an organism of indigenous rights," thus inserting itself into a transnational discourse of indigenous and human rights that would prove productive in Bolivia and Peru at least until the late 1990s. In the case of Bolivia, the reference to the Constitution was specifically aimed at highlighting Articles 1 and 171, which were amended in August of 1994, following on the heels of the LPP:

Article 1 changed from:

"Bolivia, free, independent and sovereign, built into a unitary Republic, adopts for its government the representative democratic form."

to:

"Bolivia, free, independent, sovereign, multiethnic and pluricultural, *built into a unitary Republic, adopts for its government the representative democratic form,* founded on the union and solidarity of all Bolivians." (emphasis added)

Article 171 was changed from:

"The State recognizes and guarantees the existence of the campesino union organizations." (Sanabria 183)

to:

"One is to recognize, respect and protect within the parameters of the law, the social, economic and cultural rights of indigenous nations that inhabit the national

territory, especially the rights related to communal originary lands, by guaranteeing the use and sustainable enjoyment of the natural resources, identity, values, languages, costumes and institutions.

The state recognizes the legal personhood (personería juridica) of indigenous communities, campesino communities and of the campesino associations and unions.

The natural authorities of indigenous and campesino communities will be able to exercise administrative functions as well as apply their own norms as alternative solutions to conflicts, in accordance with local costumes and procedures, so long as these are not contrary to this Constitution and to the laws. The law shall make compatible these functions and the attributions of the powers of the State." (Sanabria 280)

Article 171 remained unchanged in the new Constitution, promulgated on 7 February 2009 (Vaca).

The council of Mallkus and Amautas emphasized the failure of the Bolivian government to follow its own laws and the international conventions that it had ratified. Articles 1 and 171 of the Constitution had, after all, been reformulated in the spirit of a decade that saw much public support for indigenous peoples' issues through large donor and aid agencies, a Nobel Peace Prize awarded to indigenous activist Rigoberta Menchú in 1992, and the declaration of the period of 1995–2004 as the "International Decade of the World's Indigenous People" by the United Nations. The publicity that the LPP garnered and the massive projects to publicize the new laws were, at least in part, a calculated political move on the part of the MNR (Movimento Nacionalista Revolunionario), a traditional center-left party, to regain the support of the rural population. It may, however, have given indigenous activism a space for growth and reconfiguration that went beyond the expectations of the non-indigenous elite, which pushed the reforms in an alliance with the MRTK-L (Movimiento Revolucionario Tupac Katari de Liberación), an Aymara political party. I consider this a first cycle in the production and deployment of indigenous identity and rights discourses, one that relied heavily on foreign NGOs and aid agencies in order to give teeth to the demands of indigenous groups.

A crucial silence that opened spaces for the numerous reinventions of politically viable indigenous rights' demands was to be found in the lack of a definition of what an indigenous community was. In 2000, however, Supreme Decree No. 25763 purported to define, in formal terms, what is and is not considered an indigenous community. It proposed a system of "certification," suggesting the possibility of establishing unmovable paradigms that identify indigenous communities. This kind of fixed framework was quickly recognized as a disaster for indigenous claims and Carlos Mamani Condori, a historian and indigenous activist well known in Aymara circles, interpreted it as a move to limit the progress of indigenous demands:

Through the Supreme Decree No. 25763 (5 May, 2000), Article 255 certifies whether a community is indigenous or not when it comes to demands for land titles, such as the TCOs (Tierras Comunitarias de Origen or Originary Community Lands). This contravenes, with blatant racism, the right of indigenous peoples to their own identity. The power to certify who is indigenous and who is not is one of the most intolerant barriers for indigenous demands. (Mamani Condori, "Desaparición")

Mamani Condori thus pointed to a critical element of Bolivian law that has so far provided the flexibility to continue to inflect indigenous identity with political potentiality: its non-definition. The right of indigenous peoples "to their own identity," then, is more than a symbolic right. The ability to define themselves synchronically, if necessary, has proven to be a valuable political tool, particularly under the current legal provisions. It should be noted, for example, that the Council of Mallkus and Amautas does not spend much time defining the identity of the people it represents. Rather, it takes the floating signifier of "indigenous" as an indefinable term and proceeds to the systematic invocation of rights, rules, and laws that address "indigenous rights." This presents a crucial challenge to a diachronic definition that traces the historical development of indigenous identity and anchors it to certain stable "origins," rather than to the tactical and circumstantial new elements that might condition identity in the here and now. Certainly, in instances of collective self-definition, part of the symbolic stockpile is derived from a diachronic account of identity. However, in the case of actualizing identity in order to address a particular political grievance, these traditional and supposedly common origins are deployed only inasmuch as they are relevant to the expression of the political demand at hand and are easily combined with other, more fluid factors. The identification of the Aymara people with environmental practices and water conservancy, for example, has its roots both in the known traditions of the Aymara and in the present "routes" this group is assuming. This accords both with Paul Gilroy's mobile and blended model of identity presented in *The Black Atlantic* and Hall's assertion that identities

relate to the invention of tradition as much as to tradition itself, which they oblige us to read not as an endless reiteration but as "the changing same": not the so-called return to roots but a coming-to-terms-with our "routes." (4)

The rejection of a formula that might generate ossified or ossifying parameters of identity is not only anchored in a historical memory of externally-imposed harmful definitions and redefinitions of indigenous peoples; it is also a cautionary step away from the possibility of artificial means of exclusion from particular benefits, including community land titles.

As I stated earlier, it is not my purpose here to review the administrative and practical triumphs and shortfalls of the LPP. What I intend to emphasize is that the letter of the law, if not its application, has provided a valuable arsenal of legal recourses to interpellate the State into compliance with its purported principles of respect for indigenous identity. Although the LPP has been blasted as a superficial change produced for the consumption of external observers,[8] grassroots organizations such as the Aymara Parliament have taken the government to task over Article 171, in particular because it extends the "guarantees of rights" to issues of land tenure and the use of natural resources. Indeed, natural resources and tradition became the point of juncture for disparate groups to come together in several struggles that were originally local and group-specific, but that later acquired a national force and forced the construction (or re-invention) of a pan-indigenous discourse of identity: the coca leaf growers' rejection of the Coca Zero option,[11] the Water Wars, and the Gas Wars of October 2003.

Natural resources and respect for the "customs and procedures" of both indigenous and *campesino* communities were promised by Article 171 and later demanded by actors who assumed a fluid identity. It is precisely this ambivalence of definition (indigenous or *campesino*?) that allowed mestizo actors to embrace an indigenous struggle as they braced to fight the government to keep their embattled coca fields. Symbolically powerful, the coca leaf was constantly redefined depending on its audience: international news media, national radio and television stations, insiders and supporters. Evo Morales, the leader of the coca leaf growers' union, carved out a wide and powerful base of support that in 2002 brought to Congress, for the first time, thirty indigenous *diputados*, accounting for an unprecedented 20% of all representatives ("Indígenas").[10] By deploying numerous markers of identity that appeal to different groups at different times, and by making the coca leaf the icon of struggle even amongst poor mestizo urbanites, Morales managed to present the coca leaf growers' struggles as the "synthesis of the poverty and exclusion of Bolivians." According to him,

To speak of "Coca Zero" [the plan to completely eradicate coca crops in Bolivia] is to speak of Zero Quechuas and Zero Aymaras because the coca leaf is the essential part of the Quechua and Aymara culture. . . . It is like speaking of the Andean Apocalypse, and that will never happen, because we have resisted for 500 years. (Morales)

Though Morales was speaking in what can be understood as highly essentializing terms (coca becomes the core of Aymara and Quechua Culture), this can be understood as a tactical move, which, in later interviews, became more refined and indeed more inclusive. Whereas in this interview, Morales's focus was Andean, in a later interview with *Página Digital*, conducted soon after the resignation of Gonzalo Sánchez de Lozada in October 2003, he restated his position with a significant addition:

They want Coca Zero, but this is totally absurd: to speak of Coca Zero is to speak of zero Quechuas, zero Aymaras, zero Guaranís, *because for these cultures the coca leaf is a sacred product.* (Madariaga, emphasis added)

The tactical addition of the Guaraní to this discourse of millenarian cultural tradition and the sacredness of the coca leaf evidences how Morales deftly glossed over cultural and historical differences between indigenous groups, and refashioned the coca leaf as a repository of symbolically powerful rhetoric.

Indeed, Morales continued to shift the definitions not only of indigenous identity, but also of the identity of the coca leaf itself. He spoke, in the first interview cited above, of a resistance of 500 that "we" (Quechuas and Aymaras) have managed (Morales). In the later interview, he lauded the unity between *campesinos* like himself and indigenous peoples built over the past years of political activism (Madariaga). There is no inconsistency here. Morales was, in fact, performing the fluidity of identity that so many Bolivian migrants to urban centers recognize as their own. To be, at times, both *campesino* and indigenous, and, at other times, to be only one or the other, is not a sign of a lack of "authenticity." Rather, it is a sign of engagement with the difficulties of definitions in communities that can no longer be defined by their location. Morales and his allies have wrought an indigenous/*campesino*/*cocalero* movement not only through timely alliances, but also through an effective management of the symbolic capital of indigenous struggles, which allow for thin definitions of indigenous identity at the most crucial political moments: "the coca leaf has, of late, turned into the symbol of unity to defend the dignity and the sovereignty of the Bolivian people," said Morales in his interview with the Latin American Council of Social Sciences (Morales). Like the Council of Mallkus and Amautas, the *cocaleros* have taken up numerous markers of identity and have deployed them in moments of contestation in order to forge alliances and reassert their demands in an environment that, despite a revolution in 1952 and a progressive set of laws instated in 1994, remained highly unsympathetic to its indigenous majority.[11]

The Bolivian case study I have explored here provides a note to Hall's open conclusion in "Who needs identity?" After defining identity as a discursive practice and noting the instability with which multiple disciplines (from psychoanalysis to feminist theory) have inflected the concept of identity, Hall proposes that, in all its ambivalence, identity is nevertheless still pregnant with political possibility:

the question, and the theorization, of identity is a matter of considerable political significance, and is only likely to be advanced when both the necessity and the "impossibility" of identities, and the suturing of the psychic and the discursive in their constitution, are fully and unambiguously acknowledged. (16)

The case of Bolivian politics has shown it is possible to strategically deploy politically effective representations of non-essentialist indigenous identities to mobilize and enforce (or establish) a dialogue with the centers of power. Of course, this raises another problem in relation to national identity, which shifts from a statement of "who we are" to the question "can we be several shifting identities and still remain a nation"? The answer to this question may very well lie in the measure of Bolivians' ability to assume the impossibility of identities, the fragmentation of our national persona, and the reconstitution of politically effective symbols garnered from the various already-internally-multiple groups that comprise what in the 1990s was ironically referred to as "the pluri-multi." This, at least, would be a first step in shedding the problematic questions formulated around the assumption of indianness and would engage race relations productively as a process that does not seek a solution, but becomes a methodology for communicative encounters between groups that are already imbued in each other's identities, and whose lines of division are not black and white, but wider and wider swaths of gray.

Notes

1. This organization in particular contributed to the diffusion of a discourse of multiculturalism among NGOs and aid agencies, as it declared the period of 1995–2004 the "International Decade of the World's Indigenous People."

2. For a brief summary of these laws, see Liendo.

3. For example, the Council of Mallkus and Amautas (Quechua and Aymara terms for leaders) of the Parliament of Aymara Peoples and the CSUTCB (the national union of *campesino* workers).

4. I discuss this case at length later on.

5. Tupac Katari is an icon of Aymara resistance. He led a rebellion against the Spanish that ran parallel to Tupac Amaru's in what is now Peru. In 1781, he surrounded the city of La Paz and cut off its access to food before being defeated and executed. The Aymara movement has embraced his final words – "I shall return, and I will be millions" – as a banner of resistance. The MIP (Movimiento Indio Pachakuti), led by Felipe Quispe, is the most visible Katarista splinter group of the late 1990s and early 2000s.

6. This was the presentation by the Parliament of Aymara Peoples during the Second Inter-American Forum on Water Management, held at the IICA offices in Uruguay on 18–19 June 1999. See http://www.iica.org.uy/16-6-pan3-pon10.htm. Translated by the author. All further translations, unless otherwise specified, are also the author's.

7. The ILO's Indigenous and Tribal People's Convention (No. 169) was ratified by Bolivia on 11 December 1991.

8. Mamani Condori, in "Indios en la diplomacia boliviana?," points out that indigenous people who participated in the past two administrations were co-opted and ultimately had little say in administrative decisions that could have impacted indigenous peoples.

9. The 1997–2001 presidency of Hugo Banzer launched a project of complete eradication of coca leaf fields with little in terms of viable crop alternatives.

10. The Bolivian Congress is divided into two houses or *cámaras*: the *Cámara de Senadores* and the lower house, the *Cámara de Diputados*.

11. The deployment of indigenous identity and the tactical alliances that characterized the indigenous and rural movements of Bolivia is by no means obsolete now that Evo Morales has been President for nearly four years. The central government has engaged in the difficult process of decolonizing the state apparatus, and has made some progress, but has also faltered, as Bret Gustafson aptly illustrates in his analysis of the education policies of the MAS government. See, generally, Gustafson, Chapter 7.

Bibliography

Bolivia. Congreso Nacional. *Nueva Constitución Política del Estado*. 7 February 2009. Web. 11 Nov. 2009. <http://www.presidencia.gob.bo/download/constitucion.pdf>.

Gilroy, Paul. *The Black Atlantic: Modernity and Double Consciousness*. London and New York: Verso, 2002.

Gustafson, Bret. *New Languages of the State: Indigenous Resurgence and the Politics of Knowledge in Bolivia*. Durham: Duke UP, 2009.

Hall, Stuart. "Who Needs 'Identity'?" *Questions of Cultural Identity*. Ed. Stuart Hall and Paul du Gay. London: Sage, 1996. 1–17.

"Indígenas: un paso adelante en Bolvia." *BBC Mundo.com*. BBC Mundo, 26 Aug. 2002. Web. 11 Nov. 2009. <http://news.bbc.co.uk/hi/spanish/latin_america/newsid_2217000/2217958.stm>.

Liendo, Roxana. "Décentralisation, participation et citoyenneté en Bolivie. Una apuesta por los actores olvidados; Hombres y mujeres Aymaras frente a la participación popular." Louvain: GRIAL, 2002. Web. 11 Nov. 2009. <http://www.uclouvain.be/cps/ucl/doc/dvlp/documents/Liendo.pdf>.

"Los datos oficiales confirman la aplastante victoria de Evo Morales en Bolivia." *Clarín* [Buenos Aires], 21 Dec. 2005. Web. 11 Nov. 2009. <http://www.clarin.com/diario/2005/12/21/um/m-01111626.htm>.

Madariaga, Alexia Guilera. "Evo Morales: 'Hablar de coca cero es hablar de cero quechuas, cero aymarás y cero guaraníes'." *Noticias Pagina Digital*, 27 Nov. 2003. Web. 11 Nov. 2009. <http://www.paginadigital.com.ar/articulos/2003/2003oct/noticias2/148321-11.asp>.

Mamani Condori, Carlos. "Desaparición del Ministerio de Asuntos Campesinos Pueblos Indígenas y Originarios, fin de la administración étnica?" *Aymaranet*, Feb. 2003. Web. 24 March 2004. <http://www.aymaranet.org/a2doc010cmamani02min.html>.

———. "Indios en la diplomacia boliviana?" *Aymaranet*, Jan. 2003. Web. 24 March 2004. <http://www.aymaranet.org/a2doc8cmamani.html>.

Morales, Evo. "El movimiento cocalero es la síntesis de la pobreza boliviana." Interview with Latin American Council of Social Sciences (CLASCO). *Clasco.org*. Web. 24 March 2004. <http://www.clasco.org/wwwclasco/espanol/html/videos/morales2.htm>.

Sanabria, Floren G. *La Constitución Política de Bolivia 1967: Actualizada*. La Paz: Proinsa, 1994.

Vaca, Mery. "Bolivia promulga nueva Constitución." *BBC Mundo.com*. BBC Mundo, 7 Feb. 2009. Web. 11 Nov. 2009. <http://news.bbc.co.uk/hi/spanish/latin_america/newsid_7877000/7877041.stm>.

IV. Reinventing Tradition

Performative Constructions of Female Identity at a Hindu Ritual: Some Thoughts on the Agentive Dimension

Beatrix Hauser

Introduction

In contrast to the idea of collective identity as based on a somehow given and coherent sameness, poststructuralist scholars presume a continuous reinterpretation of identities, characterized by varying contextual and situational parameters. Thus, any kind of identity appears fluid, fragmented, imagined, shifting, and, as such, multiple in character. Since identities are understood to be contingent social constructs, they are subject to continuous affirmation, negotiation, and alteration by human beings. This process is intrinsically performative, i.e. not solely conveyed by ideology but embodied in day-to-day communicative practices, whether through habitual repetition, mimetic citation, or speech acts. To conceptualize identity as a socio-cultural construction comes as no surprise in social anthropology. Emile Durkheim already analyzed communicative processes in their capacity to raise group solidarity, yet he conceived of human beings whose given physical reality precedes its cultural transformation into a social body. The full analytical potential of a concept that regards identities as social constructs reveals itself when this dichotomy is relinquished and attention is drawn to the body as itself a cultural construct. With this intention, Judith Butler's *Gender Trouble* challenged the analytical value of disconnecting "gender" from "sex" (a paradigmatic distinction for the first generation of "women's studies"). According to Butler, even what appears to the self as a physically given sex is already a discursive product. Raising awareness of this constructiveness was supposed to have a liberating effect on women and those individuals who transgress gender stereotypes due to their sexual preferences, their "queer" self-perception, or both. Identity was not only considered as created in and through social practice, but performativity emerged as the major force in its construction process (see also McKenzie).[1]

Theorizing shared and hence also contested identities pushes the agentive dimension of the individual into the limelight and raises many questions: To what degree are human beings able to mold their identities? When and how do they refer to a specific identity *vis-à-vis* another, alluding, for example, to gender rather than regional distinctions? Under which circumstances do they invest certain behavior with semiotic meaning so that it may become normative for a community? On the one hand, human beings can no longer be seen to act as rational and autonomous creators of their identity (or identities), as was assumed in the Western viewpoint that drew on the ideas of the Enlightenment. On the other hand, they can also not be seen as fully determined by social structures and historical conditions.[2] Butler's *Bodies That Matter* emphasizes that the construction of gender should not be taken literally as a programmatic process of self-fashioning during social interaction. Performativity, rather, results from discourse and characterizes the objectification of ideas that feel natural to the subject, who, through the repeated process of enactment, explores and incorporates them once more.

The agentive dimension of human beings in the formation of identity is not only a philosophical problem; it is also relevant to the study of culture, whether defined as a discursive product, as a man-made semiotic system, or, conservatively, as a collective that shares certain values and practices. In recent anthropological research, cultural performances are regarded as particularly apt sites for the ethnographic encounter with identity politics. These events are considered not only to articulate communal identities; what is more, the process of enactment is given the authority to bring about such figurations. Scholars preferably consider the autopoietic process, the emergent qualities or the transformation of bodies.[3] Anthropologists do have a dilemma with the individual subject. This point is particularly crucial with respect to non-Western cultures associated with a concept of personhood that is driven by collectivism rather than individualism. While scholars easily conceive of identity as a social construction, when it comes to non-Western people they often hesitate to presume a reflexive monitoring of the self and its relationships with others, or the personal complexity which we perceive in ourselves (Cohen and Rapport).[4] Martin Sökefeld has argued that to deny certain cultures a conscious self in the sense of a person aware of being an agent serves as an effective strategy of othering (projecting the inverse of one's own qualities onto others, who are consequently disparaged). In general, I agree with Sökefeld's critique; recognizing the autonomous individual as a social self-construction or presuming culturally varying notions of personhood should not lead to the assumption that there is no actual reflective center to the human being. The crucial point is how we conceive of this human capacity to (re)consider identities.

My aim here is to reflect on this agentive dimension in the process of identity formation on the basis of data from anthropological fieldwork among women on the eastern coast of India (Orissa). I will introduce one case study from a long-term research project on the performative construction of female identity in this region.[5] Its subject is the performance of Mangala *puja*, a ritual that belongs to a category of votive rites associated with a woman's religious commitment to the wellbeing of her husband, brothers, and sons. Certainly, not every woman in this region defines herself (only) through religious practice, and from the perspective of a middle-class intellectual I have chosen a particular, restricting framework for my analysis. However, I am interested in the identity formation of the women who follow this highly appreciated tradition and in how they enact, affirm, and possibly challenge different notions of femininity within their ritual practice – precisely *because* these women resemble the stereotype of the devoted, submissive wife advertised by conservative Hindu scholars. If we consider the inherently contested character of identities, this case study should shed light on identity formation among those individuals who supposedly have neither the power nor the interest to question the nature of (in this case) gender identity. Therefore, I shall discuss how the participants in this ritual employ common notions of femininity and related cultural concepts. To what degree and in what way do they become agents in order to negotiate these essences? How does the performance of the ritual contribute to their vision of womanhood? While considering these questions, I do not propose a consistent image of "Orissan women," but rather focus on a popular female way to conceptualize oneself in relation to the world, as a gendered being and with reference to norms and conventions associated with different social groups. In conclusion, I will discuss the *kind* of agency involved and its social consequences in the process of (re)creating gender(ed) identity.

The concept of agency and its usage in contemporary academic debate is problematic. It gained (new) popularity in the 1980s with the sociologist Anthony Giddens (*Central Problems in Social Theory*; *The Constitution of Society*), who, in contrast to the prevailing structuralist paradigm in the social sciences, emphasized the significance of individual action. According to his theory of "structuration," human beings are considered social agents of their own, although their intention, consciousness, and choice are configured by historical, social, and other conditions. In contrast, scholars in social anthropology have focused on the idea of agency as an imaginative quality that is attributed to human beings (or denied them) for certain pragmatic reasons. With reference to spirit possession, for instance, the behavior of a human host is perceived in terms of "patiency," and agency is recognized to lie with the possessing spirit.[6] While Fritz Kramer claims that *passiones* constitutes a mode of action generally ignored in the West, other authors stress how – in any case – agency results from performative techniques only, i.e. from the *mise-en-scène* of an event. Recent works on collective or "complex agency" (Inden), which can be distributed or displaced, and on the empowerment that emerges from processions and other territorial rituals (Sax; Sutherland) evaluate the social processes involved in the collective recognition of agency. In this respect, agency is understood to be primarily associated with ideas, concepts, or artifacts (Gell), and only at times objectified in human beings. The invocation and denial of agency also characterizes much of academic writing, as Ronald Inden has argued. With reference to South Asia, the displacement of agency from persons to cultural essences (such as non-individuality) served as an effective strategy to upgrade the British colonial and also the scholarly view of the Indian other. Similarly, feminist scholars have stressed the necessity and political impact of considering women as agents (Gardiner; Kumar). However, for lack of a more suitable term to address the agentive dimension in the process of identity formation, I refer to "agency" and employ it as a "traveling concept" (Bal). This means that I refrain from defining it *a priori*, but rather confront it with my fieldwork data to conclude on its specific character towards the end of my essay. I argue that theorizing identities calls for an alternative conception of human agency that is not necessarily based on intention (and personhood), but rather constituted by both reflexivity and embodiment. If we consider the imaginative nature of an agency that is situated and objectified in and through social interaction, then it can certainly manifest itself in human beings and also with regard to the negotiation of identities.

Performing femininity
In the Hindu month of Aswina (September/October), Orissan women worship the goddess Mangala in a particularly elaborate form. For the duration of one month they abstain from certain foods and on every Tuesday they meet for several hours to pray and sing in honor of the goddess. This worship belongs to a category of votive rites (Oriya: *osa-brata*) that is defined by fasting (*osa*) and a vow (*brata*) for the benefit of a woman's husband, brother, or son. In orthodox Hindu parlance, the performance of votive rites constitutes a paradigmatic form to fulfill the *stridharma* (Skt.), i.e. their religious duty and nature as women. This concept implies that there are different, gender-specific ways to attain salvation. Since women menstruate and thus regularly face ritual pollution, they should, for instance, not engage in priestly functions. Their religious commitment is best directed towards the wellbeing and prosperity of their (marital) family. In general, votive rites are considered optional and Orissan women may choose, according to a recent manual, from eighty-three different *osa-brata* (Misra). As McGee has pointed out with reference to Maharashtra, most women feel obliged to observe at least some of these rites on a more or less regular basis. In Orissa, the collective worship of Mangala in the month of Aswina has become a rather popular choice.[7]

On Tuesday 5 October 1999, in the provincial town of Berhampur, about twenty married women from one neighborhood gathered to devote themselves to the worship of Mangala. The ritual (*puja*) was divided into two sections, each lasting about three hours. The most time-consuming sequence during the morning session was the crushing of a pile of dried turmeric, all in all seven pieces per participant. Later, the powder was mixed with water in order to renew an approximately seventy-centimeter-high relief of the goddess that was pasted on a wall. This act was performed by an elderly lady, who was respectfully called "Mausi" (literally "maternal auntie"). She was in charge of conducting the main ritual procedures and it was in her house that the women met. One of the participants was an adolescent girl, who, still unmarried, was performing this votive rite for the first year. The process of grinding turmeric with the help of a large and heavy iron pestle took quite some effort and was divided among all participants. Once it came to the turn of the unmarried girl, Mausi loudly encouraged her to do it well "so as to get a good husband." Everybody laughed.

At first glance, this teasing drew attention to the idea of *stridharma* and the girl looked down in shame. The words must have reminded her of her fragile social position. She had to get married to fulfill the female role model and to become a full member of this group. The conservative statement already offered a way to deal with this situation by hinting at the force of religious devotion. The sincere performance of the votive rite would not only secure a happy marriage, it would also help to gain social recognition. The girl had probably known this phrase since her childhood days, but in this ritual situation the ideology was sustained by her bodily reaction, the feeling of shame evoked by the laughing majority of married women. Thus, her personal somatic experience now confirmed the conservative phrase.[8] At second glance, the statement conveyed some reflective distance as well. The subjunctive mood of the phrase evoked a flavor of irony, which was realized by the laughter of the other women. To them, the power attributed to the ritual commitment obviously had its limitations. My research assistant also smiled conspicuously, possibly in anticipation of my (presumed) view of reality that privileges "love" over "arranged marriages" with divine support. In any case, Mausi's statement was ambivalent. It called on the ideology of *stridharma*, but also limited its normative status by the subtle suggestion that it was nothing more than a rhetorical formula. Even if Mausi was habituated to using this phrase, she was not bound to do so. It remained her secret whether she intended the irony that was brought about by the collective laughter. Similarly, the reaction of the adolescent girl cannot be assessed semiotically. Whether she was aware of the double meaning or not, she behaved as if listening to the conservative notion only. In this respect, she confirmed the religious ideology implied (an appropriate and decent reaction for someone of her young age). But how did it influence her sense of being a woman? When I met her a couple of days later and mentioned the incident, she did not seem to consider the force of her devotion. Very pragmatically, she spoke of her wish for an arranged marriage and for her parents to select a husband. They had made her leave college some months ago to enhance the marriage negotiations and the girl knew of the gossip about prospective candidates and of the expected amount of dowry in case of a well-educated bridegroom. During our interview, she presented herself as a mature person, aware of being a subject by herself although with limited powers. She reflected on her role of upholding her family's good reputation and on being entangled by feelings of pride, excitement, and subordination.

The votive rite in honor of the goddess Mangala is rather new to the locality. Like several women in southern Orissa, Mausi started its performance only in the beginning of the 1990s. In the course of seven years, the basic outline of the ritual developed into a sophisticated ceremony with many peculiar details like the crushing of turmeric so as to create an idol. There was no other group who did this and Mausi's neighbors proudly identified with this specific way of performing the *puja*.[9] They appreciated the initiative taken by the senior lady, who, by her convincing performance, turned into a ritual specialist and, year by year, attracted more devotees. Although from my point of view the influence and creativity of Mausi in the development of this Mangala *puja* can hardly be underestimated, she herself denied her responsibility. During a couple of visits to her house, she gradually memorized events that proved how the goddess herself had created and determined the complex procedure of the ritual. For instance, Mangala had presented her with a book of hymns that Mausi discovered somewhere "on the road" and Lord Jagannath – the Orissan deity who attracts pilgrims from all over India – had left his "toothbrush" (a wooden stick commonly used to clean teeth) in her praying room, a relic that was subsequently incorporated in the worship of Mangala. Similarly, Mausi had conceptualized herself as a divine instrument in the weekly renewal of the goddess's image. To promote the design of a ritual and to take up priestly functions is not implied in the rather restrictive idea of *stridharma*. While an outsider might suspect Mausi of using religious means for some egoistical purpose, I rather consider the situation in terms of shifting frames of reference, or in other words, shifting identification. By her mimetic citation of religious ideas, Mausi did not act in her capacity as a woman, but rather as a devotee. By doing so, the denial of her initiative as a social actor could be compensated by the ritual agency she gained through her reference to the divine. Thus, Mausi did not simply "express herself" (my cultural bias) through ritual and by inventing unusual (even from the local perspective) items like the votive toothbrush. Her self-presentation was based on the decision to follow a religious role model, rather than a gendered one. Of course, the submission of a devotee already accords particularly well with that of women. Later, I wondered to what extent the steadily rising number of memories Mausi recollected in support of her theory of divine guidance were actually triggered by my persistent questions circling around her individual initiative, acknowledging that the ability to do so was not considered appropriate. In contrast to the unmarried girl, Mausi almost forced people to regard her ritual agency as inseparable from her non-ritual self.

To engage in religion is thought to be in line with the ideal of non-individuality associated with Hindu society. From a local perspective, the performance of rituals offers a particularly suitable domain for women's commitment. While at the turn of the millennium any autonomous engagement by Indian men is appreciated within a modernist discourse (most explicitly with respect to their careers), a woman who acts similarly will face several subtle or outright objections against her alleged selfishness. Although a growing number of middle-class families put intense effort into a girl's education, most people remain much more concerned about her marriage. In provincial and conservative areas, a woman's main effort and articulation is therefore directed towards the realm of religion, especially in later life (after raising children). There is hardly any other activity available that does not challenge their role as mother and wife. According to Yumiko Tokita-Tanabe, this emphasis is a particular effect of the post-colonial discourse where the man's world was associated with economic and political progress, while women emerged as the bearers of tradition (7–9). Indeed, when on religious holidays there is a shortage of Hindu priests, women start to take on their ritual function. Occasionally, this process becomes institutionalized, since young men from hereditary priestly families (not only Brahmins) use their privilege to take up even more respected professions. In this respect, female ritual specialists like Mausi do not compete with men and hence this female activity is not understood as a subversion.

The rhetorical and non-verbal strategies to reproduce, alter, or contest different notions of femininity within a ritual context are subtle, numerous, and heterogeneous. They do not appear in a structured order, but rather as multiple and ambivalent options for interpretation. To grasp the performative dimension of identity formation seems to be even more difficult. Elsewhere, I evaluated the crushing of turmeric in terms of suffering, i.e. as an event to assess the physical effort involved (Hauser, "Creating Performative Texts" and chapter 2 of *Promising Rituals*). While women engage in this procedure (which lasts for more than an hour) they recite the legend of Khulana Sundari. The main female character of this legend is bound to tolerate immense pain and misery, which she can survive only with the help of Mangala. I argued that the sacred formulae suggest how to perceive and assess any personal experience of distress and to relate this feeling to one's self as being female. Women, as the verses suggest, are able to bear more pain than men. Moreover, women can call on the goddess's help to lighten their burden. Thus, the sacred text is given the authority to construct a reality that is revived and embodied whenever women recite the story. The physical effort of crushing becomes a means of somatic experience. Since the goddess will help women in distress, the heavy iron pestle and the exhausting process of grinding becomes "light as a flower." There is another dimension to this physical sensation. Performing any ritual jointly is also an occasion for enjoyment; the women chat and laugh a lot. The ritual therefore constitutes a gender-specific way of leisure and recreation, with participants understanding the act of crushing not only as shared burden (or household chore), but also as a competitive game.[10] This is not in contradiction to the religious significance of the ritual; the physical sensation of lightness (resulting from play) serves as a somatic reconfirmation of the ritual message, i.e. the goddess's power to relieve women's heavy burden. The most explicit bodily resonance of votive rites is certainly evoked by means of fasting. This month-long practice includes the avoidance of certain food items (meat, fish, eggs, garlic, onions, etc.), a limitation of meals, and a general preference for fruits and sweets (the "leftovers" from the weekly offerings to Mangala). A woman who assesses her own appetite in comparison to her husband's consumption of "forbidden" foods will feel like ignoring this religious observance. But if she relates her physical sensation to the religious ideal of self-control, she can recognize her released digestion tract in terms of lightness and purity. This shift of emphasis again results from her identification as a religious rather than a gendered human being. In Hinduism, self-control as well as the voluntary performance of physical austerities (*tapas*) is regarded as a means for spiritual development (exemplified by asceticism). From the perspective of Orissan women, the strength to go on a fast is intrinsically associated with their female physique. Some of my interviewees were convinced that men did not have the stamina to refrain from food (yet there *are* rituals for men that require fasting).

Although men are considered recipients of the religious fruits (*punya*) gained by their wives, husbands are often skeptical about *osa-brata* rites. Men certainly recognize that by means of performing rituals women gain power in social affairs too. They may change their cooking routine, skip household chores, or leave the family premises in order to attend female networks beyond kinship ties. Yet there is no way to stop them. To prevent someone from serving a god (or goddess) is considered a sin (*pap*). Some men still argue that fasting is harmful for the body, and thus, with reference to a medical discourse, call on their wives to limit their religious engagement. Women, conversely, often agree on their bad health but also admit to the anthropologist that meeting other neighbors is great fun.

In the end, how does the fact that their religious dedication is explicitly aimed at the wellbeing of others and not at their own spiritual or worldly benefit affect women's identities? The standard argument given among middle-class women is pragmatic. Since a woman's fate primarily depends on (the long life of) her husband, his physical and economic condition would also have some effect on her own happiness, so that the performance of votive rites finally answers immediate personal interests too. But this interpretation reflects only one viewpoint. The women who regularly worshipped the goddess Mangala did not assess the dominant explanation of votive rites as a disadvantage. Although they were very much aware of the politics involved in gender inequality, the worship "for the benefit of a husband" contributed to a rise in their self-esteem. Because it was due to their own religious practice that the prosperity of their family was sustained and realized, the women I spoke with felt responsible and confident. Their argument corresponded to a concept of femaleness perpetuated by one strand of Hinduism, which is based on the idea of *sakti*, the divine female energy that can be shared by human beings through ritual practice and self-control. Women consider themselves predestined to activate this energy, since their gender provides the most suitable access.[11] The same rationale also supports the female view that women are more religious-minded than men. Thus, the notion of *sakti* not only serves to affirm, but also to essentialize female identity. On the other hand, to sense this idea within one's female body requires repeated religious experience. Orissan women who do not practice votive rites regularly tend to doubt the necessity of their female contribution to the wellbeing of society.

Conclusion

I have evaluated how the participants of a specific ritual perceive, perform, and employ notions of femininity and how the latter are blurred through references to other concepts, such as devotion and non-individuality. My intention was to consider how this enactment contributed to the formation of female identity and to determine to what extent the participating women were agents of this process. Clearly, the performance of Mangala *puja* was more than a re-enactment and confirmation of a female *habitus*. Some of the ritual sequences had the potential to influence and alter the way in which participants recognized themselves and their position in relation to men. With the help of certain "body techniques" (Mauss) that steered the women's "somatic attention" (Csordas) towards another perception of reality, a daily household chore such as grinding turmeric came to materialize the suffering associated with womanhood. Enacted as a ritual competition game, this burden turned "light as a flower." Similarly, the fasting body was gradually sensed in terms of self-control, essentialized as an intrinsically female quality. The resonance of these experiences, however, differed from one participant to the next. For instance, the shame of being laughed at, which was realized against the background of being (still) unmarried, left its imprint on one girl. The by and large positive effect of the ritual performance on its participants was completed and sustained by a particular religious discourse. According to Shaktism, every woman literally embodies the physical capacity to realize and develop the divine generating force (*sakti*) within her. The pleasure deriving from the ritual performance thus came to prove this concept and reconfirmed the belief in the goddess and the efficacy of her worship.

The performance of Mangala *puja* was only partly motivated by its classification as a gendered religious practice; from the perspective of women, it was just an appropriate way to share the divine energy. As shown above, the logic of *osa-brata* rites dedicated to men was not questioned in terms of limiting the female scope of worship, but rather recognized as proof of women's importance to the wellbeing of society. This self-perception relied on a sense of ritual rather than social agency, and hence the recognition of oneself as a religious rather than a gendered human being. The sense of ritual agency (or action empowered through reference to the divine) emerged from its embodied practice and was not accessible to those women who did not regularly observe votive rites. However, the repeated performance of these rituals also contributed to internalizing attention towards the wellbeing of others and to its objectification as a natural female attitude.

Women could also consider their intense worship of Mangala in terms of self-presentation and in this way influence the politics of their own (joint) family household. In this respect, the potential for subversion was not so much based on the contestation of femininity as on its essentialism. The women performing the ritual were not interested in raising any doubts about their nature as submissive wives and mothers. Although they did not incorporate the Enlightenment's lesson of individualism, they certainly knew when and how to present themselves in a particular mode (see Das). Accordingly, the shy and devote girl of the ritual revealed herself as a reflective social actor as she responded to the anthropologist's questions. In contrast, the senior lady resisted a frame that indicates individuality and fashioned herself as a divine instrument, even though her initiative in the development of the ritual was widely appreciated.

In sum, the performative references during this ritual called on different facets of femininity and it was not always clear whether they were meant to affirm or contest dominant discourse. The irony that was realized by means of collective laughter was not reflected upon. Similarly, the senior lady, who through her performance emerged as the ritual specialist and hence on the behavioral level challenged the idea of a purely male priesthood, was not understood to be competing with men. In any case, a particular class of events (such as rituals) and its connotations (as being conservative) do not invite a straightforward interpretation of the issues that emerge from its performance. After all, as a contingent form of social practice, any ritual is somehow risky (Schieffelin; Fischer-Lichte). Thus, the performative construction of identity has no option but to differ from existing discourse. The crucial point is when and how alterations are made explicit and taken as a challenge. In this process, protest will not always take well-recognized forms.

When theorizing about identity formation, the question is neither whether these Hindu women are agents of this process *or* subject to it, nor whether their behavior is structurally predetermined *or* based on free will.[12] As human beings, their personality is as complex (and varied) as ours and so is their consideration of social relations. The question is rather how we conceive of the agentive dimension involved in the creation of womanhood or any other collective identity. To switch from one frame of reference to another (gender *vis-à-vis* religion) is only one strategy to increase the variety of actions. As the example of the ritual specialist has shown, new meaning does not simply emerge of itself; it always needs personal impetus as well as the reconfirmation of other women to produce either a conservative appeal or a subversive irony. But this is not the whole story. A model of human agency that is based on intention, I argue, falls short of considering the bodily impetus and hence the intrinsic directedness of human beings towards the lived-in reality that proceeds along *a continuum of reflexivity and embodiment*. To consider only the human *body* rather than the person as agent is yet another limitation.[13] With regard to the social construction of identities, I suggest acknowledging and implementing the imaginative quality of a reflexive center of the self as a potential distributed among individuals and collectives (and at times associated with deities and objects). This would offer new scope for theorizing, since we are pushed towards the varying conditions of *when* and *how* somebody is considered to challenge identity.

What about the medium and force of performativity? Which circumstances foster the perpetuation of hitherto unrecognized features into apprehensible ideas towards the negotiation of femininity? On the one hand, the performative construction of identities will always differ from the existing discourse, whether intentionally or not. As such, performativity draws on the contingency of a social event. It is not subversive *per se*, but first of all ambivalent.[14] In order to not only manifest coincidental or intersubjective meanings of womanhood, but to initiate transformation, performative reiterations (once again) need to be affirmed by others. In my case study, this happened through bodily resonance. Although subversive potential might emerge against the background of tradition, to be recognized as such it also needs the reflexivity and awareness of several participants in an event. In this case, subversion was not intended. Still, the actual performance – for example, the laughter after the conservative statement – did influence the women's perspective on themselves.

Notes

1. In recent academic writing, there have been several studies on social practices as mere performance (or *Inszenierung*). See, for instance, Willems and Jurga.

2. Here I differ from the early Michel Foucault. In his later work he revised his conception and initiated a discussion on agency (see Bartky).

3. See Parkin, Caplan, and Fisher; Hughes-Freeland and Crain; Köpping and Rao.

4. With reference to India, Louis Dumont is the most prominent scholar to have claimed that individualism is a purely Western concept. In contrast, Mines has shown the relevance of individuality in Indian social life. With respect to Orissa, Marglin argues that "the bounded unitary self does not exist for . . . Oriya villagers," but nevertheless acknowledges a deliberate construction and maintenance of their world (128).

5. Fieldwork was undertaken for about sixteen months during consecutive visits in 1999, 2000, 2001, and 2003. It took place in and around Berhampur, a commercial town in the coastal area of southern Orissa. Basically, I used participant observation and narrative interviews to explore women's representations of femininity during various cultural performances. See my "Creating Performative Texts," "Göttliches Gestalten," "Divine Play or Subversive Comedy?" "Travelling Through the Night," "Divine Possession," "How to Fast for a Good Husband," *Promising Rituals*, and "Whether Tribal or Tantric?"

6. The term patiency has become quite popular in the debate on agency; it signifies those forms of behavior where a social actor is not considered a subject but rather the recipient or instrument of another non-human force (see Gell; Inden). Patiency overlaps with the old expression of *passiones*, which Fritz Kramer revived and re-introduced to social anthropology (with reference to Godfrey Lienhard).

7. I have discussed the ritual procedure and social practice of this Mangala *puja* elsewhere (Hauser, "Creating Performative Texts," and chapter 2 of *Promising Rituals*). On female votive rites in India, see, for instance, McGee; Tewari; McDaniel. Leslie discusses the religious roles of Hindu women.

8. On the discussion of embodiment in social anthropology, see Csordas.

9. From an anthropological viewpoint, this "invention of tradition" (Hobsbawm and Ranger) is not unusual and certainly the impetus for several religious ceremonies. On the individual "personalization" of this ritual, see Hauser, "Creating Performative Texts," and chapter 2 of *Promising Rituals*.

10. Minturn also highlights this aspect in her study on women in Rajasthan.

11. Similarly, there are male ritual specialists who cross-dress in order to invite possession by a goddess; i.e. they feminize their body. See Hauser, "Whether Tribal or Tantric?"

12. With respect to the *social position* of women, however, these questions make sense. Accordingly, Yumiko Tokita-Tanabe investigated how women in Orissa are finding space for exercising agency within the socio-cultural definitions of femininity and what limitations there are to their endeavor due to the current social, economic, and political situation (3).

13. In this, I differ from Tokita-Tanabe's approach.

14. See Chapter 9 of Mieke Bal's *Kulturanalyse* on the analytical pitfalls of the seemingly clear distinction between performance and performativity.

Bibliography

Bal, Mieke. *Kulturanalyse*. Frankfurt/Main: Suhrkamp, 2002.

Bartky, Sandra Lee. "Agency: What's the Problem?" *Provoking Agents: Gender and Agency in Theory and Practice*. Ed. Judith Kegan Gardiner. Urbana: U of Illinois P, 1995. 178–93.

Butler, Judith. *Bodies that Matter: On the Discursive Limits of "Sex."* New York: Routledge, 1993.

———. *Gender Trouble: Feminism and the Subversion of Identity*. New York: Routledge, 1991.

Cohen, Anthony P., and Nigel Rapport, eds. *Questions of Conciousness*. London: Routledge, 1995.

Csordas, Thomas J., ed. *Embodiment and Experience: the Existential Ground of Culture and Self*. Cambridge: Cambridge UP, 1994.

Das, Veena. "Masks and Faces: An Essay on Punjabi Kinship." *Contributions to Indian Sociology* 10.1 (1976): 1–30.

Dumont, Louis. *Homo Hierarchicus: An Essay on the Caste System*. Chicago: U of Chicago P, 1970.

Fischer-Lichte, Erika. "Einleitende Thesen zum Aufführungsbegriff." *Kunst der Aufführung – Aufführung der Kunst*. Ed. Erika Fischer-Lichte, Clemens Risi, and Jens Roselt. Berlin: Theater der Zeit, 2004. 11–26.

Gardiner, Judith Kegan, ed. *Provoking Agents: Gender and Agency in Theory and Practice*. Urbana: U of Illinois P, 1995.

Gell, Alfred. *Art and Agency: An Anthropological Theory*. Oxford: Clarendon Press, 1998.

Giddens, Anthony. *Central Problems in Social Theory: Action, Structure and Contradiction in Social Analysis*. London: Macmillan, 1979.

———. *The Constitution of Society*. Oxford: Polity Press, 1984.

Hauser, Beatrix. "Creating Performative Texts: The Introduction of Mangala puja in Southern Orissa." *Text and Context in the History, Literature and Religion of Orissa*. Ed. Angelika Malinar, Johannes Beltz, and Heiko Frese. Delhi: Manohar, 2004. 203–38.

———. "Divine Play or Subversive Comedy? Reflections on Costuming and Gender at a Hindu Festival." *Celebrating Transgression as Method and Politics in Anthropological Studies of Culture*. Ed. Ursula Rao and John Hutnyk. New York: Berghahn, 2005. 129–44.

———. "Divine Possession as a Religious Idiom. Considering Female Ritual Practice in Orissa." *Centres Out There? Facets of Subregional Identities*. Ed. Hermann Kulke and Georg Berkemer. Delhi: Manohar (forthcoming).

———. "Göttliches Gestalten: Zur Besessenheitserfahrung von Frauen in Orissa, Indien." *Der maximal Fremde: Begegnungen mit dem Nichtmenschlichen und die Grenzen des Verstehens*. Ed. Michael Schetsche. Grenzüberschreitungen 3. Würzburg: Ergon, 2004. 139–60.

———. "How to Fast for a Good Husband? On Ritual Imitation and Embodiment in Orissa, India." *Rituals in an Unstable World: Contingency – Hybridity – Embodiment*. Ed. Alexander Henn and Klaus-Peter Köpping. Frankfurt/Main: Lang, 2008. 227–45.

———. "Periodisch unberührbar – zur körperlichen Performanz menstrueller Unreinheit in Südorissa (Indien)." *Kulturelle Ver-Wandlungen: Die Gestaltung sozialer Welten in der Performanz*. Ed. Ursula Rao. Frankfurt/Main: Campus, 2006. 73–106.

———. *Promising Rituals: Doing Gender in Southern Orissa (India)*. Halle: Martin-Luther-

University of Halle-Wittenberg, 2008 (habilitation thesis, forthcoming).

———. "Travelling Through the Night: Living Mothers and Divine Daughters at an Orissan Goddess Festival." *Paideuma: Mitteilungen zur Kulturkunde 51* (2005): 221–33.

———. "Whether Tribal or Tantric? Reflections on the Classification of Goddesses in Southern Orissa." *Periphery and Centre: Studies in Orissan History, Religion and Anthropology*. Ed. Georg Pfeffer. Delhi: Manohar, 2007. 131–52.

Hobsbawm, Eric, and Terence Ranger, eds. *The Invention of Tradition*. Cambridge: Cambridge UP, 1983.

Hughes-Freeland, Felicia, and Mary M. Crain, eds. *Recasting Ritual: Performance, Media, Identity*. London: Routledge, 1998.

Inden, Ronald B. *Imagining India*. Oxford: Basil Blackwell, 1990.

Köpping, Klaus-Peter, and Ursula Rao, eds. *Im Rausch des Rituals: Gestaltung und Transformation der Wirklichkeit in körperlicher Performanz*. Münster: Lit., 2000.

Kramer, Fritz. "Notizen zu einer Ethnologie der passiones." *Ethnologie als Sozialwissenschaft*. Ed. Ernst Wilhelm Müller et al. Kölner Zeitschrift für Soziologie und Sozialwissenschaft, Sonderheft 26. Opladen: Westdeutscher Verlag, 1994. 297–313.

Kumar, Nita, ed. *Women as Subjects: South Asian Histories*. Charlottesville: U of Virginia P, 1994.

Leslie, Julia, ed. *Roles and Rituals for Hindu Women*. London: Pinter Publishers, 1991.

Marglin, Frederique Apffel. "Gender and the Unitary Self: Looking for the Subaltern in Coastal Orissa." *South Asia Research* 15.1 (1995): 78–130.

McDaniel, June. *Making Virtuous Daughters and Wives: An Introduction to Women's Brata Rituals in Bengali Folk Religion*. Albany: State U of New York P, 2003.

McGee, Mary. "Desired Fruits: Motive and Intention in the Votive Rites of Hindu Women." *Roles and Rituals for Hindu Women*. Ed. Julia Leslie. London: Pinter Publishers, 1991. 71–88.

———. *Feasting and Fasting: The Vrata Tradition and Its Significance for Hindu Women*. Ann Arbor: University Microfilms, 1989.

McKenzie, Jon. *Perform or Else: From Discipline to Performance*. London: Routledge, 2001.

Mines, Mattison. *Public Faces, Private Voices: Community and Individuality in South India*. Berkeley, Los Angeles, London: U of California P, 1994.

Minturn, Leigh. *Sita's Daughters: Coming Out of Purdah: The Rajput Women of Khalapur Revisited*. New York: Oxford UP, 1993.

Misra, Nirmala. *Osa brata gapa*. Brahmapura: Taratarini pustakalaya, 1994.

Morrissey, Belinda. *When Women Kill: Questions of Agency and Subjectivity*. London: Routledge, 2003.

Parkin, David, Lionel Caplan and Humphrey Fisher, eds. *The Politics of Cultural Performance*. Providence/Oxford: Berghahn, 1996.

Sax, William S. "In Karna's Realm: An Ontology of Action." *Journal of Indian Philosophy* 28 (2000): 295–324.

Schieffelin, Edward. "On Failure and Performance: Throwing the Medium Out of the Seance." *The Performance of Healing*. Ed. Carol Laderman and Marina Roseman. New York: Routledge, 1996. 59–90.

———. "Problematizing Performance." *Ritual, Performance, Media*. Ed. Felicia Hughes-Freeland. London: Routledge, 1998. 194–207.

Sökefeld, Martin. "Debating Self, Identity, and Culture in Anthropology." *Current Anthropology* 40.4 (1999): 417–47.

Sutherland, Peter. "Very Little Kingdoms: The Calendrical Order of West Himalayan Hindu Polity." *Sharing Sovereignty: The Little Kingdom in South Asia*. Ed. Georg Berkemer and Margret Frenz. Berlin: Schwarz, 2003. 31–61.

Tewari, Laxmi G. *A Splendor of Worship: Women's Fasts, Rituals, Stories and Art*. Delhi: Manohar, 1991.

Tokita-Tanabe, Yumiko. "Body, Self and Agency of Women in Contemporary Orissa, India." Diss. University of Tokyo, 2002.

Willems, Herbert, and Martin Jurga, eds. *Inszenierungsgesellschaft: Ein einführendes Handbuch*. Opladen: Westdeutscher Verlag, 1998.

"We Are Like Fish That Were Reeled In": Peasant Understandings of Modernity in Zimbabwe

Guy Thompson[1]

This paper concerns the roles language, metaphor, and historical understanding play in public discourse and identity construction in contemporary Zimbabwe. In it, I explore the ways that older residents of Madziwa, Zimbabwe, frame and debate their past through two key concepts: in Shona, these are *chivanhu*, the way of the people, and *chirungu*, meaning English, European, or modern ways.[2] Peasants use these concepts to illuminate the dramatic changes they have experienced during their lives, highlighting the impact of commodification, colonization, social change, and government initiatives on rural people. The two terms are drawn from wider debates about social change, race, and identity, but older Madziwans deploy them in distinctive ways to explain and contest their memories and social position. I argue that these concepts are central to a discrete discursive field and play a key role in the dynamics of popular memory, providing peasants with a means to challenge state authority and official explanations within Zimbabwe's repressive political order. Moreover, these accounts illuminate rural people's experiences of social dislocation during the twentieth century, challenging hegemonic western understandings of modernity.

In a broader sense, *chirungu* and *chivanhu* invoke potent oppositions such as traditional and modern, or African and European, ideas that circulate widely in Africa. They emerged in state policies and national discourses about Negritude, the legitimating force of tradition in Banda's Malawi or Mobutu's authenticity policy in the then Zaire. More importantly, people draw upon similar oppositions in popular discourse throughout southern Africa. John and Jean Comaroff's "The Madman and the Migrant" highlights the pervasive dualism of *setswana* and *sekgoa*, Tswana and European ways, which Tswana speakers use to frame their history and highlight the dislocating effects of dispossession and domination. In *Of Revelation and Revolution*, the

Comaroffs explore the origins of this opposition in the missionary encounter, arguing for the "implicit structure of shared meaning" in the poetics of these terms (29). A similar pairing emerged in Belinda Bozzoli and Mmantho Nkotsoe's work in Phokeng, South Africa, as many of the elderly women they met used this contrast to contend that indigenous foods and values provided the foundations of the orderly peasant society of their childhood; Bozzoli interpreted this image as an ideology, potentially the basis for a land-based nationalism (53–5). James Ferguson also encountered a dualism between modern and traditional among residents of the towns of the Zambian copperbelt, where these ideas pervaded debates about fashion, appropriate ways of behaving, and cultural style (*Expectations of Modernity*). Research in several rural districts of northwestern Zimbabwe by Eric Worby, Pius Nyambara ("Immigrants"; "Madheruka and Shangwe Ethnic Identities"), and Jocelyn Alexander and JoAnn McGregor explores deployments of interrelated ideas about ethnicity, modernity, tradition, and backwardness in popular discourse, highlighting the association of particular cultural practices, farming techniques, and gendered behaviors with being modern. These parallel examples from different regions of Africa not only highlight the importance of popular understandings, but the role of potent dualisms such as modern and traditional in the wider processes of probing the meaning of modernity and the aftermath of colonialism around the globe.

Madziwa today is a Communal Area of 30,000 people in northeastern Zimbabwe, roughly 125 kilometers north of Harare. The designated Communal Areas are a legacy of racist land policies during the colonial period; called reserves and then tribal trust lands in Rhodesia, these areas were demarcated for black settlement and treated as marginal areas by the state, much like the South African bantustans or native reserves in Canada and the United States. Unlike most of the reserves, however, there is good quality agricultural land in Madziwa. Some residents were therefore able to make a reasonable living from peasant agriculture during the colonial period, an option that is still open to a few people today. Madziwans began experiencing intense colonial demands and capitalist pressures comparatively late, reflecting their reserve's location on the periphery of early colonial development; only in the later 1930s, as the agricultural economy recovered from the depression, did peasants in Madziwa begin experimenting with significant market production, European tools such as the plough, and new farming methods. State pressures were limited until 1945, when the white settler government forcibly relocated peasants from designated European land to Madziwa as part of its wider segregation efforts. These relocations were accompanied by coercive agricultural "improvement" schemes that introduced new landholding patterns and residential patterns along with physically demanding conservation measures. Madziwans dramatically increased crop output and sales during this period, making the area one of the leading centers of peasant maize production in the colony. Many people in the area resisted the state's aggressive efforts to direct peasant production in the later 1950s, and actively supported the nationalist movement and guerilla forces during the 1960s and 1970s. After independence in 1980, residents benefited from improved state services, particularly in health and education, and some were able to take advantage of improved market conditions for peasants. However, by the late 1990s, when the interviews for this project were undertaken, many Madziwans were frustrated by the growing signs of Zimbabwe's current crisis, including declining state services, government indifference, corruption, the failure to introduce substantial land reform, the effects of structural adjustment, and the massive impact of HIV/AIDS.[3]

Older Madziwans have therefore lived through a dramatic series of economic and political changes, remaking rural society in the process. During my interviews with 135 area residents, they frequently described their lifetime as the movement from chivanhu to chirungu, using these concepts to encapsulate their experiences with the pressures and opportunities of modernity. These concepts provide a nuanced way to understand the far-reaching changes that transformed peasants' lives, in particular to express the discrepancy between the sudden shifts brought about by state action and the much more gradual changes rooted in the influence of the market and new ideas.

The concepts of chirungu and chivanhu, presented as a binary opposition, figure prominently in debates about cultural change, identity, and race in many parts of Zimbabwe. At the most basic level, they are descriptive terms, used to distinguish indigenous and introduced items, even basic ones such as common tools and foodstuffs. Chirungu items and practices are defined as white, even though black Zimbabweans have adopted them, while chivanhu is seen as inherently African, presented in ways that essentialize racial differences. These associations emerge in subtle ways, and are evident even in the ways that people talk about food. Many black Zimbabweans think Europeans are constitutionally unable to eat chivanhu foods, and some argue that legitimate spirit mediums – key local religious figures – should only eat indigenous foods, prepared with chivanhu techniques, to ensure they keep their powers. As Louise Kutoratsoka explained:

> You know, today there are still real mediums in Mrewa. They don't eat sadza [the local staple] made from maize, no, no, they can't. They only eat millet and sorghum which have been pounded in a mortar [rather than maize ground in a mechanized mill] to make the meal for cooking sadza. They eat that [sadza] with dried cowbean leaves which have just been boiled with salt – without even oil or tomatoes.

The opposition between chirungu and chivanhu, and their wider implications of foreign ideas and authentically African practices, figure in more complex ways in contemporary Zimbabwe, surfacing in discussions of morality, the state of the nation, religion, race, and cultural practices; at their core, these debates concern identity and historical change. They also figure prominently in state propaganda and are used by Robert Mugabe to claim political and racial legitimacy in the face of widespread opposition, corruption, political violence, and electoral manipulation. The state-controlled television station, ZBC, broadcasts the series *Nhaka Yedu* – "Our Customs" – which frequently upholds "African" manners and material culture against the dangers of the west.[4] Late in 2003, the government launched an aggressive publicity campaign that invoked "African tradition" to applaud the seizure of white-owned commercial farms and their redistribution to blacks (many of whom were cabinet ministers or party officials), which has played a central role in Zimbabwe's economic meltdown. The campaign has been controversial, partly because of its political implications, but the reactions to it also illustrate wider currents of social and moral tension that enmesh ideas about tradition, culture, and authenticity:

But accompanying one [advertisement] on screen with a traditional dance, the kongonya, has prompted protests from TV viewers appalled at the pelvic grinding of young women and children. "Pornographic, sexually perverted, disgusting," some of them said. Mr Mugabe has defended the advert and this week the state-owned Herald newspaper devoted two pages to explaining that the dance epitomised the fight against colonial domination. "The sexually suggestive connotations of the waist wriggling and the fast rhythmic throwing upwards and downwards of buttocks is again a sign of defiance of the detractors of the land reform," the Herald explained. ("Be Happy")

Similar concerns about morality, values, cultural authenticity, and the meaning of race figure in wider conversation and popular culture. Ideas about *chirungu* are generally associated with modernity, while *chivanhu* is used in the sense of tradition. City dwellers, and many formally educated people in the countryside such as teachers, often use *chivanhu* as a derisive term, denoting "primitive" or "backwards" and embodying their disdain for peasants and rural practices.[5]

Debates about cultural change and social practices began during the colonial period and surfaced frequently in the African-targeted press. City dwellers and educated people often upheld the value of westernization, as the editorial in the first issue of the popular *African Parade* magazine reflected:

But there is not a shade of doubt that socially the African has made such rapid advance that there can be no misgivings in launching a magazine such as "The African Parade." The African['s] music, his art, his sense of humour, his rich gift for drama and his desire to assimilate the one hundred and one aspects of Western civilisation need full expression and there can be no better medium to achieve this than this magazine, which will attempt to put on record that aspect of African life which is as yet little known and inadequately portrayed in word and picture. While it is true that at the present stage the African is a man of two worlds, it is equally true to say that his choice to graft himself into the western political, economic and social system is an unwavering one and it is important that he finds the fullest opportunity to express himself in every way. ("Editorial")

By the early 1960s, however, cultural practices had become a key part of the intensely politicized atmosphere created by nationalist activity and state repression. Leading blacks, angered by the limits of liberal reform and the persistence of social barriers that excluded them, invoked ideas that asserted African equality on many levels. Confronting the white minority regime's ban on nationalist posters, buttons, and t-shirts, activists turned to "African" symbols such as carved walking sticks, fur hats, and animal skins to express political allegiances. *Chivanhu* and *chirungu* emerged as key identifying terms in cultural debates in this period, as a derisive government pamphlet made clear:

> There has been much talk in the urban areas of going back to your traditional ways – of wearing skin hats, of eating SADZA not tea and bread, cf paying respect to old spirits and tribal dances. It is strange, is it not, that the political speakers who talk much of this are the very ones who know nothing about the old ways, who like to live in towns and the new ways of life they call CHIRUNGU (European)? But the choice is yours. . . . There is no law about such things, although people from towns may make you think there is. ("Why ZAPU Was Banned" 11–12)

Thus, *chirungu* and *chivanhu*, and the ideas associated with the way of the people and modern ways, have been key elements of popular discourse and political debates in Zimbabwe for more than 40 years. While they are frequently invoked by the Mugabe regime to claim legitimacy and African authenticity, they take on very different meanings in peasant discourse in Madziwa, as I explain below. I hold that these terms, and the wider discursive field in which *chivanhu* and *chirungu* figure prominently, should be conceptualized on several different levels, in terms of their role in individual memory, popular memory, historical understanding, politics, and modernity itself.

On an individual level, people draw on *chivanhu, chirungu* and associated ideas to frame, understand, and present their memories, using these key concepts within the local cultural field to structure remembering. Individual recall is a dynamic process in which people draw on popular terms and understandings to reconfigure their memories, shaping them in response to contemporary and historical concerns. Oral history taps these resources, but individual recall is not my main concern in this paper. Rather, I want to focus on the level of shared and contested meaning, the cultural field in which Madziwans deploy ideas about *chirungu* and *chivanhu*, which has been conceptualized as social, collective, or oppositional memory.[6] I think the concept of popular memory developed by the Popular Memory Group (PMG) provides the best means to understand this cultural field, particularly as it foregrounds the political implications of recall that are evident in peasant accounts. The PMG argued that popular memory emerges from the interaction between, on the one hand, dominant forms of memory asserted by the state, privileged groups, and academics, and, on the other, subordinated or private memories that challenge dominant forms.

Subordinate accounts are often presented in terms drawn from dominant ones, but these terms take on new meaning, challenging dominant memory. Popular memory emerges in this process by which the disadvantaged challenge hegemonic models, drawing on and redefining the terms of dominant discourse; as I explain below, older Madziwans do this with *chivanhu* and *chirungu*, and their debates about the past, which are couched in these terms, illustrate the dynamics of popular memory and its key role in identity formation (Popular Memory Group 207–29).

Moreover, focusing on the terms and ideas in the shared cultural space of popular memory in Madziwa is also a means to highlight key areas of social change and peasant discontent in Zimbabwe, providing a deeper understanding of historical developments around commodification, colonization, and state intervention, rooted in the explanations of the people who experienced them. Thus, the conversations in which *chivanhu* and *chirungu* surface represent a discrete understanding of modernity, a discursive field in which the importance of these transitions is debated. This argument builds on Paul Gilroy's exploration of the complex and contradictory meanings of modernity in which he foregrounds black slaves' and their descendants' experiences of violence and dislocation within the Atlantic world, as well as on James Ferguson's insights into urban Zambians' understandings of modernity framed through economic decline, despair, and the broken promises of capitalism and independence (*Expectations of Modernity*). Modernity, therefore, cannot simply be presented through European narratives of progress, but should reflect the fractured, discrepant experiences, subjectivities, and identities at play throughout the world; I hold that the popular memory of people in Madziwa is one sliver within this fragmented field (see also Brown 3–4).

Among older residents of Madziwa, a few people identify strongly with *chirungu*, arguing that it brought beneficial changes to the rural areas, particularly a new sense of direction. Most members of this group are materially successful men who figure among the small peasant elite and are able to sell significant quantities of produce because they can afford chemical fertilizers and insecticides (Munaka; Musikiwa). The vast majority of Madziwans presented much more complex and critical views, echoing debates within and beyond their community. I did not encounter a unitary perspective amongst this larger group. Disagreements and even contradictory ideas within the statements of the same person were frequent, highlighting the shifting meaning and importance of ideas about *chivanhu* and *chirungu*, and ongoing processes of debate. These conversations also revealed strong common elements in the ways that peasants, including those who were generally positive about the impact of modernity, used these terms to explain the transformations in their lives, further underlining their importance and the dynamics of popular memory.

In this common usage, many Madziwans present the *chivanhu* period in an idealized and oversimplified way, as a time when peasants lived in an orderly, harmonious, healthy, and independent society. These qualities have been undermined by the impact of *chirungu*. There are many different dimensions to this view, but at its most basic it is an affirmation of Africans' past and ways of interacting with the world. Mai Ndowa neatly summarized this view early in our conversation when she said: "In the past we lived superbly. Our parents were farmers; we even grew plants near the rivers [an indigenous practice that promoted food security that was outlawed by the colonial and post-independence governments]." Many people argued that the environment was healthier and rainfall much more consistent during their youth, because people adhered to local religious prohibitions and observed the major rituals. This spiritual order is believed to have brought other benefits. People were healthier, particularly children, and they were more fertile, as Louise Kutoratsoka argued: "All the women who were of my age [in her early 70s] had given birth, and none of them had had problems. There were no operations; one could give birth to 10 children without a problem. Some people even had 20 without problems!" Greater health was also the result of eating appropriate *chivanhu* foods, as well as the careful use of indigenous medicines, drawn from roots and herbs (VaMandere and Amai Machiko; Chief Nyamaropa).

Life was simpler according to this widely held image of *chivanhu*. Households produced most of the goods they needed or acquired them by trading with their neighbors (Mai Matumba; Mai Musonza; VaMusonza). These ideas emphasize the economic autonomy of Madziwa inhabitants before 1935. Many elderly residents reinforced this by arguing that their parents had not produced surplus crops to sell, echoing VaMandere:

We just got crops to eat [when I was young], nothing was sold. We didn't know about selling. As long as you filled your big baskets with crops, you knew you would be all right for food; you had enough for the whole family for the coming year.

Thus, people largely lived beyond the reach of the capitalist economy, were free from the demands of the market, and rarely used money.[7] Residents of Madziwa had simple wants, as Amai Chaparira Paiena explained in response to my question about what things people wanted to buy when she was a girl: "Nothing, we only wanted salt, although the shopkeeper also gave us sugar. Tell me what did we need it for?" These images rest on an implied comparison with the reach of the market and pervasive use of money today, which has replaced other forms of exchange for gifts, ritual purposes, and to pay for labor and services within Madziwa.

Elderly peasants also emphasize the limited reach of the state in the years before the Second World War, contrasting the experiences of their youth with the settler administration's later intrusive efforts to shape rural life and the expansion of government services and restrictions since independence. For VaMakombe there were clear advantages to this situation: "Long ago, when I was just a boy, we were sitting pretty! The whites were here, its true, but they were very few. The *majoni* [white police and their African assistants] were only seen when there was a serious crime. This meant people were highly autonomous, largely subject to their own laws and customs" (VaMrewa and VaMushoniwa). For many, this autonomy was synonymous with freedom, an idea that has particular cogency when it is applied to the land. Mai Kondo recalled: "We were free then, it's true. There was a lot of land, and the forests were very big then, so we didn't face any restrictions." In this construction of *chivanhu*, harmony prevailed. Africans ruled themselves under the mild authority of the chiefs, mediums, and spirits, free from the demands of the colonial state and the market.

These oversimplified, nostalgic ideas about the early colonial period contrast sharply with widely held images of modernity, which emphasize the far-reaching consequences of adopting *chirungu*. As people chose to, and were forced to, change social and productive practices, there have been serious consequences in many areas. The physical environment has been degraded, with soils losing their fertility, the rain diminishing, and springs drying up, according to Amai Mushamba:

When I was young, we did not have problems with the rains. The rains would start in October, and were good. But nowadays, we don't even know when the rain will start. The problem is that people disregard the sacred places, and they are no longer conducting the rain making ceremonies. . . . The rains are also erratic now. The people of today have abandoned our spirits.

Many elders agreed with this perception of widespread spiritual and ecological decline as consequences of the growing acceptance of *chirungu*, compounded by religious dissension, as Mai Kapembeza explained:

People began abandoning the spirits when ploughs were introduced and when people began to consider themselves educated. At the same time, the spirits have disappeared, and they went together with the rain. Due to colonisation, people now want to follow chirungu, and many of them have become Christians. Along the way, people have abandoned the spirits and the medium. It was around 1940 that people started following chirungu.

People use concern about religious differences to convey their distress about growing social divisions, a key feature of *chirungu*. In part, they are lamenting the loss of a unifying practice and religious vision that upheld the role of elders. On another level, people use religious concerns to express their distress with growing social divisions, particularly along generational lines. As Morris Makaza explained, this was evident in the failure of young people to defer to their elders and show them the respect to which they feel entitled. "They [young people] just want to follow *chirungu*. Like going to the spirits for rains, they laugh about that – they are mocking us!" Older peasants often present generational tensions in terms of declining moral standards. Jojo Mandaza was particularly concerned about young people abandoning elaborate and deferential Shona greetings, which he argued was part of a wider cultural transformation brought about by European influences:

> Our children have been exposed to a lot of chirungu customs, and those customs are easy to follow. The influence of white people can now be seen even in the way our children greet their parents [elders]. Some children can even be heard saying 'Hi [in English] baba' or 'Yes [in English] baba', and they do not kneel down when they greet their elders! . . . The younger people think that chirungu practices are richer than our Shona ways. . . . Some of them think that chivanhu is very bad. They say that if someone doesn't speak English, it shows that they are not educated and are ignorant.

Moral decline and the failure to respect parents' desires have disrupted marriages and families (Mai Matumba). Women's morality and sexual behavior are considered to have particularly suffered due to the spread of chirungu. Several people complained about women wearing trousers and short skirts, which are generally considered to be far too revealing and are therefore equated with immorality and prostitution (Jera Family; VaManyika).

Peasants in Madziwa see materialism, greed, and jealousy as emotions that have been brought to the fore by the social divisions fostered by the spread of chirungu. Morris Makaza argued that jealousy of other people's success contributed to the spread of disease, obliquely referring to witchcraft and to AIDS:

Morris Makaza: Children and even elders did not just die like they do today. There were not as many diseases back then, we were just OK.

Guy Thompson: Why are there more diseases today?

Morris Makaza: I think that perhaps what we eat today has contributed. And also there are enemies who are jealous of those of us who are living well!

Desire, greed, and materialism are all raised by people looking to explain the lure of chirungu, the factors that led people away from their orderly, harmonious, and independent path. In these conversations, sugar and textiles are frequently mentioned as the key items that drew rural people towards the market and chirungu more broadly, awakening a whole range of desires:

> We were given change in sugar [at the store]. You, you whites troubled us with sugar! . . . We noticed a big change in our lives when we started using sugar. Before we were happy with two cloths, one to wear while the other was being washed. But the sugar was so good, so tasty, so sweet. So we wanted it – we grabbed it and ate it like this [demonstrates, taking handfuls and gobbling]. We mixed it with millet and made a porridge – with that and some water, you were satisfied for the whole day. Then, [with sugar] we started to want more, and we wanted many sets of clothes! (Kutoratsoka)

Sugar also figured prominently in Pearson Jera's explanation, as he connected material wants, cultural change, and environmental decline.

We are like fish that have been reeled in. . . . Sugar was given to us, that was the key thing. Once you tasted it, you would tell others to eat it. We did not eat with a spoon then, we used tree bark. Young people turned against our ways, and we have lost chivanhu now that we want a lot of things. Even the rains have been cut! (Jera family)

Elderly residents of Madziwa also tie the spread of *chirungu* to the actions of the colonial state and settlers. Mai Kapembeza argued that encouraging cultural change was an integral feature of colonialism, which she thought began with medicine.

Mai Kapembeza: When the whites came, they told people not to go into the bush and look for [medicinal] herbs and plants. It became a crime for a mother to give her child traditional medicines. We then followed the white's man's medicines, and in the process have forgotten some of the herbs that might help us to fight some of the diseases that we have today.

Guy Thompson: Why did the Europeans want the people to give up chivanhu?

Mai Kapembeza: They wanted the people to abandon chivanhu as a way of colonising them, making them give up this and that. Due to the pressure and force, people yielded and began to abandon chivanhu in favor of chirungu.

Chirungu and *chivanhu* are central concepts in the shared cultural field in Madziwa, playing vital roles in popular memory. The presentation of *chivanhu* as a time when Africans lived in an orderly, harmonious, and independent society is an oversimplification, but it is important to understand the implications of this construction. It cannot simply be dismissed as the nostalgia of the elderly, although remembering the past in romantic ways certainly plays a role. The contrast between this construction and ideas about the impact of *chirungu*, however, highlights central areas of change since 1920. Colonial rule, capitalist expansion, and cultural change have brought increased conflict within rural communities such as Madziwa. Although people speak in terms of religious differences, moral decline, and the adoption of disruptive priorities and values, I argue that these ideas illuminate key areas of conflict along gender and generational lines, as well as between members of increasingly economically differentiated communities. Moreover, these observations underline the changing bases of power as commodification spread within Madziwa, with the control of money and material resources supplanting influence over people and their labor.

The equation of *chivanhu* with independence illustrates the decline in the relative autonomy of peasants in Madziwa, who largely lived beyond the reach of the market and the state in the 1920s, but have become increasingly vulnerable to the demands, whims, and failures of both in the intervening years. Elders use the impact of *chirungu* to express the loss of peasants' economic autonomy during their lifetime, as people were drawn into the market and became accustomed to purchasing a range of goods since the late 1930s, practices that have been undermined by structural adjustment and the economic crisis. Complaints about environmental decline also reflect Madziwans' loss of economic autonomy, and the consequences of adopting new agricultural strategies that increased production but at the cost of greater risks. Chivanhu methods were designed to provide food security, sacrificing maximum yield for an assured return, regardless of weather conditions during Zimbabwe's capricious rainy season. Madziwans adopted *chirungu* farming strategies focused on ploughs, monocropping, and repeated use of the same lands because of the labor advantages of new tools, combined with the draw and pressures of the market, but they were also pushed to use them by state agricultural "improvement" schemes during the colonial period and after independence (Drinkwater 12, 88, 98–103; see also Ferguson, *Anti-Politics Machine* 254–6, 270–271).

In a similar vein, peasants use religious laments to express the loss of community autonomy to the state, as the authority of the chiefs was bound up with that of the spirits and mediums. These changing dynamics are also implicit in the association of *chivanhu* with freedom. People emphasize the changing social networks within which rural people operated, as impersonal, bureaucratic rule and relations measured in monetary terms supplanted a context wherein peasants' primary contacts were with other members of the same small community, mediated by rules that provided the relatively powerless with a variety of means to negotiate with more influential people.

The emphasis on loss that runs throughout the opposition of *chirungu* with *chivanhu* is also a veiled political critique within the context of state repression, directed against the ongoing efforts of the post-independence government to direct peasants' lives, and its failure to respond to rural people's grievances, particularly over the land question. Older residents are using the concepts of freedom and cultural autonomy to echo the ideas of the liberation struggle, which they supported at great cost to bring the Mugabe governments to power. Thus the politics of memory play a vital role in shaping not just what people are willing to publicly discuss about their past, but how they construct, understand, and debate their history.

Finally, the conversations around these terms also capture the ambiguities of modernization. The majority of peasants in Madziwa are critical of the impact of *chirungu* on their lives, even as they appreciate many of the things brought by the spread of *chirungu* – new foodstuffs, tools that reduce drudgery, formal education, radios, buses, and a wide range of commodities. Modernity, however, has come with costs, and people use the dichotomy between *chirungu* and *chivanhu* to express their underlying sense of cultural loss as they have given into the lure of *chirungu*. As Louise Kutoratsoka explained:

When they [whites] came we took to their way of life and began to follow their customs. We abandoned the hard way of living and copied the whites. We lost our culture. People did as the Europeans did, although there was a difference of skin.

Notes

1. I would like to gratefully acknowledge financial support for this project from the Social Sciences and Humanities Research Council of Canada and the University of Alberta, as well as the Graduate School, History Department, and the MacArthur Interdisciplinary Program on Global Change, Sustainability and Justice of the University of Minnesota. I would also like to thank the members of the Department of Economic History at the University of Zimbabwe for their input and support for my research, particularly Joseph Mtisi, who commented on an earlier version of this paper. Finally I would like to acknowledge the vital assistance of my research assistants in Madziwa, Rangarirai Gurure, Obert Kufinya, and Solomon Mahdi, who not only helped with introductions and translation when my Shona failed me, but provided important insights into my work.

2. *Chirungu* also means the English language. *Chirungu*, *chivanhu*, and *chishona* – meaning the Shona language – all belong to the same noun class, Class 7. In Shona, as in other Bantu languages, nouns are not divided into the categories that typify European languages: masculine, feminine, and, in some cases, neuter. Rather, nouns are grouped into 21 different classes; plural forms representing separate classes, so that the plurals of Class 7 nouns constitute Class 8, marked by a *zvi* prefix which replaces the *chi*. *Chirungu* and *chivanhu* are not used in the plural, but *chipo*, a gift, becomes *zvipo*, gifts. Most of the noun classes bring together words with common meanings and associations; Classes 1 and 2, for example, are used for people. However, Class 7 is the generic class, so the nouns in it vary widely – but it does include all languages.

3. For a full discussion of these changes in Madziwa, see my doctoral dissertation (Thompson). I use the terms Communal Area and reserve interchangeably throughout this paper. This reflects common Zimbabwean usage, in English and in Shona. I have followed this usage not only as it reflects the continuity of language patterns, but because it highlights the limited changes in the Communal Areas since independence and the constraints inherited from the colonial era that most people in the reserves continue to face. Moreover, despite the recent land seizures and related turmoil, most Zimbabweans continue to live in the Communal Areas, as the various land reform efforts have done little to undo colonial inequities.

4. For example, the episode broadcast on 22 July 2002 explored the association of language, cultural practice, and family authority, deriding western ideas and lamenting the loss of African traditions; the set and titles featured a mélange of baskets, clay pots, animal skins, and carved wooden objects drawn from different cultural groups to invoke African authenticity. The host and discussants were both academics at the University of Zimbabwe and key supporters of the Mugabe regime.

5. These ideas frequently surface on radio, TV, and in newspapers. One of Zimbabwe's leading musicians, Oliver Mtukudzi, addresses them in many of his songs, such as "Tsika Dzedu" (Our Ways) on *Tuku Music*. Debates about race, identity, and cultural practice have also moved to the Internet, linking Zimbabweans in the country with those living outside; see shonalyrics.co.zw, particularly the forum postings on the topics of Nose Brigades (MaNOZI), and Masalads neMaSadza. Tim Burke discusses these types of cultural debates within the frame of modernity and tradition, rather than *chivanhu* and *chirungu*. His examples, drawn mainly from novels, poetry, and drama, explore the resonance of these ideas in elite discussions of race, identity, and social change in the context of the development of commodity culture in Zimbabwe.

6. Understandings of the dynamic nature of memory and its use in oral history are best presented in the work of Luisa Passerini, Alessandro Portelli and Alistair Thomson. They build on the ideas of Maurice Halbwachs, but emphasize contestation, conflict, and silences. For an insightful discussion of social memory, see Antze and Lambert (xx); on collective memory, see Boym (53) and Peter Burke (98, 106–107); and for an exploration of oppositional memory, see Watson (2–3).

7. While people overemphasize the limited circulation of money in Madziwa in the early colonial period for effect, they did live on the margins of the colonial economy and had little use for money within Madziwa, except to pay taxes; there were no shops in the areas until the 1930s. Moreover, trade and commercial relations in this region were very limited in the second half of the nineteenth century, before the colonial occupation. David Beach argues that the accessible gold deposits were exhausted and elephant populations seriously depleted by circa 1850, so that the earlier commercial economy and vibrant trade links to the east coast of the continent had largely shut down.

Bibliography

Alexander, Jocelyn, and JoAnn McGregor. "Modernity and Ethnicity in a Frontier Society: Understanding Difference in Northwestern Zimbabwe." *Journal of Southern African Studies* 23 (1997): 187–201.

Antze, Paul, and Michael Lambert. "Introduction." *Tense Past: Cultural Essays in Trauma and Memory.* Ed. Paul Antze and Michael Lambert. London: Routledge, 1996. xi–xxxviii.

Beach, David. *The Shona and their Neighbours.* Oxford: Blackwell Publishers, 1994.

"Be Happy Mugabe Tells the Starving." *Guardian Unlimited.* The Guardian, 13 Dec. 2003. Web. 13 December 2003.

Boym, Svetlana. *The Future of Nostalgia.* New York: Basic Books, 2001.

Bozzoli, Belinda, with Mmantho Nkotsoe. *Women of Phokeng. Consciousness, Life Strategy and Migrancy in South Africa, 1900–1983.* Portsmouth: Heinemann, 1991.

Brown, Wendy. *Politics Out of History.* Princeton: Princeton UP, 2001.

Burke, Peter. "History as Social Memory." *Memory: History, Culture and the Mind.* Ed. Thomas Butler. Oxford: Basil Blackwell, 1989. 97–113.

Burke, Tim. *Lifebuoy Men, Lux Women: Commodification, Consumption and Cleanliness in Modern Zimbabwe.* Durham: Duke UP, 1996.

Comaroff, John, and Jean Comaroff. "The Madman and the Migrant: Work and Labor in the Historical Consciousness of a South African People." *American Ethnologist* 14 (1987): 191–209.

———. *Of Revelation and Revolution: Christianity, Colonialism and Consciousness in South Africa.* Chicago: U of Chicago P, 1991.

"Discussion Forum." Shonalyrics.co.zw. Shona Lyrics. Web. 14 August 2003.

Drinkwater, Michael. *The State and Agrarian Change in Zimbabwe's Communal Areas.* New York: St Martin's Press, 1991.

"Editorial." *African Parade* 1.1 (1953): 3.

Ferguson, James. *The Anti-Politics Machine: 'Development', Depoliticization and Bureaucratic Power in Lesotho.* Minneapolis: U of Minnesota P, 1994.

———. *Expectations of Modernity: Myths and Meanings of Urban Life on the Zambian Copperbelt.* Berkeley: U of California P, 1999.

Gilroy, Paul. *The Black Atlantic: Modernity and Double Consciousness.* Cambridge: Harvard UP, 1993.

Mtukudzi, Oliver. *Tuku Music.* Tuku/Ikwezi Music, 1998/Putumayo World Music, 1999. CD.

"Nhaka Yedu." Zimbabwe Broadcasting Corporation. ZBC 1, Harare, 22 July 2002. Television.

Nyambara, Pius. "Immigrants, 'Traditional' Leaders and the Rhodesian State: The Power of Communal Land Tenure and the Politics of Land Acquisition in Gokwe, Zimbabwe, 1963–1979."

Journal of Southern African Studies 27 (2001): 771–91.

———. "Madheruka and Shangwe Ethnic Identities and the Culture of Modernity in Gokwe, Northwestern Zimbabwe, 1963–1979." *Journal of African History* 43 (2002): 287–306.

Passerini, Luisa. "Introduction." *Memory and Totalitarianism (International Yearbook of Oral History and Life Stories, Volume 1)*. Ed. Luisa Passerini. Oxford: Oxford UP, 1992. 1–19.

Popular Memory Group. "Popular memory: Theory, politics, method." *Making Histories: Studies in History-writing and Politics*. Ed. Richard Johnson, Gregor McLennan, Bill Schwarz, and David Sutton. London: Hutchinson, 1982. 205–52.

Portelli, Alessandro. *The Battle of Valle Giulia. Oral History and the Art of the Dialogue*. Madison: U of Wisconsin P, 1997.

Thompson, Guy. "Cultivating Conflict: 'Improved' Agriculture and Modernization in Colonial Zimbabwe, 1920–1965." Diss. University of Minnesota, 2000.

Thomson, Alistair. *Anzac Memories: Living with the Legend*. Melbourne: Oxford UP, 1994.

Watson, Rubie S. "Memory, History and Opposition Under State Socialism: An Introduction." *Memory, History and Opposition Under State Socialism*. Sante Fe: School of American Research Press, 1994. 1–20.

"Why Zapu Was Banned." National Archives of Zimbabwe, File F119/E120/40 "ZAPU," date stamped 17 December 1962.

Worby, Eric. "'Discipline without Oppression': Sequence, Timing and Marginality in Southern Rhodesia's Post-War Development Regime." *Journal of African History* 41 (2000): 101–125.

Interviews in Madziwa Communal Area

Amai Chaparira Paiena. Personal Interview, 7 May 1998.

Amai Mushamba. Personal Interview, 10 November 1997.

Chief Nyamaropa. Personal Interview, 18 October 1997.

Jera Family. Personal Interview, 16 May 1998.

Kutoratsoka, Louise. Personal Interview, 8 October 1997.

Mai Kapembeza. Personal Interview, 1 November 1997.

Mai Kondo. Personal Interview, 3 November 1997.

Mai Matumba. Personal Interview, 17 October 1997.

Mai Musonza. Personal Interview, 16 April 1997.

Mai Ndowa. Personal Interview, 6 November 1997.

Makaza, Morris. Personal Interview, 30 October 1997.

Mandaza, Jojo, Amai Rita, and Amai Sophie. Personal Interview, 16 October 1997.

Mhondoro Gumboromumwe. Personal Interview, 20 May 1998.

Munaka, Laxin. Personal Interview, 14 May 1998.

Musikiiwa, Joseph. Personal Interview, 9 October 1997.

VaMakombe. Personal Interview, 24 October 1997.

VaManderere and Amai Machiko. Personal Interview, 10 November 1997.

VaManyika. Personal Interview, 14 May 1998.

VaMrewa and VaMushoniwa. Personal Interview, 18 October 1997.

VaMusonza. Personal Interview, 14 June 1998.

Silence, Absence, Loss: Chineseness in Post-Authoritarian Indonesia

Sonja van Wichelen

Introduction

After decades of complex marginalization, discrimination, and racism, Chinese-Indonesians in post-1998 Indonesia have been given back the democratic space to participate culturally and politically in Indonesian public life. The fall of the authoritarian regime of President Suharto, which lasted for thirty-two years, brought along a number of significant changes for the Chinese-Indonesian minority. Bans geared against the socio-political and cultural participation of Chinese-Indonesians in public life were lifted and various citizenship rights were restored. Manifested in the increase of Chinese temples, Chinese films on national television, a growing Chinese literary output, and the celebration of Chinese New Year, a resurgence of public "Chineseness" seemed to have taken place.[1]

In a 2004 article for the Indonesian daily *Kompas* entitled "Unintentional Racism," Ariel Heryanto – a cultural theorist on Indonesian and Southeast Asian politics – critiqued the ways in which, in this new political climate, Chinese-Indonesians were "being made Chinese" (*dicinakan*). In his observation he pointed out the ways in which they were "resinicized" according to narrow definitions of what is to be understood as Chinese culture and traditions. Instead of approaching Chinese-Indonesian identities in their diverse relations and adaptations to local cultures, the resurgence of Chinese culture in the Indonesian public sphere represented an essentialized and homogenous Chinese identity. Heryanto described this process of resinicization as yet another form of racism stemming from the New Order, although unintentionally and positively informed rather than intentionally negative.

Agreeing with Heryanto that these practices are taking place and that they are highly problematic, I would like to explore further the meanings behind this process of resinicization within a theoretical framework of trauma. Besides government-initiated activities, Chinese-Indonesians among themselves are socializing and participating in the revival of Chineseness. By analyzing excerpts from an Internet discussion forum called *Chinese Culture and History* (*Forum Diskusi Budaya Thionghoa dan Sejarah Tiongkok*), I unpack how Chineseness is imagined and desired. I argue that the process of resinicization – as promoted by the excerpts – does not merely concern an expression of cultural identity. Although intended to come to terms with the history of Chinese-Indonesians, resinicization does not enable a working through of a traumatic past. Instead, resinicization becomes constitutive of a misplaced nostalgia in which Chineseness is imagined, desired, and "acted out" as a fixed identity associated with a so-called "authentic" Chinese culture. By deploying the theoretical concepts of absence and loss from the historian Dominick LaCapra onto the framework of Chineseness, I further tease out the complexities involved in appropriating Chineseness. I argue through this framework that processes of resinicization, both externally and internally appropriated, close off rather than facilitate opportunities to recognize or value "Indonesianized" forms of Chineseness.

Contextualizing Chineseness

Most Chinese-Indonesians are so called *peranakan* Chinese; an old diaspora who came to settle permanently from the seventeenth century onwards in what was then the Dutch East Indies. These Chinese migrants came from different regions in China, derived from different ethnicities, and spoke different languages. During their settlement, they assimilated with local cultures and inter-married with local people. In contemporary Indonesia, most *peranakan* Chinese do not speak any of the Chinese languages and are more informed by local culture than by Chinese culture. The so-called *totok* Chinese are defined as either China-born or as having arrived much later in the archipelago. In contrast to *peranakan* Chinese, the *totok* Chinese do uphold some form of Chinese culture and sometimes still master their original Chinese languages. In colloquial language, the terms *peranakan* and *totok* have been used to denote proximity to Chinese culture, to indicate (often in normative ways) who is, and who is not "authentically Chinese." In recent decades, researchers have called for a re-examination of the distinction in light of New Order assimilation policies which concerned the "Indonesianization" of all Chinese.[2]

The repressive New Order regime of President Suharto submitted Chinese-Indonesians to rigorous assimilation policies in which they were thoroughly de-politicized and "Indonesianized" or *peranakanized* (Aguilar 504). During this period, all Chinese religious, socio-political, or cultural organizations were banned and discriminatory measures were forced onto the Chinese community, such as changing their Chinese names into Indonesian ones. These forms of rigorous assimilation, however, did not engender a common idea that the Chinese were becoming Indonesians.

Instead, Chinese-Indonesians remained the ultimate outsider. As the sociologist Filomeno Aguilar already argued, a central characteristic of the paradoxical way in which assimilation operated was the "juxtaposing of 'Chinese' as the internal Other of the 'true' Indonesian, a binary construct that demands re-examination" (505). These practices, coupled with a general prohibition on expressing any politics of identity, created a wedge between the so-called "indigenous" (*pribumi*) and the "non-indigenous" (*non-pribumi*) population.[3] This persistent insistence on an indigenous versus non-indigenous paradigm made it impossible for Chinese-Indonesians to become "real Indonesians."

This polarization intensified through the unremitting discourse of class disparity. By the 1980s the New Order had somewhat simplified procedures for Chinese-Indonesians to become Indonesian citizens. However, it was more a political strategy to consolidate Chinese-Indonesians under Indonesian control by confining them to the economic arena. These Chinese cronies greatly benefited from Suharto's new economic policies and established successful conglomerates. Although this group formed less than five percent of the Chinese population in Indonesia, their dominant presence gave birth to the myth that all Chinese were rich and economically influential (Suryadinata 1998). The allocation of Chinese-Indonesians to the economic realm refueled the discriminative dichotomy between the indigenous and the non-indigenous. In this context, as the cultural theorist Ien Ang argues, "class is lived in the modality of race" (*On Not Speaking Chinese*). The distinction between indigenous and non-indigenous thus comes to be read through the specter of wealth and poverty.

In post-authoritarian Indonesia, Chinese-Indonesians have increasingly started to use the term Thionghoa to define themselves. According to anthropologist James Siegel it was only after the fall of Suharto that the term Thionghoa was re-established as such in daily and public life ("Early Thoughts"). The mediation of the term Thionghoa in television, radio, and other media after the riots made it the common and politically correct term to use. As columnist and curator Amir Shidarta explains, the term Thionghoa is considered more polite than the highly charged term *Cina*, which bore connotations of racism and was often used derogatorily in everyday life.[4] Shidarta further argues, however, that by using such an explicitly Chinese term, Thionghoa also produces a form of discrimination by prioritizing Chinese rather than Indonesian terms. The younger generation of Chinese-Indonesians, he contends, prefer to call themselves *Cina* or *Chinese* rather than *Thionghoa*, because they find the latter term too much connected to mainland China, a country they know little about and have no affinity with.

Silencing Chineseness

Partly evolving out of the scapegoat status and the discriminatory practices that were geared against the Chinese, many political and economic crises went hand in hand with racialized riots that were often intricately linked to state agents. These events accounted for the pervasiveness of the stereotypes mostly associated with the communist threat in the 1960s and 1970s and economic disparity in the 1980s and 1990s. Besides numerous riots in the late 1970s, the May 1998 riots can be singled out to illustrate the connection between state violence and government-induced racism, but also with racialized sentiments in Indonesian society.[5]

The May 1998 violence witnessed widespread anti-Chinese rioting in a number of major Indonesian cities after four student protesters were shot dead at Jakarta's Trisakti University.[6] Chinese shops, buildings, and homes were looted or burned down. As many as over a thousand "looters" were caught and died in buildings and shopping malls that were set on fire. Besides arson, looting, and murdering, women were systematically raped, with most of the victims defined as Chinese. The May 1998 violence led to the downfall of President Suharto. Governmental investigation reports (eventually) acknowledged that state agents instigated the riots, although to this point no measures have been taken to put any perpetrators on trial (van Wichelen). The resulting process of exacerbating and entrenching differences contributed to a dominant racialized discourse that glossed over any reference to the political dimension of the conflict. Instead, public discussions emphasized antagonistic distinctions between "rich non-indigenous non-Muslim Chinese" and "poor indigenous Muslim-Indonesians."

The riots triggered profound emotions in Chinese-Indonesian communities and individuals. Many people, especially from the older generation, were reminded of racial riots in the past. Alarmed by the intensity of the riots, families who could afford it fled the country. Conversely, this situation led to the stereotyping of these families as securing their wealth elsewhere, putting their loyalty to Indonesia under scrutiny. A fundamental rupture between *pribumi* and *non-pribumi*, nevertheless, was prevented by the claims that the riots were state-organized (Aguilar). Moreover, the prospect of a regime change refueled the hope that full citizenship and recognition was possible and that *pribumi* and *non-pribumi* could come together as soon as citizenship rights were restored.

The 1998 violence also prompted new understandings of Chineseness. As the Indonesianist Jemma Purdey observed, "the events of 1998 necessarily led to a renewed awareness in Chinese-Indonesians of their ethnicity and for many younger Chinese, an entirely 'new' awareness of their heritage and identity" ("Reopening" 426). This confirms my own observations during my research visits to Indonesia, in which young Chinese-Indonesians would inform me that they were astounded to find out – in the aftermath of the riots – that they too were Chinese. These individuals, even though somehow they knew that they were "different" from other Indonesians, had not been aware of their Chineseness as such. They often belonged to a generation that had fully assimilated into Indonesian society. Some had lost the physical traits of Chinese appearance, but even when having these physical traits, they did not seem to mark themselves as Chinese. Occasionally, even their own Chinese physiognomy was not something that these individuals could relate to.

Although racism was prevalent, it was seldom discussed as such in the public sphere. On the contrary, matters pertaining to Chinese culture or identity, within the context of Indonesian cultural politics or history, were conveniently silenced. This silencing of public Chineseness – also referred to as "erasure" (Heryanto, "Ethnic")[7] – worked through multiple layers of Indonesian society and consistently isolated Chineseness from "Indonesianness." This had a major impact on the identity formation of Chinese-Indonesian communities in Indonesia. Most Chinese-Indonesians were stimulated (and forced) to identify with "Indonesian" culture and identity. This assimilation process went hand in hand with modes of "self-silencing." Out of fear of being confronted with exclusions, discrimination, or violence, Chinese-Indonesians actively silenced their Chineseness in the public sphere. Others silenced their Chineseness out of shame. This shame primarily evolved out of the more general social imaginary of dominant Indonesian discourse, which structurally and morally privileged "Indonesianness" over Chineseness.[8] As such, these people not only silenced their Chineseness in the public sphere, but also avoided confrontations with Chineseness in their private lives.

The fall of Suharto in 1998 can rightfully be seen as a turning point for the cause of the Chinese. The subsequent presidents have taken measures in readdressing and re-evaluating discriminative laws and regulations. Among the changes in political and public life were the sanctioning of Chinese political parties and Chinese cultural organizations in 1999; the review of discriminatory laws and the opportunity to celebrate Chinese New Year openly in 2000; and just recently the re-opening of the investigations into the May 1998 riots. However, according to Purdey's "Reopening the Asimilasi vs Integrasi Debate," the Chinese have not been given the space to consider seriously the issues of identity in relation to the May 1998 violence or to the more general debate on the assimilation and integration of the Chinese in Indonesia. She argues that this debate cannot be held until Indonesia itself addresses its future in which security, both physical and legal, is restored (437). Besides addressing the lack of security and implementing legal measures to provide Chinese-Indonesians with equal citizenship, I would argue that there is an urgency and necessity to recognize and account for the processes of silencing undertaken in the past, not only as a state, but more so as a nation. It is not until these issues of collective consciousness are raised, by Indonesians and Chinese-Indonesians alike, that Indonesia can truly work through the traumatic events in which Chineseness has been systematically silenced. The question posed in this essay, therefore, is whether resinicization in post-authoritarian Indonesia contributes to this process of working through.

Re-sinicization

In what follows, I present excerpts from a discussion forum called Chinese Culture (*Budaya Thionghoa*) that was founded on October 29, 2003, and is still active today. The Indonesian forum has 2,511 members and is run in the Indonesian language. The total amount of individual messages is about 25,414. These messages are assembled in respective threads and grouped according to returning themes. The threads reach an amount of over 10,000 initial posts that are labeled as topics or questions. The follow-up messages range from 1 to over 100 replies, depending particularly on the popularity or controversiality of the topic.

Virtual communication has been very important for the Chinese diaspora. As a means to communicate, to shape a community, and to develop a sense of (global) citizenship, diasporic Chinese have turned to the Internet en masse to connect with each other (Ong; Yang). This is also the case for Chinese-Indonesians, who, especially in the aftermath of the 1998 riots, started to connect with other diasporic Chinese on the World Wide Web to vent their anger and fear of the violent events (Ang, *On Not Speaking Chinese*; Tay). The period after the regime change has witnessed an increase in online discussion forums dealing with Chinese-Indonesian issues. Among them is *Budaya Thionghoa*.

Initially, most posted messages on the discussion forum revolved around general issues of Chinese culture, with exchange of information taking place on cultural practices (for instance, information on Chinese medicine, on the history of Chinese dynasties and the Chinese diaspora, on Chinese poetry and literature, etc.). This tendency to recount and relive Chinese culture was also found in the broader public sphere, where people not only engaged more in Chinese cultural activities, but where markets also commodified Chinese traditions and culture by promoting some of the practices as lifestyle products.[11] Alongside information on "Chinese" cultural forms, issues of authenticity were discussed on *Budaya Thionghoa*. As one message read:

What worries me and what I would like to stress from the start is that cultural values have to be preserved. The following concrete example below can maybe reflect upon this:

For instance, there is a performance of Tiongkok *Culture about* Wushu *or* Barongsai *for which the tickets are very expensive.*[9] *Then, there is a performance about* Wushu *or* Barongsai *that is adapted to local culture of which the tickets are very cheap. Now . . . which performance will be well attended? I think for surely the one from* Tiongkok, *even though the tickets are expensive. It is here that the value and meaning of culture is legitimized and more valued through its authenticity* [keasliannya]. . . .

I only want to give you something to think about. We need to preserve this rich Thionghoa *culture so that people, who are ignorant about it, can start to appreciate its value. Because when it becomes tangled [with local culture], oh my . . .* Thionghoa *cultural values will fade* (luntur) *and will lose its trail.*

United greetings (salam sinergi)
Herru Art[10]

In a cursory first reading, the above message – from someone who calls himself Herru Art – can be interpreted as a blunt case of cultural superiority. In his example of *barongsai* and *wushu*, he acknowledges but also agrees with the condition that locally adapted Chinese culture is to be less valued than non-adapted Chinese culture. He urges people from the discussion group to preserve "authentic" Chinese culture. The ones who have lost it should learn from others so that they can internalize it (again) and appreciate its worth. Rather than suggesting that Chinese-Indonesians in Indonesia need not be afraid anymore to culturally express themselves, Herru Art advises Chinese-Indonesians to return to the roots of their cultural heritage, namely the traditions of Mainland China.

However, *barongsai* and *wushu* – together with other cultural forms – have rarely been part of the cultural practice of Chinese-Indonesians. In the instances that such practices did take place, it often concerned locally adapted forms. With this in mind, the trouble with Herru Art's advice to return to the roots of Chinese culture is that for many Chinese-Indonesians in Indonesia it was not clear to what they could return to. Most were born and raised into the local cultures of, for instance, Java, where they never practiced what Herru Art refers to as "authentic" Chinese culture. Chinese culture is therefore foreign to most Chinese-Indonesians.

Herru Art's voice is not uncommon in contemporary Chinese-Indonesian discourse on Chinese culture. It represents euphoric narratives in a newly created democratic space that allows public manifestations of Chineseness. Nevertheless, these processes of resinicization essentialize ethnic identity, put mainland China and Chinese culture at the center of cultural identification, and produce a set of fundamental and deterministic authenticity discourses. They confirm the views of Ien Ang, who argues that:

[P]ractices of resinicization aimed at re-imbuing those who apparently had "lost" their Chineseness with their "true" cultural identity, can be interpreted as practices of forced inclusion*: they are attempts to prevent those who had dispersed themselves from the homeland from "going astray" and to sharpen the boundaries of the Chinese diaspora. Ironically, these very migrants cannot help but blur these boundaries through their everyday interactions with and adaptations to their non-Chinese environments.* (On Not Speaking Chinese 83, emphasis in original)

The latter becomes visible when we return to the group discussion. During its course, the virtual site also became a space in which Chinese identity in the Indonesian context is scrutinized, albeit ambivalently:

Although I am Thionghoa, I seem far away from Thionghoa culture. I am very much a layperson [in relation to Thionghoa culture] and even feel "bego" [slang for stupid] in understanding the culture of my own people ☹

I joined this Thionghoa *Culture Discussion Forum with the anticipation of gaining "something" that is useful and can be used in life. Even only one or two correct regulations/rules of the culture would be enough so that I can show myself as part of a "Thionghoa people."*

But until now, I – as a layperson – do not feel that there are advantages through this Discussion Forum that I can directly implement in my daily life.

King Hian[12]

The person using the name King Hian from the above message announces to the group that he joined the forum so that he could learn more about Chinese culture. Specifically, he wanted to be informed of certain cultural practices or regulations that he could use in everyday life. He anticipates this information in order to actualize modes of recognition from others (and himself) that he really is Chinese.

Here we have someone who, presumably, has assimilated well into a local "non-Chinese" culture, who probably does not speak or read Chinese, and who has likely learned to live in a way that does not relate directly to his Chineseness. Nevertheless, he wants to learn "Chinese ways" to *show* that he is Chinese. His inquiry is informed by a need to reach out. He feels his knowledge of Chinese culture is not sufficient to meet the standards of what he thinks his identity as a "real" Chinese should be. So he turns to the Internet to find out what the rules and codes are that could make him more Chinese. He cannot, however, identify with the forms of Chinese culture presented to him through this discussion group. Rather, he expresses his confusion about the Chineseness that is being discussed in the e-group. In other words, the rules, customs, and values that are discussed on the Internet feel alien to him. Still, he wants to become a "real" *Thionghoa* person, to represent himself as "part of a *Thionghoa* people" and to learn the "correct" way of Chinese rules. A double bind becomes visible. That which is desired does not seem to correspond to the identity politics that is practiced in everyday life and genuinely feels like one's own. His ambivalence is grounded neither in the identification with "real local culture" nor in the identification with "real Chinese culture."

How can we interpret this ambivalence? How are we to understand the ways in which this ambivalence is articulated and expressed? And how do these articulations relate to the outside world, or more specifically, to public discourses of resinicization? Suggestions have been made that anti-Chinese violence in general, and the May 1998 riots in particular, need to be placed within a larger framework of "national trauma" (Siegel, "Early Thoughts"; "Thoughts"). In the following section I make an effort to engage with the issue of trauma. But instead of focusing on collective trauma as such, I theorize how Chineseness is played out on an individual level.

Absence and Loss

In his valuable article "Trauma, Absence, Loss," the historian Dominick LaCapra differentiates between the concepts of absence and loss. Grounded in historiography and psychoanalysis, these twin concepts are theorized within the framework of remembering (cultural) trauma. He describes absence as the absence of an absolute, as that which one cannot lose because one never had it, and as applying to ultimate foundations in general, but especially to metaphysical grounds (700–02). As an example, LaCapra refers to an excerpt from Martha Nussbaum's work where she refers to the lack of a form comparable to the novel in non-western societies. Here LaCapra argues "It would clearly be more accurate to say that forms comparable to the novel are absent rather than lacking in other cultures (if indeed they are in fact absent) . . . Such a formulation might be best for all cross-cultural comparisons unless one is willing to argue that the absence represents a lack" (704). Absence, he further argues, is associated with structural trauma, which is an "anxiety producing condition of possibility related to the potential for historical traumatization" (725). Everyone is subject to structural trauma, and its association with absence implies a transhistorical character: it is not located in a past, presence, or future. In contrast with absence, loss is specific and located on a historical level. It is that which involves distinct events, such as the death of a loved one or, on a broader scale, the losses brought about by apartheid or the holocaust. Loss is therefore associated with historical trauma, which is related to particular events that involve losses. Here, trauma is specific; not everyone is victimized by its consequences or entitled to the subject-position associated with it (722).[13]

LaCapra distinguishes absence from loss and structural trauma from historical trauma[14] to come to a better understanding of how we can collectively remember and write about trauma, but also to come to an ethical position on how cultural traumas can be worked through. His contention is that "the difference between absence and loss is often elided, and the two are conflated with confusing and dubious results" (700). He observes that when absence is narrativized, t is often converted into loss. This, he explains, happens so fast and unnoticeably that it is often regarded as "natural and necessary" (700). Yet, when absence is converted into loss, "one increases the likelihood of misplaced nostalgia or utopian politics in quest of a new totality or fully unified community" (698). Rather than working through trauma or coming to a form of mourning, LaCapra points out that in conflating absence with loss, "mourning may (perhaps must) become impossible and turn continually back into endless melancholy" (715). Instead of a mode of working through, mourning becomes a form of acting out, in which "the past is performatively regenerated or relived as if it were fully present . . . : it hauntingly returns as the repressed" (716). Put simply, the misrecognition of absence as loss could ultimately lead to a misplaced victimhood, which appropriates another's loss as identical to one's own.

As mentioned earlier, public manifestations of Chineseness are to be set against the newly created democratic spaces in which Chineseness is not only allowed but at times also celebrated. In these open spaces, performatively engendering a self-image

(Chineseness) through forms of overexposure can be very empowering. One could compare this with the forms of self-empowerment involved in "coming out" as gay.[15] Similar to what Herru Art and King Hian are doing, a gay person can correspondingly turn to the Internet to find out how gay subcultures live, move, "act up," and "label" themselves. This can have an empowering effect on the subject, who now gives voice to a part of her/his identity that was not recognized before.

Besides the empowering effect, however, performatively evoking gayness – or in this case Chineseness – through forms of overexposure can also become a form of acting out. In acting out, Chineseness is not only informed by a lack of belonging to a unified group identity, but the absence of Chineseness is turned into lack or loss through the simple confrontation with a Chineseness to which one is forced to relate. In this case, the individual's need to affiliate with Chineseness to give legitimacy to her/his notion of Self is informed by an empty or (en)forced meaning of racial, ethnic, or cultural identity.[16]

In enticing people to go to the "authentic" cultural performance rather than to the culturally adapted one, and in distinguishing what is and what is not authentically Chinese, Herru Art defines Chinese-Indonesian culture as lacking cultural values. King Hian further emphasizes this lack by explaining that he longs for and desires to appropriate this Chinese identity. Both Herru Art and King Hian have conflated absence, namely the absence of Chineseness, into a loss or lack. A misplaced nostalgia evolves out of this conflation, namely a desire to belong to a unified community. Yet, whereas Herru Art dismisses a Chineseness that is not inextricably linked to an "authentic" Chinese culture, King Hian attempts to reconcile the double bind he experiences. Thus, while Herru Art seems to act out the idea of identity that privileges "authentic" Chinese culture over a locally adapted form of Chineseness, King Hian attempts to work through or to come to terms with his own Chineseness.

The conflation of absence and loss should be set against the nostalgic mood of Chinese diasporic communities. Here, a unifying community is desired and sometimes forced upon "fellow" others. The denial of ambivalence towards Chineseness affects how Chinese-Indonesians are presented and represent themselves in public space and the diasporic community. As illustrated by the case of Herru Art, there exists a tendency to convince fellow Chinese to re-appropriate a form of Chineseness that they supposedly lost along the way. Ang analyzes these tendencies in the virtual narratives of the global diasporic Chinese community in relation to the May 1998 riots and explicates how these narratives created "an imagined community that constructs itself through a massive sense of beleaguerednes, a paranoid closure of its discursive boundaries, and the absolutization of a singular normative truth" (*On Not Speaking Chinese* 71). The closure of these discursive boundaries denies any form of ambivalence and, correspondingly, closes the space to confusion, disarray, or, for that matter, embarrassment; conditions that are necessary in reconfiguring self-identity.

Thus, the resinicization discourse of both post-authoritarian politics and the diasporic Chinese community anticipates the conflation of absence and loss. Post-authoritarian processes of resinicization force all Chinese-Indonesians to relate to Chineseness, whether they have or have not engaged themselves with Chineseness in the past. Also, these processes are racially informed: Chinese-Indonesians are confronted with a situation that involves them only because they are "marked" as Chinese through their physical features. The role of visuality is crucial here. The May 1998 events and the Chinese revival led to a situation where people who looked remotely Chinese were once again marked as such in daily life. As described earlier, this led to confusing moments for a generation that did not "see" itself as having these Chinese physical features. In that sense, the slanted eyes and fair skin – that which is marked as Chinese in Indonesia – only became Chinese when they were defined as such.

With respect to the diasporic community, the conflation of absence with loss is made visible through modes of acting out, where escapism and nostalgia seem to replace or cover up ambivalence and past silencing. Chinese-Indonesians are expected to relate to a Chinese culture that does not recognize Chineseness as traveling, transformative, or adaptable. Similar to Herru Art's plea for the re-assertion of Chinese identity, the revival of Chinese culture produces, as Heryanto argues in "Rasisme Tak Sengaja," a form of "unintentional racism" by persistently emphasizing "authenticity" rather than acknowledging that the notion of Chineseness differs within and through the complex histories of the Indonesian nation-state.[17] Rather than allowing for an ambivalent subject, the revival still suggests that as a Chinese person, one should choose to be here or there, with us or them.

As intimated earlier by LaCapra, the specificity of historical trauma (traumatic experiences by the Chinese of state-sanctioned discriminatory events and practices) poses problems when consolidated with structural trauma (the absence of "Chineseness"). The process of resinicization has exacerbated the effects of conflating absence and loss, as well as structural trauma and historical trauma, resulting in a discourse of misplaced nostalgia and utopian politics. What is important is to see how this recognition can help us to come to a historical understanding and ethico-political judgment in relation to remembering cultural trauma. It is reasonable to argue that discriminatory practices toward the Chinese throughout the Indonesian past are constitutive of a historical trauma. The emphasis, however, on a "revival" of Chinese culture (instead of recognizing, recording, and remembering past events) seems to displace or even dismiss the traumatic related to that historic silencing. In such a way, the discourse of resinicization functions as a mode of "forgetting," or even as a form of compensation for past silences.[18]

Conclusion

As indicated above, distinguishing between absence and loss informs us of the complexities involved in studying Chineseness in Indonesia. It explicates to what extent it can facilitate a working through, in which one can come to terms with one's Chineseness, or an acting out, by conflating these moments. Notwithstanding the possibility that expressing one's cultural identity can be very empowering, or the likelihood that forms of Chinese revival could facilitate a working through of a complex history, I have contended that the discourse of resinicization, as portrayed above, makes of the Chinese revival a "spectacle"; a process of disavowal and fetishism through which Chineseness, silencing, and "the traumatic" are actively forgotten. Analyzing how these modes of identity politics were played out, I argued that by reviving Chinese culture without taking measures to deal with the Indonesian discriminatory past, the Chinese-Indonesian quest for fully recognized citizenship is made more complex and ambivalent. The twin concepts of absence and loss have helped us to understand some of the unexplored dimensions of Chineseness. The next step would be to investigate how Chinese and non-Chinese citizens are able to rework Chineseness in contemporary Indonesia in such a way that the past is dynamically worked though rather than actively forgotten.

Notes

1. I use the term "Chineseness" in the manner deployed by the cultural theorist Ien Ang, who uses the term to point out the multiple constructions of Chinese identity in diasporas, detaching it from the cultural or "authentic" center of Mainland China. See Ang, "Can One Say No to Chineseness?," "Migrations of Chineseness," and *On not speaking Chinese*.

2. For a more elaborate background of Chinese history and politics in Indonesia and a discussion on the *peranakan* and *totok* distinction see Coppel, *Indonesian Culture in Crisis*, and Suryadinata, *Pribumi Indonesians* and *Interpreting Indonesian Politics*.

3. This general prohibition is known as the politics of SARA, which is an abbreviation for Ethnicity, Religion, Race and Regional Affiliation (Suku, Agama, Ras dan Antar Golongan). During the Suharto era, public discussions or debates containing SARA elements were strictly prohibited in the name of stability, peace, and development.

4. Around 1911, Chinese-Indonesians, especially from Java, started to call themselves Thionghoa and to refer to the country of China as Tiongkok. These terms are Hokkien, stemming from the Zhonghu and Zhonggou region of Mainland China. See also Aguilar.

5. See Heryanto's "Rape, Race and Reporting" for a background on the state discourse during and after the May 1998 violence. See also Jemma Purdey's *Anti-Chinese Violence in Indonesia, 1996–1999* and the edited volume by Tim Lindsey and Helen Pausacker. Agreeing with Purdey ("Anti-Chinese Violence") that the anti-Chinese riots cannot be solely explained through state violence, but that racist structures in Indonesian society were equally responsible for the exacerbation of the violence, it is useful to look at the ways in which forms of racism have been produced and sustained in Indonesia. This, however, is not my aim here. Instead, my focus is on "self-racism" and the ways in which the process of resinicization is reinforcing this internalized racism.

6. The students who were shot were demonstrators in a protest against the corruption, collusion, and nepotism of the Suharto administration.

7. In coining the term "erasure," Heryanto emphasizes the extent to which forms of Chineseness or Chinese identities were not necessarily wiped out but "carefully and continually reproduced, but always under erasure" ("Ethnic Identities and Erasure" 104).

8. The notion and problem of shame implies another extensive theoretical discourse that I, unfortunately, cannot elaborate on in this essay.

9. *Wushu* is a Chinese generic term for all kinds of combat sports or martial arts. *Barongsai* is a traditional Chinese dance often performed at Chinese New Year.

10. Herru Art, "Reply to 'Evolusi dan Transformasi Budaya adalah Mutlak.'" http://groups.yahoo.com/group/budaya_tionghua/?yguid=106719433, posted on 11 May 2004, translated from Bahasa Indonesia by the author.

11. Exemplified, for instance, by the enormous popularity of Feng shui (the Chinese practice of organizing harmonious living and work spaces), Chinese horoscopes, Chinese medicine, and other lifestyle-related products in Indonesia today.

12. King Hian, "Reply: [budaya_thionghoa] 'Apa milis ini dpt bermanfaat?'" http://groups.yahoo.com/group/budaya_tionghua/?yguid=106719433, posted on 2 May 2004, translated from Bahasa Indonesia by the author.

13. Often, loss is correlated with lack: while loss is referred to as that which is of the past, lack is situated in the present or future (LaCapra 703).

14. Absence and loss, as well as structural trauma and historical trauma, should not, as LaCapra notes, be approached as binary

oppositions. The two interact in complex ways and often, especially in post-traumatic situations or periods of crisis, absence is transformed into loss (700).

15. The same mechanisms can be found in performatively evoking blackness or Muslimness.

16. Many thanks to Marc de Leeuw for suggesting this comparison.

17. Heryanto further argues that the cultural forms that are now presented in public life (such as Chinese New Year) are the ones that are most readily subjected to capitalist industry. In this respect, the "Benetton-effect" of multiculturalism, where transgressing race, sex, and religion amalgamates with the free market, has also reached Indonesia, but this time by virtue of Chineseness.

18. See Abidin Kusno for an elaboration on how this "mode of forgetting" works out spatially. According to him, revival and displacement are articulated in re-imaginings of urban space. Without reference to the horrific events, new buildings (in colonial Batavian-style architecture) replaced the buildings that were burned down during the May riots. While silencing the traumatic, these new spatial allocations also revive a colonial exoticism.

Bibliography

Aguilar, Filomeno V. "Citizenship, Inheritance, and the Indigenizing of '*Orang Chinese*' in Indonesia." *Positions* 9.3 (2001): 501–33.

Ang, Ien. "Can One Say No to Chineseness? Pushing the Limits of the Diasporic Paradigm." *Boundary 2* 25.3 (1998): 223–42.

———. "Migrations of Chineseness." *SPAN* 34/35 (1993): 3–15.

———. *On Not Speaking Chinese: Living Between Asia and the West*. London and New York: Routledge, 2001.

Coppel, Charles. *Indonesian Chinese in Crisis*. Kuala Lumpur: Oxford UP, 1983.

Heryanto, Ariel. "Ethnic Identities and Erasure; Chinese-Indonesians in Public Culture." *Southeast Asian Identities; Culture and the Politics of Representation in Indonesia, Malaysia, Singapore, and Thailand*. Ed. Joel S. Kahn. Singapore: Institute of Southeast Asian Studies, 1998. 95–114.

———. "Rape, Race and Reporting." *Reformasi: Crisis and Change in Indonesia*. Ed. A. Budiman, B. Hatley and D. Kingsbury. Clayton: Monash Institute, 1999. 299–333.

———. "Rasisme Tak Sengaja." *Kompas* 6 February 2004.

Kusno, Abidin. "Remembering/Forgetting the May Riots: Architecture, Violence, and the Making of 'Chinese Cultures' in post-1998 Jakarta." *Public Culture* 15.1 (2003): 149–77.

LaCapra, Dominick. "Trauma, Absence, Loss." *Critical Inquiry* 25 (1999): 696–727.

Lindsey, Tim, and Helen Pausacker, eds. *Chinese Indonesians: Remembering, Distorting, Forgetting*. Singapore: ISEAS, 2005.

Ong, Aihwa. *Flexible Citizenship: The Cultural Logics of Transnationality*. Durham: Duke UP, 1999.

Purdey, Jemma. "Anti-Chinese Violence and Transitions in Indonesia: June 1998-October 1999." *Chinese Indonesians: Remembering, Distorting, Forgetting*. Ed. Tim Lindsey and Helen Pausacker. Singapore: ISEAS, 2005. 14–40.

———. *Anti-Chinese Violence in Indonesia, 1996–1999*. Leiden: KITLV Press, 2006.

———. "Reopening the Asimilasi vs Integrasi Debate: Ethnic Chinese Identity in Post-Suharto Indonesia." *Asian Ethnicity* 4.3 (2003): 421–37.

Shidarta, Amir. "Cina, Thionghoa, Chunghua, Suku Hua." *Kapok Jadi Nonpri: Warga Thionghoa Mencari Keadilan*. Ed. A. Hamzah and B. Trim. Bandung: Zaman Wacana Mulia, 1998. 79–81.

Siegel, James T. "Early Thoughts on the Violence of May 13 and 14, 1998 in Jakarta." *Indonesia* 66 (1998): 75–108.

———. "Thoughts on the Violence of May 13 and 14, 1998, in Jakarta." *Violence and the State in Suharto's Indonesia*. Ed. Benedict Anderson. Ithaca: Southeast Asia Program Publications, 2001. 90–123.

Suryadinata, Leo. *Interpreting Indonesian Politics*. Singapore: Times Academic Press, 1998.

———. *Pribumi Indonesians, the Chinese Minority and China*. Kuala Lumpur: Heinemann, 1975.

Tay, Elaine. "Global Chinese Fraternity and the Indonesian Riots of May 1998: The Online Gathering of Dispersed Chinese." *Intersections: Gender, History and Culture in the Asian Context* 4 (2000): n. pag. http://wwwsshe.murdoch.edu.au/intersections/issue4/tay.html.

Wichelen, Sonja van. "The State and Gender-Based Violence in Indonesia: A Study into the May 1998 Riots." MA thesis, University of Utrecht, 2000.

Yang, Guobin. "The Internet and the Rise of a Transnational Chinese Cultural Sphere." *Media, Culture & Society* 25.4 (2003): 469–90.

Moving Identities: Mythology and Metaphor in André Brink's *Praying Mantis*

Saskia Lourens

As the introduction to this volume has suggested, the term identity, although subject to an overuse that possibly dilutes its usefulness as a critical term, is inevitably significant when it comes to any consideration of political hierarchies, social structures, and inequalities. This is especially so in the context of contemporary South Africa, where, more than ten years after the end of legislated apartheid, both social and political inequalities remain unresolved. By entangling myself in the historical and mythical aspects of South African identity that are highlighted in a recent novel of South African author André Brink, I aim to explore the continued usefulness of this concept as a tool for political engagement.

In his 2005 novel *Praying Mantis*, Brink returns to the world of Khoi mythology as previously explored in his *First Life of Adamastor* of 1993, this time juxtaposing it with the colonial landscape of eighteenth-century South Africa. As with the earlier novel, which presented a Khoi protagonist, the focalization of *Praying Mantis* is characterized by a marked shift in worldview from Brink's other novels, and reads somewhat like that of a fairytale or dreamscape. The novel's setting is the dry and barren hinterland of South Africa, where overt activity and incident seems to be lacking. Its last section, consisting of about 55 pages, is, in fact, entirely taken up with the protagonist's residence in Dithakong, a missionary outpost in the desert without church, houses, or inhabitants. However, there is much going on beneath the surface.

As Inge Boer argues in "No-Man's-Land? Five Short Cases on Deserts and the Politics of Place," the consideration of desert space as empty (conquerable) space is one that is conventionally focalized from the outside and therefore overlooks what she terms the "palimpsestic traces of human histories" that populate the desert. The narrative of *Praying Mantis* is desert-like in that it is one in which not much happens, but much is said to happen, and it presents the reader not so much with a historical account, on which its endnote claims it to be based, as with a mythology.

By examining the novel in terms of myth, a fruitful connection can be made between the concepts of history, religion, and narrative that the narrative foregrounds. Because myth is "a mode of signification" that is "open to appropriation" by its very nature as speech or discourse, as Roland Barthes puts forward in his *Mythologies*, the interpretation of history and religion as unyielding certainties is emphatically discarded. Instead, the structure of history and religion as themselves made up of stories and narratives that are inconstant and subjective is stressed, as is the value of these stories, because of their very changeability, in interpreting the South African context. In reading the novel as a myth "open to appropriation," the conventional opposition between African mythology and Western rationality can be disabled and replaced by a more productive reading of myth as shaping (yet never exhaustively defining) identity.

Before commencing with an analysis of the novel as myth, not even so much of South Africa's colonial past, I will argue, as of its postcolonial present, I will comment on the complicated narrative structure that has been chosen to present the reader with the story of its protagonist. After this, I will examine the concept of myth, as proposed by Barthes, in terms of discourse and as a semiological system. This will lead to a more specific consideration of myth as mythology in terms of language and metaphor, as evident in Derrida's "White Mythology: Metaphor in the Text of Philosophy," and to the more specifically postcolonial critique of metaphor, myth, and discourse in Robert Young's *White Mythologies*. These frameworks will then be linked to the use made of metaphor in understanding colonial history in *Praying Mantis* in order to finally consider this novel's narrative as the story of South Africa today.

Hatched from stories

As asserted above, there is not much that explicitly happens in *Praying Mantis*, but much is said to happen. Brink's narrative ostensibly concerns itself with the history of Cupido Cockroach (or Kupido Kakkerlak, as he was actually known), who, as historiography would have it, became the first Khoi person to be employed by the London Missionary Society as a missionary at the Cape of Good Hope in the early years of the nineteenth century.[1] The novel was written over a period of twenty years (as its author confesses in the endnote) and, perhaps partially because of this, retains a somewhat schizophrenic character that nevertheless corresponds pleasingly with the interpretation of myths as "productions of the human imagination" (Campbell, 27). It is divided into three parts that represent various narrators and a plethora of linguistic conventions.

Part one makes use of an omniscient narrator who instantly frames the narrative in terms of fable rather than history, despite dealing with the child- and boyhood of the historically verifiable character Cupido Cockroach. The potency of narrative is confirmed right from the onset of the novel, where its first line states: "Cupido Cockroach was not born from his mother's body in the usual way but hatched from the stories she told" (3). Stories, like origin myths, are here represented as having the power to shape physical reality, and it is this story-generated reality that forms the (only) basis for the reader's understanding of the protagonist.

The initial story of Cupido's "birth" is instantly complemented (or destabilized, depending on your point of view) by at least four other versions that the narrator describes Cupido's unmarried mother as offering to explain her son's appearance, each adjusted to her audience and mood. One of these stories has Cupido dropped in her lap by an eagle. Later on, the reader comes to understand that the motif of the eagle carries great significance throughout Cupido's life, as he continues to link the foretold reappearance of this eagle to his future fortune.[2] Another version sees the baby Cupido being stillborn and close to burial when a praying mantis settles on his winding sheet and halts the funeral proceedings. The baby draws breath and is "born again." The figure of the praying mantis, too, reappears throughout the novel as a harbinger of destiny that aids Cupido in making crucial decisions.[3]

These and the other various stories that Cupido grows up with shape his sense of identity and expectations for the future, and take on solid form in the events that befall him at later stages in part one of the novel. As he grows into manhood, for example, Cupido's status on the farm where he lives is affected materially when the Khoi God Heitsi-Eibib leaves the confines of the stories told to him by his mother and appears to him in person, helping to transform him into a successful and respected hunter. Cupido braves lions, speaks to meerkats, and comes to an understanding with a water sprite. All of these occurrences receive the same dry consideration by the narrator of the novel's first part as do, for example, his nausea on first discovering alcohol and his attempts to have intercourse with various farm animals.

The turnaround in this part arrives not so much with a change in attitude towards the credibility or materiality of these stories as with the transformation of their content. On becoming enamored of a visiting preacher, Cupido's physical and identitarian immersion in the story world of Khoi mythology is replaced by his material participation in the stories of Christianity. This, the narrator recognizes, is achieved by means of three specific devices, which he terms "magic tricks" in the language of Cupido and tabulates as follows: "The mirrors are the first of these. Music is another. And the third is stories" (44). All three of these reach across the gap between the material and the abstract and combine, in their features, something of both reality and myth that Cupido deems magical.

The association of these "magic tricks" with Christianity effects Cupido's conversion, as he ponders that:

> [h]e could no longer be quite sure about Heitsi-Eibib anymore. Not even about Tsui-Goab or Gaunab. It was beginning to look as if there might be more to the world than he had known before. The very thought made his chest contract. (52)

The physical discomfort that Cupido feels at the upheaval of his view on the world (and himself) due to the intrusion of another mythology into the order of his Khoi belief-system exemplifies the function of myths as structures that help us interpret the world and ourselves, as "tools with which we organise the mass of incoming data" (Midgley 4). In the sense that these tools, as proposed in studies of mythology by the likes of Barthes, are intricately tied to historical context, they can be, and often are, replaced when historical circumstances change. In spite of this, as Mary Midgley notes in her study on myth, "myths do not alter in the rather brisk, wholesale way that much contemporary imagery suggests" because, as she recognizes, "(t)hey are organic parts of our lives, cognitive and emotional habits, structures that shape our thinking, So they follow conservation laws within it" (4–5). This, perversely, accounts for both Cupido's preservation of certain habits, such as that of relying on the appearance of portents from the natural world in making decisions, and his unnecessarily violent performance in rejecting his old belief system, as displayed, for example, in his upturning of the stone monuments to Heitsi-Eibib as he encounters them throughout the South African landscape. It is during this period of his most expressive rejection of his old identity and way of life, and his most manifest insertion in the new mythology, that the second part of the novel commences and the Reverend James Read takes over the narration.

The part narrated by James Read relates the story of Cupido's actual conversion and his appointment as first Khoi missionary for the London Missionary Society. Read's narration presents a markedly different voice from that of the first narrator, making self-conscious use of the "I"-form and repeatedly voicing his insecurity about the language that he has at hand. At the same time, Read follows the first narrator in placing his narrative firmly in the service of the telling of Cupido's life. All three parts are about Cupido and easily characterized as such by their perpetual return to his legend. Upon opening it, Read qualifies his narrative by recounting:

> The first time I may be said to have properly made the acquaintance of Cupido Cockroach (although I had been afforded glimpses of him before) must have been at his baptism in the Sunday's River at Graaff-Reinet on that stormy day at the end of 1801. (114)

The careful evocation of place and time, as well as of the deviant or even foreshadowing conditions, communicates Read's awareness of the importance of his recollection in terms of a historical recording of a person of note. All that Read narrates is valued according to its ability to explain Cupido's ultimate fate and, as such, is colored by the historical outcome of his story. Indications of this abound in the text: "How could

I ever, then, have foreseen . . . ?" (114), Read asks, using phrases like "I know now, too late perhaps" (127) and "Where did we go astray?" (183), all of which serve to link the time in which his account is set to its ultimate significance at the time of telling. Hindsight plays a significant role in the mythologizing of Cupido's story and identity, as the use of knowledge after the fact allows for an association of concepts and meanings in a metaphoric sense that was not available on first experiencing events.

After the sense of foreboding instilled by James Read in his narration of the second part of the novel, the third part returns to an omniscient narrator. This, however, is not the same jocular storyteller passing on a legend for posterity of the first part. The third narrator is quieter, more serious and often relinquishes his focalization to Cupido himself, who battles with disillusionment after realizing that the conclusions he had previously drawn about the hard lessons learned throughout his life have left him without the solid ground of certainty in interpreting the world around him and his own self. This in a metaphorical sense only, of course, since solid ground, in fact, constitutes all that is left to him in the isolation of the missionary outpost of Dithakong, where he spends the last years of his life.

To be counted

Aside from the division of the novel in three parts, several other features give it the character of a complex narrative structure that opposes all considerations of history as chronologically verifiable or comprehensible. In this way it opposes the notion that simplicity stands for truth, which, in itself, is a myth perpetuated by Enlightenment thinking, and is isolated and examined by Midgley in her 2004 *The Myths We Live By* as one of three myths that continue to influence intellectual and moral thinking in the Western world today. In a section entitled "Complexity is not a Scandal," Midgley exposes the conviction, held in the social sciences as well as in much of the humanities, that "only one very simple way of thought is rational," as a misleading doctrine (21). This "Enlightenment myth," which she dubs both "imperialistic" and "strangely ambitious," is described by Midgley as centering on two claims, that of infallibility and of unity of thought. In fact, she states, "[r]ationality does not require us to be infallible, nor to have all our knowledge tightly organised" (23). She goes on to argue that "we need scientific pluralism – the recognition that there are many independent forms and sources of knowledge – rather than reductivism, the conviction that one fundamental form underlies them all and settles everything" (27).

This, perhaps, is the aim of *Praying Mantis*'s complexity. Its narrative structure is marked as a metafiction in terms of the many fictions and texts that interrupt its surface. Direct literary references are made by means of a series of epigraphs that open the novel and set up expectations about its content. One of these dates from the time in which the narrative is set and comprises a nineteenth-century commentary about the insignificance of the "name of Hottentot," believed by the cited article to be of "little note." The effect achieved is a contrary one, in that its use as an epigraph in a postcolonial novel anticipates that these low expectations will be refuted. Considering the hailed subject of the novel as being "the first 'Hottentot' missionary enlisted by the London Missionary Society" in a colonial country beset with racial barriers, this expectation takes on a special urgency. The second epigraph dates from 1984, the year, as we read in the endnote to the novel, in which Brink began this novel. The quote comes from a work by Don DeLillo, *White Noise*, which deals with the meaninglessness of modern-day life through the spectrum of the experiences of an American professor of "Hitler studies" who becomes contaminated by an unknown toxin and faces his death in the meaningless surroundings of small-town America ("white noise" refers to random or uncorrelated signals). The quote plays believers and non-believers out against each other in an unexpected way, in its assertion that it is the existence of non-believers on which belief itself is built. The third and last epigraph dates from the time at which Brink once again took up the novel after a long period of neglect (this was in 1992), and comprises a deliberation on Erasmus's concept of "free will," which begs the question of whether a man can choose to be mad, and, more importantly, of whether he can, on the other hand, choose not to be. The proposition of being "compelled" to a way of life or course of action by something beyond mere human "will" is here set up.

The implications of the quotes prefigure the implications of the other narrative voices of the novel. All of them contribute to conjuring up the story of Cupido, but no one voice is presented as having "the last word," least of all The Word itself. As mentioned, aside from the variety in narrative voice and focalization discussed earlier, an interspersion of other textual devices occurs within the three narrative voices, influencing their interpretation. One of these forms is that of the endless lists that appear in the first and third parts.

In the first part, the reader encounters lists of, variously, wild game that Cupido's first master shoots on a hunting trip; names of places he encounters on his journey into the hinterland; and the unlikely items transported by rogue missionary Servaas Ziervogel on his visits to lonely farmer's wives – including, among the recording of "sugar and coffee" and "needles and cotton," items such as "the skull of St Peter as a child" and "two white-plumed wings of an angel from Macedonia" (40). At first glance, these tabulations take on the appearance of the pseudo-scientific charts of colonial record, associated with a colonial power structure that lends the overarching metanarrative the framework of an ideological grid of colonial documentation. The first encountered list reads:

>   *eleven lions*
>   *forty-two elephants*

> *seven hippopotamuses*
> *ninety-eight springbok*
> *twenty-three hartebeest*
> *two rhinos*
> *seventeen zebra*
> *thirty-one wildebeest*
> *a single camelopardalis (a rare beast, almost as*
> *improbable as a unicorn)*
> *and eight Bushmen* (5)

The list provokes distaste at its dry and objective tone, and ends on a repulsive note when it includes human death as well.

In her consideration of scientific myth, Midgley characterizes the use of the list as a "favoured way of appearing scientific. . . . [P]olicies can be called scientific if they involve counting or measuring something, never mind whether that particular thing needs to be counted or not, and never mind what use is being made of the resulting data" (19). The pretence of objectivity that accompanies scientific appearance is exposed in the novel as grotesque, considering the brutal practices that must have preceded this tabulation. At the same time, the narrator of the third part of *Praying Mantis* also undermines the (Western) association of lists with order by including in his catalogues both reasonable and unreasonable items.

In his final capacity as missionary of Dithakong, Cupido tells a group of visiting travelers of his own travails by recalling various place names:

> . . .
> *Okavango and the lake at Ngami*
> *as well as Kgalagadi and the Chella Mountains*
> *and Lebebe and Omabonde*
> *and the Okawabga River and Andra and Humpata*
> . . . (230)

He goes on with his list until he comes to:

> *Samarkand and Sumatra*
> *Vladivostok and Nizhni-Novgorod*
> *and the Great Bear and Orion with his girdle and the*
> *Southern Cross*
> *and, for all one can tell, Saturn and Uranus*
> *and the New Jerusalem*
> . . . (231)

All pretence to scientific objectivity is abandoned with this use of the list, and the erstwhile tool for colonial control begins to take on the form of a song or chant, which evokes the mentioned places rather than try to capture them in a catalogue.

Another repeated variation intruding on the three narrators takes the form of the letters that Cupido writes to God. These vary in quality and language as his mastery of written language improves and his emotional state vacillates, and they give a view on events decidedly different from how they are described by the other narrative voices. It is through this first-person account of Cupido's understanding of the events that befall him that we can trace the progress from his desire to adopt a single mythology in order to cope with the world, to his acknowledgment of the folly of linking his life to any one single narrative. This advancement in understanding, from when he comes into contact with the stories of the Christian religion and instantly adopts these as his new reality, violently and brutally forsaking his Khoi beliefs, to an espousal of a syncretistic worldview, only comes towards the end of the novel, when every kind of misery and misfortune has befallen him, and it is strongly linked to Cupido's transformed understanding of the workings of stories and words. By plunging the reader into various experiences of numerous manifestations of discourse (in the form of quotes, letters, and lists), the narrative follows Campbell's interpretation of myth as delivering "not simply the idea, but a sense of actual participation in . . . a realization of transcendence, infinity, and abundance" (xx). Because these different discourses are also different ways of organizing the world, the reader is immersed in a story presented as myth, and, as such, invited to probe its propositions, both in the sense of interrogation and infiltration.

The founding of the world
Praying Mantis presents itself as a narrative straddling the divide between history and fable, and, as such, introduces its underlying concern with complicating systems of ideological imposition by making use of the dual meaning of the concept of mythology. By profiling itself on the surface as an exploration of the stories that explain the nature of reality in Khoi culture, for instance in the sense of narratives traditionally passed down about divine and heroic beings and linked to the spiritual life of the Khoi community, the other, broader meaning of mythology as a presentation of the practices of power as naturalized truth in a specific cultural context is achieved. In this case, the specific cultural context is that of colonial South Africa, and, by extension, that of South Africa in the present day.

The distance between the two perceptions of myth is not all that great, but whereas both arguably focus on what Mircea Eliade terms sacralization, the importance given to the practice and study of language as a structuring device is underplayed in the first. The role of religion in this novel, which deals with a converted Khoi missionary who comes to serve the faith perpetuated by his colonial oppressor, is, however, uncontested in both. In the still widely read *The Sacred and The Profane: The Nature of Religion*, first published in 1959, Eliade shows how religion emerges from myth, insofar as the desire to explain and control the world gave rise to the desire to experience the world as sacred or religious. This actively called a world into being: "the experience of sacred space makes possible the 'founding of the world': where the sacred manifests itself in space, *the real unveils itself*, the world comes into existence" (63). Eliade, in this way, already foresees later considerations of myth as constructed, and acknowledges that socio-historical factors play a central part in this. "(T)here are," he begins, "differences in religious experience explained by differences in economy, culture and social organisation – in short, by history" (17).

History, indeed, is what directly gives rise to myth for Barthes. For him, myth is "a system of communication, a message" (109) closely tied to the workings of history. He challenges the "naturalness" of cultural practices and texts by demonstrating how they are artificial constructs subject to an imposition of meaning. These constructs create a mythological reality intended to maintain existing structures of power, and, as such, are determined by history. "(M)ythology can only have an historical foundation," Barthes states, "for myth is a type of speech chosen by history: it cannot possibly evolve from the 'nature' of things" (110). It is in connection to signification and giving value to things that Barthes places the concept of myth within the realm of semiology, where language is interpreted as conceptual rather than referential. "Semiology has taught us," he writes, "that myth has the task of giving historical intention a natural justification" (142). By uncovering the hidden myths that mask power structures as truths to be taken for granted, Barthes's brand of mythology inevitably engages with political issues.

One scholar who delves into this engagement between mythology and politics in the specific context of missionary intervention in nineteenth-century South Africa, is Elizabeth Elbourne. In her article "Word Made Flesh: Christianity, Modernity, and Cultural Colonialism in the Work of Jean and John Comaroff," Elbourne responds to the Comaroffs' seminal *Of Revelation and Revolution: Christianity, Colonialism, and Consciousness in South Africa* (1991), which previously formed the pinnacle of analysis of South African missionary influence. In her reply to their interpretation Elbourne puts forward the intriguing proposal that, rather than seeing missionary undertakings from the vantage point of the Christianization of Africa, they can be interpreted as bringing about the Africanization of Christianity.

Elbourne believes that a reading of missionary work as essentially furthering the oppositions that served colonialism focuses too much on the Western origin of Christianity, which "contains deeply embedded culturally specific assumptions" (par. 43), ignoring African agency. Interpreting Christianity as a language of cultural domination gives an oversimplified view of the performative process of "colonizing [African] consciousness" (par. 8). Elbourne asserts that conversion was "an act, with attached rituals and beliefs" (par. 35), and she follows the Comaroffs in reading missionary endeavors as *performances*. By performing civilization it was hoped that South Africa's indigenous population would follow suit and adopt Western practices. By the notion of one universal truth, the rejection of existing traditions would ostensibly also be achieved. Elbourne complicates this situation, however, when she notes that it was not the straightforwardness of its worldview that converted Khoi people to the Christian faith, but the promise of power that its exclusive vision implied. This is also what motivates Cupido to learn to read and write, as this written language can run "farther and faster" than his spoken word (Brink 22).

So while an immersion in the Christian word to a certain extent achieved the adoption of a Western world view and, by extension, an acceptance of Western authority, it concomitantly gave Khoi converts a way of negotiating a better position for themselves in the colonial context, even to the extent that, as Elbourne notes, "prophetic figures emerged from time to time to use aspects of the Christian message in a context that suggests how quickly its language became unhinged from missionary guardianship" (par. 26). The context referred to here was that of the Christian doctrine of equality, which was used by indigenous converts to oppose assumptions of authority by white farmers. This "African prophetic innovation" (par. 26) caused much anxiety among white South Africans, who, in order to re-establish authority, forwarded race, and not religion, as the determinant of colonial status. Christian ideology and language, once unhinged, proved impossible to re-attach to the idea of exclusivity.

Language inevitably plays a role in our observation of the world and language is always complicit in structures of power. Thomas MacLaughlin explores this idea of language as "a conceptual grid, a system of values, through which we experience reality" by linking this conceptual grid specifically to figurative language (86). Metaphor, which stresses connections based on the logic of words as they refer to aspects of the outside world, plays a central role in this.

In "White Mythology" Jacques Derrida challenges the traditional opposition between concept and metaphor in philosophical theory. Metaphor, he argues, has been regarded as a "loss of meaning" and a "detour" from "proper meaning" (270). But as a matter of fact, Derrida argues, philosophy exists precisely by means of metaphor, as assertions of truth are made in the form of metaphors. This admission does not necessarily devalue a statement or finding, because meaning does not diminish simply because it is transported by means of language. Metaphor, in this way, is not alien to metaphysics but is itself a metaphysical concept. As Derrida states: "Metaphor remains, in all its essential characteristics, a classic philosopheme, a metaphysical concept" (218). It is not possible to speak about metaphor non-metaphorically. This is so because a metaphor must be performed in order to grasp its meaning. The very word "metaphor" itself, as Mieke Bal notes in her article "Metaphoring: Making a Niche of Negative Space" (2006), is a metaphor, since the Greek root translates as "to carry from one place to another."

Bal's article proposes a development of Derrida's deliberation on the absence of a clear distinction between literal and figurative language. Where Derrida infers that a purely literal language may not exist, but only a language where the figurative origins have become invisible (or "white") because of over-use, Bal puts forward the concept of "metaphoring" to reconceptualize metaphor within the context of a performative understanding of language (164). As a verb, metaphoring performs a transferal of meaning that does not necessarily rely on referentiality. Instead of assessing the appropriateness of a metaphor by its proximity to what is referred to, the act of metaphoring, Bal contends, does not transfer "meaning in a referential or representational sense, but a preoccupation that *requires re-enactment* in each event of occurrence" (165, emphasis added).

Bal warns against what she terms the "disabling abstraction" of generalizations. Instead of essentializing truth claims that, as she warns, "easily mislead . . . us into believing that states and situations are inevitable," and so deny "the possibility of political agency" (165), she pleads for agency and performance as entailed in the act of metaphoring. By metaphoring the particularity of one idea or experience onto another, while retaining the connotations specific to their configuration, the gap between distinct situations *can* be bridged. The meanings of both elements augment each other in the dynamic process of metaphoring, without one connotation acting in the service of another. This retention of particularity returns us to what Campbell called "the vitality of [a myth's] symbols as metaphors" (18), allowing for an immersion in myth by participating in its central ideas, such as the idea of transcendence, infinity, or, in the case of the nineteenth-century Khoi, of a radical equality among Christians.

Extending this train of thought, I argue that the understanding of God that Cupido demonstrates in Brink's novel is not presented as simplistically literal in a laughable, quasi-primitive manner, but shows a sophistication of conceptualization that renders Western traditional notions of a divide between the literal and the figurative comical. Cupido's amalgamation of the Khoi way of making sense of the world with the textual conception of reality of the white missionaries not only makes *visible* the invented nature of both, but makes perfect *sense* in the context of the Khoi missionary.

Robert Young, in *White Mythologies: Writing History and the West* (1990), takes this idea a step further. He departs from Derrida's notion of metaphor as the inescapable (both excessive and deficient) access point for western philosophical thought to a consideration of Western history as the inevitable point of departure for considering all histories. Hence, history is a "white mythology" that sets the limits for any project for knowledge about history. So-called "world histories," whether Marxist, capitalist, liberal, or conservative, are always histories of the west, seen from a Eurocentric viewpoint. In this way, Western ideology is a mythology that is "white" both in the sense that it becomes transparent as a mythology and in the sense that it is a mythology that "makes white," that erases divergence. Young posits colonialism as the "dislocating term" in the debate between theory and history, as both of these are implicated in the history of European colonialism, and both continue to provide the contemporary framework for the conditions of institutional knowledge and practice (vii). The field of postcolonial study, Young seems well aware, provides the terrain needed to do justice to the complexity of history and its multifaceted composition in political, social, and linguistic terms. The simple oppositions of Hegel's binaries, such as that of master and slave, colonizer and colonized, can be circumvented in the spirit of Foucault's critique of the sovereign model of power, which presumes that, as power resides on a single basis, it can easily be reversed (5). "You cannot get out of Hegel by simply contradicting him," Young posits, "for your opposition is likewise always recuperable, as the workings of ideology or psychic resistance" (6). Contradiction, in Young's analysis, is replaced by Derridean deconstruction in effecting a decolonization of history, brought about within the realm of language.

The realization that dialecticism can never be opposed by its reversal (as that would preserve the dialectic) also formed the focal point of Elbourne's analysis of the historical interpretations of South African missionary endeavors. Her insight that the Christianizing of indigenous South Africans did as much to alter the nature of South African Christianity and *all* South African Christians (not only the indigenous members) as it changed the world view of those it newly converted, goes a long way towards making sense of the attitude towards the Word exhibited by Cupido Kakkerlak in Brink's narrative.

Considering "The Word"

Brink's novel fights the war waged by language and words in the creation of myths that uphold the political status quo on the battlefield of religion. The conflation of the meaning of "the word" and "The Word" plays a central role within its narrative, in the same way that the dual meanings of "mythology" are brought to life within its pages. According to Jonathan Culler, in *The Pursuit of Signs: Semiotics, Literature, Deconstruction*, metaphor expands its reach in modern considerations of language, and has become the "figure of figures, a figure for figurality" (189). The myth that metaphor is capable of transcending the oppositions it straddles to access a truth undermines the power of metaphor, as demonstrated by Derrida's and Bal's considerations discussed above.

Thomas MacLaughlin attributes to metaphor the capacity for a "magical sharing of meaning." Unlike metonymy, which relies on connotations built up over time in a specific historical context, metaphor creates associations "on the basis of a deep logic that underlies the use of words" (84). This "deep logic," whose connotations, for MacLaughlin, already seem to approximate those traditionally aligned with magic, characterizes the performance of myth as it is borne out by *Praying Mantis*. As Cupido becomes increasingly aware of the power that resides in the tenacity and flexibility of words, he connects their deep logic with his conception of magic in that they are both able to construct and change reality. The magic that Cupido detects in words, and, specifically, the written word, can be attributed to his finding their "logic" not so much "deep" as unreasonable.

This inappropriateness also characterizes metaphor, as Jonathan Culler explains in "The Turns of Metaphor." In this piece, Culler explains metaphoricity as the result of interpretative processes that are performed on being confronted with "textual incongruity" (232). The suggestion is that surface descriptions sometimes fail to express what is salient, and require the enhancement of figurative conceptualizations. Again, this would point to a clear-cut distinction between the real and the figurative, of which Derrida and Bal remain unconvinced, and which fails to acknowledge the real as constructed by language in the first place.

Cupido, in pointing to the artifice inherent in the white mythology of textual associations, differs in his understanding of words from those used in his mother's, and later his wife Anna's, oral stories, as these are set up in the text as participating in a different logic, one that engenders rather than describes. When Cupido's mother's describes the land "far away" that she came from to her young son, she tells him:

> "It is a bare place"
> "How bare?"
> "Just bare. No word has come to lie on it yet to say how bare it is. So it is just bare." (17)

This exchange appears to hark back to a world before words at the same time as it characterizes these words as unnecessary in recalling a history and maybe even obstructive to the process. Marshall McLuhan, in his 1962 *The Gutenberg Galaxy: The Making of Typographic Man*, asserted that the advent of print culture caused the cultural predominance of the visual over the oral by its privileging of writing over speech. "The technology and social effects of typography," he notes, "incline us to abstain from noting interplay and, as it were, 'formal' causality, both in our inner and external lives. Print exists by virtue of the static separation of functions and fosters a mentality that gradually resists any but a separative and compartmentalizing or specialist outlook" (126). The domination of writing over other forms of language is, in itself, a mythology of the west, and acts prescriptively in the way in which it frames perceptions of the world. This bias of writing over speech has been called *graphocentrism* or *scriptism*. McLuhan argues that its effect extends to social organization, especially in terms of the "specialist outlook" he mentions.

When Cupido adopts the written form of language as his new god because of the magical powers he attributes to it, this absorption of power turns out to be anything but empowering, as it ties him to a restricted set of values and ultimately leads to the narrowing of his worldview. In taking The Word of Christianity at its word, Cupido displays violently intolerant behavior in his aggressive conversion of non-Christians and his destruction of non-Christian sacral sites. Thus, the progress and development that graphocentrism attributes to writing are undercut. Cupido contributes to this immobility by counting on the solidity of words. One day, after Reverend James Read has presented him with a Bible of his own, he encounters Cupido sitting on the ground with a much-depleted Bible on his lap, intently reading every word on a page and then, when reaching the end of the page, tearing it out, crumpling it, and stuffing it into his mouth. Read is horrified and confronts Cupido, at which Cupido replies:

I am consuming the Word of God . . . . There is so much that I still do not understand, Brother Read, . . . So I decided I must eat it and swallow it to absorb it in my body. Only then will the Word of God be fully part of me. Then no one can ever take it from me again. (185)

The need for material absorption is at odds with Read's understanding of written language as transmitting value via an abstract absorption. Yet the tension found in the symbolic language of the Christian Bible, with its bread and wine becoming blood and body, and its word being made flesh, provides an apt context for Cupido's questioning of the boundaries between the physical and the abstract.

In *Transfiguration*, Frank Brown makes an analysis of metaphor and religion in a way that opposes this idea of an inhibiting conflict between literal and figural meaning. He disagrees with the conventional characterization of both poetic metaphor and religious language as sign-systems that are purely "self-authenticating" (149). Instead, he argues that "however self-referential or noncognitive some function of religious language may be, the 'game' played by such language as a whole becomes trivial and even incomprehensible unless it is understood as concerned, ultimately, with more than itself" (150). Because he assumes that these systems of symbolic language are neither trivial not incomprehensible, he deduces that the complex relationship between experience, words, and what he calls "a higher or deeper Word" can be successfully explored. The way in which he foresees this happening is by the realization that our sense of reality is related directly to the language we use, and that metaphoric and conceptual discourse both mediate what lies beyond the confines of language (151). Brown speaks of "the dynamics of metaphor" as serving "to incorporate and help create the vital tensions and awareness fundamental to the religious dimension of human experience" (173) in the same way that Derrida recognizes metaphor to function as a "transfiguration," both remaining within language and pointing to that which is beyond it.

Conclusion: Moving Identities

In his introduction to *Questions of Cultural Identity*, Stuart Hall reserves the first of his questions for a consideration of identity as related to agency, but is careful to specify that his notion of agency relates less to a theory of the knowing subject and more to Foucault's notion of discursive practice (2). The fictional nature of what he calls "the narrativization of the self," which attends identity constructions, does not undermine its political effectiveness, but, rather, situates the potential for their subversion or transformation within the imaginary and the symbolic as well (4). As the above analysis of *Praying Mantis* demonstrates, the story of Cupido's life ultimately reveals identities as continually re-constructed and re-invented, both in terms of public memory that crystallizes as consensual myth, and in the light of the dynamics of political developments and actual interaction and participation in discourse. By acknowledging the untenability of notions of "fixed" identity (or a word that can be digested whole), the hierarchical opposition between an "ignorant" African mythology and a "developed" Western rationality can be destabilized and a more productive metaphorical reading of myth as capable of transforming identity reached.

Notes

1. The London Missionary Society was an Anglican (non-conformist) missionary society formed in England in 1795 with missions on the islands of the South Pacific and in Africa.

2. By the end of the novel, the desolate, neglected, and emaciated Cupido is finally facilitated in leaving his deserted missionary outpost by a runaway slave whose name is "Arend," which translates into English as "Eagle."

3. The praying mantis also figures as the embodiment of the Khoi god Heitsi-Eibib, the son of the good god Tsui-Goab of Khoi mythology.

Bibliography

Bal, Mieke. "Metaphoring: Making a Niche of Negative Space." *Metaphoricity and the Politics of Mobility*. Ed. Maria Margaroni and Effie Yiannopoulou. Thamyris/Intersecting: Place, Sex and Race 12. Amsterdam and New York: Rodopi, 2006. 159–79.

Barthes, Roland. *Mythologies*. London: Vintage, 2000.

Boer, Inge E. "No-Man's-Land? Five Short Cases on Deserts and the Politics of Place." *Mobilizing Place, Placing Mobility: The Politics of Representation in a Globalized World*. Ed. Ginette Verstraete and Tim Cresswell. Thamyris/Intersecting: Place, Sex and Race 9. Amsterdam and New York: Rodopi, 2002. 155–72.

Brink, André. *Praying Mantis*. London: Vintage, 2006.

Brown, Frank Burch. *Transfiguration: Poetic Metaphor and the Languages of Religious Belief*. Chapel Hill and London: U of North Carolina P, 1983.

Campbell, Joseph. *The Inner Reaches of Outer Space: Metaphor as Myth and as Religion*. Novato, CA: New World Foundation, 2002.

Culler, Jonathan. "The Turns of Metaphor." *The Pursuit of Signs: Semiotics, Literature, Deconstruction*. Ithaca: Cornell UP, 1981. 188–209.

Derrida, Jacques. "White Mythology." *Margins of Philosophy*. Trans. Alan Bass. Chicago: U of Chicago P, 1982.

Elbourne, Elizabeth. "Word Made Flesh: Christianity, Modernity, and Cultural Colonialism in the Work of Jean and John Comaroff." *The American Historical Review* 108.2 (2003): 44 pars. Web. 8 December 2009.

Eliade, Mircea. *The Sacred and the Profane: The Nature of Religion*. San Diego, New York, London: Harcourt, 1959.

McLaughlin, Thomas. "Figurative Language." *Critical Terms for Literary Study*. Ed. Frank Lentricchia and Thomas McLaughlin. Chicago and London: U of Chicago P, 1990. 80–90.

McLuhan, Herbert Marshall. *The Gutenberg Galaxy: The Making of Typographic Man*. London: Routledge & Kegan Paul, 1962.

Midgley, Mary. *The Myths We Live By*. London and New York: Routledge, 2004.

Young, Robert. *White Mythologies: Writing History and the West*. London and New York: Routledge, 1990.

The Contributors

Huub van Baar is a doctoral candidate at the Amsterdam School for Cultural Analysis, Faculty of Humanities, University of Amsterdam, and has published on Romani memorial practices, Romani transnational networks, and minority governance in Europe. His current work focuses on past and current forms of Romani minority governance in Europe and the ways in which these forms relate to different conceptualizations of Europe.

Nimrod Ben-Cnaan completed his thesis – entitled "A Comparative Study of Tropes of Cultural Pessimism in Postwar Britain and France" – at the Centre for European Studies at University College London in 2008.

Marc Brudzinski studies twentieth-century Francophone and Hispanic Caribbean literature, and teaches at Purchase College, State University of New York. His book *Island Secrets*, on the discourses of insularism and secrecy in Caribbean cultural debates, is forthcoming from Lexington Books.

Gülru Çakmak is an art historian specializing in the eighteenth and the nineteenth centuries, who received her BA and MFA degrees at Bilkent University (Ankara, Turkey). Gülru's growing interest in the politics of representation was supported by a full scholarship from the Department of Gender Studies at the Central European University (Budapest, Hungary), where she followed an intensive curriculum of feminist criticism and acquired an MA in Gender Studies. She received her MPhil degree at one of the leading programs in the field of visual studies, the Amsterdam School of Cultural Analysis at the University of Amsterdam. Currently an advanced PhD candidate at Johns Hopkins University (Baltimore, Maryland), Gülru is working on her dissertation, *Jean-Léon Gérôme: The Formative Years (1855–1864)*, under the supervision of Michael Fried and Kathryn Tuma.

Sudeep Dasgupta is Associate Professor at the University of Amsterdam, and teaches media studies with a focus on visual culture, postcolonial theory, queer theory, and critical theory. His recent publications include "Conjunctive times, Disjointed Time: Philosophy between Enigma and Disagreement" in *Parallax* 52 (2009), "Words, Bodies, Times: Queer theory before and after itself" in *borderlands* 8.2 (2009), and "Jacques Rancière" in *Film, Theory and Philosophy: Key thinkers*, edited by Felicity Colman (Acumen, 2009). He wrote the critical introduction to the joint Dutch translation *Het Esthetisch denken* (Valiz, 2007) of Jacques Rancière's *Partage du sensible* and *L'inconscient esthétique*. He is the editor of the volume *Constellations of the Transnational: Modernity, Culture, Critique* (Rodopi, 2006).

Beatrix Hauser is presently interim professor of Social Anthropology at the University of Heidelberg. In 1989 she received her Magister Artium from the University of Hamburg and in 1997 her PhD on the basis of her research on a contemporary Bengali tradition of storytelling that is performed with the help of scroll paintings (*Mit irdischem Schaudern und göttlicher Fügung: bengalische Erzähler und ihre Bildvorführungen*, Berlin 1998). In 2009 she passed her habilitation at the University of Halle with a study on Hindu women in Orissa in their religious practices (*Promising Rituals: Doing Gender in Southern Orissa, India*, Halle 2008). Hauser's research interests are the anthropology of religion (Hinduism, subaltern and transreligious practices, spirit possession, notions of im/purity), the anthropology of the body (cultural concepts of body and self, body techniques, embodiment), the anthropology of performance (changing aesthetics of religious plays, ritual and political performances), and gender (self-images and identity, female religiosity).

Anette Hoffmann is a postdoctoral researcher at the Centre for Humanities Research at the University of the Western Cape in Cape Town, South Africa. She obtained her doctorate at the University of Amsterdam in 2005 with a dissertation on praise poetry in Namibia and its poetic construction of landscape and identities. Currently, she is working on the history of an anthropometrical project by the German artist Hans Lichtenecker in Namibia in 1931, and curating an exhibition (shown in Cape Town and Basel) containing visual and sound materials of the collection. The exhibition catalogue, edited and co-authored by Hoffmann, appeared as *What We See. Reconsidering an Anthropometrical Collection from Southern Africa: Images, Voices, and Versioning* (Basel Afrika Bibliographien, 2009).

Niamh Ann Kelly is an art writer and researcher. She lectures in Critical Theory at the School of Art Design and Printing at the Dublin Institute of Technology, Ireland. She also works as a freelance art critic and is currently completing her PhD entitled "History by Proxy – Imaging the Great Irish Famine" at the Amsterdam School for Cultural Analysis, University of Amsterdam.

Saskia Lourens earned her PhD degree at the Amsterdam School for Cultural Analysis researching a dissertation on South African literature and cultural identity formation. She holds an Honor's Degree in Fine Art from the University of Cape Town as well as a Master's Degree in English from the University of Leiden. She currently teaches English at the Amsterdams Lyceum.

Esther Peeren is Assistant Professor in Literary Studies at the University of Amsterdam. She is the author of *Intersubjectivities and Popular Culture: Bakhtin and Beyond* (Stanford UP, 2008) and co-editor, with Silke Horstkotte, of *The Shock of the Other: Situating Alterities* (Rodopi, 2007) and, with María del Pilar Blanco, of *Popular Ghosts: The Haunted Spaces of Everyday Culture* (Continuum, 2010).

Hanneke Stuit is a PhD candidate at the Amsterdam School of Cultural Analysis (ASCA), at the University of Amsterdam. She received her MA in Literary Studies from the same university in 2007. Her research deals with the concept of ubuntu and the ways in which it relates to other (predominantly Western) concepts of communality and intersubjective relations. She is particularly interested in the possibilities of using ubuntu as an analytical tool when working with cultural expressions, especially novels.

Vannina Sztainbok currently teaches in the Department of Sociology and Equity Studies in Education at the Ontario Institute for Studies in Education, University of Toronto, where she recently completed her PhD. Her research interests include race, belonging and citizenship in Latin America; the politics and psychodynamics of space, and black femininity in the Americas. This chapter comes from her MA thesis of the same name. Her doctoral dissertation, titled *The Afro-Uruguayan Conventillo: Belonging and the Fetish of Place and Blackness*, explores the symbolic place occupied by a racialized neighborhood within the Uruguayan national imaginary.

Guy Thompson is an Associate Professor in the Department of History and Classics at the University of Alberta in Edmonton, Alberta; he completed his PhD at the University of Minnesota in 2000. His older work explores rural social dynamics, agrarian change, indigenous knowledge and rural protest in colonial Zimbabwe. In his current research he is considering how black Zimbabweans understood historical and cultural change in the colonial period, work that began as an exploration of the concepts and debates that run through his contribution to this volume. He is particularly intrigued by the ways in which ideas about race, morality, gender, and the meaning of modernity figure in these disputes.

Claret Vargas is an independent scholar whose main areas of interest are poetics and ethics, indigenous rights and indigenous movements, exile and violence in literature, and human rights. She received her PhD in Romance Languages and Literatures from Harvard University in 2003 and was Assistant Professor of Spanish at the University of Miami. Her work appeared in *Hispanic Review* and *Neophilologus*, among others. In 2010, she will receive her JD from Harvard Law School, where she worked with the Harvard International Human Rights Clinic, led the student Advocates for Human Rights, and was an editor for the Human Rights Journal.

Sonja van Wichelen is currently the Nancy L. Buc Postdoctoral Fellow with the Pembroke Center at Brown University where she is working on her new project *The Cultural Pragmatics of Global Adoption*. She was a Postdoctoral Fellow at Yale University's Center for Cultural Sociology (2007–2009) and received her Ph.D. from the University of Amsterdam. Her book *Religion, Politics, and Gender in Indonesia: Disputing the Muslim Body* is forthcoming with Routledge (2010) and together with Begüm Firat and Sarah De Mul she co-edited the book *Commitment and Complicity in Cultural Theory and Practice* (Palgrave Macmillan, 2009).

Index

A

Abdulaziz   111n4
Abella, Gonzalo   182
Acevedo, Eduardo   177, 179, 181, 186
Acevedo Díaz, Eduardo   185, 189n7
Achugar, Hugo   176, 177, 179
Acković, Dragoljub   124
Acosta y Lara, Eduardo F.   177, 178, 179
Acton, Thomas   117, 121
Adorno, Theodor   16, 34, 35–38, 41–43, 44n3, 44n6, 44n8, 45n12, 45n13, 119
Aguilar, Filomeno   238, 239, 240
Alexander, Jocelyn   224
Alexander, M. Jacqui   74
Alfred, Taiaiake   22, 23, 27n15
Alonso, Ana Maria   177, 178, 179, 183, 188
Amaru, Tupac   202n5
Anderson, Benedict   37, 95, 176, 186
Andrews, George Reid   189n6
Ang, Ien   10, 239, 242, 243, 246, 249n1
Anselin, Alain   63
Antón, Danilo   182
Antonescu, Ion   124
Antze, Paul   234n6
Appadurai, Arjun   19, 23, 78, 119, 180
Arnold, Matthew   70
Augé, Marc   78

B

Baar, Huub van   19–20, 115–131
Bal, Mieke   16, 27n11, 170n4, 210, 218n14, 262–63, 264, 265

Balibar, Étienne   176
Banda, Hastings Kamuzu   223
Banzer, Hugo   202n9
Barany, Zoltan   123–24
Barben, Tanya   85, 99n3
Barber, Karin   170n8
Barrios Pintos, Aníbal   177, 178, 179, 182
Barthes, Roland   254, 261
Bartky, Sandra Lee   218n2
Baumann, Zygmund   10
Bauzá, Francisco   185, 189n7
Beach, David   235n7
Beck, Roger G.   99n13
Ben-Cnaan, Nimrod   17, 67–81
Benítez-Rojo, Antonio   47
Bennett, Tony   151n4
Bernáth, Gábor   125
Bey, Salaheddin   107
Bhabha, Homi   16, 33, 36–37, 41, 42–43, 44n1, 45n10, 73, 150, 176, 180
Bizos, George   90
Blanco Acevedo, Pablo   177, 179, 181
Bloom, Kevin   27n5
Boer, Inge   253
Bollig, Michael   171n11, 171n12
Bongie, Chris   14, 27n7
Boorman, John   88
Boulanger, Gustave   105, 107, 108, 111n3
Bourdieu, Pierre   23, 44n2, 44n3, 44n4
Bourke, Marie   143
Boym, Svetlana   234n6
Bozzoli, Belinda   224

Brathwaite, Edward Kamau   55
Brawne, Michael   136, 151n2
Breton, Jules   141
Brincker, Heinrich   163, 170n7
Brink, André   25, 253–268
Brown, Frank Burch   266
Brown, Wendy   228
Brudzinski, Marc   16–17, 47–65
Burke, Peter   234n6
Burke, Tim   234n5
Buthelezi, Mangosuthu   12
Butler, Judith   18, 95–8, 189n5, 207, 208
Byers, Thomas   11, 27n3

C

Caetano, Gerardo   176
Çakmak, Gülru   18–19, 103–112
Campbell, Joseph   254, 260, 263
Campbell, Stephen J.   141
Caplan, Lionel   218n3
Castagnary, Jules-Antoine   110
Castells, Manuel   17, 76
Çelik, Zeynep   105
Certeau, Michel de   78
Césaire, Aimé   48, 51
Cezar, Mustafa   104
Chakrabarty, Dipesh   74
Chamoiseau, Patrick   49
Clifford, James   12, 26, 157, 160, 164
Coertze, R.D.   99n4
Cohen, Anthony P.   208
Comaroff, John and Jean   157, 223–4, 261
Condé, Maryse   41, 63
Condon, Stephanie   48
Connery, James   144–45
Constantine   68
Coolighan Sanguinetti, María Luisa   177, 179, 181, 182
Coplan, David   170n8
Coppel, Charles   249n2

Corntassel, Jeff   22, 23, 28n15
Cosse, Isabella   176
Crain, Mary M.   218n3
Crawford, Margaret   141, 142, 148
Crow, Thomas   109
Crowe, David   124
Csordas, Thomas J.   215, 218n8
Culler, Jonathan   264, 265

D

Damon, Matt   11
Danielová, Helena   125
Das, Veena   216
Dash, J. Michael   47
Darsières, Camille   64n4
Dasgupta, Sudeep   16, 23, 33–46
David, Jacques-Louis   109
Dawson, Ashley   13
Decamps, Alexandre-Gabriel   106–7, 109
Delaroche, Paul   107, 111n3
Deleuze, Gilles   61, 64n6, 78
DeLillo, Don   258
Derrida, Jacques   9, 27n9, 37, 44n1, 44n3, 44n6, 44n9, 45n13, 45n17, 69, 254, 262–263, 264, 265, 266
Desportes, George   17, 47–59, 61–62
Diocletian   69
Donnelly Jr., James S.   151n1
Drinkwater, Michael   233
Drouais, Germain-Jean   109
Du Camp, Maxime   106–7
Duffy, P.J.   141
Dumont, Louis   218n4
Duncan, Carol   135
Dunne, Tom   141
Durkheim, Emile   207

E

Edgeworth, Maria   151n1
Edwards, R.D.   151n1

Eisenstadt, Shmuel N.   72, 75
Elbourne, Elizabeth   261–62, 264
Eliade, Mircea   260–61
Enwezor, Okwui   13
Erasmus   258
Ersoy, Ahmet   105

F

Fabian, Johannes   164–65
Fanon, Frantz   42–43, 71
Fares, Fares   35
Fares, Josef   16, 34, 35
Ferguson, James   224, 228, 233
Ferreira, Luis   189n8
Fikeni, Somadoda   13
Finkelstein, Norman   118
Fischer-Lichte, Erika   216
Fisher, Humphrey   218n3
Flood, Henry   140
Foster, Roy   144
Foucault, Michel   68, 164, 178, 218n2, 264, 267
Fraser, Nancy   12, 26, 27n5
Friedman, Steven   12
Fructuoso Rivera, José   178, 186

G

Gandon, James   140
Gardiner, Judith Kegan   210
Gates Jr., Henry Louis   27n8, 170n1
Gaulle, Charles de   51
Gay, Paul du   9
Geertz, Clifford   159, 170n4
Gell, Alfred   210, 218n6
Germaner, Semra   105
Gérôme, Jean-Léon   103, 105, 107–110, 111n3
Gewald, Jan-Bart   167, 171n11, 171n12
Gheorghe, Nicolae   117
Giddens, Anthony   209

Giesen, B.   75
Gilroy, Paul   10, 165, 198, 228
Glenny, Micha   124
Glissant, Édouard   17, 47–48, 52–62, 64n3, 64n5, 64n6, 64n7
Glucksmann, André   44n4
Goldberg, David Theo   181
González Laurino, Carolina   185–6, 189n7
Gotovitch, José   124
Graham, Richard,   184
Gray, Peter   137, 141, 142
Guattari, Félix   64n6, 78
Gunner, Liz   12–13, 27n5
Gustafson, Bret   202n11

H

Hahn, Carl Hugo   167, 171n11
Halbwachs, Maurice   234n6
Halkes, Petra   161
Hall, Stuart   9, 13, 15, 21, 22, 44n1, 61, 62, 160–61, 169, 180, 194, 195, 198, 200, 267
Hamdi, Osman   18, 103–11
Hamon, Jean-Louis   111n3
Hancock, Ian   125–6
Hannerz, Ulf   17, 72, 77–78, 80n4
Haragal'ová, Jana   125
Hauser, Beatrix   23–24, 207–221
Hegel, Georg Wilhelm Friedrich   264
Heidegger, Martin   37–38, 44n1, 44n3, 44n9, 45n12, 45n13
Heim, Susanne   124
Hekman, Susan   27n1
Hendry, Joy   28n14
Henrichsen, Dag   167
Heryanto, Ariel   237, 241, 247, 249n5, 249n7, 250n17
Hever, Hannan   72, 73
Heywood, Annemarie   158

Hirsch, Marianne   125, 128n6
Hobsbawm, Eric   23, 151n9, 218n9
Hoffmann, Anette   9–29, 157–73
Hoffmann, Deborah   89
hooks, bell   26
Horkheimer, Max   34
Horstkotte, Silke   19, 27n10
Hoskins, Andrew   125
Hubert, Marie-Christine   124
Hübschmannová, Milena   125
Hughes-Freeland, Felicia   218n3
Husserl, Edmund   45n13
Huyssen, Andreas   118–120

I

Inden, Ronald   210, 218n6
Irle, Jacob   163, 170n7

J

Jackson, Samuel L.   88
Jacobs, Jane Margaret   186
Jameson, Fredric   41, 42
Jasper, James M.   74, 75
Johnson, Mark   169
Joyce, James   151n5
Julien, Isaac   44n5
Jurga, Martin   218n1

K

Kandiyoti, Deniz   93, 94
Kapralski, Slawomir   117
Kaputu, Alexander   167, 171n10
Katari, Tupac   195, 197, 202n5
Katjivena, Uazuvara   163, 170n7
Kavari, Jekura   158
Kelleher, Margaret   140, 151n1, 151n7
Kelly, Niamh Ann   20, 133–53
Kelso, Michelle   124
King, Martin Luther   117
Kissane, Noel   141, 142

Klímová, Ilona   117, 121
Klopper, Dirk   99n12
Köhler, Oswin   170n7
Köpping, Klaus-Peter   218n3
Kramer, Fritz   209, 218n6
Krog, Antjie   88, 92, 99n3, 99n7, 99n11
Kumar, Nita   210
Kureishi, Hanif   35
Kusno, Abidin   250n18

L

Lacan, Jacques   37
LaCapra, Dominick   25, 238, 244–45, 247, 249n13, 249n14
Lacková, Ilona   125
Laclau, Ernesto   60
Lakoff, George   169
Lambert, Michael   234n6
Leerssen, Joep   146, 151n5
Lefebvre, Henri   177
Lemaires, Gérard-Georges   103
Leslie, Julia   218n7
Lessing, Gotthold Ephraim   146
Lévi, Bernard-Henri   44n4
Lévi-Strauss, Claude   44n6, 45n9, 180
Levy, Daniel   118, 120, 124, 128n4
Libin, Mark   87, 99n3, 99n4
Liendo, Roxana   202n2
Lienhard, Godfrey   218n6
Liman, Doug   11
Lindsey, Tim   249n5
Linenthal, Edward   118, 126
Litton, Helen   141, 142
Lloyd, Mona   27n1
Lorente, J. Pedro   151n2
Lourens, Saskia   25, 253–268
Lozano, Pedro   181
Lucassen, Leo   124

M

MacKenzie, John   103
MacLaughlin, Thomas   262, 264–65
Madariaga, Alexia Guilera   199
Madikizela-Mandela, Winnie   91–92, 94, 97, 99n10, 99n11, 99n12, 99n14, 99n15
Mahon family   134, 137, 146–49, 151n1
Mahony, James   142
Malan, J.S.   166, 171n9
Malkki, Liisa   166, 180, 181
Mamani Condori, Carlos   197–8, 202n8
Mandela, Nelson   86
Marglin, Frederique Apffel   218n4
Markarian, Vania   176
Marshall, Catherine   141
Martin, Denis-Constant   11
Martínez Barbosa, Rodolfo   177, 178
Marx, Christoph   85, 94–95, 99n3, 99n4
Marx, Karl   70
Mauss, Marcel   215
Mbeki, Thabo   13
Mbembe, Achille   86
McClintock, Anne   73
McDaniel, June   218n7
McGee, Mary   210, 218n7
McGregor, JoAnn   224
McKenzie, Jon   207
McLuhan, Herbert Marshall   78, 265
Meijer, Mia   125
Meissonier, Ernst   108
Memmi, Albert   36, 45n10
Menchú, Rigoberta   197
Midgley, Mary   256, 257, 259
Migdal, Alicia   176
Mignolo, Walter D.   175, 184
Mihok, Brigitte   124
Miller, J.C.   165
Millet, Jean-François   141
Mines, Mattison   218n4

Minh-Ha, Trinh T.   151n8
Minturn, Leigh   218n10
Mirga, Andrzej   117
Misra, Nirmala   210
Mnyaka, Mluketi   85, 99n3
Mobutu, Joseph-Désiré   223
Mohanram, Radhika   177, 180, 181, 182, 185
Molina, Lucía Dominga   189n6
Morales, Evo   23, 195, 199–200, 202n11
Morooka, Junya   44n4
Morrison, Toni   180
Mothlabi, Mokgethi   85, 99n3
Mtukudzi, Oliver   234n5
Mugabe, Robert   24, 226, 227, 233, 234n4
Murphy, David   168

N

Nahum, Benjamín   177, 179–80, 181
Nazzari, Muriel   189n6
Ndlovu, Nosimilo   84
Nečas, Ctibor   123, 124
Nicolas, Thierry   17, 48, 57–63, 64n8
Niezen, Ronald   22, 27n13
Nkotsoe, Mmantho   224
Nora, Pierre   17, 73
Nussbaum, Martha   245
Nyambara, Pius   224

O

Ogden, Philip E.   48
Ó'Gráda, Cormac   151n1
Ong, Aihwa   242
Ong, Walter   170n1

P

Pape, Markus   124
Parkin, David   218n3

Passerini, Luisa   234n6
Pausacker, Helen   249n5
Pavelić, Ante   124
Pearce, Susan   134, 136
Peeren, Esther   9–29
Peritore, Silvio   128n5
Persaud, Walter   178
Petrova, Dimitrina   121
Pi Hugarte, Renzo   177, 178, 179, 182
Pineau, Gisèle   63
Polletta, Francesca   74, 75
Portelli, Alessandro   234n6
Porzecanski, Teresa   176
Praeg, Leonhard   99n4
Preziosi, Donald   151n8
Purdey, Jemma   240, 241, 249n5

Q

Quispe, Felipe   202n5

R

Radcliffe, Sarah A.   175, 176, 177, 188
Radhakrishnan, R.   14, 26
Ranger, Terence   151n9, 218n9
Rao, Ursula   218n3
Rapport, Nigel   208
Razack, Sherene   186
Reid, Frances   89
Reinhartz, Dennis   124
Reuter, Frank   128n5
Reyes Abadie, Washington   178
Ricoeur, Paul   140, 142
Robinson, Mary   145
Rodriíguez, Romero Jorge   176
Rose, Gillian   189n5
Rose, Romani   122
Rosello, Mireille   47
Rushdie, Salman   157, 168

S

Said, Edward   18, 106, 149–50, 180, 184, 189n4
Sanabria, Floren G.   196
Sánchez de Lozada, Gonzalo   195, 199
Sanders, Mark   99n4
Sapriza, Graciela   176
Sarmiento, Domingo   176
Sax, William S.   209
Sayer, Derek   116
Schieffelin, Edward   216
Schluchter, Wolfgang   72, 75
Schmid, Wieland   128n2
Schurmann Pacheco, Mauricio   177, 179, 181, 182
Schwarz-Bart, Simone   63
Scott, Joan W.   11, 178
Shaw, Wendy   105, 108, 109
Shenhav, Yehouda   72, 73
Shidarta, Amir   239
Shohat, Ella   189n4
Siegel, James   239, 244
Skidmore, Thomas E.   175, 184
Smith, Linda T.   181
Snow, D.A.   17, 75–76
Soja, Edward   177
Somerville, Edith   151n7
Sommer, Doris   177, 183
Sökefeld, Martin   208
Sontag, Susan   136, 150, 151n6
Sparks, Allister   99n3
Spivak, Gayatri   36, 41, 43, 44n3, 45n17, 73, 136, 142, 150
Stabile, Carol A.   44n4
Stallabrass, Julian   151n4
Stam, Robert   189n4
Stoler, Ann Laura   184
Stuit, Hanneke   18, 83–101
Suharto   24, 237–241, 249n6

Suryadinata, Leo   239, 249n2
Sutherland, Peter   209
Suzman, James   170n6
Szabolcs, Szita   124
Sznaider, Natan   118, 120, 124, 128n4
Sztainbok, Vannina   21–22, 175–92

T

Tansuğ, Sezer   104
Taussig, Michael   157
Tay, Elaine   242
Tewari, Laxmi G.   218n7
Thalasso, Adolphe   106, 111n2
Thatcher, Margaret   35, 70
Thompson, Guy   24, 223–236
Thomson, Alistair   234n6
Tokita-Tanabe, Yumiko   213, 218n12, 218n13
Torres, María Inés de   186
Tutu, Desmond   85, 88–89, 90, 91–92, 94, 97, 99n5, 99n12

V

Vaca, Mery   197
Vargas, Claret   22–23, 193–203
Vasconcelos, José   176
Vásquez Romero, Andrés   178
Vedder, Heinrich   167, 170n7, 171n11, 171n12
Venn, Couze   74
Verdesio, Gustavo   175, 176, 180, 181, 187
Vidart, Daniel   177, 179, 181, 182,

W

Wade, Peter   175, 176, 184, 185
Walcott, Derek   44n7
Wallach, Alan   135
Watson, Rubie S.   234n6
Watts, George Frederic   141
Weaver, Hilary N.   14, 22
Weiner, James   164
Westwood, Sallie   175, 176, 177, 188
Wichelen, Sonja van   24–25, 237–252
Wilkinson, Jennifer   92
Willems, Herbert   218n1
Williams, Raymond   10, 17, 69–72, 77, 78, 80n3
Williams, T.D   151n1
Wood, Nancy   73
Worby, Eric   224

Y

Yaeger, Patricia   61
Yang, Guobin   242
Yeats, Jack   143
Yeğenoğlu, Meyda   106
Young, James   118–119, 125, 128n6
Young, Robert   74, 254, 263–64

Z

Zajoncová, Dana   125
Zanón, Angel J.   178, 179, 182
Zapiro (Jonathan Shapiro)   83–86
Žižek, Slavoj   80
Zorrilla de San Martín, Juan   182
Zuma, Jacob   12–14, 25, 27n4
Zum Felde, Alberto   177, 179, 181, 182